Witchcraft and Magic in

The Middle Ages

WITCHCRAFT
AND MAGIC IN EUROPE

General Editors
Bengt Ankarloo (University of Lund)
Stuart Clark (University of Swansea)

The roots of European withcraft and magic lie in Hebrew and other ancient Near Eastern cultures and in the Celtic, Nordic, and Germanic traditions of the continent. For two millennia, European folklore and ritual have been imbued with the belief in the supernatural, yielding a rich trove of histories and images.

Witchcraft and Magic in Europe combines traditional approaches of political, legal, and social historians with a critical synthesis of cultural anthropology, historical psychology, and gender studies. The series provides a modern, scholarly survey of the supernatural beliefs of Europeans from ancient times to the present day. Each volume of this ambitious series contains the work of distinguished scholars chosen for their expertise in a particular era of region.

Witchcraft and Magic in Europe: Biblical and Pagan Societies
Witchcraft and Magic in Europe: Ancient Greece and Rome
Witchcraft and Magic in Europe: The Middle Ages
Witchcraft and Magic in Europe: The Period of the Witch Trials
Witchcraft and Magic in Europe: The Eighteenth and Nineteenth
    Centuries
Witchcraft and Magic in Europe: The Twentieth Century

Witchcraft and Magic in Europe
The Middle Ages

KAREN JOLLY

CATHARINA RAUDVERE

EDWARD PETERS

Edited by
Bengt Ankarloo
and Stuart Clark

PENN

University of Pennsylvania Press
Philadelphia

First published 2001 by
The Athlone Press
A Continuum imprint
The Tower Building, 11 York Road, London SE1 7NX

First published 2002 in the United States of America by
University of Pennsylvania Press
Philadelphia, Pennsylvania 19104-4011

Library of Congress Cataloging in Publication Data

Witchcraft and Magic in Europe: The Middle Ages / Karen Jolly, Catharina
Raudvere, Edward Peters; edited by Bengt Ankarloo and Stuart Clark.
   p. cm
Includes bibliographical references and index.

   ISBN 0-8122-3616-5 (alk. paper) -- ISBN 0-8122-17-86-1 (pbk. : alk.
paper)
   1. Witchcraft--Europe--History--Middle Ages. 2. Magic--Europe--
History--Middle Ages. I. Catharina Raudvere. II Edward Peters. III.
Ankarloo, Bengt, 1935-. II. Clark, Stuart

                          2001023964

Typeset by Columns Design Ltd, Reading
Printed and bound in Great Britain

Contents

Introduction

Bengt Ankarloo and Stuart Clark

The aim of this volume is to demonstrate how a common European concept of magic emerged during the Middle Ages; how the classical and Christian heritage from the late Roman empire was fused with local and regional creeds in the missionary areas of central and northern Europe; what such a regional, non-Christian belief-system could look like, using as an example the rich material from the magic lore of pagan Scandinavia; how the Church modified its attitude towards magic in contact with other traditions, sometimes by absorbing them, sometimes by trying to suppress them; and how Church and State, centralized powers in a decentralized Europe, in which empire gave way to nation states and the political multiplicity of late medieval Europe, gradually sharpened their attitude to magic in general, and to sorcery and witchcraft in particular, paving the way for the violent outbreaks of witch persecutions in early modern Europe.

While doing all this we should nevertheless remember that by narrowly focusing on magic we run the risk of overstating its place in medieval consciousness, and in the source material it has left behind for us to explore. In his essay on the place of magic in legislation and politics Edward Peters rightly points out that 'superstition, magic and witchcraft [were] not always matters of great concern to authorities. Even in the fourteenth and fifteenth centuries the laws and theoretical literature concerning sorcery and witchcraft remained a very small part of an immense literature that was chiefly devoted to the social and spiritual life of Christian Europeans.'

Another caveat is called for as well. The term Middle Ages (*medium aevum*) came into use in the seventeenth century to designate an emptiness, the long parenthesis from the fall of the Western Empire to the revival of classical culture in the Renaissance. To this emptiness, this perceived absence of artistic refinement, were eventually added other deficiencies such as gross ignorance, superstition, social oppression, and devastating wars and epidemics. This crude misrepresentation of a historical period comprising over a thousand years has now generally been abandoned, but the uneasy feeling of something dark and sinister still clings to the term medieval, and all the more strongly when it is used in connection with magic and witchcraft. We are repeatedly reminded of this almost subconscious danger of simplification when the authors of this volume caution us against too easy generalizations about medieval mentalities and ideas in the face of such a complex and multifarious history as that of magic and witchcraft from St Augustine to the *Malleus Maleficarum*. In the words of Karen Jolly, 'the European-encoded ideas of magic as demonic, evil and fearful, as medieval and backward, as unscientific, irrational and uncivilized, as something "other", are hard to exorcize. These notions of magic pervade the way we think as moderns and are ingrained in modern scholarship of the Middle Ages.'

For magic is in the mind. As a historical category it is constantly created and recreated. It can therefore be understood only in relation to other categories which are also undergoing this process of continuous redefinition. Sometimes it is not only in relation to, but in direct opposition to certain concepts that it gets its meaning: magic is not religion, nor is it science. Such a tripartite and mutually exclusive subdivision of the mental world was long used by scholars trying to envisage the historical development of man's thinking about the world around him as a consecutive series of cosmologies starting in the magic mode and ending, triumphantly, in the scientific. This is the positivist paradigm as formulated by Condorcet and Comte and the social anthropologists of the late nineteenth century. Magic in their view was associated with early man as he childishly tried to make sense of the dangers and exigencies around him. In so far as magic is still found in more advanced societies, it is, therefore, according to this view, to be regarded as an atavism, the last remnants of a superannuated mentality.

The criticism of the positivist developmental paradigm has resulted in a strong tendency in recent scholarship to dispense altogether with the term 'magic' as an absolute scientific category. It is no longer regarded as a useful tool in describing certain beliefs and practices in the past. But the concept itself has a history. It has been used in the past in a polemical and derogatory way to emphasize certain aspects of those beliefs that were considered to be outside the accepted way of thinking about the world. The history of magic has, therefore, increasingly become conceptual history (or *Begriffsgeschichte* to use the term coined by the the German historian Reinhard Koselleck, who defined the genre). The purpose is no longer to give an account of what magic was, but of what it was perceived to be at any given time.

In the Middle Ages magic was rejected as non-religion, because the main concern of the times was true religion. Today we condemn magic as non-science because our faith has long been in science. Take the category of superstition. To the medieval scholar it meant those practices and beliefs that were outside or in opposition to Christian doctrines. Today superstition instead means conceptions with no foundation in, or in direct contravention of, logical and scientific knowledge. First meaning 'irreligious', the word superstition has taken on the meaning of 'irrational' or 'unscientific'.

In both cases truth finds its identity with reference to its perversion, i.e. to the untrue. There were different ways of handling this dichotomy, the extreme alternatives being inclusion and violent rejection. Missionary Christendom transformed and incorporated bits and pieces of pagan lore and practices; and medieval magic used elements from the Christian Mass. This symbiosis of opposing but closely related doctrines gives rise to ambiguities and doubts. The borderland between orthodox and heretical positions is sometimes so narrow that it takes a real expert, a demonologist inquisitor like Bernhard Gui for example, to tell which side anyone is on.

But the representation of this opposition between true religion and false magic is altogether the work of a learned elite of church men and university scholars, 'the clerical elite whose literate voices dominate the surviving evidence'. It is doubtful whether this dualism pitting saint against magician gives a true picture of popular attitudes and practices. Furthermore, this learned and clearly visible opposition between magic and religion is blurred by the revival in the twelfth century of the classical concept of natural magic as a particular cognitive skill, the ability of philosophers to manipulate the natural world to create effects that appeared as miracles to ordinary people.

This 'white' magic eventually gained a certain position by being entertained both at the new universities and at the royal and noble courts. A doctrinal precondition for this was the emerging distinction between the supernatural and the occult, between the divine, and by extension saintly, realm of true miracles and the immanent secrets still to be found and used in the sublunar world. That is why a modern scholarly tradition, most prominently represented by Lynn Thorndike, has studied this medieval white magic as a kind of proto-science with experimental procedures as a key element. But this 'white' tradition was open to criticism from the guardians of faith. In 1277 the bishop of Paris issued a formal condemnation of 219 propositions drawn from the work of ancient thinkers. And Thomas Aquinas, in a famous dictum, declared that 'everything that visibly occurs in this world can be the work of demons'. The devil could intervene in the course of natural causation, thereby working what seemed to humans to be wonders.

Nevertheless, the sophisticated and versatile definition of 'white' magic might have opened the way for a more relaxed and tolerant attitude of the church to popular superstition as a minor aberration but for another important change of focus taking place with the appearance in the high Middle Ages of organized heretical movements. Large scale doctrinal dissent was suddenly seen to be threatening the very foundations of society, the Church itself as well as all Christian states. It became a matter of great concern for those in power to protect the peasantry and the growing urban proletariat from the temptations of subversive creeds. Rejection was gaining ground as the Church consolidated its position and secular rulers

organized royal judiciaries throughout their territories. Magic became ultimately both a spiritual and physical crime, especially, of course, in its
demonized forms of sorcery and witchcraft.

The account of medieval magic given in this volume is indeed a complex one. It is certainly not the grand and simple story of a journey from
darkness towards light, but a survey of multiple tendencies, of contrasts and
oppositions between learned and folk traditions, between a
classical–Christian tradition and different substrata of Celtic, Germanic and
Slavic 'paganisms'. These shifting paradigms of magic are developed in a
multiplicity of sources–sermons, laws, learned treatises, and, towards the
end of the period, even in court records produced by the inquisition and
the secular courts.

Leaving aside the notion of progress there is still the problem of developmental stages and historical periodization. Are there times of crucial
transformations? Is the timing of these transformations the same over the
whole European area? These complexities notwithstanding it is possible to
discern the main characteristics of different periods within the medieval
millennium. Jolly recognizes three: first, the early missionary campaign
with acculturation, an accommodation between Chistian and pagan faith,
as its pervading strategy; then the twelfth century renaissance, when
scholasticism under the influence of classical, Arabic and Jewish thinking,
reflecting on the nature of knowledge, developed a more complex model
of magic including the natural or 'white' variety; and finally the cultural
dislocation associated with the demographic and economic crisis of the
mid-fourteenth century, when magic was gradually being interpreted as a
coherent and organized demonic cult, pointing the way to the early modern consciousness with its 'heightened discourse over witchcraft and the
increase in accusations of witchcraft and heresy'.

This timetable is, of course, valid only for west-central Europe. In the
trans-Elbian and Baltic north the impact of Christian acculturation was
first felt in the high Middle Ages. The case of the Scandianvian north is
particularly interesting as an example of this later incorporation into the
European mainstream. At least in the eleventh and probably long into the
twelfth century, pagan and Christian culture lived side by side in the north.
The literate Christian elite was, therefore, as in the case of Snorri
Sturluson, closely familiar with the heritage of the older pagan culture
with its cosmological and heroic poems and the family sagas produced for
and centred around the chieftain clans, the ruling strata of Viking society.
This happy overlapping of pagan and missionary Christian culture has left
behind a rich source material for the study of a magic tradition which was
still unaffected by classical and Christian influences, and which, possibly,
could tell us something about the magic prevailing in the Germanic areas
of central Europe before they were Christianized. It might be rewarding to

compare the world of magic in the scattered legal and ecclesiastical sources of the early Middle Ages with the *trolldómr* of pagan Scandinavia, where sources are abundant. In fact, the list of known practices in the early continental Germanic law codes is long. The practices and beliefs condemned there include a large number of charms, and the practices of ritual blessing and cursing, healing, divining, lot casting, fortune telling, storm raising, herb lore, and the use of amulets and talismans. But Catharina Raudvere in her essay on the Old Norse *trolldómr* concept is careful to avoid such comparisons. The theoretical and methodological pitfalls are too many to allow for a direct juxtaposition of eleventh century Iceland and, say, sixth century Saxonia. But in recompense the material allows for an admirably plastic image of an aristocratic peasant society where magic was an important and on the whole tolerated part of daily life even among the ruling elite and across the gender lines.

Periodization pays attention to discontinuities, to the emergence of new paradigms and dramatic social transformations. Still, there are questions about continuities and long-range developmental tendencies that are legitimate to ask, in particular in a series of six volumes like this one, starting with the early beginnings of European witchcraft and magic and ending in the present. One such set of questions about continuities might deal with the converging factors which encouraged the linking of simple popular creeds and rituals with the sophisticated depravity of demonic worship and ritual murder, in short the relationship between popular magic lore and the learned doctrines as they emerged in the late Middle Ages and were fully employed during the great persecutions of the sixteenth and seventeenth centuries. We are intrigued to learn, for instance, that the identification of sorcery and magic with heresy and both with diabolism increased from the mid-twelfth century on; and that in 1217 confession in church was made mandatory for all Christians at least once a year. That of confessor became one of the most important pastoral roles for the clergy. The missionary zeal of this period of the high Middle Ages, when the mendicant orders walked the streets to fight against the sin of heresy, can be compared to the intense clerical energies mobilized by the Protestant and Catholic reformations of the early modern period. In the same category is the observation that the literature of canon law and inquisitorial procedure between the late thirteenth and the early fifteenth centuries laid down both the substantive and procedural groundwork for trying both heretics and sorcerers, particularly as it came to consider the latter guilty of idolatry and violation of the First Commandment.

Yet in the end it must be emphasized that the essays in this volume should be read as contributions to the history of magic in the Middle Ages in its own right. Looking into the past and finding only that which has led up to the present, the precursors of ourselves, as it were, is another distortion of history that we should try to avoid. This can only be done if we pay attention to all those tendencies and sensibilities that did not survive, that perished under the impact of reckless acculturation perpetrated by colonizers of various creeds and persuasions: conquistadors, explorers, missionaries and scholars.

PART I

Medieval Magic: Definitions, Beliefs, Practices

Karen Jolly

Magic is more a concept than a reality. The term is a way of categorizing a wide array of beliefs and practices, ranging from astrology and alchemy, charms and amulets, to sorcery and necromancy, trickery and entertainment, as practised by both laity and clergy, by those of high and low social status, educated and uneducated, and found in diverse sources and contexts, including scientific and medical treatises, liturgical and other religious documents, and literary texts. How certain practices in medieval Europe come to be labelled magic, as opposed to scientific or religious, depends on the perspective of the person using the label, whether a medieval commentator or a modern scholar. Consequently, the study of magic is the study of the systems of thought that defined magic in particular ways, and the changes in these systems over time. The concept of magic is, then, a window into medieval mentalities precisely because it was (and is) a problematic and evolving category in European history. This definitional problem is further complicated when examining the common and courtly traditions of magic because they raise issues of class: those of the literate elite who dominate the written sources privilege certain rationalities over others, making various distinctions between demonic magic and Christian miracle, natural versus supernatural forces, black versus white magic, and high and low forms; moreover, literary treatments add a fictional element to magic as entertainment or trickery, particularly in the court environments. Consequently, these varied sources for magic may or may not reflect the reality of common practice, for which we have less direct evidence. As a consequence, much of the study of popular and courtly magic must consider the impact of the perceptions expressed in literate sources: religious legislation regarding magic, the 'high' tradition of magic/science among intellectuals, and the literary use of magic, treated in greater depth in other essays of this series. Moreover, these perceptions are further elaborated in the early modern and Modern periods, creating another layer of meanings that impinges on the scholarly treatment of magic.

Thus, various authors, both medieval and modern, use the construct magic in different ways to describe collectively a group of practices that the authors want to link under this rubric as exceptional. What is exceptional about magic in these definitions usually arises from a perceived difference in magic's rationality. Magical modes of rationality often involve a way of knowing centred in the principle that nature contains hidden virtues that practitioners can possess or tap for practical purposes, good or ill. Magic as an alternate rationality emerges in response to some normative category, an acceptable way of knowing – for example, revealed, religious knowledge or learned, scientific knowledge. Thus what holds the group of excluded, magical practices together depends upon the theoretical framework of the persons employing the term magic, and its opposite, whether that be religion or science. Further, social distinctions play into these views, particularly when a literate elite employing emergent religious or scientific rationalities dominates the discourse, often leaving the common practices of magic in an excluded category, as demonic or low magic versus the more progressive thinking of religion and science.

Consequently, the use of the word magic in most of the sources tells us more about the world views of those using it than about actual practices. That being the case, it is essential to distinguish between modern and medieval notions of magic, and to dissect some of the processes that produced these notions, before examining actual practices that were classified as such. Since the construct is so deeply embedded in the knowledge systems of European history, the topic of magic is central to the study of medieval culture. This centrality is evident in three interrelated ways.

First, magic is critical to the modern study of medieval thought because of the western intellectual model of 'progress' that posits development from magic through religion to science. This paradigm of magic as an early developmental stage of rationality affects the way modernity conceptualizes the Middle Ages within the larger scope of European history. For example, if magic is construed as a first stage preceding progress to a second stage of religion, then the process of 'Christianization' is understood, by both medieval Christian authors and many modern scholars, as the triumph of 'religious thinking' over 'magical thinking.' In so far as magic persists, it indicates a failure of the religion. In this anachronistic paradigm, the so-called Christian Middle Ages, with their retention of magical thinking, slowed down or even impeded the march of progress toward scientific rationality.

Second, magic is central to the study of medieval society not only because of these problematic modern constructions of progress, but also because the conceptualization of magic was a central issue in the Middle Ages as well. Changing definitions of magic were indeed part of the cultural shifts in the period 500–1500, especially in the intellectual changes that increasingly separated and defined elite, academic cultures from popular cultures, evident in the evolving distinctions between high and low, white and black, natural and unnatural magic.

Third, the study of medieval magic in context highlights the convergence of three lines of tradition in European societies: the classical or Graeco-Roman heritage, Christian belief and practice, and local 'indigenous' (Celtic, Germanic, Slavic, Scandinavian) traditions. The complex interplay between theology, medicine and folklore, the tensions between orthodoxy and heresy, and the growing gap between popular and formal religion are reflections of this multicultural heritage that emerges in the discourse over magic.

In light of this phenomenology of magic, this essay takes a three-pronged approach to the subject, examining it from three perspectives, historiographical, conceptual and contextual or pragmatic. Part One, 'Definitions of Magic,' examines the wider historiographic issues in the study of magic as a relative term, focusing on some major shifts in this century, partly as the result of influences from cultural anthropology as well as changing conceptions of medieval Christianity. Part Two, 'Beliefs about Magic,' proposes a theoretical model of paradigm shifts in the Middle Ages that caused redefinitions of the concept magic in the dominant discourses of the period. These shifts are located at the initial conversion periods, in the twelfth-century renaissance, and in the charged environment of the fifteenth century. Part Three, 'The Practice of Magic', examines the particular practices associated with magic in the common and courtly traditions in five categories, healing, protection, divination, occult knowledge and entertainment, with examples drawn from Ireland to Russia, Scandinavia to Italy in the period 500–1500.

This tripartite approach is in some ways like eating an artichoke, by stripping the outer layers of the modern constructs to expose the inner medieval, predominantly Christian, concepts arising out of the heart of the matter, magical practices themselves. Much of what we take to be the essence of magic practice will turn out to be only the outer layers of perceptions of magic, each giving a mere taste of actual practices and beliefs that are no longer available to us directly.

CHAPTER 1

Definitions of Magic

The Greek μαγεία and Latin *magia* contain within them the seeds of the paradigm for magic as developed in succeeding ages, primarily the sense of 'otherness' (Luck 1985: 3–9, 25–46; Mathiesen 1995: 157; Tavenner 1966: 1–8). Magic is most often a label used to identify ideas or persons who fall outside the norms of society and are thereby marked as special or non-normative, either for the purpose of exclusion or to heighten a sense of mysterious power inherent in their status. This alien quality of magic appears also in the Christian tradition. The three Magi at Christ's birth are educated Persians, foreigners in the Roman world, who enter the story as keepers of the arcane knowledge of astronomy/astrology, creating a tension in the Christian tradition of the *magi* as both sorcerer and wisemen (Jacobus de Voragine 14, 1993: I: 79). Christian resistance to the kind of secret knowledge and manipulative power implied by the label *magus* is evident in the New Testament story of Simon Magus (Acts 8: 9–25), often elaborated upon in later legends and adapted in saints' lives (Jacobus de Voragine 89, 1993: I: 340–50; Ferreiro 1996). Simon's attempts to buy divine power from the Apostles to supplement his own magical prowess contributes to the dichotomy between magic as demonic and heretical versus the miraculous and divine power bestowed by God. This distinction becomes fundamental in the minds of medieval European clerics. In theory, a sharp line existed between magic as illusions of the devil and the very real, divine power exhibited in the Eucharist and in miracles performed by saints. This ecclesiastical dualism pitting saint against magician – a figure often demonized with the other scapegoats in medieval society, heretics, Jews and witches – is a powerful model, but should not be taken at face value or applied too literally to popular practice. Popular culture, of which the common tradition of magic is a part, is an amorphous entity that exists in a symbiotic relationship with the more clearly articulated formal culture promulgated by the primarily clerical elite whose literate voices dominate the surviving evidence.

Popular practices in medieval Europe, including folk knowledge of medicinal remedies, special plants or holy places, amulets, charms and curses, often arise out of the Celtic, Scandinavian, Germanic and Slavic cultures of Europe, as well as derive support from residual Graeco-Roman traditions. European vernacular languages in the Middle Ages had no word that functioned like 'magic' to encompass these various practices under a single rubric of problematic or excluded practices; rather, classical *magia* intertwined with paganism and heresy as large categories of exclusion (Muchembled 1994: 9). *Superstitio* was often used by churchmen as a milder term of opprobrium to indicate the illogicality of false belief (Brown 1996: 35). Thus popular practices are only magic in so far as the classical Christian template is imposed on them by churchmen, who do so for different reasons, with different results, in different contexts. The same applies to practitioners of such arts, who fall under a variety of condemnatory labels in laws, canons, and sermons – as sorcerers, witches, death-workers, magicians and diviners, with strong associations with heathenism and heresy. However, we know very little about these putative magicians beyond the condemnations; the unifying labels of magicians or heretics only tell us something about the world view of the ecclesiastical authors.

In essence, modern scholarship is confronted with two intertwining strands interacting in medieval Europe: the continuity of folk practices that are rapidly absorbing and adapting Christian and classical ideas, and the shifting paradigms of magic developed in sermons, laws and treatises as a way of categorizing illegitimate versus legitimate knowledge and practice (and as a way of establishing the authority of the church over knowledge). These latter, authoritarian models dominate the written evidence; consequently it is easy to assume these intellectual distinctions about magic pervaded medieval society. However, popular practices of healing, divination or protection from invisible forces, less readily accessible in the surviving documents, do not always fit neatly into these intellectual categories. The symbiotic relationship between the common tradition and the elite definitions of magic, each shaping the other, creates a large grey area of popular practices in Christian Europe that are not clearly magic or miracle, but lie on a spectrum in between. The popular practices lying across the middle of this spectrum, while often conservative in handling traditional knowledge, are constantly adapted to changing circumstances, including the ecclesiastical and intellectual winds of change. In turn, the intellectual changes in the magic-religion paradigm, evolving out of new assumptions about knowledge and nature, then seek to recategorize existing practices towards one end of the spectrum or the other. Thus, the degree to which European folk remedies adapted to a Christian world view creates a contested zone in the changing definitions of magic over the coming centuries.

Historiographic Models

This complexity of practice versus theory is not limited to the medieval period itself. The subsequent evolution of the magic–religion–science distinction in early modern and modern European intellectual history has left its stamp on scholarship and still dominates the way scholars approach medieval practices. Thus, another reason why some medieval popular practices earn the designation magic, in addition to the dominance of medieval Christian writers, is the subsequent elaboration of this Christian model of 'magic versus religion' into the modern (and now disputed) paradigm of 'progress' from magic to religion to science. In this evolutionary view, magic is manipulative in its focus on effective results, compared to the supplicative quality of religious prayer; and magic is unsystematic and irrational compared to the rationality of scientific thought.

The chief implication of this view of magic as incoherent and unsystematic thought in need of replacement by religion and science is found in the notion of magic as degenerate religion. If people 'fall back into' manipulative, superstitious rituals and prayers because they have 'lost' the religious meaning, they have in effect degenerated into incoherence (Merrifield 1987: 6, 36). This 'origins' bias privileging the original over subsequent meanings also works in reverse: when religions like Christianity take over an older practice and 'Christianize' it (Christmas trees, for example), the modern tendency is to see this as the retention of paganism with a veneer of Christianity, rather than as a transformative process in which old and new ideas interact to create a new and meaningful ritual with ties to the past.

A second problematic assumption of the magic–religion–science evolutionary paradigm is the oft deployed distinction between manipulation and supplication as the dividing line between magic and religion, charm and prayer. The historical evidence, however, contains more grey areas than clear examples of one versus the other. To cite just one pair of examples, note the coercive power of the prayers of saints found throughout hagiographical literature – the saints' holiness and hence closeness to God allows them virtually to compel God to do their will – while at the same time charm rituals incorporate supplicative prayer, appealing to the Creator of all nature to empower the natural elements with healing virtue. To call the manipulative saints magic-workers is to make nonsense out of the medieval world view they represent; likewise, to categorize medicinal remedies employing charms with Christian prayers as 'magic' is to miss something essential in the development of religious thought in the Middle Ages.

Because this magic–religion–science progress view is so deeply entrenched in modern consciousness, some sense of how this model was deployed in nineteenth and twentieth-century scholarship, and how it is now disputed, is a necessary preliminary to examining the medieval evidence. The European-encoded ideas of magic as demonic, evil and fearful, as medieval or backward, as unscientific, irrational or uncivilized, as something 'other,' are hard to exorcize. These notions of magic pervade the way we think as moderns and are ingrained in modern scholarship on the Middle Ages.

Modernity has two main attitudes towards the medieval past that have an impact on the study of magic, one emphasizing continuity with the Middle Ages by identifying modern roots in the period, the other emphasizing discontinuity with the past by highlighting the otherness of the Middle Ages (Freedman and Spiegel 1998). In the continuity view, with its concern for establishing the roots of modernity in the medieval past, magic has either been marginalized as peripheral to progress or as an early, and hence disposable, stage of progress in rationality. In particular, the common tradition of magic becomes in this view a remnant or leftover of superstitious thinking superceded by more important intellectual developments. With the rise of social and cultural history and the study of mentalities, the 'otherness' view of medieval culture has come into greater prominence, emphasizing its dissonance with modernity by bringing into the centre of the stage elements of popular culture such as magic and other forms of dissidence in the Middle Ages, evident in the work of Emmanuel Le Roi Ladurie, Carlo Ginzburg, and Michel Foucault (Muir and Ruggiero 1991; Hunt 1989). In this view, magic as well as religious mysticism and other distinctively non-modern phenomena become alternative rationalities from a world now lost to us, the path not taken by the rise of scientific rationalism (Murray 1978: 404).

The implications of these differing views on the relation between modernity and the medieval can be traced in twentieth-century historiography of magic, from the evolutionary model of magic–religion–science in anthropology to the post-modern deconstruction of that model.

The evolutionary model of progress in rationality from magic through religion to science emerged in late nineteenth and early twentieth-century anthropological studies (Tylor 1889; Frazer 1911; Malinowski 1948). In part, this magic–religion–science view is a product of early modern European intellectual history and the construction of a progressive rationality from the Renaissance and Reformation through the Enlightenment to the Scientific Revolution, and influenced in the modern period by pseudo-Darwinian notions of social evolution. But the view of magic as 'primitive thought' is also the product of European contact with other cultures through colonization and Christian missions. The colonial and mission efforts to assess developmental phases in human societies based on a European model led them to categorize non-urban, non-literate societies as 'children', or 'primitive', to see their non-Christian beliefs and practices as magic, not religion, and to associate their lifestyle with 'Dark Age' Europe. While early anthropologists rejected the political and religious elements of these early encounters in an effort to establish a neutral, objective view of human societies, they did not escape the progressive developmental bias implicit in the magic–religion–science model they produced. Further, this identification of some non-western cultures with pre-modern Europe also reversed itself, as medieval Europe became the site of the 'primitive' in the European past and therefore subject to anthropological study.

It was in the context of this dominant paradigm of magic–religion–science that Lynn Thorndike wrote *The Place of Magic in the Intellectual History of Europe* (1905) and produced his magisterial multivolume *History of Magic and Experimental Science* (1923). Thorndike presents magic primarily as a primitive philosophy of the preternatural, but secondarily as a tradition that manifests itself in literate historic periods in residual shreds of beliefs and practices, and in attempts by intellectuals to rationalize and define the parameters of the preternatural. As a consequence of these traits, magic in Thorndike's view lacks within itself any coherent system or rationality, but survives within more organized systems (religion or science) as a remnant of the primitive past. Yet while some of the terminology Thorndike employs betrays an essentially nineteenth-century sensibility ('primitive') and progressivist notions, nonetheless his conclusion that the history of magic in Europe is bound up with that of science, folklore and religion still holds. The premise of universality, and the problematic nature of words such as 'occult' and 'superstition' in his work should not obscure two innovative arguments in Thorndike's approach. First is his thesis that magic and experimental science are intimately connected within the context of medieval Christian thought; and second is his willingness to allow a definition of magic to emerge from the texts over time, to the point of asserting that any understanding of the twelfth and thirteenth-century views could only be understood by looking at the preceding centuries and traditions (hence his multivolume work). Despite the now-disputed anthropological model of magic he employs, Thorndike's work has enduring value because, as a historian, he allowed the texts to speak from their own contexts. His focus on the complex conjunction of magic and science in the twelfth and thirteenth centuries, as a formative period for the development of European theories of knowledge and systems of thought, in many ways laid the groundwork for the later challenges to the magic–religion–science paradigm.

Nonetheless, it is hard to escape the pervasive influence of this universalizing paradigm even in more recent attempts to alter it. The work of Keith Thomas, *Religion and the Decline of Magic* (1971), and Valerie Flint, *The Rise of Magic in Early Medieval Europe* (1991), significantly modifies the relationship between magic, religion and science in European history by suggesting a 'rise and fall' paradigm. Thomas's book is a masterful study of the early modern evolution of the concept of magic as incoherent and unsystematic and its decline under the pressure of more coherent religious and scientific rationalities, linking the decrease in clerical claims to supernatural power with a decrease in magical arts. Flint's equally erudite and detailed study of early medieval Europe examines the period of rise in magic before the decline described by Thomas. Flint adopts a universalist definition of magic as preternatural control over nature, similar to Thorndike, but goes on to explore the problematic nature of magic as a historical construct in relation to religion and science, acknowledging the dangers of a single definition (Flint 1991: 4). Like Thomas, Flint sees magic not so much as a system of thought but as a historically conditioned set of phenomena lacking coherence; this incoherence of magic is the result of acculturation between the religion of Christianity and the magic of pre-Christian practices and beliefs. This rise-and-fall model of magic, like the evolutionary-progress model of magic–religion–science, presupposes that magic and religion can be distinguished from one another according to some universal formula.

Recent anthropological theory, however, has challenged that presupposition by demonstrating that the magic–religion–science distinction is the product of historical forces in early modern European history and is not a universal phenomena (Geertz and Thomas 1975: 71, 76–77; Hsu 1983; Tambiah 1990; Herbert 1991). It becomes an anachronism, therefore, to measure medieval Europe by the standard of a later period and define its beliefs and practices as magic. However, the implications of this anthropological deconstruction of magic–religion–science have not yet been fully assessed in the field of history or medieval studies. Meanwhile, other scholars in search of a universal paradigm have turned to new models in literary studies, religious studies and sociology, but nonetheless continue to emphasize incoherence and non-rationality as essential to magic's definition. In literary approaches, semiotics endeavours to chart or compare magic's efficacy to empirical science (Nöth 1977; Mathiesen 1995). Sociological approaches to religion offer systematic ways of treating magic and religion together and bypassing the distinction between the two, evident in Ninian Smart's six dimensions of world views, James Russell's BAVB model, and Jacob Neusner's neutral rubric of 'modes of rationality' (Smart 1983; J. C. Russell 1994; Neusner 1989: 3–7, 61–81). These efforts in religious studies reflect the search to find a common ground or Foucaultian *tabula* on which to place the varieties of beliefs and practices called magic or religion (Foucault 1970: xv–xxiv).

A viable alternative, however, is to reject any effort to arrive at a universal definition of magic and instead work towards contextual definitions of the concept. It is in this arena of a contextualist approach that the otherness of the Middle Ages converges with new efforts to understand medieval magic. Some medieval historians, responding to changes in anthropology, have rejected the notion of magic as essentially unsystematic, non-rational and incoherent compared to the more rational and systematic nature of religion (Kieckhefer 1994b: 814). Rather than reading magic as either 'surviving' despite inroads from religion, or religion 'compromising' itself by accommodating magic thinking, the shifting notions of Christian, pagan and magic can be explicated in terms of dynamic interactions amid their inherent commonalities. The 'subterranean attraction of deep homologies', in Peter Brown's terminology, allows so-called pagan beliefs or magic thinking and religion to 'sidle up to each other' (Brown 1995: 12–13). In a similar fashion, Alexander Murray suggests that avoiding the two-sided view of magic versus religion allows us to see the 'religious aspirations' of magic and points to the complexity and inconstancy of medieval beliefs and practices: 'Everyone, intellectual or rustic, actually accepted both modes of thinking, magical and non-magical, but in ratios widely differing, and, in each person, with a boundary of uncertainty between what they did and did not believe' (Murray 1992: 203–4). Cultural studies in general, or ethnohistory in particular, offer an opportunity to study magic in a broader context, for example by examining popular religion as Gábor Klaniczay has done (Klaniczay 1990).

In sum, the most recent work is more concerned with commonalities and accommodation than with defining boundaries between magic and religion, in part because all such boundaries are artificial and all definitions suspect. The shared ground of both religion and magic – whether one calls it world views, modes of rationality or beliefs and practices – is becoming the centre of attention in current scholarship (Meens, 1998). This is abundantly clear in Richard Kieckhefer's *Magic in the Middle Ages*, where magic is a crossroads central to a medieval culture that is alien and 'other' to a modern mentality. If magic is a way of 'understanding how different cultures relate to one another', then the study of medieval magic is a multicultural study focused on the interactions between different traditions, classes and regions (Kieckhefer 1990: 2; Muchembled 1994: 11, 317–20). Consequently, the study of medieval magic means engaging in conceptual history. History of concepts traces not only intellectual constructs but also popular notions – in effect, the full complexity of encoded beliefs and ideas across the social spectrum and in all media, whether written or visual, abstract or concrete (Russell 1987: 9). As a concept, magic has a history and a tradition from which changing definitions emerge. The following section (Part II) looks at the broad picture of that tradition in medieval European history, marking out certain phases when historical conditions brought the concept of magic into contention and hence provide evidence for the ways the concept was evolving. These contexts form the basis for understanding the common and courtly practices of magic outlined in Part III.

CHAPTER 2

Beliefs about Magic: Conceptual Shifts and the Nature of the Evidence

Three periods in medieval European history constitute phases of change for the concept of magic, the conversion period, the twelfth-century renaissance, and the late-fourteenth and early-fifteenth-century cultural dislocations. In each of these eras, changing economic, social, political, intellectual and religious conditions caused shifts in both belief and practice. More importantly, each of these periods involved some kind of dynamic cross-cultural exchange accompanied by tensions between different traditions. Out of these periods, new, sometimes competing, conceptions of magic, religion and science emerged (Kieckhefer 1990: 72). This section surveys the conditions in these three shifts and the attendant changes that ensued in the following period. The first conceptual shift, during the conversion phase, is not easily datable because of regional differences, but occurred variously in the centuries between *circa* 300 and *circa* 1100 as different European cultures came to terms with Christianity. In this phase, acculturation is a prominent pattern, as older beliefs and practices began to adapt to the new religion. The second shift is located in the twelfth-century renaissance, but had wide-ranging implications beyond scholasticism. Scholastics redefined the nature of knowledge, in part through Arabic and Jewish influence; they also fostered a divide between natural and supernatural and increased the distance between the much more holistic popular experience of nature and intellectual apprehensions of nature in Aristotelian terms. The third shift occurs amidst radical social and political dislocation in the late Middle Ages, beginning *circa* 1350 when magic becomes a coherent and organized demonic cult in the minds of church authorities who prosecuted it. Significantly, lay people's conceptions of their relationship to the material world were changing, at the same time that Renaissance humanists were experimenting with new ways to manipulate the natural world.

Oddly enough, the larger pattern evident in these three phases is the increasing prominence of magic as a definable phenomenon within the growing tradition of rationalism, culminating in the late Middle Ages in the emergence of the Renaissance *magus*. If, then, magic as a construct 'rises' during the Middle Ages, it does so in the context of scientific development and reaches its peak at the brink of the early modern period, in a way similar, and parallel, to the heightened discourse over witchcraft and the increase in accusations of witchcraft and heresy. The concept of magic in the Middle Ages is a product of these intellectual and legal developments.

The Conversion Phase and the Early Middle Ages

In this first phase, the late antique synthesis of biblical and classical concepts of magic intersected with Celtic, Germanic, Scandinavian and Slavic peoples through conversion. The Celtic inhabitants of the British Isles converted in the fifth century and produced an influential bilingual written Christian culture; charms and other formulas appear in the later texts of the invading Anglo-Saxons, and Irish penitential literature, including prohibitions against magic, spread to the continent. Various Goths, Franks, Angles, Saxons and other Germanic groups gradually converted to Roman Christianity, sometimes from Arianism, over the course of the fifth and sixth centuries, producing the bulk of the synthesized Roman–Christian–Germanic literature in England, France, Germany, Iberia and Italy (Behringer, Muchembled, Sharpe, and Bethencourt in Muchembled 1994: 65–7, 100–2, 133–4, 159–61). The later Scandinavian conversions, in Sweden, Denmark, Norway, and Iceland, left a larger body of evidence of pre-Christian practice embedded in the written traditions of the Christian era – runes, sagas of the gods and heroes, charms and amulets (Ankarloo in Muchembled 1994: 195–7; Raudvere in this volume). In eastern Europe, Slavic groups in Poland and Bohemia and the invading Magyars in Hungary converted to Roman Christianity in the ninth and tenth centuries, while the Scandinavian-Slavic kingdom of Rus under Prince Vladimir chose Eastern Orthodoxy (Klaniczay in Muchembled 1994: 215–18). Even later, in the thirteenth century, the conversion of pagan Baltic peoples like the Lithuanians introduced new elements, or hitherto lost components, of pre-Christian practice that survive better in the more highly literate environment of the high Middle Ages. In most of these cases, the converting rulers purposely aligned themselves with an international church body, either the Roman or the Byzantine, that then entered the region as an authority figure with permission to introduce their own ideas into the indigenous culture, creating a tension between local/pagan and outsider/Christian in the ongoing process of conversion and negotiation.

Consequently, two kinds of early medieval evidence survive from these conversion syntheses of Roman Christian and indigenous practices, from which the beginnings of a common tradition of magic in Europe emerges. On the negative side are laws, canons, penitentials, saints' lives, sermons and other treatises that condemn a range of practices; these sources derive their notions of magic from the late antique Roman Christian tradition supplemented by intriguing, but by no means complete or reliable, references to and descriptions of local practices condemned as demonic, pagan superstition. On the positive side, hagiographical literature, medicinal manuals, and liturgical rituals written down primarily by clerics indicate at least a textualized, Christianized set of practices that may partially reflect common practices and beliefs that some people in some places might label magic, but which were, at least in the Christianized form we have them in these texts, acceptable to many. Because both of these types of sources are overwhelmingly Christian in world view, they must be used with care as evidence for magic in early medieval Europe. And yet since the practices listed in these texts form the bulk of our knowledge about magic and are widely cited as evidence, their use by modern scholars bears examining.

The period of European conversion to Christianity is one of the chief points at which modern scholars argue for the continuance or rise of magic, based on the evidence of practices and beliefs that seem to be 'non-Christian'. Thus the problem of magic in the early Middle Ages is closely connected with the larger question of the Christianization of Europe (Van Engen 1986). The difficulty with examining the continuity of pre-Christian practices into the Christian era as evidence of magic or of the survival of 'paganism' is that this approach assumes the binary thinking of medieval Christian writers (Stanley 1975). The ecclesiastical sources of the first type, those condemning magic, pit Christian religion and true belief against pagan magic and superstition, thus eliding the differences between pre-Christian religions and magic. The essential divide for these Church writers is between Christian/religion/divine miracle and pagan/magic/demonic illusion. For example, in Bede's account of the mission to England, he describes how Æthelberht, king of Kent, received the missionary party of Augustine of Canterbury in the open air because the king, based on an old tradition of augury, feared their *maleficae artes* (Bede, *Ecclesiastical History* I: 25, 1994: 39–40). However, as Bede points out, the monks came 'endowed with divine not devilish power' carrying the cross and singing litanies, a scene comparable to Constantine's miraculous victory against the magic-using rival emperors Maxentius and Licinius in Eusebius' biography of Constantine (I: 27, 37, II: 4–7 in Jolly 1997: 40–2). Likewise, Gregory of Tours has the Burgundian Christian princess Clotild arguing with her husband, the Frankish king Clovis, that his idols, specified as the Roman deities Jupiter, Mars and Mercury, are immoral, powerless, and what they do achieve is done through 'magical arts' (Gregory of Tours, *History of the Franks* II: 28, 1974: 141–3; cf. Bede, *Ecclesiastical History* II: 10,

1994: 87–9). Early medieval Christian historians like Gregory of Tours and Bede used the label magic as a way of condemning paganism as false by identifying it with magic as a pejorative concept.

When we turn to the 'positive' evidence of Christianized practices that might appear magical to some, the problem of this binary thinking is exacerbated by modern scholars, who read into the early medieval rejection of magic as 'not religion' a modern rejection of magic as 'not science'. Practices found in the second type of sources (hagiography, liturgical medicine) appear magical in the sense of unscientific manipulations of nature, at least from a modern definition which sees miracle-working saints as closely resembling magicians in their ability to transform natural phenomena; but they would not necessarily appear magical from the perspective of an early medieval Christian writer, who identifies magic primarily as antithetical to right religion and venerates the saints precisely because of their validating miracles. For example, using the mass or other liturgical formulae to 'enchant' herbs for healing is a ritual practised by early medieval Christians that a later age would classify as manipulative magic and not legitimate Christian religion. Some scholars have interpreted these liturgical 'charms' as evidence of a survival of earlier pagan/magical beliefs with a mere Christian veneer and concluded that Christianization failed to displace this magical thinking (Storms 1948; Jolly 1996: 100–1, 118–19; 141–2, 163–4).

An alternative approach is to posit the existence of a form of Christianity in late antiquity and into the Middle Ages that did believe in the power of words for healing in a way similar to local converts, and to explore the possibility that folk practices such as charms are not essentially religious in nature and hence are free to adapt to a new religious system (Jolly 1996). The issue in early medieval Europe was not so much whether words had power or invisible spiritual forces existed – they certainly did in the minds of most Christian thinkers – but *whose* words and *whose* spiritual forces (divine or demonic). Early medieval Christianity thus shared three fundamental assumptions with local folk world views: belief in the power of words, in the existence of invisible entities, and in the power of hidden virtues in natural objects.

Whether these assumptions constitute 'magical' or 'religious' thinking is hard to determine, since both the magic thinkers and the religious thinkers, both the local culture and the missionary, are active participants and members of communities coping with change by adapting new to old (Murray 1992; Nie 1995). In essence, during the conversion phase, the macrocosm or larger world view shifted to a Christian monotheism, while the microcosm of everyday practices adapted to this new world view. This principle was fostered self-consciously by the missionaries themselves, evident for example in Pope Gregory's famous advice to Abbot Mellitus to convert temples of idols into churches, keeping the customary festivities with animals now sacrificed not to the devil but in thanksgiving to the one God who gave the animals to humans as food (Bede, *Ecclesiastical History* I: 30, 1994: 56–7). The doctrinal elements of Christianity, its monotheism and Christology, eventually dominate, but the experiential dimension of religion shows continuity, for example, in the belief in invisible spiritual agents such as demons or elves, or the reliance on words of power in charms or in the Mass. Consequently, the major shift in this period is seen in the incorporation of Christian monotheistic ritual and theology into everyday practice and belief and vice versa, evident in the textualizing and legitimizing of oral practices by literate Christian authors. These adaptations are culture-specific, but overall indicate a conscious desire to identify and build on the commonalities between Germanic and Christian practices while at the same time confronting the differences between pre-Christian and Christian beliefs (Karras 1986). In general, then, during conversion the cosmology changes, but everyday life and practice go on, including medicinal and protective rituals that might in a later age be classified as magic but are here Christianized with the inclusion of appeals to the one God, creator of all nature, and reliance on the power of the Eucharist.

However, undeniably objectionable pre-Christian practices did continue and were condemned by Christian leaders. Practices that seemed to circumvent the power of the one God or his priests were more troublesome to Church leaders because they did not fit the Christian cosmology or did not point to the centrality of the church and its altars. These, such as astrology, divination, curses and graveyard rituals were the items that earned clerical condemnation as magic. The most influential treatise condemning magic is Book VIII of Isidore of Seville's *Etymologies*. He focuses on divination of various kinds, such as auguries, oracles and necromancy, as well as 'execrable remedies' that use incantations, signs and amulets, rejecting them as both demonic in origin and unscientific in practice. Popular sermons, for example by Martin of Braga and Agobard of Lyons, castigated rustics for un-Christian and illogical *superstitio* that imperilled both soul and body (Hillgarth 1986: 57–64; Dutton 1993: 189–91).

Similar views are expressed in early medieval laws and penitentials, which tend to be conservative and repetitive, copying and building on each other (McNeill and Gamer 1965). Burchard of Worms's masterful collection reflects the dominant threads, condemning magic practices with both Roman and Germanic roots, such as the Roman divinitory practice of auguries and Germanic pagan rituals (McNeill and Gamer 1965: 321–45). A number of the prohibitions focus on pagan rituals, such as funeral wakes with diabolical songs and dances, eating offerings to idols at tombs, springs, trees, stones, crossroads, honouring Jupiter on Thursday (i.e.

Thor's Day), dressing as a calf or stag on the Kalends of January or beginning weaving that day for luck, women running water under a dead man's
bier, or anointing a dead man's wounds to heal them in the next life. One
curious practice indicating animistic belief in nature spirits is that of putting child-sized bows and arrows and shoes in the barn for satyrs and gob-
lins to play with, in order to bribe them to increase one's store, with the
suggestion that they would do so by stealing from one's neighbours. Other
superstitions include belief in supernatural beings, such as werewolves,
amorous forest nymphs, and the three Fates, sisters for whom women set
extra places at the table. A disturbing number of Burchard's items concern
rituals performed by women in death rituals and love magic, as well as
belief in women being able to ride with demons at night with the Roman
Diana or the Germanic witch Hulda. Driving a stake through an unbaptized infant or a mother and infant dead in childbirth to prevent harmful
revenants is condemned, as is burying a baptized child with a wax host in
the left hand and a wax chalice in the other. The most curious ritual he
describes, for getting rid of an unwanted husband, involves the woman
stripping naked and coated with honey, rolling in grain, and then making a
deadly bread from the flour, milled backwards. These penitentials and laws
are intent on condemning belief in these practices as much as the actual
practitioners. In some cases, the laws go so far as to condemn accusations
against magicians as demonstrably false. For example, Burchard condemns
belief in women dedicated to Satan being able to go out of the body, slay
baptized people and cook and eat their flesh, leaving straw or wood in
place of their hearts. Nor, according to Burchard, can women actually
harm people by cutting turf from their footprints and using it in magical
rituals, although, ironically, there are instances of Christian saints whose
holy footprints produce miracles.

Thus much of this critique in early medieval Christian literature identified magic practices with paganism and asserted that they are demonic
illusions. This created a battleground, then, between the delusory, evil,
demonic, pagan magic and the very real, good, Christian religion and its
miracles. For example, in Gregory the Great's *Life of St Benedict*, the saint
sees through the demonic illusion of a kitchen fire that befuddles his
monks, a fire caused by a heathen idol buried underneath (*Dialogues* II,
1959: 75–6). Macarius likewise has the saintly ability to perceive truly the
form of a girl believed by everyone else to have been turned by magic into
a horse; making the sign of the cross removes the delusion (Ælfric 1966: I:
470–1). Consequently, the common Christian view of witches and magicians as agents of the devil is that they do harm primarily through deception or creating illusions in the mind. Christianity renders them powerless
by denying their efficacy and proposing a substitute. The antidote to magic
is then manifested in the miraculous power of the one God as wielded by

his saints and emissaries. For example, in a typical hagiographical account of demon possession, from sixth-century Gaul, St Eugendus heals a tormented young woman (Hillgarth 1986: 14–15). Others had attempted to exorcize the demon using written formulas hung around her neck, but the demon jeered at them by pointing out the sinful failings of their authors; many such papyri amulets containing written formulas from saintly persons survive. However, no amount of saints' papyri would satisfy this demon, who revealed that only one would work, that of Eugendus, whose written exorcism subsequently drove out the demon even before the text was half way back to the woman. Clearly Eugendus' written formula, and any others from saints, are operating as real sources of divine power in opposition to illusory demonic power.

To call both the saint's efforts and the demon's activities magic would render the story non-sensical. However, one can still raise the question: were early medieval Christians perpetuating a new form of 'Christian magic', for example, by encouraging idol worship in the reliquaries of saints? Bernard of Angers in the eleventh century confronts the issue fairly directly in his defence of St Foy (Sheingorn 1995: 77–9). In the midst of recounting numerous stories of Foy punishing those who deny her power, slander her or show disrespect to her shrine, Bernard uses his own initial, scholarly doubt about saints' idols to argue that it is 'an ineradicable and innate custom of simple people' that does not, in fact, contribute to lapses into paganism. In fact, he seems intent on demonstrating the validity of relics even for intellectuals like himself, moving them beyond the realm of popular *superstitio*.

The self-consciousness with which early medieval Christian writers distinguished between magic and religion is instructive. One clear result of drawing the battle lines in this way was to open the door to the power of Christian ritual. Early medieval Christianity offered the power of Christian words and rituals as substitutes for believers, both in the realm of religious practice and in folk medicine. Just as Pope Gregory advised the English mission to convert pagan sites and rituals into churches, so too the great missionary to the Saxons, Boniface, fought pagan practice by displacing it. In the famous story of the oak told by Willibald, Boniface was so disgusted with the continued practice by converts of divination, legerdemain, incantations, auguries and other practices carried out at trees and springs that he attacked the Oak of Jupiter with an ax (Jolly 1997: 208). After it miraculously fell into four equal lengths, Boniface built an oratory from it. While on the one hand, many sermon writers roundly condemned the continued practice of devilish worship found in auguries, invocations and charms, they also urged Christians to resort to the powerful signs and incantations of the cross, the Creed, and the Lord's Prayer, using these blessings over herbs instead of diabolical pagan ones (McNeill and Gamer 1938: 41–2).

As substitutions and as antidotes, these Christian prescriptions functioned as words of power, but unlike the demonic incantations, they were efficacious rather than illusory or deceptive because they appealed to the one God, creator of all things.

The binary structure of demonic magic versus divine miracle, harmful incantation versus efficacious prayer is clear in early medieval Christian writings, as is the transformative power of Christianity. The repetition of the same condemnations in the surviving documents, using the same language to reject magic/paganism as demonic, illusory and deceptive, indicates a dominant tradition imposed on the converting populace from above. Pagan magic, Germanic or classical in origin, merged in condemnatory lists. In all of these cases, the Christian cosmology is asserted as obliterating, demonizing, or demoting pre-Christian cosmological structures, while particular folk practices, such as blessing herbs, were adjusted to fit that Christian cosmology. This paradigm shift resulting from the conversion phase colours everything we read about popular practice in the early Middle Ages and suggests caution in making assertions about the actual practice of magic in this period.

Paradigm Shifts in and after the Twelfth Century

If early medieval Christian writings tended to combine or overlap categories, twelfth-century thinkers tended to expand and redefine categories. The pre-twelfth century views described above merged so-called paganism and various forms of magic under the rubric of condemned, demonic, illusory practices. The post-twelfth-century world, a period of rapid intellectual change under the impetus of a variety of economic, social, and cross-cultural influences, began to define magic in new ways and to make distinctions between different kinds of magic (high and low, white and black), definitions that had far-reaching implications. These changes among the intelligentsia had the effect of leaving the popular practice of magic as a substratum that, while maintaining continuity of practice with the past, appears curiously different in the light of the new scholastic definitions propounded by the elite. The creation of a high, scientific study of something that might be called magic (for example, astrology) stands in contrast to what now becomes the low, practical efforts of the common cunning man or woman. This has the effect of creating a new dimension in the good versus evil distinction. Common magic is wrong because it is *illiterata* as well as *superstitio*. Simultaneously, a courtly and literary tradition of magic created an artificial world where power took on occult dimensions, for good or ill. In many ways, the courtly tradition of magic has more in common with the intellectual changes of the high Middle Ages, creating a gap between itself and the common traditions.

These distinctions evolve gradually over the course of the thirteenth century, but are the product of changes beginning in the twelfth century 'renaissance' (Benson and Constable 1982; Ward 1982). This changing mentality is the result of three main currents: the new urban environments, the reform movements and the development of Aristotelian logic versus early medieval Augustinian thought. First, the economic and social changes of the eleventh century toward urbanism created new classes of people, with new needs, and new distinctions between urban and rural, with the consequence that rural herbal medicine now existed in relation to towns and cities, with their imports and trade connections. Second, the reform movements that sought to purify the Church from secular influence and establish its primacy in relation to secular authority, while primarily concerned with the upper echelons of medieval society, nonetheless had an impact on the local parish level in terms of the reform of clergy and increasingly specific lifestyle recommendations for the laity. Third, the new schools of thought and the subsequent importation of classical and eastern Mediterranean learning through Jewish Arabic sources – most importantly the recovery of Aristotle – led to new conceptions of *scientia*, knowledge, and new ways of classifying magic as an intellectual category.

The official Church stance regarding magic shifted from a demonic association with paganism to a demonic association with heresy (J. B. Russell 1980: 52–8; Peters, in this volume). However, the bias of these religious sources towards binary thinking makes it difficult to ascertain the reality of popular practice, if only because most of the cases of prosecution arise, and are dealt with, on a local and personal level, rather than on an institutional level. The sources for condemnation of heretical magic include laws, canons, parochial handbooks, inquisitorial records and sermons. Although the demonic component of magic still included the illusory or delusional quality, increasingly popular stories of diabolical magic indicate the reality of these activities and therefore the guilt of the sorcerers, witches, heretics, Jews and Muslims who are accused of practising them. For example the popular *Golden Legend* presents Mohammed as a sorcerer, while Peter the Venerable's tracts against Islam present it as a diabolical heresy (Jacobus de Voragine 1993: II: 370; Tolan in Ferreiro 1998). The mentality cultivated by religious leaders to counteract heresy, and by the rhetoric of the Crusades, creates an environment fraught with spiritual battles, often getting out of the control of Church leaders. The most insidious is the blood libel against Jews that accused them of using the Eucharist wafer for diabolical rituals and stealing Christian babies to perform horrific rites (Marcus 1938: 121–7).

Although condemned by Church authorities as a myth, this potent storyline recurs in hagiography and sermon literature, drawing on latent Christian fears of 'the other' in medieval society and leading to virulent attacks on Jewish communities.

In the context of both the official church condemnations of magic as heresy and the popular outbursts attacking minority groups as diabolical magicians, the common tradition of magic in the twelfth and thirteenth centuries becomes inseparable from popular religion. Both belief in the dangers of diabolical magic in one's neighbourhood and the potential for recourse to Christian antidotes are part of the mental landscape of the medieval populace, both urban and rural. What increases the tension, though, over these practices and beliefs, is the increasing legal and theological distinctions that marginalize or demonize popular practices as heresy or as ignorant superstition. Some practices accepted for centuries now come under censure, as various folk remedies, herbal preparations and rituals mildly condemned as ignorant superstition are now identified with demonic heresy. It is also possible, though, that attention paid to popular practices by church authorities concerned with heresy actually increased popular belief in diabolical practices. This phenomenon is particularly evident in the way that many of the popular stories mirror not so much earlier ancient, pre-Christian rituals but appear to be perversions of Christian doctrine and ritual generated in these centuries by a predominantly Christian society increasingly obsessed with establishing and maintaining that identity. For example, the accusation of misuse of the Eucharistic host in Satanic rituals or in popular practice parallels the increased emphasis on the power of the Mass by the Church and in popular devotion evident in Eucharistic miracles.

Within the courtly environment, a distinctive set of traditions about magic evolved, connected to the earlier popular trends but altered by the dynamics of court life. On the negative side are accusations of magic and witchcraft made against persons in power, against a backdrop of court intrigue that purportedly includes astrologers and sorcerers among court advisors, as well as the ubiquitous love magic. Astrologers and diviners in particular became common in the courts of twelfth-century rulers (Kieckhefer 1990: 97). In the twelfth and thirteenth centuries, however, accusations of magic remained localized and comparatively innocuous, compared to the development of an international inquisitorial process in later periods. On the positive side, fascination with magic is evident in courtly literature and entertainment. The romances of Alexander the Great, Virgil and the Arthurian material, fanciful as they are, do reflect courtly interest in the power of objects such as gemstones, the potential for trickery and intrigue found in illusory magic, and the symbolic value of prophetic and visionary experience, suggesting the emotive and symbolic power of the occult.

When the literary and courtly evidence is correlated with the legal condemnations, intellectual distinctions, and popular practices, magic emerges as an ever more complex construct. It remains thoroughly occult, in both the sense of illicit, potentially heretical activities and in the sense of tapping hidden power to change the human condition, whether as a common person seeking material well-being or a courtier seeking to alter fate. Moreover, the divide between good and evil, white and black magic, is problematized, both in the realm of popular remedies that use chants, amulets or gems and in the fantasy world of romance. In so far as magic works through appeal to demons, it is clearly evil, but in so far as it taps virtues in the God-created natural world, it may be justified as a means to an end. Despite continued assertions from churchmen condemning magic as heretical, demonic, and ultimately ill-fated and illusory, and despite the rise of a new rationalism, references to magic that actually *works* proliferate, particularly magic relying on the power of Christian rituals to coerce spiritual forces like demons to do the will of the practitioner. Why and how these forms of magic develop in this high medieval environment continues to be a puzzle.

The Rise of Magic in the Late Fourteenth and Fifteenth Centuries

Something different began happening to and with magic as a concept in the late fourteenth and fifteenth centuries, partly as the result of the earlier trends toward a heightened interest in spiritual powers, and partly in response to new conditions after circa 1350. In the realm of popular practice, the increase in lay literacy contributed to a proliferation of self-help manuals in the vernacular offering remedies and divinatory techniques, popularizing what was once a magic tradition exclusive to the literate clergy (Kieckhefer, 1990: 63–64, 72). The elements of this magic tradition were still intensely Christian, though, and for the most part do not reflect continuity with some intact pagan religion surviving underground the centuries since conversion. Rather, late medieval popular magic reflects a sophisticated synthesis of folk ways, classical medicine, and Christian liturgy in its use of herbs, blessings or adjurations, and ritualistic behaviors. Clerical involvement in necromancy continued to draw on Christian ritual while intellectual magic, embodied in the 'Renaissance *magus*', overlapped with scientific experimentation. On the negative, prohibition side, magic as a phenomenon takes on a life of its own in the late Middle Ages. Magic becomes more than a list of objectionable practices in the minds of its persecutors, but an organized demonic sect of sorcery, witchcraft, and necromancy prosecuted throughout Europe as both heretical and criminal. Magic accusations moved out of local affairs onto a larger stage and were punished more severely – not as ignorant superstition, but as evidence of membership in a diabolical conspiracy worthy of the death penalty, visible from the inquisitorial records of Bernard Gui to the *Malleus Maleficarum*.

In both the positive and negative sources, magic in the late Middle Ages became more real than illusory; the reality of ritual pacts with the Devil and the like became a dominant feature of late medieval and early modern obsessions with witchcraft. In the 'clerical underworld' of necromancy, rituals coercing angels, saints, and demons granted occult knowledge and power to those who possessed the manuscript or mastered its texts (Kieckhefer, 1990: 151–75). In the Munich Handbook, a fifteenth century necromantic manual, the reader learns of techniques and formulas to produce illusions, in some cases akin to rather elaborate party jokes, to command spirits through conjurations, and how to divine hidden knowledge, including the future (Kieckhefer, 1997). The reality of this kind of magic is rooted in a set of assumptions about the power of words and texts and the existence of invisible spiritual powers and virtues which the magician can command.

Although late fourteenth century condemnations continued to emphasize the worthlessness of magical practices while linking them to heresy, in the fifteenth century legislation against magic confirms its reality rather than denouncing it as illusory. In a 1385 manual for priests, copying from a long tradition of such manuals, the priest is told to warn his parishioners not to practice incantations and sorcery since these arts are worthless as cures and unlawful (Shinners, 1997: 19). However, a generation later, Bernard of Siena's popular 1427 sermon condemning divination and charms as heretical worship of the devil strikes a different note (Shinners, 1997: 242–5). He asserts that those who claim to have the power to break a charm are obviously the kind of people who know how to make one, lumping together maleficent and beneficent practitioners. 'There is nothing better to do,' he trumpets, than to cry out 'To the fire' with them, condemning them as heretics. Those who know of such practitioners and do not accuse them are equally guilty of the crime, resulting in a multitude of accused, primarily women, whose confessions of horrible activities were accepted as proven when names of victims were verified. Accusations of witches killing children for their blood, making sacrifices to the devil, or concocting unguents to make themselves appear as animal illusions led to the stake. Bernard's call to accuse 'every witch, every wizard, every sorcerer or sorceress, or worker of charms and spells' as an act of faith appeals to both his audience's charity, inducing sympathy for the hapless victims of sorcery in their community, and to their piety, by accusing those whose spells deny God. This acceptance of guilt and consequently of the reality of such magical powers is quite different from the early medieval warnings against belief in the reality of such false accusations made against persons suspected of successfully performing such magic. A corner has been turned here, somewhere around 1400: the illusory nature of demonic magic is no longer a possible defence.

At the same time, late medieval magic and magicians were irredeemably Christian in mentality, even if their practices were perversions of Christian ritual or condemned as heretical. The world of the saint and the world of the magician were remarkable similar (Kieckhefer 1994). Both operated in a material world that concealed and revealed a spiritual realm and yet both were locked with each other in a battle between the forces of good and evil. The consequence was that both saints and magicians possessed the means to command these spiritual forces. Saints, existing in a blessed state in the afterlife, could make demons serve them or do their will, while magicians, recognizing the supremacy of Christian spiritual forces, utilized aspects of Christian ritual to coerce demons to do their will – sometimes for allegedly good ends such as revealing the identity of a thief, but also for self-serving or even harmful ends, such as cursing an enemy. For example, in the condemned *Ars Notoria* tradition, practitioners could acquire knowledge of the seven liberal arts through special prayers. In a complex twist on this tradition, the *Liber Visionum* text claims to replace the condemned magical art with a holy set of rituals and prayers. Their orthodoxy is authenticated through a vision from the Virgin Mary, connecting this 'magical' practice to the visionary traditions prominent in the late Middle Ages (Watson in Fanger 1998: 163–215).

Likewise, Christian piety is the dominant context for many of the late medieval popular practices associated with magic in the modern mind (Kieckhefer 1992: 242; Duffy 1992). The emotionalism of late medieval piety, evident in Eucharistic visions, devotion to the suffering Christ, and the excesses of flagellants, resonates with many of the 'magical practices' relying on Christian rituals and materials, such as the Eucharist for healing, holy salt for divining heretics, or relics of the blood of Christ as an amulet. Thus the boundary between magic and religion is obliterated or crossed so frequently as to make it impossible to tell where one leaves off.

Although the evidence for popular and courtly practice of magic increased exponentially, given the numerous tracts, court records, manuals and popular stories circulating, it is questionable whether an actual increase in the practice of magic occurred as cause for this outburst in the literature (Peters, in this volume; Kieckhefer 1990: 92). It is more likely that as the rhetoric about magic increased, and ideas spread more rapidly in Europe, more people were passing stories about magic so that we hear more accounts of persons claiming to have the powers associated with magicians – because it now means something quite specific to make such a claim. What is most characteristic of this period, however, is the seriousness of magic and its potential to both empower and to disrupt Christian society. Anyone can now perform magic, with a little training or access to a text, endowing ordinary lay individuals with the power to heal or harm through appeals to occult resources. On the other hand, the danger of magic, or the perception of danger from very real magic, increases. In earlier centuries, Christian antidotes to magic as illusory were more than powerful enough to coerce and contain demonic powers invoked through magic; in the fourteenth and fifteenth centuries, any crisis (of which there were many, from natural disasters, famine, disease, political dislocation, financial disasters and wars) was cause to accuse some persons of membership in an occult conspiracy. The self-proclaimed magician who concocted love potions, herbal remedies, and performed illusory tricks was dangerously close to the heretic in a pact with the devil, which could get the lay magician in some trouble.

By the fifteenth century, magic was no longer, as in the earlier periods, a list of superstitious and potentially harmful practices needing to be eradicated through pastoral correction of the ignorant and through the elevation of Christian ritual as an antidote. On the one hand, magic and magicians were everywhere throughout medieval society and seemingly impossible to eradicate. Now any lay person could claim occult knowledge to cure or curse. On the other hand, magic was increasingly perceived as part of a monstrous, dangerous pan-European cult threatening to destroy Christendom and needing to be stamped out. Popular religion, and popular practice in general, now looked far different in the eyes of those who adopted this view – less innocent, more devious, in need of harsher remedies. And once popular culture adopted this attitude towards magical practices, that it was a real threat to the community that normal Christian practice was not strong enough to counteract, mass persecution was an inevitable outcome whenever economic, social or political dislocations occurred, targeting minority groups of various ethnic and religious types. In some senses then, magic as a social phenomenon rises in the late Middle Ages and reaches a peak in the early modern period, not as a consequence of a now distant 'pagan' past but as the result of a dominant Christian mentality.

CHAPTER 3

The Practice of Magic: Popular and Courtly Traditions

After sifting through the modern layers of interpretation and medieval paradigms that construct magic as a category, we come to the actual practices found in medical remedies using herbs, stones, animal parts, incantations and ritual actions, in protective amulets and talismans, in divinatory techniques, and in manuals of sorcery and necromancy. Whether all of these practices belong in a single category called magic is questionable (Murray 1992). The nature of popular practice is such that it does not articulate its underlying premises. Any shared assumptions must be derived either from categories created by medieval elites seeking to define these practices in some way or those created by modern commentators extracting from the sources some unstated internal logic governing magic practices. As is evident from the survey in Part II, the first path of looking at literate elite treatments of magic is problematic because these views changed radically over the course of the Middle Ages, moving from a loose list of practices in the early and high medieval to a hardened view of magic as cult in the late Middle Ages. Medieval labels such as sorcery, witchcraft and incantations only gradually came to be defined in clear ways, beginning as a series of overlapping designations used at different times in different ways, often in the context of rhetorical or legal condemnations of such practices. Practices condemned in the penitentials find their commonality in their association with each other through common themes of the demonic and the unnatural, more than by specific defining features. Using these sources as a way of defining popular practices is best avoided, since they tend to read later definitions backward, as noted below in Edward Peters' essay. The second path, looking for common elements that define magical practices, is therefore more promising, even if it is difficult to classify these practices into subcategories.

This third section therefore makes certain choices regarding what constitutes the common and courtly traditions of magic and how to subdivide these categories. For the purposes of this essay, magic consists of *practices* found within medieval society that are in some fashion classified as magic or share characteristics associated with magic as defined by one of the dominant medieval paradigms explored in the previous section. This focus on practices excludes both the high/intellectual traditions and the legal prohibitions, both discussed elsewhere, that helped create the conceptual categories of magic, although both will of necessity be brought in as source material for popular practices.

These popular practices do not fit neatly into boxes, since there are a number of ways of dividing up these practices, and even the distinction between common or 'low' magic, courtly traditions and intellectual 'high' magic is problematic, as is the division between 'white' and 'black' magic. Common magic emerges as a separate category primarily in the minds of post-twelfth-century thinkers distancing themselves from popular practice as they developed theoretical models for natural magic derived from classical, Arabic and other eastern Mediterranean sources coming into their possession. Nonetheless, shared concepts about nature evident in certain practices cross the boundary between popular and intellectual. Similarly the division between 'white' and 'black' magic is an effort to isolate the practices with a positive result through godly means from those with a purposely negative or harmful effect derived from unwholesome, demonic impulses. This can also be a grey area, however, as when someone tries to acquire good ends through bad means, or vice versa. The distinction is not always clear, as when a bishop asks a necromancer to use his knowledge of spells, full of Christian liturgical formulas, to call up demons and force them to reveal information that will allow the bishop to defeat evil heretics (Caesarius of Heisterbach V: XVIII, 1929: I: 338–41). The same materials may be used in both black and white magic – healing through certain herbs with spells and causing illness through similar means. Magic practices can thus be divided according to a variety of criteria, whether by their origins or their sources, or an examination of their materials, means and results.

Tracking the origins of magical practices, for example to their Egyptian, Graeco-Roman, Germanic, Celtic or Scandinavian roots is useful, but because these traditions are so intermixed in adaptations within Europe, categories by origin do not represent a true understanding of medieval practices. For example, identifying the pre-Christian origins of a 'pagan' vernacular charm found alongside Latin liturgical prayers in a tenth-century monastic manuscript does not explain how the practice was accepted as Christian by the people who produced the texts in the tenth century (Stanley 1975; Jolly 1996). Moreover, similar practices are found throughout the Mediterranean region, from Syriac, Arabic, Egytian, Greek, Indo-European and Slavic traditions ranging from ancient sources to the fifteenth century and recorded as living practice right down to the present century, as evident for example in the work of Moses Gaster (1971). Classifying magical practices according to their textual sources allows us to evaluate their production and use in their manuscript context, as more recent work in necromantic manuals has shown (Fanger 1998).

Magical practices themselves, and references to the practice of magic, are found in a wide array of manuscript types. Primary evidence of magic – actual remedies, formulas and rituals produced for someone to use – are found in medical handbooks both lay and clerical, in monastic and liturgical texts, as marginalia in other texts, in scientific treatises, and in specifically magic handbooks prevalent in the late Middle Ages (necromancers' manuals for example). Secondary sources describing, and usually condemning, magic practices include the law codes, penitentials, theological treatises, sermons, histories, saints' lives and other religious literature, as well as literature of entertainment such as fairy stories, romances and fables.

Magic practices thus occur in different contexts, whether medicinal, liturgical, scientific or literary. So, for example, Lynn Thorndike's work discussed earlier examined the phenomenon of magic in the context of experimental science, treating them together as a single area of study (Thorndike 1923). Many of the incantatory healing rituals and formulae found in the written evidence are heavily derived from Christian liturgy, making it difficult to study magico-medical texts apart from the monastic contexts that produced the manuscripts (Murdoch 1989, 1991). Prescriptions for physical ailments might include incantatory words offensive to a narrow-minded clergyman, while at the same time invoking the miraculous power of a saint whose cult is promoted by the said clergyman. A pilgrim's relic, authentic or not, from an authorized shrine might be sold as an amulet, spreading the saint's fame at the same time that it irks the guardians of the shrine.

Examining the materials and results of magic takes us closer to the practices themselves, but is a very utilitarian approach that has a certain modern bias to it, in that practices drawn from very different contexts are grouped together. For example, Richard Kieckhefer divides his chapter on the common tradition of magic into six groupings based on their materials or tools: (1) medical magic using herbs and animals; (2) word magic such as charms, prayers, blessings and adjurations; (3) protective objects, such as amulets and talismans; (4) sorcery as a form of 'black' magic that misuses the means employed in the first three categories; (5) divination and astrology; and (6) trickery (Kieckhefer 1990: 56–94). Similarly, and overlapping with Kieckhefer's categories, practices can be organized into groups according to what they endeavored to achieve as an outcome rather than the means they used to achieve them. Braekman, for example, has a fourfold schema based on outcome, healing, protection, divination and entertainment, while acknowledging the potential for both positive and negative outcomes – white or black magic, those things bordering on the miraculous versus those that fall off into sorcery (Braekman 1991).

Recognizing that no organizational scheme is completely satisfactory given the nature of the topic, the following five sections organize popular practices according to the results or intended outcome: healing, protection, divination, occult knowledge and entertainment. Within each section, the sources and methods are examined, although they often overlap from one category to the next. For example, both healing and protective practices occur in medical manuscripts and use similar materials, such as herbs, stones and animal parts, as well as similar words and rituals to empower these objects. While both use verbal and written formulas to counter invisible attacks, healing rituals produce medicines taken either internally as potions or applied externally as unguents to cure; whereas protective practices to ward off disease and harm use the same tools to make amulets and talismans. Likewise, divinatory practices overlap with occult knowledge acquired through sorcery or necromancy. Divination, however, is more closely allied with healing and protection in that it provides means for reading signs as meaningful in the natural world, whether lunar cycles, the cry of birds, or the entrails of an animal. Some divination is based on the occult knowledge of the skilled practitioner, a seer or sibyl, similar to the sorcerer whose occult knowledge is used to produce particular effects, such as theft detection, curses or love magic. Necromancy achieves similar ends through calling up spirits such as demons or angels. 'Entertainment' crosses over these categories, both in terms of magicians performing for courtly audiences and literature telling stories of magicians. Astrologers, sorcerers and necromancers at court might produce tricks to astound or illusions to deceive willing audiences. Literary accounts of these magical practices reflect popular and courtly perceptions of magic and also contribute to notions of magic as mysterious, illusory, powerful and dangerous.

Medical Magic: Healing Body and Soul

Magic associated with medicine is the largest, and most amorphous, category of common magical practices in the Middle Ages, existing at the boundary between the natural and unnatural manifestations of illness. The distinction between material and spiritual causes of illness is a fuzzy one in medieval medicine, particularly in the early Middle Ages, where the distinction is more between visible and invisible causes. Most folk and classical remedies identified illness with specific material causes and prescribe combinations of herbs or other natural products to cure or alleviate symptoms, often based on rebalancing the four classical humours or on sympathetic association (eg. liver of the vulture for liver complaints). Other ailments had invisible causes – from airborne poisons, elves, dwarves or demons – that required invisible help from spiritual forces to conteract them and hence required the use of ritual actions derived from ancient practice or from Christian liturgy. In Christian practice, God was the

Divine Healer and the ultimate source of health; consequently medieval liturgy was full of prayers for health and relief from infirmity, including blessings and exorcisms of patients and of objects and materials used in healing, such as herbs, holy water and amulets. This convergence of Christian and Germanic concerns is visible for example in the exorcisms of demons and illness found in both liturgical and medical manuscripts that include Germanic elves and nightmares in their list of exorcised evils (Jolly 1996; Hunt 1990: 80–1).

Because of this duality of meaning in healing, both spiritual and physical, we have a range of practices that might be declared magic in a later age. Rituals derived from folk Germanic practice as well as from Christian practice show up in a variety of contexts. Although most remedies are found in medical treatises, they can also appear in liturgical texts and as marginalia in religious texts. On the one hand, remedies for physical ailments rely on classical medical paradigms, evident in the medieval manuscript traditions of herbals, lapidaries, animal parts and practical manuals for treatment of both human conditions and illness in animals. Interlaced with these medical remedies using natural materials are prescriptions that use ritual actions and charms, sometimes derived from earlier Germanic folk practice. On the other hand, Christian remedies occur in the context of liturgical prayers for healing and in the margins of religious texts, curiously intermixed again with Germanic components. This synthesis of Germanic, Christian and classical traditions in the early Middle Ages is unsurprising in the context of a shared set of presumptions about the integration of the natural and spiritual worlds and the existence of hidden 'virtues' in natural objects that can be tapped or activated through ritual actions and verbal formulas, a theory found in both Pliny and Augustine.

In the twelfth century, a distinction between natural and supernatural emerged among scientific thinkers that led to a greater distance between natural remedies and those appealing to supernatural forces, with a consequent distancing of elite medicine from folk medicine. It is wise to keep in mind, however, that professional physicians in the early Middle Ages were uncommon and in the high Middle Ages they existed primarily in rarified environments, either as theoreticians in the universities or as court physicians to the highest nobility (Rubin 1974, 1989; Siraisi 1990). Most medical practice was carried out by more ordinary folk, such as herbalists, barber-surgeons and some religious, although the clergy was prohibited from practising medicine in 1131 at the Council of Rheims, another indication of the intellectual separation between spiritual and physical concerns. To a great degree, the practices of herbalists and midwives, and hence often of women, are relatively invisible in the predominantly male clerical texts that survive, although more evidence is apparent in archaeological evidence (Weston 1995; Meaney 1989). Nonetheless, the continued existence in these manuscripts of folk remedies employing ritualized cures not only grants these popular traditions some authority but also suggests the existence of widespread oral traditions involving 'medical magic'.

However, the components deemed magical from a modern medical view do not all originate in pre-Christian folk practice; rather, a high percentage of the 'magical' rituals found in medieval medicine have a Christian basis, particularly in the use of Latin formulas and the sign of the cross. Moreover, hagiography substantiates the power of saintly words and actions in medicine. For example, Gregory of Tours tells the story of St Martin taking pity on a wind-blown tree fallen across the road (Gregory of Tours, *Confessors* 7, 1988: 25). Martin raises it by making the sign of the cross over it. Subsequently, people scraped bark off this tree and dissolved it in water to make medicine.

Given this Christian world view dominant in the sources, the 'magic' components of medicine cannot be easily isolated from the medical or liturgical contexts in which these remedies occur. Even trying to separate these components into categories is difficult because they overlap to such a great extent. For example, herbal remedies with verbal formulas can be used both for healing and as amulets for protection against disease or harm; some of the same tools and methods used for healing in medicine can also be used for causing illness or harm in sorcery. Nonetheless, the following analysis breaks medical magic into two parts, medical materials and verbal formulas, even though they overlap within remedies. The first part examines remedies with ritual characteristics employing herbs, stones and animal parts, derived from the classical tradition of herbals, lapidaries and animal compendiums, but also found in other medical treatises. The second examines the much larger category of verbal (oral and written) formulas, often combined with ritual actions used to activate the healing potential of herbs, stones and animal parts.

Materia Medica: Herbs, Animals, Stones
The classical medical tradition contributed two main conceptual frameworks to medieval medicine: the idea of the four humours which medicine seeks to rebalance, and the medicinal properties of natural objects found in scientific compendiums. Herbals, the animal books and the lapidaries are organized by item and thus function more as reference works than actual practical manuals. Although the medieval manuscripts are copies of Latin, Greek and Arabic treatises, they sometimes show enough innovations and alterations to suggest a conscious application of some of the remedies in medieval European practice. Some of the items gain potency through ritual actions or verbal formulas, in addition to proper preparation of the substance. Others function through association, identified in modern thought as 'sympathetic magic'.

Herbals are the largest category, derived from a complex history of Greek, Roman and Arabic transmission, primarily from the works of Dioscorides, Apuleius Platonicus and Pliny. These herbal compendiums occur in both an illustrated tradition and in manuscripts without illustrations (Collins 1999). The first herb in the Pseudo-Apuleius *Herbarium* is betony or *betonica*, bishopwort in English, and its uses are indicative of the nature of these texts (de Vriend 1984). Betony is good for soul or body because it protects from nocturnal visitors and frightening dreams as well as healing head injuries, sore eyes and ears, nosebleeds, toothache, fatigue, fever, gout and internal ailments of the loins and stomach. It can also be used as a purgative against ingested poisons and for snake bite. The preparation varies depending on the use, but most involve drying and pounding the root to a powder and then combining it with other ingredients, usually liquid (wine, beer, honey, water); such mixtures are prescribed for both external and internal use. Betony also occurs in a wide range of remedies in medical treatises organized by complaint. For example, in the Anglo-Saxon *Leechbook*, betony figures prominently in cures for invisible afflictions, such as madness, nightmares, and demonic oppression (Jolly 1996: 135).

In some cases, the collection, preparation or application of herbal remedies is accompanied by ritual actions and verbal formulas (Stannard 1977). Although Burchard of Worms condemned the use of incantations in collecting medicinal herbs, he granted that Christian prayers thanking God for the herbs were appropriate, and much of the medical literature follows that prescription, not to mention blessings of herbs found in liturgical manuals. Further substantiating this Christian view of medicinal herbs is the apocryphal legend of the young Jesus collecting herbs for his mother Mary, illustrated in a fourteenth-century herbal showing Christ and Mary blessing herbs (Kieckhefer 1990: 68).

Classical knowledge of herbs, Christian formulas and Germanic elements come together in many of these prescriptions. For example, the herb *dracontium*, according to classical herbals derived from the blood of the mythical wormlike dragon, is useful in a sympathetic way against snakebite and against worms, one of the most common complaints in Germanic medical lore; but it is also used against both migraine and toothache, ailments often attributed to worms. Narrative incantations derived from Christian legends bring out the inherent virtues of this herb (Pinto 1973). The story of Peter healed of a toothache by Jesus is recited in one popular remedy. Another recites Psalm 90: 13 (*super aspidem et basiliscum ambulabis, et conculcabis leonem et draconem*), a verse that recurs frequently in medical charms and is often portrayed in manuscript illuminations, with Jesus standing victoriously treading on the beasts (Siller 1982: 134–6; Gallée 1887). For another equally common complaint, bleeding, the fourteenth-century physician John of Gaddesden gave a remedy for nosebleed that recommended collecting the herb shepherd's purse with recitation of the Our Father, Hail Mary and a special prayer to the Precious Blood (Hunt 1990: 27; Shinners 1997: 286). The herb was then hung around the neck like an amulet. Such prayers for staunching blood are very common in medical and religious manuscripts, with obvious spiritual overtones connected to the Blood of Christ.

Like herbals, treatises explaining the medicinal properties of animal parts transmitted classical knowledge into the Middle Ages, often in the same manuscript with herbals. The *Medicina de Quadrupedibus* of Sextus Placitus opens with an impeccable pedigree for these cures, attributing them to Aesculapius as transmitted from Caesar Octavianus to his friend the king of the Egyptians (Cockayne 1961: I: 326–73). Some of the remedies involving animal parts are purely 'natural' if bizarre from a modern perspective. For example, a British compendium asserts that cat faeces are useful for curing baldness or fever (Kieckhefer 1990: 66). But, like the herbals, some animal-part remedies involve ritual preparations and formulas. In a Carolingian manuscript, an epistle containing seventeen remedies from the vulture was inserted at the end of Dioscorides' *Materia Medica* and attributed to the king of Rome as sent to the province of Babylonia Alexandria, giving it an exotic, foreign flavour (MacKinney 1943). Among other things, it recommends a special formula when decapitating the vulture in order to use parts of its head or brain for corresponding human complaints, such as migraine: 'Angel Adonai Abraham, on your account the word is completed.' Vulture body parts could also be used as amulets for protection against demons, thieves and sorcerers. Despite these dubious practices, these texts for the most part contain methods for extracting chemical components from natural products, in most cases without the aid of ritual, and, despite their often mistaken theoretical basis, form the foundation for later scientific experiments. For example, Albertus Magnus furthered the scientific study of animal derivatives, as well as herbs and gemstones, in his *Book of Secrets*. The sharp line between science and magic as construed in modern terms distorts the fact that much of science evolved from magical experimentation (Tambiah 1990).

Lapidaries list the various uses of stones and gems, again derived from classical Mediterranean traditions and merged with local practice (Evans 1922; Evans and Serjeantson 1933). Evidence for the use of stones in early medieval medical practice, as for example in the Anglo-Saxon *Leechbook*, suggests a conscious adaptation of Latin knowledge to local knowledge (Kitson 1989). The lapidary tradition became much more highly developed in the High Middle Ages, beginning with the late eleventh-century *Book of Stones* by Bishop Marbode of Rennes; gemstones were common among the nobility as protective amulets (Kieckhefer 1990: 102–5). The theory of humours allied with a Christian cosmology lies behind much of the medicinal use of stones. Jewels seemed to contain a concentrated form of power greater than herbs, placed there by God for humans to use for various ills. For example, the twelfth-century abbess, visionary, composer, philosopher and herbalist Hildegard of Bingen notes that stones are hot and humid and that the devil hates and avoids all gemstones because they remind him of the City of God (Hildegard, *Patrologia Latina* CXCVII: 1247–52; Bozóky 1992: 88–9). Jacinth accompanied by a Latin narrative formula is therefore useful for dementia and magic-induced fantasies. Like herbs and animal parts, stones for medicinal use could be ground and put in a drink to take internally, or could be placed on the body, often as protective amulets, as discussed below.

Ritual Performance: Words and Signs
As evident in the discussion of medical materials above, the label 'magic' as applied to the medicinal use of herbs, animal parts and stones is largely derived from the employment of ritual formulas or actions in the gathering, preparation and application of some of these natural products. In many ways, this is an anachronistic measure, in that it isolates out of context many remedies that only a later age would consider magic, whereas in their own time they were considered part of healing methods. The power of words to effect changes in the material world, now discredited in modern science, is the chief reason why much of medieval medicine is classified as magic instead of science. Nonetheless, the bulk of medical remedies in the medieval tradition do not contain ritual formulas, but use entirely natural, if not scientifically reliable, methods. Those remedies that do have such formulas tend to use them for ailments that have an invisible cause (airborne poisons, for example), a demonic association (such as madness or nightmares) or a pagan association (afflictions caused by demonized elves, witches' curses or sorcery). They also occur with the three most common medical complaints, worms, bleeding and childbirth (Pinto 1973), perhaps because these conditions were so much a part of daily life and frequently life-threatening that recourse to higher powers was common.

Much has been made of the pagan roots of such verbal formulas, highlighting the actually very few charms that lack any Christian component found primarily in early medieval vernacular traditions, but also in Latin. The oft-cited Latin appeal to Mother Earth to bless the earth and an adjuration of herbs to bring out their healing powers is found in a twelfth-century English manuscript (Coulton 1928: 41–2). However, this is a copy of a classical text found in one line of the herbal tradition, and hence is not the product of Germanic paganism surviving into the high Middle Ages (Collins 1999). Moreover, Christianized versions of such prayers that address Mother Earth and Father God produced in early medieval texts and Latin liturgical blessings of herbs demonstrate an ongoing conversion process (Jolly 1992). The retention of 'pure' pagan remedies in the context of these Christianized remedies raises many questions about the relationship between pre-Christian Germanic folk practice and conversion to Christianity. For example, the famous 'Lay of the Nine Herbs' and 'Lay of the Nine Twigs of Woden' occur together in an Anglo-Saxon medical text, the *Lacnunga*, that is otherwise full of formulas calling on God using Christian prayers (Grattan and Singer 1971: 150–7). The German Merseberg charms from tenth-century Saxony narrate the fetter-breaking powers of the 'valkyries' and relate the horse-sprain charm of Wodan; similar charms for horse sprain occur elsewhere with Christ substituted for Wodan (Hampp 1961: 247–65; van Haver 1964: 463–5; Remly 1979). These two remnants of 'untouched' paganism in the Merseberg charms appear to date back to the forcible conversion of the Saxons by Charlemagne in the eighth-century; yet they are arguably a product of tenth-century historical conditions in Saxony and may represent a form of cultural resistance (Fuller 1980; Karras 1986). On the other hand, some scholars now suggest that charms lacking any Christian reference and yet copied within a Christian manuscript may represent an allegorized Christianization of the older tradition (Holton 1993). 'Pagan' cannot just mean the absence of overt Christian references, but is relative to the manuscript context.

What is more surprising than the survival of these so-called 'pagan' remedies is to recognize the thoroughly Christian character of the bulk of charm formulas and their closeness to liturgical prayers, even in the early Middle Ages soon after conversion (Murdoch 1991). This is partly the function of the texts as products of monastic and clerical environments; but it is also a reflection of a widespread Christianization of folk practice rather than a complete rejection of its methods. The terminology is also deceptive. Incantation (derived from the Latin), spell (an Anglo-Saxon word also used of the Gospel), and charm (Old English *galdor*, 'song') imply to the modern mind 'magic' as opposed to prayer in 'religion.' However, many so-called charms employ Scripture and prayers found in the liturgy, while liturgical prayers often function rhetorically in the same way as charms, as effective means of cure. Kieckhefer makes a useful distinction between prayers, addressed to God, blessings, addressed to the patient, and adjurations, addressed to the infesting agent (Kieckhefer 1990: 69). All three can be found in both medical and liturgical manuscripts that contain exorcisms of the devil, blessings of herbs and prayers to God on behalf of the patient.

The common assumption in these prayers and charms, Christian or pre-Christian in origin, is that words are effective. In particular, Christian literature argues that Christian words, pronounced by the clergy in the

Eucharist or by saints in miraculous cures, are effective, either in conjunction with medicinal herbs or alone. St Monegundis healed blisters by preparing a paste of leaves and her own saliva, making the sign of the cross over the sore; she also blessed water that healed sore throats and fevers (Gregory of Tours, *Confessors* 24, 1988: 39–40). The relics of such saints continued to offer the power for healing after their death, as for example the medicine people obtained from the moss on St Tranquillus' tomb (Gregory of Tours, *Confessors* 43, 1988: 55). Empowered object-oriented healing is thus fostered by Christian teaching. On the other hand, St Foy contrasts her painless verbal formulas to the trauma of medical treatments and witches' cures. 'She doesn't scrape away diseases with an iron hook, or twitter old witch's songs over rotting wounds, but wields all her power with a potent command' (Sheingorn 1995: 215). In many ways, the advent of Christianity increased the use of verbal formulas because of the predominance of the spoken and written word in Christian liturgy and a theology that emphasized Christ as Incarnate Word. Thus the opening words of St John's gospel, *In principio erat verbum*, was a common formula in remedies, both spoken and written. Christian words dominated literate modes of transmission, hence they form the bulk of the manuscript evidence for verbal healing formulas.

Christian stories also take over in what are called 'narrative charms', a form of sympathetic magic in which the recitation of a story channels healing power to the patient. A few Germanic samples survive that refer, for example, to Wodan, as noted above. But the vast majority in both the vernacular and Latin rely on Christian narrative and are incredibly popular given the number of versions and copies from throughout Europe that survive from medieval and later periods, including Germany (Müllenhoff and Scherer 1892; Steinmeyer 1916; Spamer 1958; Hampp 1961), Scandinavia (Ohrt 1921; Bang 1990; Grambo 1990), the Netherlands (van Haver 1964), and England (Cockayne 1961; Hunt 1990). Remedies involving the spear of Longinus, for example, are widespread; in one case a late eleventh-century German version is close enough to a contemporary English one to suggest direct contact between the two traditions (Selmer 1952). Most of these remedies occur in medical collections, but others in the margins of religious texts. For example, the Three Angels narrative charm in Latin occurs, among other places, in a twelfth-century German manuscript of St Bernard's sermons (Bartsch 1873: 45–6).

Representative examples of narrative formula include the story of Jesus healing St Peter's toothache, the story of Longinus' spear for staunching blood, the Three Angels narrative adjuring the seven demons of illness, the Jordan River formula for staunching blood just as the river stood still at Jesus' baptism, and the story of the 'Three Good Brothers'. The story of the 'Three Good Brothers' dates to Greek and Egyptian texts of the fifth and sixth centuries, but shows up in Latin and vernacular traditions throughout Europe in the twelfth and later centuries (Hampp 1961: 196–201; Ohrt 1921: 51; Bozóky 1992: 87; Köhler 1868: 184–8). In the narrative, three brothers encounter Jesus on their way to gather healing herbs. Jesus offers to give them a secret remedy, if they swear by the crucifix and the milk of Mary not to pass it secretly or sell it. In the wound remedy, wool soaked in olive oil from the Mount of Olives staunches blood when accompanied by a 'just as' formula invoking Longinus' spear: just as Longinus' spear pierced the side of Christ and the wound did not fester, so too this present wound on the patient will not fester because of the words chanted over it, done in the name of the Trinity.

Narrative formulas are essentially 'hagiographic reliquaries': their ritualized narration or invocation of a saintly story contains a verbal relic powerful enough to cure. Often, the narrative may be connected to actual relics or the legends of relic recovery from the Holy Land, as in the remedies referencing the spear of Longinus, the Holy Blood or the three nails from the crucifixion (Bartsch 1873: 52; Bozóky 1994: 94). Consequently, the cross, whether invoked in word or in sign, is one of the most common and powerful ritual actions incorporated into medicinal remedies. Many of the medical texts, like liturgical texts, insert graphic crosses into the text to indicate the action of signing as part of the performance of the remedy. For example, Carolingian charms for heart problems and for eye problems combine a mixture of Graeco-Latin gibberish with crosses (Riché 1973), as do many of the Anglo-Saxon medical texts such as the *Leechbook* and *Lacnunga* (Cockayne 1961: II; Grattan and Singer 1971), and on into the later Middle Ages in remedies to ward off evil in the form of serpents or demonic oppression (Gallée 1887).

Moreover, invocation of biblical narratives in liturgical prayers or in visionary literature is quite common, so their appearance in healing remedies is as much a product of Christian influence as anything else. Visions can substantiate the use of a biblical narrative in healing, as in the case of the young Gregory of Tours who relieved his father's gout by following the instructions given in a vision, in a seeming play on his budding literacy (*Confessors* 39, 1988: 51–2). The first vision referred him to the biblical story of Joshua and told him to put his name on a chip and place it under his father's pillow. The second vision instructed Gregory to use the remedy from the book of Tobit, that is, burnt aroma of fish gall, revealed to Tobias by the archangel Raphael. This hagiographic tale confirms the use of narrative charms found in the medical manuscripts, as well as being an early example of the healing uses of the Tobit narrative. The apocryphal book of Tobit contains an engaging and memorable story of the righteous Tobit's blindness caused by bird droppings, his son Tobias' journey with, unknown to him, the archangel Raphael, and his subsequent marriage to the ill-fated

Sarah, whose first seven grooms died in the wedding chamber through the antics of the demon Asmodaeus. Raphael, known in the Middle Ages as the 'healing archangel', solves these problems by instructing Tobias to keep the gall, heart and liver of a fish he caught. The aroma of the burnt fish liver and heart drives off the demon on his wedding night and the fish gall is used to cure his father's blindness. Aspects of this story show up in wedding blessings for exorcizing demons, in eye remedies and, curiously, in a remedy for scaring birds away from the fields (Gallée 1887: 457; *Durham Ritual*, 1927: 145–7).

The basis for the power of narration lies in a particular view of language, that words represent reality and their performance can therefore alter reality. This view held sway from the early Middle Ages and remained unchallenged in religious practice and popular culture into the early modern and modern period, despite the advent of nominalism with its disjunction between words and reality among intellectuals in the thirteenth century. This power of words is visible in three healing practices: the use of language to shape the actions desired, the use of multiple languages, and the use of written words.

Verbal formulas shape actions both directly and indirectly. As noted above, some narrate stories in an effort to sympathetically reduplicate the consequences in the original events, such as staunching blood through reference to Christ's wounds. Similarly, some charms rely on sympathetic association between the action of the words and the actions desired, as in the 'reduction' charms where the performer counts down to diminish the size of a swollen gland or to eradicate worms, almost all counting down from nine, a number considered significant in Germanic lore (*Lacnunga* in Grattan and Singer 1971: 184–5; Hunt 1990: 82–3). Curiously, studies from modern Corsica record very similar reduction charms for worms, performed by female 'Signadori' (Bertrand-Rousseau 1978: 58–64). Other remedies use chant and poetic forms to give rhythm and shape to these powerful words. As a consequence, some scholars include these charms, extracted from their medicinal context, as examples of the aesthetics of poetry (Dobbie 1942: 116–28). Other literary scholars analyse them as oral genre or using semiotics (Halpern and Foley 1978; Nöth 1977), while more recent anthropological approaches note the shamanistic function of such chants (Glosecki 1989). The performative elements of these remedies are hard to reconstruct from the textual remnants we possess, since most of the records are designed to give the essential ingredients for a particular remedy to a practitioner who will know what to do with them. Tantalizing hints to 'sing this charm' or 'recite this psalm' followed by an *incipit* do little to convey the place, timing, or body language of the performance.

Charm remedies also utilized a variety of languages, both vernaculars and the learned languages of Latin, Hebrew and Greek. Medical texts were frequently bilingual, mixing vernacular instructions with Latin formulas or combining English and French (Hunt 1990: 91). The vernacular generally indicates everyday or practical usage in oral culture, while the Latin the literate traditions of Christianity; and yet we have many cases of translation from one to the other of similar formulas, indicating the bilinguality of those who transmitted these remedies in writing. The translation of a Latin formula, such as a blessing of herbs or a biblical narrative charm, into the vernacular demonstrates a downward spread of classical and Christian practice. On the other hand, the Latinization of a vernacular formula, such as the gradually Christianized bee charm, seems to show movement in the other direction (Elsakkers 1987).

The use of several languages, whether Greek, Hebrew, Latin, Scandinavian runes or Celtic languages, can lend the remedy learned authenticity by appealing to an ancient heritage, or at least the claim to it. Some of it comes out as gibberish, intentionally or through transmission errors. While 'gibberish' to modern eyes could be unintentionally garbled due to the ignorance of the scribe, it also could function on principles of performative sound rather than intelligibility. Often reduplicating sounds, rhythm, and alliteration are central to these chants, as in this example from the *Lacnunga* for theft, 'Luben luben niga / efith niga efith fel ceid fel, delf fel cumer orcggaei ceufor dard giung farig widig delou delupih'; or this one for corns on horse's feet, 'Geneon genetron genitul catalon care trist pābist etmic forrune naht ic forrune nequis annua maris scāna nequetando' (Grattan and Singer 1971: 179, 185).

Greek and Hebrew words in early medical remedies are mostly drawn from the liturgy, such as the 'agios, agios, agios' in parallel to 'sanctus, sanctus, sanctus', or *Adonai* and *Sabaoth*. Both languages come into greater use and prominence after the twelfth century with the rise of universities and the influx of learning from Jewish and Arabic sources. As the language of the divine names and God's angels, Hebrew occurs frequently in high and late medieval necromancy and in association with the Kabbalah, but it also turns up in more ordinary cases of miracles and healing. The script used to write these 'foreign' languages varies in the manuscripts. In many cases, the words are transliterated into the Roman alphabet, not without errors. In some instances, Greek and Hebrew script are used, demonstrating the erudition of the scribe and the presumed literacy of the practitioner using the manuscript. On the other hand, the appearance of Greek and Hebrew script does not necessarily imply literacy in those languages. The physical script itself may lend authenticity to the remedy and be employed as an amulet. Mark Zier has noted, for example, the curious use of a manuscript and the Hebrew psalms for healing in late thirteenth-century England (1992).

Some of these bi- and trilingual charms also gain authority by attributing their source to heroic or angelic beings. An Anglo-Saxon charm says that an angel brought the writing from heaven and laid it on the altar of St Peter's in Rome (Cockayne 1961: III: 232–5). The prayer, a combination of Latin and Greek, is equivalent to 'all the psalms in the psalter' and to attendance at Eucharist on the day of death. It is also good against airborne poisons and epidemics, illnesses and bad dreams. The angelic source gives assurance that the words are exact and pure heavenly ones, rather than corrupt human ones, despite the fact they appear gibberish to us today. A fifteenth-century English formula was brought by the archangel Gabriel to Susanna (Hunt 1990: 90–1). Others come from famous ancient rulers and exotic sources associated with magic in legend, such as Alexander the Great.

One example combining many of these linguistic features comes from the fourteenth-century friar John of Greenborough, who produced a compendium of recipes including many of the narrative charms discussed above, in Latin, Anglo-Norman and English. In the remedies for toothache narrating how Peter was cured by Jesus, Greenborough includes both an Anglo-Norman narrative, preceded by a Latin formula asking for relief in the name of 'Messias, Sother, Emanuel, Sabaoth, Adonay, Panton, Craton, Permocraten, Iskiros, agios, ymas, eleyson, Otheos, Athanatos, Alpha et Omega, leo, vermis, vitulus, agnus, homo, aires, usion, serpens, prius et novissimus, finis, Pater et Filius et Spiritus Sanctus, amen'. There follows an appeal to the cross to ward off all evil and a list of saints (Hunt 1990: 86, 359; Shinners 1997: 287). This listing tendency is common in many remedies. Lists of the names of God, angels, and saints, found in medical remedies and in necromantic magic, are in some ways similar to a martyrology listing the saints. In other cases body parts, demons or other sources of affliction are listed, particularly in exorcisms and protection remedies or loricas discussed below. Part of the functionality of the words is to 'cover' everything or invoke all possible agencies.

While most of these formulas are performed orally as noted usually in the instructions in the remedy to chant, sing, or say the words, some formulas are prescribed as written objects to be worn as amulets or to be eaten. Although most amulets are protective, for warding off disease or harm as discussed below, some written amulets are prescribed as cures. The written word as compared to the oral has the added strength of being a sacred object, akin to a relic. The written word has both pre-Christian roots, evident in the Scandinavian use of runes for protection and cure (Kieckhefer 1990: 47–9, 141; Raudvere, in this volume), but also Christian roots in the power of the incarnate Word inscribed in Scripture. An Anglo-Irish medical treatise prescribes a written charm wrapped around a woman in labour, ostensibly as a protective amulet. The words to be written are interspersed with crosses, which function in writing like the action of signing. The Latin formula names the Trinity, Mary Mother of God, and the blood of Christ, concluding with the very appropriate Ave Maria: blessed are you among women and blessed is the fruit of your womb (Hunt 1990: 233).

In other cases, however, the written words are eaten and therefore work internally, usually as a remedy for fever but also for other mind-altering afflictions (see Thorndike 1923: I: 729–30). They seem to have an exorcistic function, as evident in the *corsnæd* ordeal, where the accused must eat bread inscribed with his crimes (Keefer 1998). In the Anglo-Saxon *Leechbook*, the words of John 1: 1 are written on a paten and washed into a drink for fever, while in the *Lacnunga*, a longer passage is used (Jolly 1996: 119, 140–1). The exorcistic power of John 1 occurs in a later English manuscript where the words are scraped off parchment into a bowl and administered to the demon-possessed, authenticated by the fact that a demon taught it to a person afflicted in this way (Kieckhefer 1990: 74). In the rather obscure Anglo-Saxon remedy against 'a dwarf', the names of the legendary Seven Sleepers of Ephesus – Saints Maximianus, Malchus, Iohannes, Martimianus, Dionisius, Constantinus and Serafion – are each inscribed on a wafer, followed by an Old English metrical charm lacking any overt Christian references (*Lacnunga* in Grattan and Singer 1971: 162–3; Stuart 1977). Presumably, although no instructions are given, the wafers are to be consumed by the patient. The Seven Sleepers are also consumed on bread in a German fever remedy (Murdoch 1991: 30). The connections to the Eucharist and Christ as Word seem to be the obvious source for these practices.

While most of these performance rituals, involving natural materials and words spoken or written, are used for good, healing purposes, some of the same techniques can be inverted to curse and thus fall into the category of sorcery. Inverted blessings and adjurations can cause illness or bring down invisible agents of harm on an enemy (Kieckhefer 1990: 82). Consequently, much of the protective magic in the next section is geared to counteract these curses and sorceries, often relying on the same principles discussed here in healing: classical knowledge of herbs, animal parts, and stones combined with Christian ritual and Germanic folklore ward off the threat of invisible harm from human or spiritual enemies.

'Deliver us from Evil': Protective Formulas, Rituals, Amulets and Talismans

Operating on some of the same principles as healing, protective magic seeks to ward off invisible causes of illness or harm before it reaches the victim, using natural materials, classical and folk prescriptions and Christian components. These practices include amulets and other talismans empowered by rituals as well as verbal formulas and ritual actions. Amulets are constructed from herbs, animal parts, or stones, while talismans utilize written words. These items could be worn around the neck, wrapped around the body, or contained in a ring. The concentrated virtues of gemstones, often engraved with incantations, were popular amulets and talismans among the nobility, while their less potent counterparts, herbs, were more accessible to common folk. Oral formulas recited for protection include blessings, adjurations and exorcisms, often combined with ritual actions such as the sign of the cross. These preventive measures inoculate against disease, keep demonic forces at bay, provide an antidote for curses and sorceries and protect animals, fields and travelers from natural and unnatural disasters. Some formulas, however, are all-purpose or serve several functions; these reveal the basic principles underlying protective magic and are thus addressed first, followed by an examination of specific protective rituals for disease and other natural disasters, and then counter-magic for malevolent forces such as demons and sorcery.

All-purpose Devices

Certain protective devices are ubiquitous and of great antiquity. Amulets, talismans, and formulas to deflect invisible attacks, sudden death or poisons are common in many ancient and medieval cultures, Christian and otherwise. For example, Moses Gaster traced a number of Samaritan amulet artifacts and their uses (1971: I: 387–461). Coptic 'wizard's hoard' texts from the fourth to seventh centuries give lists of angelic powers for the practitioner to call upon; one protective remedy against bites, enemies and bad dreams uses Hebrew formulas with honey, licorice root and a hawk's egg (Mirecki 1994; see also Meyer and Smith 1994). Graeco-Roman, Egyptian and Hebrew adjurations, spoken or written, calling on angels or daemons and using ritual objects, can acquire protective knowledge from the heavenly realm (Lesses 1996). Consequently, it would be wrong to conclude that European magical devices are a peculiarly Germanic perversion of the Judaeo-Christian heritage when these practices were common throughout other Christian and monotheistic societies.

One major channel of transmission and development of protective Christian devices is the Celtic tradition, which draws on diverse sources from Latin, Greek, Hebrew and even Syriac and is transmitted from the Irish to the Anglo-Saxons and other Germanic peoples on the Continent (*Lacnunga* in Grattan and Singer 1971: 67–8). The *loricas*, for example, are protective verbal 'shields' that embody St Paul's instructions in Ephesians to arm oneself with the armour of God as spiritual protection against the devil. The eighth-century *Faeth Fiada* or 'The Deer's Cry', known traditionally as the Breastplate of Patrick, is the most well-known example of an Old Irish *lorica* (Carey 1998: 127–38). It opens with a command formula invoking the Trinity and the Incarnation. In the middle, the prayer enumerates all of the protections in an incantatory repetition against a list of ills, a reduplicating pattern found in Scandinavian and Germanic formulas associated with Woden as well (*Lacnunga* in Grattan and Singer 1971: 150–7). Other loricas and Latin prayers follow a similar pattern of shielding through repetition. The Old English *Lorica of Gildas*, found in six manuscripts, calls on heaven's army, the named ranks of angels, prophets, apostles and saints, for defence against a wide range of dangers, enumerating all body parts external and internal (*Lacnunga* in Grattan and Singer 1971: 69–71, 130–47). Two similar protective formulas, a Latin exorcism of body parts and an Old English command formula against all invisible evils, occur in the margins of another Anglo-Saxon manuscript, a copy of Bede's *Ecclesiastical History* (Grant 1979). The enumeration of body parts also shows up in Latin in the *Leechbook* and in the *Leofric Missal* (Jolly 1996: 163–4). This appears to be a case of translation from a vernacular tradition to a Latin one, but it would be unwise to assume it moved from pagan to Christian practice, since the source is the earlier Christianized Celtic tradition. The oral-performance aspects of these formulas resonates with Christian liturgical practice more than anything else.

Christian thought, particularly neoplatonic philosophy, gravitated towards the notion of a universe governed by divine principles and mathematical proportions that have great power when named or described in words. For example, the 'magic square' talisman constructed of the letters SATOR-AREPO-TENET-OPERA-ROTAS dates to the first century but appears in medieval texts throughout Europe (Kieckhefer 1990: 77–8; Grant 1979: 19–22). An apparent anagram for the words Pater Noster when written out in cruciform shape with A and O (for Alpha and Omega), it shows how words assume a logical, mathematical power in their perfection. Likewise, another common protective device, found in texts from Iceland to the Balkans, uses the measurement of Christ's body, the nails of the cross or the spear of Longinus in an amulet (Bühler 1964). The precise measurement of the cross on the page is essential, since multiplied (by fifteen, for example) it equals the height of Christ. Some of these scrolls were wrapped around labouring women, but they were generally beneficial both for protection and prosperity (Shinners 1997: 289–99).

The sign of the cross is the most common ritual action deployed in all protective, as well as healing, remedies, certainly as a consequence of Christian liturgical practice, sermon literature and hagiography to which the general public was exposed. For example, the *Golden Legend* of Jacobus de Voragine contains numerous stories designed to show the protective power of the cross, either as a physical object or in the act of signing, against sorcerers and the devil. St James the Greater freed a new believer from magical fetters by sending a relic, his kerchief, and powerful words to break the bonds. 'The Lord upholds all who are falling; he sets the prisoners free' (Jacobus de Voragine 1993: II: 4). St George makes the sign of the cross over his wine thus neutralizing the poison a magician placed in it (Jacobus de Voragine 1993: I: 240). The hideous dragon that appears in St Margaret's visions disappears when she makes the sign of the cross; the dragon bursts open to release her when she does it again – although Voragine allows that this part of the story is apocryphal and not to be taken seriously (Jacobus de Voragine 1993: I: 369). St Justina likewise uses the sign of the cross to ward off demons who try to seduce her, called up by a powerful pagan magician (Jacobus de Voragine 1993: II: 192–5). The reverse is also true, since failure to perform a blessing as an acknowledge- ment of Christ's protection is dangerous, illustrated for example in the story of the nun who ate a little demon on her lettuce leaf because, as the demon complained afterward, she failed to bless it (Gregory the Great 1959: 18). Likewise, in stories of saints or necromancers compelling demons, one slip in one's protective rituals allows the demon to pull his tricks. Given the importance of the sign of the cross in popular Christian literature, it is unsurprising to find signing as a common ritual action in protective remedies or inscribed crosses in amulets.

Hagiography and sermon literature also reveal the protective power of angelic and divine names as well as the power of the Eucharist and relics. Often, a formula is authenticated by a narrative explaining its transmission from an angelic source; for example, the numerical knowledge in the measurement amulets was given to Charlemagne or Constantine by an angel (Bühler 1964: 277). According to Jacobus de Voragine, the angels have power against demons in three ways, of which one is

> through impressing on our minds the memory of the Lord's passion. This is what Revelation means where we read: 'Do not harm the earth or the sea or the trees, till we have sealed the servants of our God upon their foreheads' [Rev. 7: 3]; and in Ezechiel we find: 'Mark *Tau* upon the foreheads of the men that sigh' [Ezek. 9: 4]. *Tau* is the Greek letter that is written in the shape of a cross, and those who are marked with this sign have no fear of the avenging angel. Hence we read in the same place: 'Upon whomsoever you shall see the sign *Tau*, kill him not.' [Ezek. 9: 6] (Jacobus de Voragine 1993: II: 206).

Christian literature therefore fostered the talismanic use of Christian words and signs, most clearly evident in the use of relics and the increasing prominence of the Mass and the feast of Corpus Christi (Kieckhefer 1990: 78–80). The prominence of pilgrimage to holy shrines containing the relics of saints as sources for healing contributed to the replication of non- authenticated relics as well as the theft of authenticated ones.

Thus, the ritual of the Mass and Eucharistic objects were often used for protection, despite certain church prohibitions, for the very reason that the Church taught that the power of the priests resided in the words and

rituals they performed. Gregory of Tours tells the story of the poor woodman who housed a travelling priest and had the priest bless his breakfast
crumbs; later, invisible voices, presumably demons, discuss drowning the
woodman as he crosses a river but cannot because he carries the bread
crumbs blessed by the priest (*Confessors* 30, 1988: 44–5). Unsurprisingly,
then, amulets and other objects were often empowered or blessed by placing them under the altar during Mass. Preachers and canon law frequently
reproach people for secreting the wafer out of church to use for other purposes (Browe 1930). For example, Etienne de Bourbon tells the story of
the man who took the wafer home to place in his hives to increase his
bees' productivity (Jolly 1997: 435–6). The bees, recognizing God in their
midst, built an altar around the relic. The miracle attracted attention and
the new reliquary was removed to a church. The moral of the story
remains somewhat ambiguous. The man was chastised for stealing the
Eucharist and his greedy plan fails. On the other hand, Etienne, as a
Dominican preacher intent on stamping out heresy, is reasserting the
power of the priest to transform bread and wine into the body and blood
of Christ. Since the Church is the source for many of these practices and
ideas that slip from authorized usage to unauthorized *superstitio*, it is hard
to know where to draw the line between magic and religion in these
cases.

Warding off Disease and Natural Disaster

Protection from illness, plague, famine and other inexplicable disasters in
life often had recourse to divine or spiritual agencies, those invisible forces
that hold the world together. In a Christian world view, God as Creator
made an orderly world that, though fallen, nonetheless functions on divine
principles and by his command. Conjuring, adjuring or appealing to those
spiritual forces was a common response to the hardship of an often marginal rural life, where one accident or illness could wipe out a family or
village. However, it would be reductionist to suggest that medieval people
believed in magic or religion in the absence of adequate science to explain
the mysterious in life. Although moderns have devised a new explanatory
system, a science that observably and experientially works in a very real,
material sense, this system of thought offers no better explanation for
chance or so-called 'acts of God' than any other. Medieval practices for
protection offered a way of coping with reality that reflected a larger belief
system about the nature of the cosmos and the human condition. Like
most people, medievals sought meaningful explanations for life experiences, beyond just an immediate cure. Protective devices offered a reference point to, and a reminder of, that larger cosmic belief system. Whether
these devices were effective or not is therefore not the sole criteria for
measuring their worth to medieval society.

Physical ailments warded off by protective rituals or devices, like the closely related healing rituals, were generally complaints with an invisible cause, such as madness, poison or contagion. For example, amulets for epilepsy, often associated with spiritual assault, could cure or protect patients from attacks as prescribed by physicians, utilizing a formula with the names of the three magi (Kieckhefer 1990: 77; Bozóky 1994). Amulets and talismans were also frequently deployed for childbirth assistance. For example, the life of St Margaret, protector of women in childbirth, offers protection in a prayer for those who carry her book, contributing to parchment leaf amulets (Bozóky 1994). As noted, childbearing remedies are one of the three most common type of 'medical magic', in addition to blood-staunching and worm remedies. Despite the generally male-dominated textual tradition for medicine, this exclusively female domain appears frequently in the texts and raises questions about female practitioners of the healing arts, their access to texts, and their use of manuscript parchment in talismans of this type (Weston 1995). They also show that one of the predominant concerns of protective magic is in preserving and maintaining life and productivity.

A large number of protective rituals were associated with agricultural life, such as the protection of crops from pestilence or vermin, the recovery of lost or stolen animals and weather control. The most elaborate 'field blessing' is the day-long ceremony from an Anglo-Saxon text, the 'Æcerbot Ritual', a remnant of which was retained into the modern period in 'Plough Monday' (Jolly 1992, 1996: 6–11). The ritual combines appeals to the earth reminiscent of the Latin Mother Earth prayer, Christian formulas, a Mass, and ritual actions to incite productivity. Four sods are taken from four corners of the field and taken into church where Masses are said over them. Samples of all forms of sustenance – honey, oil, milk from each type of animal, yeast, woods and herbs – are anointed with holy oil and placed on the sods. The sign of the cross, as well as the names of the four gospel writers, are used throughout the ritual, and a common liturgical formula drawn from Genesis and repeated here in both Latin and Old English: *Crescite*, grow, *et multiplicamini*, and multiply, *et replete*, and fill, *terre*, the earth (for a modern example, see Bertrand-Rousseau 1978: 107). Despite earlier attempts to reconstruct a Germanic pagan origin for this ceremony, its components can be clearly traced to a Latin literate tradition closely allied with liturgical practice. Far from being evidence of the retention of paganism, this ceremony is evidence of the Christianizing of rural practice.

Less spectacular protective formulas and rituals ward off natural disasters using holy objects, such as wax or ringing church bells (Kieckhefer 1990: 78). Prayers and exorcisms in liturgical manuscripts drive out of the fields vermin such as rodents or birds. Belief in weather magic, although condemned in the penitentials, was widespread according to Bishop Agobard of Lyons (McNeill and Gamer 1938: 331). Burchard describes the details of a rain-inducing ritual performed by women (McNeill and Gamer 1938: 341). A girl is stripped and sent to gather henbane, which she digs up with the little finger of the right hand and ties with a string to the little toe of her right foot. She then drags the henbane in a procession with other girls carrying twigs and sprinkling water on her. The girl is then guided walking backwards to the village. Agobard condemns the persecution of storm-makers, those accused of destroying crops by calling up destructive winds, cautions people against paying weather magicians to protect their crops from storms, and exposes the myth of a cattle-killing dust, evidently an actual scare in 810 (Dutton 1993: 189–91). He also contrasts those who curse at a storm, blaming the person who caused it, with those who instead call on God and his saints. Nonetheless, weather charms persist throughout the Middle Ages and into the sixteenth century, often adjuring the devil and his angels as the cause of trouble (Siller 1982).

Another common type of protective formula wards off predators. Such formulas assist in the recovery of stolen animals or in the detection of a thief (Siller 1982: 131–4). The Anglo-Saxon *Lacnunga* version for lost or stolen cattle narrates the birth of Christ, the recovery of the cross, a reference to the popular legend of Helen, and includes a troubling reference to the Jews as Christ's killers and as thieves (Grattan and Singer 1971: 183). Other versions show the same propensity to use Christian narration that connects to Christian antiphons as well as the powerful sign of the cross (Barkley 1997; Hollis 1997; Hill 1978) One fourteenth-century Middle English narrative formula from a medical text protects animals against both wolf and thief (Smallwood 1989). It uses a combination of English and German charm motifs that show the spread and interaction of these traditions, including elements of the Anglo-Saxon cattle theft and recovery charm and a version of the Jordan river formula.

Other protective rituals for rural life include the bee swarm formulas noted earlier and journey amulets and charms. One Old English metrical journey charm is found in the margin of a copy of Bede's *Ecclesiastical History*, along with other marginalia that include cattle-theft charms, the bee swarm formula, remedies for sore eyes, liturgical prayers and homilies (Grant 1979). The journey charm offers protection while en route against a wide range of evils, both spiritual and physical, and appeals to a long list of biblical saints from Abraham and Isaac to the four gospel writers, as well as the Trinity and all God's angels. But the performance of the words themselves offers powerful protection (Nelson 1984). The opening asserts, 'I gird myself with this rod [presumably the cross] and give myself into God's fealty' and later brags 'I chant a victory charm; I carry a victory rod, word victory and work victory' (Cockayne 1961: I: 388–91).

Among the nobility of the high Middle Ages, gemstones became popular amulets, and when inscribed with formulas, functioned as talismans (Kieckhefer 1990: 102–4). Precious and semi-precious stones could be worn as rings or other jewellery, not only as a mark of luxury and status, but also for the heightened protection they offered, more concentrated than herbs. Gems carried as amulets could protect against disease, madness, wild beasts, fire, and assist in theft detection. Gervase of Tilbury in the early thirteenth century defended the use of gemstones for such purposes, citing ancient authority in the person of Solomon (Kieckhefer 1990: 105). Empowered with inscribed words, talismanic gems served as all-purpose protection. One of many such rings still in existence, a fourteenth-century Italian example, is inscribed with two Scripture verses that function as narrative protection charms. The first is Luke 4: 30, 'But Jesus passed through their midst', and the second John 1: 14, 'And the word became flesh' (Kieckhefer 1990: 102–4, with picture). Together, these two verses suggest that the wearer will be able to pass through enemies unharmed, as Jesus, incarnate God, did. The opening passage of St John's gospel is a favourite one in talismans and other charms because it is a reminder of the central truth of Christianity, that Word was enfleshed, and therefore words have virtue from God.

Whether performed in a ritual, spoken over an amulet or carried in written form as talismans, such words have power because they connect the participant to the cosmic structure of the universe. Consequently, it is somewhat artificial to separate 'natural' disasters from unnatural ones, since often the natural elements have a spiritual component evident in these rituals. Nonetheless, assault from malevolent forces – demons and sorcerers – constitutes a large and somewhat separate category of 'unnatural disasters' that require spiritual protection through appeals to God and counter-magic.

'Unnatural disasters': protection from demonic assault, sorcery and heresy
Although evil perpetrated by demons and by humans constitute two different sources of harm, they are often connected in the protective remedies to counter them. The devil and his minions were held responsible for direct assaults that delude people's minds or cause illness, but increasingly in the medieval period it was believed that human sorcerers derived their power to curse from those same demonic powers. In late antiquity and in the early Middle Ages belief in such human power to curse was often denied (Brown 1972a; Agobard in Dutton 1993: 189–91). However, the continued teaching of the Church regarding the spiritual threat of demons led to a convergence of the spiritual and physical threats. By the late Middle Ages, sorcerers, witches and others who perform maleficent magic were associated with a widespread cult of the devil. A curious muddle of

practices evolved throughout the Middle Ages, including exorcisms of both people and natural objects that provided a spiritual shield from further demonic manipulation, prayers and Scriptural formulas that scared off demons, and protective words against all kinds of enemies such as sorcerers and witches. These practices coexisted with stories of both necromancers and saints who had the ability to conjure demons and force them to do their will, along with manuals offering formulas and rituals for doing so. These are treated below under necromancy, but they provide an important context for the counter-magic offered by protective devices.

Exorcisms are forms of adjuration in that they command the infesting agent to depart. The power of the command is based on the names or powers invoked, obviously in a Christian context God, his angels, his saints or their relics. Such exorcisms are found not only in the Christian liturgy, but also in medical remedies banishing elves, demons, poisons and diseases. Within the liturgy, exorcisms were performed not only on persons – in the baptism ritual for example – but also in the blessings of holy water, holy oil and holy salt, as well as medicinal tools such as herbs and unguents (*Durham Collectar* 1992: 214–15, 226–35; *Missal of Robert of Jumièges* 1994: 280–2; *Leofric Missal* 223–5; *Lacnunga* in Grattan and Singer 1971: 202–5; Kieckhefer 1990: 77). These liturgical manuals also contain exorcisms of the instruments or materials used in the judgement ordeal, iron, water or bread and cheese (Keefer 1998). These items would need to be purified and sanctified so that they would report the truth about the accused. In all of these cases, exorcism itself, and the exorcized items, can serve as a means of protection as well as cure.

Exorcistic words are command formulas, then, for resisting the devil and thereby avoiding the harm he can cause. Any number of Scriptural formulas, spoken or written, can ward off the devil, as evidenced in hagiography and popular sermon literature where the motif is quite common (Thompson 1955–8: G303.16). Caesarius of Heisterbach tells the story of a possessed woman who revealed the three words that bind the devil by pointing to them in the missal: 'through Him, and with Him and in Him', a reference to Mark 3: 7 and binding the 'strong man', here seen as the spiritual enemy bound by the liturgical invocation of the Trinity (V: XIII, 1929: I: 333). Curiously, the idea of a demon forced to reveal the truth about himself or how to bind him is a common motif in Christian literature, a means of showing the supremacy of God and his methods over demonic powers. In his long section on demons (book V), Caesarius records other instances of demons scared off by recitations of holy words, including the power of John 1, invoking the Word made flesh, and the *Benedicite* (1929: I: 355, 378, 381). While Latin liturgical formula would be best known by clergy and monastics, their use in vernacular literature and in remedies suggests widespread transmission of these phrases into popular culture and practice. The *Pater Noster* and the Creed, which the canons specify that all Christians should know, appear frequently, along with phrases any regular attender at Mass could pick up quite easily – the Sanctus, Trinitarian formulas, and names of God, not to mention the sign of the cross, perhaps the most instinctive exorcistic ritual when confronted with danger.

Revenants or reanimated corpses are a related source of spiritual harm in a physical form, often associated with demonic forces in a Christian view. Stories of ghosts, wraiths, and revenants in Celtic and Scandinavian tales remained popular in the medieval period, and indeed seemed to multiply in the late medieval and early modern period with stories of corpses reanimated by magician/scientists, mixed with accounts of vampires. The Old Icelandic *draugr* is a dangerous form of revenant, sometimes associated with treasure-guarding (Caciola, 1996: 15). Although Christian commentators asserted that corpses that appeared to move were reanimated through demonic possession, the belief in human reanimation – an evil person returning to their body and harming the living – persisted and grew throughout Europe in the twelfth through fifteenth centuries (William of Auvergne and William of Newburgh, discussed in Caciola 1996: 10–11, 17–24). Many of these tales are horrific and do not posit a clear antidote to ward off such evil, other than some mentions of reburial of the culprit or other preventative burial rituals. In some ways, these stories represent the mirror opposite of saint's relics, especially the incorruptibles, saints whose ascetic bodies showed no signs of decay. Although walking corpses usually bring death in these medieval stories, for the most part they are not vampires, blood-hungry revenants popular in post-medieval literature. Purposeful reanimation of corpses through experimentation, or the artificial creation of life forms as in the Jewish tradition of the *golem* or the miniature test-tube homunculus made by Paracelsus, appears to be a related motif associated with learned men and experimentation with automatons (Higley, 1997). The *golem* is given the spirit of life through placing sacred Hebrew words on its forehead; the creature often is a protector for the rabbi and his people, even though it is a terrifyingly dangerous procedure to perform.

Suspicion of harmful sorcery is not a unique trait of Christian society. Magic at its roots in classical, Judaeo-Christian and Germanic lore stood in an ambivalent position in relation to normative behaviours. Counter-sorceries from pre-Christian Germanic traditions and ancient Near Eastern cultures fed into medieval culture. Woden was the master of magic formulas and counter-spells, according to Scandinavian lore. The last section of the Hávamál lists eighteen chants of Óðinn (Woden) offering help against all kinds of trouble, including protection against weapons, fetters, runes and witches (Page 1995: 212–15). Gaster tracked a series of Romanian narrative charms and amulets against a child-stealing witch (1971: II: 1037–8). They contain both pre-Christian and Christian elements traceable to Assyria or Egypt and transmitted throughout Romania, southern Russia, the Balkans, Byzantium and Syria. He also traced the development of the verbal formula known as the 'Sword of Moses', a list of divine names used for protection against witchcraft and other harm as well as for healing (1971: I: 288–337).

Some of these formulas are all-purpose, against all kinds of enemies, physical and spiritual, while others are specific. For example, one herbal conjuration in a fourteenth-century hand runs: 'In the name of Christ, Amen. I conjure you, herb, that I may conquer by lord Peter ... by moon and stars ... and may you conquer all my enemies, pontiff and priests and all laymen and all women and all lawyers who are against me' (Thorndike 1923: I: 598–9 n. 1). Others that appear generic become specialized against witches in the late medieval period. One fifteenth-century talisman against a witch sounds like a general protective charm: 'In nomine Patris ... By the power of the Lord, may the cross + and passion of Christ + be a medicine for me. May the five wounds of the Lord be my medicine +. May the Virgin Mary aid and defend me from every malign demon and from every malign spirit, amen. +A+G+L+A+ Tetragrammaton + Alpha + O ...' (Kieckhefer 1990: 84–5). Both of these examples demonstrate how these categories of medicine and liturgy, charm and prayer, magic and religion, were interwoven in medieval society. Much of the protective magic discussed here only makes sense in the context of the healing practices discussed earlier and the necromantic traditions discussed below.

The belief that human beings can be the agents of the devil's activities is a socially disruptive one, leading eventually to witchcraft trials, inquisitions and mob persecutions scapegoating Jews, gypsies, heretics and other marginalized groups. However, throughout the Middle Ages, the accused sorcerer or witch held an ambiguous position, with the Church initially teaching that such power was illusory and accusations of witchcraft therefore false, but later asserting that these activities were harmful because they channelled demonic force into society. The association of heresy, magic and demonic pacts with the devil began as early as the twelfth century. In an incident at Rheims *circa* 1176–80, a condemned woman about to be taken to the flames defied and escaped her accusers by throwing a ball of thread out of the window, saying 'catch' and then magically flying away, assisted, according to the accusers, by the same evil spirits who helped Simon Magus to fly (Wakefield and Evans 1991: 249–54). Ironically, such heretical sorcery is often combated by equal or greater assertions of spiritual authority using similar tools (Kieckhefer 1990: 82–5). For example, in another twelfth-century incident involving the Patarine heresy, an orthodox knight carried consecrated salt as a protection against this heresy;

when he applied it to his food at his nephew's house, he was horrified to discover that his fish shrivelled up into pellets like rabbit's dung, implicating his nephew in the heresy (Wakefield and Evans 1991: 254–6). He then imprisoned the knights who had misled his nephew, and set fire to the building. When the men appeared untouched, a riot ensued, with a mob insisting this was a miraculous sign of their righteousness. Undaunted, the orthodox knight calmed the crowd, then took the advice of the archbishop and placed the men in a larger house around which he sprinkled holy water to counteract the magic of these heretics. When the house refused to ignite, the angry mob broke through to free the men, only to find that their bodies were completely burned while the wood around them remained untouched. Thus the contest between opposing spiritual forces was often unclear in the popular mind, when miracles were the proof of sanctity and righteousness.

Controlling the Future: Popular Forms of Divination

As with healing and protection, divinatory practices helped connect everyday life with the cosmic structure. They provided meaningful ways to cope with seemingly chance-driven events in a supposedly divinely ordered world. Divination does not necessarily mean predicting the future or laying out someone's destiny; rather it is most often a way to interpret signs and to make decisions as to a right course of action. Next to healing, divination is one of the most common realms of 'magical practices', yet one of the most emphatically rejected by Christian authorities, with or without the Christian components that in healing could shift a remedy from condemned magic into acceptable Christian practice.

Divination operates on the principle that the microcosm and macrocosm are interlinked, that human experience and natural phenomenon are interconnected, one reflecting the other. This holistic view is compatible with animistic and polytheistic world views as well as a monotheistic belief in a divine creator who orders all things. Nonetheless, Judaeo-Christian teaching generally condemned divination on the grounds that it denied or bypassed divine will in favour of human control and manipulation. Augustine of Hippo condemned divination in all its various forms and explained how demons contrived to fool people through it (Augustine 1995: 90–101). Astrology, divination by stars, or predictions based on lunar patterns were strenuously rejected by Christian teaching, partly on rationalist grounds that questioned how the stars or the moon could possibly influence human destinies. Nonetheless, despite these condemnations, Christian calendars computing Easter, charting lunar cycles, or listing safe days for blood letting easily came into use as divinatory devices, bringing along with them Christian texts and concepts. Divination continued to be one of the first and most frequently mentioned accusations of magic in laws, sermons, stories and historical accounts, indicating its endemic nature. Paschasius Radbertus mentions, for example, the corruption at the Carolingian court with all kinds of 'soothsaying and sorcery in demand' (Dutton 1993: 277). In the thirteenth century, the Dominican Etienne de Bourbon railed against village sorceries, including divination and worship at elder trees in association with the famous St Guinefort legend (Shinners 1997: 460–1; Schmitt 1983).

Much of the knowledge needed for interpreting significance in divination is found in evidence designed for the literate, and often elite, practitioners. Charts and manuals for reading signs in the sky, in the animal world, on the body or in devices are found in special manuals devoted to the subject or as short treatises added to other manuscripts. We can only speculate about knowledge and practices passed down orally, as gleaned from references in sermon literature, penitentials and canon laws. Augustine of Hippo and Burchard of Worms condemn a wide range of practices from consulting seers, reading auguries, palms, and omens in nature to belief in lucky and unlucky days, times and signs. Popular forms of divination included not just astrology, which became a high form of magic-science, but also the reading of omens and signs in nature, in human experience and in various man-made devices. Finally, there are diviners, those with the special abilities to discern knowledge or acquire it in occult ways, which shades off into the next category of necromancy.

Divination from Nature
Based on the proposition that the created world is orderly and that it is connected to human experience, a high proportion of divination looks to nature for answers and advice. An adept could 'read' messages in celestial patterns, weather, geological phenomena, plant life and the behaviour and anatomy of animals. Observations of nature and correlations of cause and effect are common to all human speculation and scientific inquiry. Unique disruptive events such as earthquakes, unusual tides or comets could be read in different ways, depending on the context. Patrick Geary explores the various explanatory systems that the eleventh-century monk Arnold tried out when he remembered how he saw a dragon in the sky while travelling through Pannonia. As Geary points out, Arnold is writing natural history when he recounts this experience, not millennial speculations about signs and portents; consequently, he is more intent on demonstrating that the crystalline spheres are not solid by showing that a literal, solid dragon could pass through them (Geary, 1994: 164). Signs in medieval thought were multivalent, containing potentially many meanings. Divination was one of the possibilities, but by no means the only explanation.

Chroniclers frequently recorded unusual natural phenomena, sometimes, but not always, correlating them to human events for dating purposes or as omens of good or ill. For example, the comet drawn in the bottom margin of the *Eadwine Psalter* was noted as a portent but lacks any interpretive signification (1992: 157–64). Thus observations of natural phenomena and their interpretations can range in a modern view from scientific to magical, with a great deal in between.

Popular astrology, as compared to intellectual branches of astrology and astronomy, focused primarily on lunar cycles and their influence (Kieckhefer 1990: 86). This led to 'good' and 'bad' days on which to do certain activities, such as beginning a journey, although early medieval churchmen railed against such beliefs as illogical, unnatural and superstitious. For example, the Anglo-Saxon homilist Ælfric of Eynsham, echoing Augustine, condemned this practice of making decisions about journeys or other life affairs according to the sun, moon, stars or day of the week as illogical. He countered that it is natural according to the divine order, and not sorcery, to understand that the moon affects nature in the tides and in the fact that trees cut down at full moon are harder (Jolly 1996: 87–8). Nonetheless, treatises expounding on the 'Egyptian days' were common throughout the Middle Ages, especially those listing safe and unsafe days for blood-letting, practised regularly in monasteries where calendars form an important textual tradition for liturgical purposes. For example the *Prognostics by the Moon's Age* is found in two eleventh-century Anglo-Saxon manuscripts that, ironically, contain Ælfric's own tract on dating, *De Temporibus Anni*, as well as a *Horalogium* and a calendar with diagrams and charts for the lunar cycle, computations of time by shadows, and calculations for Easter (Cockayne 1961: III: 150–73). Divination by reading calendars, celestial patterns or weather phenomena continued throughout the Middle Ages in a strong textual tradition, alongside new astrological tables derived from Arabic learning in the twelfth century. For example, a fourteenth-century manuscript charts divination by thunder, while a fifteenth-century leechbook lists thirty-two evil days on which one would not want to have blood let, start a journey or get married (Burnett 1996: XVIII; Dawson 1934; Kieckhefer 1990: 87).

Plants, stones and animals could also reveal vital information. One physician recommended placing the herb vervain in a patient's hand to gain an accurate prognosis, because the person would speak his or her fate truthfully as a consequence of the herb; likewise, placing the heart and left foot of a toad over a sleeping person's mouth will force them to reveal whatever you ask (Kieckhefer 1990: 89–90). Certain gemstones could also induce someone to reveal the truth – a magnet placed on the head of an unfaithful wife will cause her to fall out of bed (Kieckhefer 1990: 104–5). The more common form of animal divination was augury, the reading of

fortunes in the entrails of animals. Augury dates back to the Greeks and
Romans, and was heavily condemned by Christian commentators; it is
unclear how widespread it was among Germanic peoples. Less well-
known forms of divination from animals include scapulimancy, or divination by sheep shoulder blades, an Arabic tradition imported into Europe in
the twelfth century, although Gerald of Wales claims the Flemings introduced it into England (Burnett 1996: XII–XVI). The logic behind this
form of divination, as explained in Arabic treatises translated into Latin, is
that the divinely placed secrets of the upper world are brought down to
earth in rain and transferred through grass to herbivorous animals like
sheep (Burnett 1996: XIII: 35). Likewise, William of Auvergne posited that
animals and humans have a type of extra-sensory perception that allows
them some premonition of future events (Kieckhefer 1990: 90). These
attempts to provide scientific theory behind divinatory practices are part of
the post-twelfth-century intellectual world. In popular practice the belief
in the interconnectedness of things may have been more intuitive and
based on experience.

Divination from Human Experience and Man-made Devices
As noted above, natural phenomenon can be read as omens of good or
evil. Likewise, specific human experiences – a bird call, a dream, finding a
horseshoe – can be interpreted as a sign. Stories of good-luck objects that
a person finds (a halfpenny, a needle, or a horseshoe, for example) were,
and are, common, despite attempts by the clergy to demonstrate their
illogicality; usually such practices were condemned as *superstitio* rather than
magic. One anecdote told how a priest encountered a woman who super-
stitiously crossed herself to avoid bad luck upon seeing a priest; he then
threw the woman into a ditch on purpose to give her bad luck, despite the
fact that she had crossed herself (Kieckhefer 1990: 88). Burchard mentions
the false beliefs in the success of a journey if a crow croaks from a person's
left side to their right, in watching grain jump on a hot place in the
hearthstone to predict danger, or looking for bugs under a stone outside a
sick person's home to determine if they will get well (McNeill and Gamer
1965: 335, 337). Caesarius of Heisterbach also warns about false signs and
demonic tricks in an ominous tale of a lay brother who thought the
twenty-two cries of a cuckoo meant he would live twenty-two more
years; unfortunately, two years later, in the midst of a planned twenty-year
spree of worldly living (he saved two years at the end for penance), the lay
brother died (Caesarius V: XVII, 1929: I: 337–8). Nonetheless, the tendency to read 'chance' encounters as significant and to collect meaningful
objects for good luck continued to thrive, down to the present day.
    More systematic forms for interpreting one's destiny relied on charts
and numerical systems. Fortunes could also be read on palms (chiromancy),

through numerological analysis of names (onomancy), in dreams (oneiro-mancy) or through talking heads. Chiromancy, traceable to classical times, became popular only in the thirteenth century, as evidenced by numerous scientific and divinatory treatises describing it. Surprisingly, this system of palm-reading made its first appearance in the twelfth-century *Eadwine Psalter*, which Burnett links to John of Salisbury's *Policraticus* and the Canterbury clerical sphere of activity (Burnett 1996: X). *Eadwine* also has a text on onomancy, in part derived from the Arabic Pseudo-Aristotelian *Secret of Secrets*, but also containing an earlier version of the 'victorious and vanquished' numerology system (Burnett 1996: XI). This system for deter-mining which combatant will win in a contest is found in Greek, Arabic, Syriac, Hebrew, Russian, Spanish, Latin and English languages and scripts. *Eadwine* includes four tables that give the numerical equivalents for the planetary weekdays, the victorious and vanquished numbers, the numbers to divide by according to type of person and the numerical equivalents for the alphabet. No instructions are given, but we can deduce them from other such treatises, including onomantic texts found in liturgical books such as the *Leofric Missal* (Burnett 1996: XI: 144). The practice of ono-mancy is rooted in the same presuppositions noted in protective magic using magic squares and numbers, that language has a mathematical corre-spondence to reality. Talking heads, mechanical idols animated by demons, or androids are another source of information, generally associated with learned experimentation dating from ancient sources such as Hermes Trismegistus and often found in legends of famous medieval scholars as necromancers (Higley, 1997: 130–34, 137–43).

These forms of divinatory practice increased in sophistication and use in the high and late Middle Ages in professional treatises. For example, the physician John of Mirfeld used onomancy as a means of medical prognosis, while the dream book of Hans Lobenzweig outlined rules for oneiro-mancy in great detail (Kieckhefer 1990: 85–86; 89). Charts of lunar cycles, calendars of lucky and unlucky days, or maps of hand-palms became increasingly common in the late twelfth and thirteenth centuries, in part, as we saw above, through the influx of Arabic and Jewish tracts and transla-tions of classical sources. The 1184 'Letter of Toledo', purportedly sent by sages and astrologers of Toledo to Pope Clement III and others, predicts apocalyptic doom in 1186, based on occult knowledge of astrological events (Gaster 1971: II: 985–1004). A fourteenth-century Hebrew astro-logical text with Chaldean roots works calendrically by assigning angels to specific days (Gaster 1971: I: 338–55). Texts with Egyptian, Greek, Hebrew or Arabic roots gained wide currency among the intellectual dabblers of the late Middle Ages, the Renaissance *magi* (Kieckhefer 1990: 144–50).

Treatises with charts and diagrams for interpreting individual experi-ences are closely related to other man-made divinatory devices for casting lots, such as dice and gemstones (Braekman 1980). Burchard of Worms noted in the early Middle Ages the oft-condemned practice of *sortes sortilegum*, whereby one randomly points to a text in the Scriptures and uses it to decide an issue or determine a fate (McNeill and Gamer 1938: 331). It is easy to see how this practice could emerge from monastic practice and the contemplation of the Scriptures, whereby a reader might assume that God is speaking directly to him or her in the daily reading. Christian teaching relied on revealed truth, located primarily in the Scriptures but also transmitted through saintly visions. However, in charting a middle course away from extremes, the Church was often suspicious of those claiming special knowledge, not only to quell heretical challenges to Church authority but also to suppress recourse to magicians and diviners as rivals to the Christian clergy.

Sybils and Diviners
Many of the divinatory practices described here required professional assistance, either in the form of a text or a person knowledgeable in reading the signs. While some are learned in such magic through study, often such persons were considered to have a 'gift', or special *gnosis*. Gifted seers are found in many of the Celtic, Scandinavian and Germanic sagas and myths. Germanic and Scandinavian divination in the pre-Christian era was dominated by female seers or sibyls; men apparently entered the practice later, mostly in sorcery and rune magic, heavily condemned after Christianization (Jochens 1993). In the *Prose Edda*, Snorri Sturluson tells the story of the 'Deluding of Gylfi', a king famous for magic who travels to Ásgarðr, the home of the Æsir, to find and bring back knowledge from Óðinn and his wife Frigg, both of whom were gifted in prophecy. The tale is interspersed with quotations from the *Poetic Eddas* (including *Vǫluspá*, the 'Sibyl's Prophecy') that explain how the world came into being through the gods and goddesses. Attribution of divinatory power to women also derives from the ancient Near East, and survived for example in the legend of Sibyl and the dream of one hundred suns found in Old Slavonic and Romanian (Gaster 1971: I: 211–25). Sibylline literature in the Middle Ages was generally apocalyptic, with oracles describing the Antichrist and the Last Judgement (McGinn 1979).

Magicians skilled in divination, however, often derived their insights from conjuring spirits, especially demons. This art has come to be known as necromancy and involves a whole sphere of knowledge acquisition in addition to foreknowledge of events.

Occult Knowledge: Sorcery and Necromancy

Sorcery is one of the generic terms used to describe magic that relies on occult powers. Magicians or sorcerers who possess this knowledge provide their expert services to others, for such tasks as finding a thief, recovering lost property, or performing 'love magic'. Necromancy is a slightly more specialized term for magic that gains its power or knowledge from conjuring spirits, whether angels, demons or ghosts; the necromancer forces these spirits to perform amazing feats of transportation or illusion or to provide knowledge of the secrets of the universe. Stories of necromancy and sorcery, manuals containing spells and conjurations and persecution of known necromancers were on the rise from the thirteenth century, reaching a peak in the fifteenth century. For the most part, medieval necromancy is the product of a 'clerical underworld' (Kieckhefer 1990: 151–75), and is part of a literate intellectual tradition of magic. However, stories about occult knowledge do appear in popular literature, often as cautionary tales in sermons, and thus have an influence on popular perceptions of magic.

Occult knowledge is at the heart of the way magic is perceived as something 'other' and dangerous. The magician is one who has access to secret knowledge, often derived from ancient, foreign or supernatural sources. Evidence from the early Middle Ages of pre-Christian Scandinavian and Germanic practices often associates women with the art of knowing or finding information, as with the norns who weave fates. Burchard of Worms condemns women weaving webs with incantations and spinning magic skeins on the first of January. The association of women, weaving and magic is also documented in archaeological evidence of bracteates of weaving goddesses and the burial of spindle whorls with women, as well as crystal balls, work boxes, and bags that might have had medicinal or magical functions (Wickham-Crowley 1996; Meaney 1989).

With sorcery in general, often the knowledge sought is specific information, such as finding a thief or lost property. Some of the spells are similar to narrative charms for healing. A popular element in these recalls the story of Helen finding the true cross. In a fourteenth-century Flemish version, the magician lies down on the ground arms outspread in cruciform shape, four times pointing to the four compass directions, and calling on the earth to reveal the location of the stolen property, just as the earth hid, and then divulged, the true cross (Kieckhefer 1990: 90). A more diabolical procedure is recounted in the *Grandes Chroniques de St Denis* (Coulton 1928: I: 160–3). A group of Cistercians hired through an intermediary a sorcerer to catch a thief who had stolen money from the abbey. They buried a black cat underground in a chest at a crossroads, including an air pipe, water, and food in the form of bread soaked in chrism, consecrated oil and holy water. Unfortunately for the conspirators, some shepherds and their dogs discovered the cat before the required three days were up; but they had planned to flay the cat and use the hide to form a circle, then eat the cat's food and call up the devil, who would reveal the thief to them. The perpetrators, along with the cat, were burned at the stake in 1323.

Often knowledge is revealed through visions in reflecting objects empowered through incantations. In another case of foiled sorcery from an early fifteenth-century collection of ghost stories, a lord paid a magician to find out who was a thief in his house (Shinners 1997: 235–6). The sorcerer used incantations and anointed the fingernail of a small boy who could then see in the reflections on the nail who the thief was. However, while this revelation was in progress, the thief went to confession and hence disappeared from the boy's vision. In most of these accounts, the moral of the story is that Christian ritual is more powerful than sorcery, which may be why so much sorcery deployed Christian elements in its methods. Etienne de Bourbon goes a step further, however, to demonstrate that such sorcery does not work, in the story of a scholar whose books were stolen (Coulton 1928: I: 85–6). The scholar tried going to several wizards who failed before finally finding one who showed him in a vision on a swordblade the thief, his own much-loved cousin. After accusing his cousin and causing a split in the family, the scholar belatedly hears new evidence that reveals the real thief. In a story found in the *Gesta Romanorum*, a knight discovers his wife's affair with a necromancer (Tale CII, 1959: 174–6). The betrayed husband goes to a learned man who gives him a mirror that allows him to see what the evil necromancer is doing – trying to kill him through an effigy. This foreknowledge saves the knight's life as he is able to duck under water to avoid the necromancer's curse. In many of these cases, magic is used by both sides, to curse and and as a counter-spell.

The same is true in another major category of sorcery, the ubiquitous love magic, used both to cause impotence and to seduce. Popular in legend and romance, actual cases and methods occur throughout the medieval period. They work through methods similar to healing, using herbs, potions or amulets with incantations. Knowledge of such magic is associated with both curses and poisons. Causing impotence is a form of curse, similar to magic that causes death. Similarly, some love potions were thought to have accidentally caused death and were condemned as evil sorcery (Kieckhefer 1990: 81–2). Nonetheless, successful stories of both forms of love magic persisted.

Magic spells that cause male impotence occurred with alarming frequency, along with remedies to undo them. Whether impotence was a common medical problem in medieval Europe is unknown, but most of the documented cases and stories attribute its cause to magic curses placed by jealous women. Burchard of Worms accuses adulteresses of performing such magic to prevent their lover from consummating a marriage with a legitimate wife (McNeill and Gamer 1965: 340). Actual cases of induced impotence include the account in the *Memoirs* of Guibert of Nogent of his parents' marriage, unconsummated for seven years (1996: I: XII). His father's impotence was attributed to the envy of a stepmother using magical arts to break up the marriage so that one of her nieces might seduce him. Guibert compares this bewitchment to conjuring illusions, and claims that this form of magic is common practice among ignorant people. Nonetheless, Guibert's father was also cured by recourse to 'a certain old woman', presumably using a counter-spell. Another famous account of magic-induced impotence is the mysterious story of Martin Guerre in the sixteenth century, again blamed on jealous family rivalry (Davis 1983: 19–21, 27–9). In this case, both husband and wife apparently were under a curse that was undone, after eight years, by the advice of an old woman who 'appeared suddenly as if from heaven', and recommended a cure to lift the spell involving four Masses, sacred hosts and special cakes. The case and later trial as Jean de Coras describes it gains in complexity, but the essential features of the impotence curse is similar to Guibert's father's case.

Magic to seduce is just as common. Positive views of love potions occur in romance literature, where they are a common motif. In the eighth-century Celtic fairy story 'The Adventure of Conle', the hero is wooed by a woman from the Land of the Living (Jackson 1971: 143–5). The druids' spell holds her off, but Conle eventually succumbs to a magic apple. Interestingly, the seductress makes predictions that Christianity will end the evil magic of the druids, a comment found in other post-Christian retellings of earlier tales. The most famous literary love potion, however, is in the story of Tristan and Isolde (Gottfried von Strassburg 1967: 191–7). In this highly romanticized view, the love potion was intended to help the bride Isolde fall in love with her groom King Mark, but the young hero Tristan accidentally drinks the potion with Isolde; the drink is powerful enough to erase Isolde's previous hatred of Tristan and the two fall helplessly in love, leading to a tragic contest between loyalty and the overwhelming power of Love personified in this romance.

A more negative view of love potions is recounted in sermon literature. Jacobus de Voragine in the *Golden Legend* story of St Justina points out the evils of love potions (1993: II: 192–5). The pagan Cyprian calls up demons to help him seduce the virgin saint; the demon instructs him to sprinkle a certain lotion outside her house, but the procedure fails due to her constancy and faith. Later attempts by the demons to inflame lust in her also fail, as does Cyprian's attempts to get near her by transforming himself into a bird or a woman. Justina sees through all of these demonic illusions. Even saying her name aloud breaks the spell when the demons pretend to be her in order to satisfy Cyprian's desire. Caesarius of Heisterbach tells of a nun driven mad by the 'magic arts of a miserable brother' tempting her to lustful passions; the young woman eventually committed suicide (IV: XLII, 1929: I: xx). On the other hand, he tells the story of a woman in purgatory who deployed love magic not for lust but for a good intention, so she was capable of being saved; she was afraid her husband would commit adultery, so she used a love potion to keep him in love with her (1929: II: 316–17). In some ways this story provides an antidote to impotence-causing adulteresses who try to prevent consummated love in marriage.

Most of these stories in hagiographic and homiletic stories are designed to point out the evils of sorcery, although some are ambiguous. Necromancy, calling on demons for information, recurs frequently in stories by Christian authors, sometimes denying the effectiveness of such practices as illusory, but in other cases seeming to support the reality of demonic-derived knowledge. Guibert of Nogent, whose own father was cured of impotence by some kind of magic cure, was intent on showing the demonic evil of sorcerers, asserting that 'they admit no one to instruction in their magic except those whom they rob of the honour of all their Christianity by a horrible sacrilege' (1996: I: XXVI). He gives two examples that show some of the biases and beliefs about the source of these practices. In one, a monk-priest learned sorcery from a Jew that involved a pact with the devil (libation of his own seed, which he drinks), and an ongoing sexual affair with a nun. At one point, he conceals her visits by creating an illusion so that she appears to be a large dog. In the second story, a clerk takes up with a sorcerer who will show him how to get rich. The procedure involves preparing a cock in a special way on a specific day in order to attract the devil; however the clerk disobeys the instructions, calling on the saints in his fright, and the devil cannot complete the pact.

Aside from showing the power of the saints, these stories illustrate how beliefs about magic associated with a cult of the devil, and unfortunately implicating Jewish people, came to be widespread in Europe from the twelfth century through monastic and mendicant sermon literature. Even more so than Guibert of Nogent, Caesarius of Heisterbach fosters these associations in his *Dialogues*, particularly in book V on demons. Caesarius clearly associated necromancy with demonic pacts and heresy, and seems intent on showing how easily Christians are caught up in it. In one story, two heretics are caught and burned at the stake for their magic, revealed, ironically, through necromancy (V: XVIII, 1929: I: 338–41). These two had power to perform a variety of illusions because they had made a pact with the devil, whose indentures were sewn under the skin in their armpits. The bishop discovers their secret through recourse to a clerk who knew sorcery, and though he had renounced it, used the art to help the bishop in his holy cause. The reality of such powers is clear, but in Caesarius' monastic view, what makes one side right or wrong is holy versus unholy intent, and true conversion. Even the recluse Bertradis is deceived into thinking a demon is an angel of light, and she follows his visions until she adjures him by the Trinity. In this context Caesarius explains the possible counter-medicines to demonic attack, including the Ave Maria, Benedicite and the sign of the cross. He lays little blame on

Bertradis, saying that not everyone has the gift of discerning spirits and the devil is wily, appearing in many forms, both beautiful and ugly, or as animals (V: XLVIII, 1929: I: 381–2).

Thus Caesarius' intent is to induce true conversion in a Cistercian view. Several of his stories in book I on conversion tell of reformed necromancers who renounce their art after seeing a colleague in torment in hell for practising that 'accursed science' (I: XXXIII, 1929: I: 42–3). In a peculiarly ambiguous case, a reformed necromancer in the monastery is convinced to revive his art for the sake of finding out the fate of someone who has died (I: XXXIV, 1929: I: 43–6). He rides on the back of a demon to visit hell in a fairly typical underworld journey found often in vision literature; although he comes back pale and exhausted, he is not punished for using nefarious means to gain a true vision of the afterlife, since he was obeying orders and returns to his converted lifestyle. In telling this tale, Caesarius seems to substantiate the reality and effectiveness of necromancy. In fact, he goes out of his way to prove the existence of demons and their powers to those who might doubt, describing in detail the procedures used by masters and their pupils to call up demons using a circle drawn at a crossroads followed by fantastic illusions (V: II–IV; 1929: I: 315–20). Another Cistercian source, the *Grandes Chroniques de St Denis*, also describes the use of a circle with crosses, but in this case used to protect a lay brother from assault by the devil while on a journey, begun before daybreak despite the fear of beginning journeys before sunrise (Coulton 1928: I: 157–8). Caesarius in his tales gives specific details of Swabian and Bavarian scholars going to Toledo to study necromancy, suggesting the importation of the art through Arabic and Jewish practices, spreading throughout the education system of Europe to create a network of cult necromancy.

Mendicant sermon literature, aimed more at common lay people than the Cistercian conversion tales, is just as explicit about the reality of a demonic cult of necromancy, as evident for example in tales of the devil, relics and miracles by Etienne de Bourbon (*Translations and Reprints* II. 4: 2–20). Another Dominican, Rudolf von Schlettstadt, tells the story of a woman who went to a sorceress, a widow, who knew incantations to call up demons to give you whatever you desired (Shinners 1997: 216–17). The sorceress prescribed an amulet made of plaster, wood from a consecrated altar and the shin bone of a thief hung for three nights. The amulet worked, although not in the woman's favour. The devil in the form of a black man appeared, grabbed the woman, and twisted her head killing her. Although in this story the woman's unholy desires earn her punishment, in another story a wandering scholar/necromancer named Walravius calls up demons not only to prove their existence to doubters, but also to take revenge on a servant who abuses him (Shinners 1997: 218–19).

If this kind of sermon literature were our only source for a cult of necromancy, we might have good reason to doubt the actual practice of the art. However, trials of accused necromancers and manuals of necromancy corroborate the existence of at least a belief in the ability to conjure spirits and gain occult knowledge, not only in western Europe but in related traditions in Christianity, Islam, and Judaism. For example, in Byzantine demonology, control of demons by sorcery is used for coercion, protection and divination (Greenfield 1988). Astral magic found in a fourteenth-century Italian manuscript is a Latin version of an Arabic Hermetic treatise known as *Picatrix* in its Latin form, dating back to the thirteenth century. This particular manuscript also uses Scandinavian runes as a cryptic alphabet to write the names of the planets (Burnett 1996: VIII). Much of this form of magic shared between these monotheistic traditions belongs to an intellectual tradition closely associated with philosophy. The *Ars Notoria* tradition, for example, achieves knowledge of the seven liberal arts through necromantic means, confirming Caesarius' suspicion that the magic art was rampant in the world of scholars and secular clerics (Burnett 1996; Fanger 1998).

By the fifteenth and sixteenth centuries, despite infamous cases of condemnation and book-burning, manuals of necromancy were quite popular. An Italian manual from *circa* 1510 included recipes for everything from conquering cities and becoming invisible to love magic and astrology (Burnett 1996: IX). It employs Latin, Greek and Hebrew, along with magic squares, talismans, rings, cabbalistic and Arabic techniques. One of the more intriguing recipes explains how to make women think they are wading through a river so they lift their skirts above their waists (6–7). Similar recipes occur in the fifteenth-century *Munich Handbook*, which Kieckhefer divides into categories of 'illusionist experiments', 'psychological experiments', 'divinatory experiments', and 'conjurations and exorcisms' (Kieckhefer 1997). Creating illusions of banquets, horses and castles seems akin to party jokes and perhaps reflects a courtly environment of magic for entertainment, treated below.

Manipulating people into falling in love or driving them mad seems more devious, but provides evidence for some of the magic condemned by sermon authors. Creating an illusory banquet is found in an earlier, twelfth-century case of heresy, wherein a rather simple-minded man named Eon proclaimed himself God because he was the 'eum' of the liturgical formula 'per eum ...'. According to William of Newburgh, Eon provided his followers with sumptuous banquets that were completely ethereal, supplied by invisible spirits; evidence of their illusory quality was manifested at the first belch, whereupon the partaker immediately felt hunger (Wakefield and Evans 1991: 143–4). That later necromancers' manuals like the *Munich Handbook* supply elaborate Latin formulas for producing such banquets indicates not so much a direct connection with heresy but a set of common themes and motifs associated with magic. The *Munich Handbook* and related late medieval manuals seem to be a culmination of all of the suspected sorceries involving divination through enchanted mirrors and fingernails and the use of magic circles and spheres to conjure spirits.

Thus the *Munich Handbook* seems to confirm the worst nightmares of writers like Caesarius of Heisterbach, as well as later inquisitors, about demonic magic produced by a clerical underworld of scholar-necromancers. Yet the *Munich Handbook* seems equally to be a product of the very environment and mentality that condemned it. It is, to state the obvious, in clerical Latin, deploys common Christian formulas, and calls on divine, angelic and demonic names derived from a range of ancient Near Eastern sources attractive to the intelligentsia of late medieval Europe. The rituals described therein, while they may seem to operate on similar principles of magic to a modern eye, are quite different from some putative pagan magic surviving from the early Middle Ages or even the popular healing rituals in medicinal manuals. They are arguably the product of high and late medieval Christian theology, philosophy and science.

Nonetheless, some of the ambiguity surrounding demonic magic in popular culture is evident by comparing motifs found in this intellectual branch of necromancy, in sermon literature condemning commerce with demons, and in the hagiography extolling the power of saints over demons. For example, magic transportation through conjuring demons is a common literary device found in romances, sermon literature and saints' lives, but also found with complete instructions in necromantic manuals. The magician/saint conjures demons into producing an illusory means of transportation (horse, chair, magic carpet) to a far-away land, such as Rome, Jerusalem or even hell. Usually there is a proscription against committing a sin, as minor as omitting a blessing, since that will cause the traveller to lose control of the conjured demons (Kieckhefer 1997: 42–3). For example, the *Munich Handbook* has several incantations for obtaining a horse, as well as one for a boat and one for a flying throne, that are essentially illusory but allow the magician to travel magically across land or water (Kieckhefer 1997: nos. 8, 9, 14, 15, 17, 43).

In the saintly story of Great John, Archbishop of Novgorod, the archbishop captures a demon in his water bowl using the sign of the cross and a prayer (Zenkovsky 1974: 310–14). He then commands the demon to appear as a horse and take him to Jerusalem to visit the holy places, which the demon does, placing a condition on the archbishop that he should not tell anyone the story. Later, the archbishop relates the events in the third person, which the demon takes as a violation of the condition. The demon takes revenge by creating an illusion of a woman visiting

the archbishop's quarters in private, which causes the townspeople to
drive him out. The angry parishioners place him on a raft in the middle
of the river, whereupon the gracious archbishop forgives them. The
demon is so abashed by the archbishop's behaviour that he weeps and
then confesses. Archbishop John is carried back in procession to the city
by his repentant people.

Likewise, Caesarius of Heisterbach tells an ambiguous tale of demonic
transportation (V: XXXVII, 1929: I: 368–70). An honourable knight, suffering from some madness or disease of the brain, has taken to hating his
wife. A demon offers to transport him magically to Rome to obtain a
divorce, in spirit, since his body remained at home, pale and bloodless.
Along the way, besides a detour to Jerusalem, the knight observes a thief
robbing his neighbour, information he uses to assist the neighbour. When
the knight is restored to his body and his senses, he loves his wife again, but
retains vivid memories of his journey while ill. It would be simple to follow a reductionist argument and attribute this story to high fever, as some
scholars erroneously do to explain the visionary experiences of mystics
and saints. However, for Caesarius, this is a story about a moral universe
where demons, despite their ill-will, can turn people to good. The knight's
journey was more real, in terms of the spiritual life of his soul, than a physical journey; consequently it would be a mistake to dismiss such accounts
as products of a diseased imagination. Rather, what these stories about
magical transportation reveal is a complex world view in which humans
interact with spiritual forces in a variety of ways, sometimes humorously,
but always meaningfully. Sorcery and necromancy were taken seriously, as
evident in the prosecution of magicians, and yet the belief in and practice
of conjuring spirits existed in the context of a Christian moral framework
that often treated supernatural forces lightly, as motifs in an ongoing moral
and spiritual drama. This same view of magic is evident in the realm of
entertainment.

Magic as Entertainment

Although entertainment may be a modern anachronism, some examples of
illusory magic in the necromantic manuals and many of the stories of
magic in Christian literature noted above seem to have entertainment as a
secondary motive. In addition, magic with entertainment as a primary
function occurred in two venues, the court and literature. In both cases,
illusions were the focal point, involving deceiving or fooling the mind as a
way of exploring ideas and human relationships.

In the sense that magic was illusory, a deception of the mind, magic acts
could be considered an art performed for an audience. Most of the evidence

comes from courtly entertainment, but the existence of popular entertainers travelling through towns and villages can certainly be posited; certainly we know of minstrels, acrobats, acting troupes and other performers who all, in a sense, create illusions in their performances. Sleight of hand, optical illusions, secret writing and making objects move mysteriously appear in late medieval manuals, along with other more mischievous tricks such as some of the illusions found in necromantic manuals and performed in courts (Kieckhefer 1990: 91–2).

In particular, the aristocracy seemed fascinated with automatons, mechanical devices that moved mysteriously through the illusion of mechanical technology (Higley 1997). Automatons are often associated with medieval legends of Virgil as a powerful magician, recounted for example in the *Gesta Romanorum* story of a magic statue Virgil constructed for emperor Titus that communicated to the emperor any secret offences committed during the day (1959: 97). The technology for such wizardry was absent in early medieval Europe, causing some consternation for the German ambassador Liudprand of Cremona when he saw the mechanical wonders at the Byzantine court. But by the thirteenth century, the engineering skills had developed through experimentation by scientists like Roger Bacon and in more entertaining fashion at the courts of Europe; for example, mechanical birds that sang (Kieckhefer 1990: 101). One fully equipped room of 'entertaining' mechanical marvels included overhead pipes that wet the ladies and pipes below that blew flour on unsuspecting guests, a veritable funhouse (Eamon 1983: 176). Of course, the danger in presenting these technological feats as magic acts is they lend themselves to accusations of actual necromancy, since the line between natural science and natural magic was unclear, leaving court magicians in a precarious position.

As masters of arcane knowledge, magicians, and particularly astrologers, were known at court especially from the twelfth century, a major turning point in occult knowledge in Europe. John of Salisbury in the twelfth century complained of magical arts used by courtiers, castigating a classically derived list of divinatory practices but also recounting his own memory of a priest using incantations of demonic-sounding names to see images in the boys' fingernails anointed with chrism (1938: 146–7; Kieckhefer 1990: 151). Nor were astrologers always trusted or believed. In the fifteenth century, Louis XI tried to test an astrologer who had correctly predicted the death of a court woman whom Louis had loved (Kay 1988: 319). The king arranged a signal with his courtiers to indicate that they should throw the astrologer out of the window at his command. The astrologer was then asked to predict his own death. Cleverly, he answered that he would die three days before the king died, whereupon the king made sure he did not signal to his courtiers and thereafter was careful to keep the astrologer alive. The anecdote, true or not, indicates the fragile balance between belief and doubt in the political context of magic. In fact, court intrigue lent itself well to accusations of magic directed at political figures, with obvious political motives. Especially popular were accusations of assassination through magic poisons and seductions through love magic, both clearly related to disputes over political succession and power (Peters, this volume; Kieckhefer 1990: 96–9).

While magic at court thus had its dangerous side, it also has its light side in entertainment. Tricks as performed in illusory magic by their nature admit to deception and suggest a willing suspension of belief on the part of the audience. The same is true with magic as portrayed in literature. Literary magicians played a role in medieval notions of magic and its operations. Stories popular in the Middle Ages have their roots both in the classical Judaeo-Christian heritage and in the Celtic, Scandinavian and Germanic traditions.

Medieval Europeans inherited and expanded on legends from late antiquity: Solomon, Alexander, Aristotle and Virgil became literary examples of the powerful magician, both feared and respected for their occult knowledge (Higley 1997). The romance stories of Alexander the Great and his magicians demonstrate the continued interest in divination among the nobility (Cary 1956). Of the five categories in Gautier de Châtillon's Alexander romance, most have to do with divination (Townsend 1996). Under prophecy, he lists pyromancy, aeromancy, hydromancy, geomancy and necromancy (the basic elements, borrowed from Isidore of Seville); under mathematics he lists haruspicy, horospicy, and auspicy; meanwhile he defines *maleficium* as using demons to find out the future and identifies fortune-telling with casting lots. The only non-divinatory technique in his list is conjuring, specifically invisibility and shape-shifting, both practices involving deception or illusion to trick others. Similarly, Virgil is transformed in medieval legend into a necromancer whose extensive knowledge and abilities are derived from demons (Spargo 1934; Comparetti 1997). These legends cross cultural lines, appearing in Latin, European vernaculars and Hebrew. For example, Gaster has located Hebrew versions of the Alexander romance, of the *Secretum Secretorum* attributed to Aristotle and the Arthurian motif of the destruction of the round table (1971: II, 814–78, 742–813, 942–64). The role these ancient and foreign magicians played in the actual practice of magic is evident in the frequency with which magic treatises attribute their remedies or spells to these men as sources.

The image of the powerful magician also derives from Celtic legends and Scandinavian sagas (Higley 1995). These stories often present gods and heroes – the Irish Cú Chulainn in the *Táin*, the Scandinavian Gylfi in the sagas – as powerful in magic, combined with heroic quests into magic realms, lands or islands inhabited by the gods or fairies. Irish and Welsh tales are full of voyages exploring strange lands, such as the mysterious voyage of Mael Dúin (Jackson, 1971: 152–9). Magicians in the Icelandic sagas have a special gift of second sight which they can use for good or ill; often they are perceived as self-serving (Bayerschmidt 1965). The most revered of the seven known Icelandic magicians is Sæmundr Fróði, a Christian priest who studied magic, apparently without much conflict of beliefs (Aðalsteinsson 1994, 1996).

Prophecy and divination, games of power, and love magic are common motifs carried through from Celtic, Scandinavian and Germanic lore into high medieval romance literature and the Arthurian tradition. Often set in another world, or involving interaction between two worlds, medieval romances explored human character through tests and quests outside the realm of ordinary human experience. In the Breton *lai* retelling of the Orpheus legend, the hero Sir Orfeo recovers his queen from the fairy land after she was bewitched away (Sands 1966: 185–200). In *Sir Gawain and the Green Knight*, the hero accepts the traditional Christmas challenge at King Arthur's court and must confront a powerful 'magician', a knight in the form of a green giant who can survive having his head chopped off. While scholars may debate the Celtic and pre-Christian origins for the 'Green Man' motif, it is abundantly clear that these romances derive most of their supernatural material from Christian ritual and story (*Sir Gawain and the Green Knight* 1967: xx). For example, Sir Gawain's arming and the pentangle represent Christian virtues, while his shield reflects penitential doctrine (*Sir Gawain and the Green Knight* 1991: xvii–xix, 243).

Arthurian romances are also full of magic devices, such as swords, gemstones and illusory banquets, that are reminiscent of practices found in magic treatises and manuals of necromancy, calling into question the boundary between fiction and reality. Christian mysticism is infused into some of these motifs, most clearly evident in the stories of the Holy Grail, the search for which takes the heroes through many magic lands and castles. The Arthurian Grail legends evoke both the mystical power of relics and the magical power of gemstones and other objects to transform and reveal in a way that obviates the difference between mystical and magical (*The Quest of the Holy Grail*, 1969).

Most of all, Arthurian romance offers the most renowned magician in the Middle Ages, Merlin. His complex story evolved over the centuries, reflecting a combination of earlier legends as well as changing ideas about magic over the course of the Middle Ages. The twelfth-century historian Geoffrey of Monmouth is responsible for the main storyline embroidered in later legends (1966). Although Merlin remains a secondary character in the literary versions, such as Malory's *Morte D'Arthur*, he is an essential component in the narrative, foretelling and shaping events almost as a *deus ex machina* (Malory 1971: I). According to Geoffrey, Merlin was the child of a nobly born nun impregnated by an incubus demon. Carnal commerce with demons was a frequent preoccupation in Christian condemnations of magic. Merlin's demonic origin is somewhat mitigated in later tellings by his baptism, but his magical powers are retained. Geoffrey includes an extensive – and much quoted – recitation of Merlin's prophecies regarding the kingdom of Britain. He justifies his inclusion of Merlin's prophecies by asserting that the Bishop of Lincoln, a man of 'great religion and wisdom', requested them. The prophetic basis for Britain's rule is essential for the kind of legendary history Geoffrey was writing. Orderic Vitalis quotes from it in his *Historia*, as does Abbot Suger in his biography of Louis VI (Suger 1992: 69, 185). The animal symbolism is particularly striking in these prophecies, reminiscent of classical and medieval lore and medicine using animals. Merlin is most renowned, however, for his 'love magic' creating an illusion that allows Uther to beget the future King Arthur on his enemy's wife, and for assisting Arthur in the creation of his kingdom. The political context for these stories is clearly that of the high medieval court. For example, rival necromancer Morgan le Fay in many ways personifies the evil magic of court intrigue involving jealousy and political rivalry. Magic in the Arthurian tradition remains both potent and dangerous, mirroring magic in the courtly environment.

Literary magic not only reflects the self, in this case medieval Europeans, but also their perception of 'the other'. Medieval travel literature often contains highly illuminating descriptions of magic and magicians in foreign lands, in part because magic by definition is alien and 'other'. Early medieval travel literature, such as the Irish voyage tales, describe encounters with the marvelous. In fact, 'wonder' seems to be a dominant theme in both magic and travel literature, even in stories of actual encounters with foreign cultures (Greenblatt 1991). For example, Marco Polo frequently associated idolatry with magic. He attributed magical prowess to the people of Kashmir and to the Brahmans of India, and found magic among the Tibetans, in a variety of provinces between China and India, at the court of Kublai Khan, and even among the Christians on an island called Socotra (1958: 78, 109, 131, 173, 182, 223–4, 261, 298). The most frequent forms of magic he describes are weather-control and divination, although he also notes medical incantations as well. Even taking into consideration the fact that he is witnessing a variety of religions – Hinduism, Buddhism, Islam, ancestor worship, shamanism – in foreign languages, his observations seem to reflect more his own European assumptions about magic and religion than a real understanding of these religious traditions.

These European responses to other cultures bring us back to the definitional problem of magic and remind us that magic is a European construct, the product of a complex social, political and religious history. Two corollaries of this proposition best summarize this history. First, the application of the term 'magic' to other cultures and beliefs outside of Europe should be avoided. Second, an understanding of the evolution of the concept of magic in the Middle Ages is essential for understanding European culture.

PART 2

Trolldómr *in Early Medieval Scandinavia*

Catharina Raudvere

Introduction

The aim of the present survey is to give some glimpses of the cultural and social context in early medieval Scandinavia that produced a system of beliefs and rituals linked to the assumed special capabilities and extraordinary knowledge of certain persons. In this system, reference to witchcraft/*trolldómr* was considered a sensible and acceptable truth.

The world of the peoples of Scandinavia was geographically on Europe's periphery, *Ultima Thule* as Roman writers regarded it. However, culturally it was not an archaic isolated society as older, more romantic, scholarship emphasized (Burke 1992a: 79). Recent writings on the Norse world stress the continental influences more and more (DuBois 1999). Through travelling and trade, groups in the Norse communities were in regular contact with the Continent, as well as other parts of the world. Both material culture and social structures show early influences from Europe. The period covered by this study is to a large extent parallel to the process of Christianization, approximately 800–1300 CE, which involved significant changes at all levels of Scandinavian society. The greater part of the sources relevant to this study were written during the last of these centuries by Christians. Labelling the time covered as either pre-Christian or Christian confirms a dichotomy that does not take into account that the Christianization was a long process, or the fact that what the texts reveal is to a large extent products of a mixed culture.

Images of the Past

In this essay almost exclusive use is made of written Old Norse sources from the Scandinavian Middle Ages, mainly of Icelandic and Norwegian

This study was made possible by generous support from the Knut and Alice Wallenberg Foundation. I am also grateful for the kind hospitality shown me during the academic year when this essay was written by the members of the Scandinavian Department, University of California, Berkeley, especially Professor John Lindow. Several studies with relevance for the present work have been published after this essay was finished. As far as possible references to those studies have been integrated during the proof-reading.

origin. For comparative reasons some texts in other languages will be discussed. With the exception of runic inscriptions no written texts were produced in Scandinavia before the introduction of Christianity, although, along with the Anglo-Saxons and the Irish, the Scandinavians used their vernacular extensively. The texts written in Old Norse deal with a long period of time, but were principally composed during the thirteenth century. Their relation to the previous – and to the contemporary – oral culture is a complicated matter. Though form and style indicate a background in oral transmission, radical changes must have taken place during the process of writing. To suppose a verbatim transcription seems unrealistic. Two major text groups, the sagas and the mythological narratives, provide us with the basic material for an understanding of the Old Norse world and its belief systems (Andersson 1967; Clover 1985; Lindow 1985; Clunnies Ross 1994, 1998).

The first group of texts is the various kinds of sagas. Without discussing the classification of the sagas into distinctive subgroups, it can be said that they constituted the Norse form of history writing. Most sagas were written down in the thirteenth century and are generally by anonymous authors. They recall important events from the time of the settlers' colonization of Iceland (the ninth-century *landnám*), and continue in some texts up until the writer's own time. Although it is impossible to give any exact demographic statistics, it can be noted that the population of Iceland in the Middle Ages mainly originated from Norway and other parts of Scandinavia, and also from the British Isles. Formally the sagas are chronological prose texts with insertions of skaldic poetry with its metaphoric language. Mostly the persons, places and events that appear have historical relevance and the texts also give probable indications of religious and moral concepts.

The focus of many sagas is power and power relations. In many senses these texts were a mode of articulating political conflicts. The whole motivation for establishing an Old Norse written literature originated in a period when a distinct Icelandic identity with a specific history was formulated. The Icelanders were involved in harsh political conflicts, especially with Norway and Denmark, and in 1262–4 the Icelandic 'freestate' perished. Iceland came under the rule of the Norwegian king and later under the Danish crown. Therefore the texts reveal several discourses of national identity along with those of local and individual identity. After the early settlement the land was principally divided between independent chieftains, even though the tendency in the thirteenth century was for some few families to dominate the political and social scene. The landscape is a significant entity in the sagas, closely connected to family history. James Fentress and Chris Wickham have made an analysis of how Icelandic memories were structured by geography and genealogies and they write:

'Icelandic social memory needed to develop genres which preserved the complexity of their [the Icelanders'] social topography' (1992: 163f.). To the authors of the thirteenth century the era of colonization was the background against which social and spatial mobility were understood. Places had their specific history and were related in the narratives to special persons. Social borders between families were established and maintained through discussions about claims to land and places were named after important persons and consequential events.

Every saga text is part of these conflicts and the histories of the families and their feuds are all told from highly subjective angles. The sagas were a way of explaining why certain conflicts had arisen, who took part in them, who was claiming authority over what area and, not least, how loyalties and alliances were broken. 'The logic of feud, in effect, constituted a narrative form in itself, which could underpin texts several pages long', write Fentress and Wickham (1992: 167). An accusation of *trolldómr* was in this perspective a useful category of either claiming a certain authority or explaining why evil things had happened.

With its background in classical antiquity the Church inherited a link to divination, astrology and healing rituals. But these ceremonies were placed in a new context. Belief in witchcraft was therefore not necessarily contradictory to Christian dogma. As Valerie Flint points out, 'early medieval Europe was remarkably well supplied with influential and respected *harioli*, *auspices*, *sortilegii* and *incantatores*' (1991: 60). It is necessary from this perspective to comment on the impact of conversion and the process of Christianization, with its many cultural, political and social implications. Despite significant changes, continuity can be observed in areas where we might at first not expect to find it: in the religious and moral universe. Most conceptions of *trolldómr* seem at first sight totally contradictory to central Christian beliefs. If those destructive deeds were to be associated with anything in the sphere of the Church it had to be the devil himself. But in a Christian perspective the performances of cunning people were certainly not seen as a way of gaining victory over enemies, or looking into the future, or assisting women in childbirth. 'Yet, the sagas were copied in monasteries and all the accounts of witchcraft we have witnessed would hardly have survived had those who copied the Family Sagas subscribed to a world-view very much opposed to heathen customs' (Pálsson 1991: 165). Practices very similar to the Old Norse ones are recorded much later as folk beliefs and folk medicine. It seems as if the Reformation in the sixteenth century was a shift as important to Scandinavian spiritual life as the establishment of Christianity in the early Middle Ages. Still, certain themes can be observed in popular religious discourse over the centuries.

The second group of texts relevant to this study concern mythology, and are much less homogeneous in form than the sagas. The principal sources for knowledge of Old Norse mythological narratives are the two so called *Eddas*: the *Poetic Edda* and Snorri's prose *Edda* (Harris 1985; Lindow 1985; Faulkes 1987; Hallberg 1993; Clunies Ross 1994, 1998). The name *Edda* is of disputable origin; some commentators claim the etymological interpretation of 'great-grandmother' (i.e. the texts are supposed to be the source of old wisdom and lore) while others claim that *edda* means inspiration or writing (from the Latin *edo*, 'to express in public, distribute, edit'). Both text collections were written down in the middle of the thirteenth century and both are part of the same ideological project to establish Icelandic cultural autonomy. Knowledge of mythology was crucial for the possibility of constructing metaphors. The literary aspects of these texts must be stressed from the beginning to avoid any misunderstanding of them as religious documents or arguments against Christian dogmas. In relation to the themes of the present study it can be noted that the myths tell in an ahistorical perspective how *trolldómr* had been used in the realm of the gods since the dawn of time.

The *Poetic Edda* in its standard editions consists of twenty-nine individual poems written down anonymously. The major manuscript, *Codex Regius*, was more or less accidentally rediscovered in 1643 after being lost and forgotten for some centuries. The individual texts are well arranged by the medieval editor who apparently saw the poems as linked to each other in a specific succession. The songs deal with mythological themes in the realm of the gods as well as poems about heroes acting in the dawn of history. The poetic mythological texts are unique in the corpus of preserved Germanic literature, while the latter group correspond to Continental poetic traditions as expressed in *Das Niebelungenlied* and *Beowulf*. The Eddic poems are generally considered to reveal some of the characteristics of an older oral literary form. The complex use of mythological metaphors is an indication of the audience's general awareness of the mythological content. 'Many texts refer to alleged pagan ritual, and these references have precipitated a vigorous debate on their trustworthiness and meaning', John Lindow writes (1993). Given the creative dynamics of oral transmission, it is impossible to claim any age or *Urform* for the Eddic poetry; instead, it gave room for many individual modes of understanding (Finnegan 1992). In perhaps the most important lay of the collection, *Vǫluspá*, *trolldómr* plays an important part, as it is used and abused in the different phases of the history of the universe.

Snorri Sturluson (*c.*1179–1241) was a well-known politician and historian in his time, born to power and wealth. Through family and relatives he was deeply involved in political and other conflicts. Despite – or perhaps because of – this involvement Snorri cultivated antiquarian interests. His comparatively extensive writings cover a variety of different genres, though predominantly Norse history. Snorri's *Edda*, a part of his attempt to write a handbook for poets, is a systematic survey of the Old Norse mythology. Yet the motivation for the compilation was not based in religious sentiments. In order to preserve Old Norse poetics in style and content, especially the elaborate use of metaphors, he realized the need to explain the old mythology and offer future poets as many details as possible. It is obvious that Snorri is making use of known and unknown earlier texts together, as he generously quotes songs almost identical with the texts of the *Poetic Edda*. Without the systematic and pedagogical structure of Snorri's survey it would be difficult for a modern reader to understand the many metaphors and hints about myths in the *Poetic Edda*. Snorri's choice of form is both traditional and innovative for the time. The dialogue of his *Edda* that takes the shape of a competition about wisdom is a form frequently used in Old Norse literature when it comes to draw up comprehensive overviews. Snorri gives the impression that he was a learned man in terms of his time. Margaret Clunies Ross characterizes his strategy in formulating the pagan world view as inspired by Continental ideals of style. The mythic narratives of the *Edda* have, she writes, 'Aristotelian form, with well-defined beginnings, middles and ends, they are extended narratives and they deal in the main with myths of gods and giants on the horizontal plane' (1994: 231).

The social setting of the Old Norse mythological narratives has a clan-like character and the gods are represented as living under family-like patriarchal conditions. Many texts reflect an ideology based on warrior ideals from the upper part of a society with a distinct social hierarchy. Both poetry and history were created for an audience in the upper parts of society and were performed by a skilled poet. The question of representation must therefore be at the core when trying to extract supposed meaning from them. Whose myths and whose history are we reading? To a large extent they are echoes from the halls of the chieftains. Nevertheless, pictorial representations and archaeological artefacts from several centuries and from vast geographical areas give clear indications that the stories, the characters and the symbols were known to a wide range of communities all over the Scandinavian peninsula.

Too often Old Norse mythology has been presented as a reflection of static and homogeneous conditions rather than as part of dynamic processes and changes in northern Europe. The same stories must have been given highly different meanings in different times in different areas among different social groups – and presumably also by men and women. 'Change is structured, and structures change', writes Peter Burke, indicating the dangers of giving a petrified image of Old Norse society and its conceptions (1992a: 2). But with sources as scarce as the Old Norse ones it is frequently hard to maintain an animated image that gives the full flavour of complexity.

Witchcraft or Trolldómr?

There are difficulties with any attempt to formulate a definition of witch-craft as a universal category. The Old Norse concept of *trolldómr* and related terminology was frequently used and given meaning in specific Scandinavian contexts. In order to avoid terms like 'witch', 'witchcraft', 'magic', etc., as far as possible, as they are loaded with miscellaneous mean-ings from totally different contexts (Burke 1992a: 87f.), the emic terminol-ogy: *trolldómr, seiðr, galdr, at spá* etc. is used and there is no need to establish a taxonomic structure that does not exist in the sources. Precise classifications are impossible to formulate since the texts give contradictory statements – not because the Norsemen had confused opinions, but because the con-cepts of *trolldómr* and related ideas were used for explanations in so many very different areas of life. The empirical material of the present study is divided into three sections starting with the belief system and conceptual framework, following on with the ritual implications of *trolldómr*, and end-ing with some examples of how the conceptions and rituals were dealt with in the legal system. The earliest Christian laws deal to some extent with pagan beliefs and practices in stating penalties for those who kept up the old sacrifices or did not follow the commandments of the new reli-gion. Penalties for practising *trolldómr* are also mentioned in this Christian context and there are interesting parallels with some of the accounts in the sagas where cunning people are punished. There are certain analytical advantages to using a broad term like *trolldómr*, when trying to avoid homogeneous categories that contradict the emic use. In what follows a picture of *trolldómr* based on readings of Old Norse texts is presented, in which emphasis is put on the idiosyncracies and the multiple use of termi-nology. A basic distinction is made in the disposition of this study between contexts where *trolldómr* is used for malevolent deeds and other situations where it is connected to divination rituals with supposed positive effects. In other words, there is a spectrum in the Old Norse construction of *trolldómr* ranging from local political strategies to individual peasants' con-cerns about the coming year. It is the context of the narrative that deter-mines whether a deed was to be considered as malevolent or beneficial. The act or words were only a method. The distinction is definitely not meant as any indication of a dichotomy between so called black and white magic.

As with 'witchcraft in general', the history of *trolldómr* is sometimes rep-resented as women's history in the sense that it is a topic more or less exclusively related to women as victims and men as accusers. One of many problematic aspects of such an opinion is that it fixes the conceptions of *trolldómr* in the realm of social relations, leaving out its religious and ideo-logical aspects. The relation between sex/gender and conceptions of *trolldómr* is a complicated matter for several reasons. Both men and women were thought to be involved in *trolldómr* practices, although women did take part more actively in *trolldómr* narratives than is customary elsewhere in Old Norse literature. Women's frequent appearance in this arena does not mean that we can pinpoint a specific and separate women's culture with a more intimate connection with *trolldómr*, as has been stressed (Kress 1990, 1993). Men were apparently equally involved (Dillmann 1986, 1992; Aðalsteinsson 1994, 1996). The saga authors were obviously making use of gender politics in an attempt to construct as appealing a story as possible (Clover 1986a, 1988, 1993), and social differences as well as age were important when hierarchies were constructed. The result in the saga texts is intriguing interplays between sex/gender and power games.

Neither can *trolldómr* accounts be used to formulate a 'history from below', since accusations were to some extent part of elite politics (cf. Sharpe 1992). *Trolldómr* is, in many popular essays, emphasized as something 'underground' and as hidden lore. On the contrary, mythology and popular beliefs were used in literary motifs to express norms, ideas and values, not necessarily in exact reproductions but as metaphors and symbols. In this sense, literature mirrors society. Sagas formulated collective social memory (Connerton 1989; Burke 1992a; Hastrup 1992a). The Icelanders of the thirteenth century interpreted their contemporary situation through the art of telling history. James Fentress and Chris Wickham write in their essay 'Medieval memories': 'Whatever they did with the past, they were writing in – and ususally for – worlds that had their own ideas about the nature of the usable past, the current, functionally relevant past, and the collectively remembered past' (1992: 146).

The rural conditions are always present in the texts and most social interaction occured within the local community. Although it was a small scale society there were important and emphasized social differences: between free men who owned land, *bændr*, and slaves, between chieftains and their subjects, between the generations, and between men and women. To this can be added a certain emphasis in some texts on ethnic difference. The social background to the *trolldómr* stories is still very much that of a pioneer society. The times of settlements and the formation of liaisons between the families are apparently living traditions in the sagas. As in the case of the mythological narratives, I think it reasonable to assume that there were several other ways of telling history than those variants preserved in written texts today. 'The medieval world was as heterogeneous as that of today, or indeed more so, and it would be improper to attempt to generalize too precisely about any aspect of it, least of all its social memory' (Fentress and Wickham 1992: 172).

In the process of demonization the old gods were sometimes adapted to the collective of demons. They were transformed from more distinct characters in the Old Norse mythological narratives to members of a much more diffuse group of demons and devils. From later medieval texts and Church paintings we know that such themes played a crucial part in the didactic ambitions of the clegymen. The Church did not deny the existence of such creatures, but the power of God was greater.

The Old Norse corpus is a unique collection of texts. This is not only because of its magnitude, but also because of its variety in form and content. Magical deeds are referred to in the epics and other kinds of prose text from outside Scandinavia, but do not provide many suggestions of actually performed rituals. The only really meaningful comparisons in relation to the conceptions of *trolldómr* that can be made with literature from other parts of Europe are with the Old High German and Anglo-Saxon spells. To a large extent they indicate a mythology and religious conceptions of similar kinds, but lack descriptions of social context. As stressed above *trolldómr* was not an independent entity, but closely related to the social operations of a local community.

The present study is structured in three major sections. The first deals with the belief system that surrounded *trolldómr*. Basic concepts such as fate, the human soul and knowledge are discussed. The second section on practice and performance makes a distinction between mythological narratives where various gods are told to be involved in *trolldómr* rituals, and saga texts relating to the behaviour of humans. The question whether mythological structure is prototypical for the human is debatable. Nevertheless, the similarities are apparent. The last part of the study concerns legal texts and the administration of justice as it is described in the saga texts. The first text group is explicitly the voice of Christian authorities whereas the latter hint at older legal procedures.

CHAPTER 1

The Concept of Trolldómr: Mentalities and Beliefs

The following words of advice are uttered by the mother of Grettir, an outlaw with many enemies, as she is parting from her sons: 'Be on your guard against treachery. You will not be killed by weapons; I have had strange dreams. Be vary of sorcery; few things are mightier than black magic.'[1] The statement certainly gives us an image of how conceptions of *trolldómr* can be represented in Old Norse literature. The scene occupies a very limited part of the saga text but, although far from being one of the more spectacular episodes, this quotation from one of the Icelandic family sagas is a significant *trolldómr* narrative in its own right. In this case, the saga tells, the source of the old woman's knowledge is her dreams. Through them she can foresee much more trouble for Grettir in the future, and even predict his death. She uses the events of the dream to clarify and analyse the incidents of the daytime. Foreseeing in Old Norse literature is closely related to the protection of family interests, which is also a significant feature of the context of *trolldómr*. No ritual or performance is needed; the mother's action is exclusively oral, but with a strong connection to complex conceptions of fate. Through her foresight the climax of the saga is anticipated and her urgent request thereby constitutes a vital part of the narrative structure. Her words are like a sudden chilly breeze indicating that bad things will become worse. However, the warning turns out to be fruitless, since Grettir's enemies will prove to be stronger; and not only are they more capable, but this is the way destiny had predicted things to be.

By choosing this text as the first example of Scandinavian *trolldómr* conceptions it can be demonstrated that these ideas are not necessarily presented framed by very spectacular events. As we shall see further on, this particular saga also carries some highly dramatic narratives of performed malevolence, but, generally, artless statements are as important in expressing fundamental conceptions and world views.

Trolldómr and associated conceptions were to a great extent part of social events and must therefore be placed in their specific cultural contexts. No *trolldómr* story is found in Old Norse literature without a background of conflicts and related strategies. As will be discussed below, both the performances and the accusations of *trolldómr* dealt with claiming the right to speak in an authoritative mode. Authority, as discussed at length by Bruce Lincoln, could be understood as 'the effect produced by a conjuncture of the right speaker, the right speech and delivery, the right staging and props, and the right time and place' (Lincoln 1994: 90). In an intriguing essay entitled 'The name of the witch' Gísli Pálsson has discussed the implications of social dynamics of Icelandic society in the texts.

> In the Family Sagas both sorcery and the accusation of witchcraft tend to be described as powerful speech acts performed in particular contexts by conscious persons and for particular purposes, not as rule-governed activities. The accuser and the accused are creative agents, not the instruments of culture. Thus, sorcery, divination, and the gossip and the accusations which followed were closely related to the micro-politics of the early Commonwealth. (Pálsson 1991: 168)

Evidently both transformation and hybridity can be said to characterize the period of Christianization in Scandinavia, and a mentality into which *trolldómr* fitted as an explanation must have been prevalent for a long time. Despite bloodshed and violence, a conversion can also be a creative process where new forms are constructed, totally dependent on the meeting of cultures; or to use Mary Louise Pratt's terminology, conversion can be a contact zone. Although her perspective is colonial travel writing, her approach to the interaction between diverse cultural systems is illuminating when considering the time of the saga writers.

> 'Contact zone' is an attempt to invoke the spatial and temporal copresence of subjects previously separated by geographic and historical disjunctures, and whose trajectories now intersect. By using the term 'contact', I aim to foreground the interactive, improvisational dimensions of colonial encounters so easily ignored or suppressed by diffusionist accounts of conquest and domination. A 'contact' perspective emphasizes how subjects are constituted in and by their relations to each other. (1992: 7)

Some parts of the Old Norse world view were kept and some rejected in the transformation into Christian theology through a process of demonization where anything conceived to be pagan was associated with the devil, a copresence in Pratt's terminology. 'There has to be consensus. There has to be an imputation of immorality', as Mary Douglas says about the techniques of rejection and control (1992: 85). The degrading of the old religion as superstition in theological discourse also turns out to be crucial in the interplay between continuity and change, and in relation to the construction of meaning. The spatial aspects of Pratt's term 'contact zone' are worth consideration; in an Icelandic perspective they could comprise a variety of aspects from negotiations over actual cult places to more abstract struggles over social space and ideological dominion.

Old Norse studies have traditionally been dominated by philological and literary approaches. But the last ten or fifteen years have revealed an increasing interest in the social context and cultural background of the Old Norse world. With their anthropological approach to historical documents scholars like Kirsten Hastrup and Gísli Pálsson have influenced the present view of the Old Norse conceptions of *trolldómr* as clearly structured interactions between protagonists in a social arena. Three aspects of these social studies, in particular, can be emphasized when applied to historical materials like those in the Old Norse *trolldómr* narratives.

Mary Douglas uses the phrase 'strategy of rejection' when she compares European medieval conceptions of leprosy to contemporary African witchcraft beliefs (Douglas 1992). She thereby touches on the complicated question of the marginality of the performers. A marginal position for these persons is in many cases apparent in the Old Norse texts but certainly not for all of them. As we shall see further on, some persons related to *trolldómr* activities could also be in a central position in the field of social activities. Rather than being marginal in the first place, a process of marginalization of the performers (or the suspected performers) takes place in some of these texts.

Victor Turner's criticism of the very much used distinction between witchcraft and sorcery, which was appropriate for Evans-Pritchard's Zande studies but has not necessarily proved so for other cultures is highly relevant for the present study (Evans-Pritchard 1937; Turner 1971). In his discussion of taxonomy versus dynamics in witchcraft beliefs Turner points out: '[the dichotomy] is likely to sidetrack investigation from the study of actual behaviour in a social field context to an obsession with the proper pigeonholing of beliefs and practices as either "witchcraft" or "sorcery" ' (1971: 126). A classification of performances as either good or bad per se cannot be made in the Old Norse material, as far as I can see.[2] Attempts to establish categories like 'white' and 'black' magic fail to integrate the social context of the *trolldómr* stories and the narrative construction of the texts.

Kirsten Hastrup has dealt with the correspondence between mythological and social geography and raises questions about the relation between ideology and ritual practice. In her studies on Icelandic culture she has maintained a highly contextualized perspective, and at the same time she has been pointing at continuities and an emphasis on long-term development. 'There was such a close fit between the ancient Scandinavian cosmology and the spatial and social realities of Iceland that each level of reality reaffirmed the others' (1981: 66). Hastrup, from a pronounced structuralist point of view clearly inspired by Russian scholars like Meletinskij and Gurevich, has continuously situated the discussion within the field of historical anthropology (Hastrup 1985, 1990a, b, 1992a, b). When analysing the Old Norse world view Hastrup stresses a basic cosmological conflict between chaos and order. The struggle between disorder and harmony is represented in mythological narratives by the spatial imagery of Útgarðr, inhabited by demonic and destructive forces, and the structural harmony of Miðgarðr, the home of gods and men. In Hastrup's model this is a relevant picture for the social geography; she also regards the farm and the cultivated soil as clearly defined in opposition to the wildness of nature. From Hastrup's perspective the same structure is visible in the legal system where outlawry was an existence outside society in every respect, with a status inferior to that of animals. It is debatable how far these corresponding oppositions can be taken, but when studying the world view of *trolldómr* a certain contrivance with such dichotomies is apparent.

The term 'conception' is used in this essay to cover the ideological framework and the cognitive base that formed what was conceived to be a coherent system linking cause and effect. This abstraction is to be compared with the ritual practices and legal codes discussed in the following two parts of this chapter. The following discussion will not be of conception as a particular spiritual quality but of the different ways in which they were expressed. When writing on 'the power of knowledge', Kirsten Hastrup states: ' "beliefs" are not an empirical category, because at the empirical level belief cannot be separated from knowledge' (1990a: 197). This is certainly true in a discussion of *trolldómr* where a recurring question must be whether practice corresponded to the images presented in mythological narratives and other texts formulating more normative discourses. To put this another way: the relationship between literature and lived experience must be taken into consideration. When the expression 'belief in *trolldómr*' is used it is not referring to extraordinary supernatural experiences but to a system of knowledge and explanations that take into account that mischief, envy and famine were factors to deal with in everyday life.

It must be stressed once more that there were also positive aspects to *trolldómr*. Beliefs and actions did not only cause or point at inauspicious things. *Seiðr*, the more elaborate divination ritual, was also spoken of as equivalent to performing *trolldómr*, and was used not only to predict the future, but also to gain power over a certain situation (Strömbäck 1935; Dillmann 1986, 1992). What was manipulation and destruction from one perspective was good advice and healing from another. Knowledge and knowing always ambiguous.

The Concept of Trolldómr

Common ingredients in the Continental mythology of the early modern 'witch craze', like the witches' sabbath or other nocturnal gatherings, ritual murder of small children, orgies of perversion or cannibalism,[3] are not found at all in Old Norse literature. Altogether different matters were the focus of interest. *Trolldómr* conceptions dealt with certain persons' abilities to have an influence on fellow humans and on nature – for better or worse. References to such abilities are given in various texts and cannot be limited to a particular genre. Individual accounts of *trolldómr* in most sagas fit into a pattern of local conflicts; hence it would be incorrect to isolate these texts from their social relations, ideas, and values. In some respects *trolldómr* is also a literary motif with a genuinely wide use. Arguments in saga texts based on *trolldómr* had to refer to commonly shared beliefs and assumptions to make sense and be valid.

Trolldómr is chosen here as an umbrella term to indicate the notions, rituals, and social interactions in the Old Norse traditions relating to conceptions about the influence certain persons had – by innate qualities or through skill – on the world surrounding them. *Trolldómr* covered an extensive field and complex combinations of abstractions and ideas as well as ritual practices. Conceptions of *trolldómr* were always related to ideas about power and the experience of the balance of power. The stories are always well integrated into a social setting. There is always a distinct purpose for a sender or an acting person. The target for the activities can be a person, an animal, the landscape of a certain vicinity or more abstract entities like prosperity and fortune. Focused as they are on actions committed, no text gives any formal definition of *trolldómr*. It covers a wide field of assumed abilities to change the visible reality by means invisible and unreachable to ordinary people. In most texts *trolldómr* is said to generate destruction and harm, and is almost always described from the perspective of the affected. When a cause was asked for, *trolldómr* could serve as a plausible and sensible reason for the mishap. With few exceptions performances of *trolldómr* for the purposes of creating destruction, sickness, or misfortunes were clandestine and solitary activities, while the positive applications of such knowledge used in acts of divination were collective events, executed more or less in public. The talk about cunning deeds was also a highly social matter. The very idea of accusations was the fuel of much gossip and slander. In Old Norse tradition, *trolldómr* was first of all a way of explaining the hardships of life – misfortune, illness, theft, unexpected death, etc (Hastrup 1990a: 197ff., 1992b; Flowers 1993; Mitchell 1998). It served as a diagnosis of an uncontrollable situation. As no established terminology existed, a rich variety of terms to describe the extraordinary capabilities was used, many of them with the connotations of traditional ancient learning and knowledge.

Troll is used as the first element of the term to indicate the mythological background to the concepts and acts discussed. The resemblance of words in modern Scandinavian languages is intentional. The motive is to mark a distance to terms derived from the German word 'Hexe', a concept that was first introduced in Scandinavian languages during the witch-craze of the seventeenth century. *Trolldómr* is also wide enough to cover many aspects of extraordinary knowledge and cunning deeds in Old Norse literature. Different compounds with *troll-* are frequent, although the use of the form *trolldómr* is more rarely found. Even less common is the term *troll-skapr*. A plausible reason is that the sagas focus on concrete deeds, *gerningar*, and not on abstract discussions. *Troll* is a term in the neuter case and is not, as such, gender specific. The trolls of the text can appear in both male and female shape and the word is therefore suitable as a technical term.

It seems that the various compounds served as signals in the texts and as indications that mighty powers were in the wind. When analysing them it is an advantage to use a broad term and not very fruitful to try to establish a *trolldómr* 'genealogy' that stems from supernatural beings or humans. *Troll* is the name of a rather vaguely defined group of supernatural beings in Old Norse mythology (Halvorsen 1982a, b; Lindow 1993). They are demonic beings, sometimes acting as individual characters but mostly spoken of as a harmful collective. However, the term is also used to characterize humans with special capabilities, and is even associated with giants, *jǫtnar*, or related to the dead. The word is also frequently used in early Scandinavian Christian literature as an equivalent of devils, demons, monsters etc. But mostly *troll* refers to the enemies of the Æsir and as a threat to the harmony of Miðgarðr (Hastrup 1981, 1990a, 1992b; Clunies Ross 1994).

Words associated with *trolldómr* could point in several directions, particularly those concerning knowledge and speaking out loud. There was a rich variety in terms relating to knowledge and knowing, and persons affiliated with *trolldómr* in Old Norse texts were generally described as knowledgeable. The verb *kunna*, meaning both 'to know, to understand, to know by heart' as well as 'to have insight in the old traditions and lore' and 'to behave properly', is at the core of this semantic field. When 'know' or 'knowledge' are used in an Old Norse context the words have a far more elaborate signification than is usual in modern English. Therefore, the emic (folk or local) terms will be used here, as a constant reminder of the implications of knowledge in the original context.

A person could be said to be *fjǫlkunnigr* or *margkunnigr*, i.e. to have much knowledge about many things. But this was certainly never used in a neutral way; the consequences of such knowledge would always tell of the ultimate purpose. In *Eyrbyggja saga* 15 and 16 the two women, Geirríðr and Katla, are both depicted in terms of a very similar terminology as regards their knowledge and their abilities. But when it comes to practice their very different characters become manifest. The intention in the use of knowledge always turns out to be a disclosure; as always, knowledge could be both used and misused. *Eyrbyggja saga* does not give any exact descriptions of what the women really do, only that one of them is prepared to share her knowledge with a young man while the other uses it to harm him severely when he resists her erotic invitations.

There is a rich variety of terms relating to knowledgeable persons and their activities, good or evil (Mundal and Steinsland 1989; Hastrup 1990a: 197ff.; Pálsson 1991: 158ff.; Flowers 1993; Mundal 1993b). A rough division of the terminology can be made between words relating to descriptions of men and women assumed to be, or accused of being, knowledgeable and performing *trolldómr*, and different activities or deeds based on assumed *trolldómr* and age-old lore. The vocabulary deviates in different genres of Old Norse literature and some of the terms have already been mentioned above. There was mostly a sender and these persons – or maybe 'personalities' is a better word – always had a name with a visible gender. Males could be called *galdramaðr, vitki, skratti, trollmaðr*; and females *gýgr, seiðkona, spákona, trollkona, vǫlva*, the latter often in connection with *seiðr* rituals. A radical way of desecrating a person thought of as knowledgeable was to give him or her the name of a supernatural being like *illvættr, meinvættr*, or *úvættr*. In contrast to males, human females in the sagas could be given the names associated with the many evil-minded mythological women.

Action and result were the focus of the terminology related to the knowledgeable persons' activities, *gerningar* or *fordæðuskapr*. Deed, *dáð*, and advice, *ráð*, were loaded terms that flavoured the texts when used. To be *fróðr* meant to be knowing and well informed in a general sense, but it also included the traditions of old (*forn*) times, *fornfróðr, forneskja* and having access to the old knowledge, as we saw in the terminology used to portray what Grettir's mother had to say. *Fræði* hinted at both the abstract aspect of knowledge and learning and the exercise of charms and spells. To predict the future, *at spá*, was an instrument to protect the coming season and the future of children.

There is a general tendency to historicize extraordinary knowledge in Old Norse literature. Such insights are represented as the innate traditions of old times, *fornfróðr, forneskja*. A term like *fornfræði* referred both to the abstract aspect of knowledge and learning and to the actual performance, i.e. charms or spells. Terms in this semantic field pointed to some individuals having or exhibiting the capacity for discerning and the intelligent application of knowledge, or to the ability to act in situations where other people with more limited mental capacity had reached their limit.

The multiplicity of meanings is a crucial feature of the *trolldómr* texts and a key to understanding them. As mentioned in the introductory discussion of the sources, the saga texts can certainly not unconditionally be read as historical documents. As social memories they formulated an ideal of times past in which knowledge of the old days was a powerful resource. Still, they express attitudes and standpoints, if not accurate descriptions of conceptions and rituals; modes of how to relate to the past, as much as relating to something necessarily 'supernatural'. 'Magic, witchcraft, and healing constitute a field of indigenous explanations of individual success or misfortune' (Hastrup 1990a: 197). Knowledge about the past was a way of establishing authority. References to what was *forn* had a significant effect as an argument, and added to that was a flavour of the capacity to see into the future.

With the exception of *seiðr* no activity is more closely connected to *trolldómr* than the art of carving runes with the aim of cursing or healing. Runes are letters, adapted in part from Latin, and mostly preserved as inscriptions on wood, bone or stone. Most of the stone inscriptions were memorials of individuals and their deeds, but in the sagas scenes with the carving of runes were also a way of telling of people who made use of their *trolldómr* knowledge. The runic alphabet was not just an ordinary writing system used for straightforward communication, but to a large extent associated with the carver's special abilities. These Old Norse letters were kept in use for several hundreds of years after the introduction of Christianity and Latin letters, for writing charms, notes, and also prayers to the Holy Virgin and the saints. The technique of formulating a plea remained, but the religious context changed. Sometimes the Old Norse texts do not reveal any real difference between writing runes and the art of singing powerful songs. When a phrase like 'carving runes' appears in the texts it can also connote performing *trolldómr* in a more general sense. Of all poets and knowledgeable characters Óðinn is described as the master of all these potent crafts. His quest for wisdom and powerful runes is a major theme in mythological narratives. In the Eddic poem *Hávamál* we read about the most wise of gods and men:

> The runes you must find and the meaningful letter,
> a very great letter,
> a very powerful letter,
> which the mighty sage stained
> and the powerful gods made
> and the runemaster of the gods carved out.[4]
> (trans. by Larrington 1996: 34)

The mythological images of Óðinn's complex relation to runes and *trolldómr*, with its strength and ambiguities, constitute a paradigm for other forms of narratives.

Speaking Out

The most important terms connected to *trolldómr* either refer to knowledge or to the spoken word. The importance of the latter in Old Norse literature is well documented (Boyer 1986; Hastrup 1990a: 197ff.; Pálsson 1991). The pronouncement of words was recognized to have a tremendous influence over the concerns of life. The impact of a sentence uttered aloud could not be questioned and could never be taken back – as if it had become somehow physical. Strong and powerful words reappear throughout the sagas. Words create reality – not only the other way around. Concrete expression and utterance had a dignity and a status, as is common in oral cultures. Many of the deeds of cunning people were not necessarily done but spoken. The formulaic elements were supposedly vital when performing *trolldómr*. Therefore, the verb *gala*, 'to say, speak out loud, utter, sing' is the focus in this context. Metaphorically the word also meant chanting and singing, but not always with pleasant sounds: it could comprehend 'to crow, to cry', or even refer to animal sounds, e.g. repulsive noise, wild cries. The associations of the verb *gala* are clearly negative. A participal form of the verb, *galinn*, could also be used for describing a person out of his or her mind – insane or bewildered. It is unclear whether this referred to the state of the performer or to the effect of the song or perhaps both. This particular state of mind was characteristically interpreted as honourable and at the same time indicated the ambiguous position of the poet and his praised abilities, *skáldskapr*. The bard was therefore keeper of social memory and the key to days gone by. Many terms themselves do not indicate any estimation, and connote the possibility of destruction. Bestiality or madness were powerful images of the enemies of the harmony and order that characterized the ideals of Miðgarðr. Not surprisingly a usual punishment for performing *trolldómr* was outlawry.

The power of the spoken word is an apparent example of cultural continuity. Although paganism was strongly condemned by the Church, many of its practices were transformed into modes of religious expression acceptable to the Church. Among them was the trust in prayers and blessings, the latter often accompanied by some kind of ritual behaviour. In much later recorded rural folklore, uttered phrases were thought to have a tangible effect. Spells describing ceremonies accompanied by minimal movements seem to work out as a kind of fictive rituals; the narration of a ritual – sometimes in a formulaic mode and maybe accompanied by symbolic bodily movements – was thought to have the same impact as if actually performed (Raudvere 1993: 157ff., 301f.).[5] When formulated in words the healing or destruction was believed actually to take place. 'In Old Icelandic *galdr* referred to a song, mainly in the sense of "charm" or "spell". The corresponding verb was *gala*, to "chant" or to "cast spells". This linguistic derivation is an important key to the semantics of magic', Kirsten Hastrup writes (1990a: 200). The second feature connotes the performative aspects of the use of words. *Galdr*, songs or poetry with special power, was the instrument for the performer (Halvorsen 1981). Just as a poet could enchant his audience, so a person with the right insights could use loudly uttered words for protection, healing, or cursing. In general, what was said in public had a certain epistemological status. But since women were excluded from public speech acts to a large extent, the conceptions of authoritative speech formed the basis of a gendered social space. Due to this women were also more or less excluded from trials. The texts therefore hint at words uttered in secrecy, when women were supposed to practise *trolldómr*.

Snorri Sturluson's handbook for poets *Háttatal* gives a catalogue of different metres used in different genres. Also *trolldómr* had its poetics and distinctive forms of expression in *ljóðaháttr* and *galdralag* (st. 101). A whole section of metric spells at the end of *Hávamál* is named 'Ljóðatal' and puts powerful songs into the mouth of Óðinn. Carolyne Larrington characterizes the section in the following way: 'The Ljóðatal is a list of eighteen spells, whose contents are briefly sketched, but whose text is never given'(1993: 62). The themes for the area of use are given, but not spells as such. It must be remembered as we read that *Hávamál* was never meant to be a documentation of spells, but a poet's visualization of the meanings of powerful words, *galdr* songs. An example is stanza 151 where Óðinn speaks of the situation of being exposed to attacks from evil runes and bad speech and the poet makes us understand that the insightful god can turn the assault back against the sender:

> I know a sixth one if a man wounds me
> with the roots of the sap-filled wood:
> and that man who conjured to harm me,
> the evil consumes him, not me.[6]
> (trans. by Larrington 1996: 36)

The field of extraordinary knowledge is encompassed in the stanza. *Galdr* can also be synonymous with practised *trolldómr* as in the phrase: *galdrar ok gǫrningar*, crafty words and deeds. Kirsten Hastrup calls *galdr* 'the original term for magic' (1990a: 200). Knowledge and utterance were closely associated, for example in the expression *galdrar ok fjǫlkyngi*. From *gala* and *galdr* a rich variety of compounds emanates. People could be called *galdrakona, galdramaðr*, or *galdrarumr*, and their art or character *galdralist, galdrafullr*, and *galdrligr*; and the presumed equipment of the performers *galdrabók* (book of *galdr* songs), or *galdrastafr* (*galdr* wand). The terminology indicates that the performers were thought to need instruments to be able to mediate their insights.

A recurrent theme in Old Norse literature is men and women in possession of strong words who give their assistance to people in need by teaching them powerful verses. The didactic theme is apparent as regards both form and content. We have seen some brief examples from *Hávamál* that teach Óðinn's abilities. In another poem of the *Poetic Edda*, *Grógaldr*, a young man addresses Gróa, a *vǫlva* whose son he claims to be, asking for her assistance in his quest to win his bride. From the first stanza it is evident that the young man is communicating with the *vǫlva* in her grave and commanding her to arise. The same situation is prevalent in *Vǫluspá* 28 where before *ragnarǫk* – the end of the world – Óðinn visits the grave of a *vǫlva* to obtain the advice he needs before facing the final battle. In *Grógaldr* the wise woman Gróa responds to her son's plea and gives him nine *galdrar* for protection against enemies and harm, and ends her monologue in this very motherly way:

> Never now go
> where danger appears;
> and may no evil bar you from bliss!
> On a stone firm in the earth
> within doors I stood,
> while I chanted you spells.
>
> A mother's words
> take with you, son, away from here,
> and keep them stored in your heart;
> ever abounding good fortune
> shall you have throughout life,
> as long as you mind my words.[7]
> (trans. by Robinson 1991: 66)

Although the context is fragmentary we can notice the claimed mother–son relationship which is also a manifest motif in the sagas where fostermothers often act to protect their sons, sometimes by means of *trolldómr* and powerful words. Gróa is not referred to in any negative terms, in contrast to yet another Eddic poem, *Hyndluljóð*, where Freyja is addressing a *vǫlva* to gain advice and the answering tone is quite cold and reluctant. Gróa's enumeration of beneficial advice is quite similar to equivalent catalogues and could in some aspects be compared to Óðinn's list of *galdr* songs in *Hávamál*.

From the Continent some interesting examples of early medieval spells and charms are preserved. Compared to the advice in *Hávamál*, Carolyne Larrington remarks, 'The Ljóðatal is an index to spells, but spells which are not "genuine", in that sense that the Old English charms, or the Old High German Merseburg Charms are' (1993: 63). In the second of the two Old High German so called Merseburg Charms help is asked for from pagan gods, whose names are recognizable from Old Norse mythology (Hampp 1961; Wolff 1963; Wipf 1975). The purpose of the spell is the healing of a horse and it was written down in the tenth century, definitely in a Christian context. It reads in a prose translation:

> Phol and Wodan [the Old High German name of Óðinn] rode into the wood; the foreleg of Balder's horse was dislocated; then Sintgunt and

Sunna, her sister, sang over it, then Friia and Volla, her sister, sang over it, than Wodan sang over it, for he could do that well: be it dislocation of bone, be it an ailment of the blood, be it dislocation of the limbs: bone to bone, blood to blood, limb to limb, as if they were glued.[8]

The gods are urged to sing over the wounded limb and seemingly their song as such had the assumed healing power.[9] In comparison with much later recorded spells a formal similarity can be noted. The healing situation was almost always expressed as a meeting or a confrontation – a meeting between the healer and the patient and a confrontation of curing and destructive forces. A parallel situation is constructed (the gods are riding their horses and an injury springs up) which is followed by a threefold parallel structure: 'bone to bone …' The first Merserburg Charm also shows thematic resemblances with Eddic poety. This Old High German text deals with releasing prisoners and breaking up fetters by means of the spoken word, a theme prevalent also in Eddic poetry. Here is *Hávamál* 149, where Óðinn claims

> I know a fourth one [*galdr* song] if men put
> chains upon my limbs;
> I can chant so that I can walk away,
> fetters spring from my feet,
> and bonds from my hands.[10]
> (trans. by Larrington 1996: 35)

The few Old High German spells that are preserved are generated from a distinctly Christian context and reveal another characteristic feature also apparent in later charms: the seemingly unproblematic mix of pagan conceptions with references to Christ, the Virgin, the saints etc. The structure seems to be an indication of continuity not only in form but also in the understanding of the power of the spoken word. The text quoted above shows striking conceptual and formal similarities with the well-known Anglo Saxon 'Journey Spell' that begins:

> I protect myself with this rod, and commend myself to the grace of God,
> Against the grievous stitch, against the dire strike of disease,
> Against the gruesome horror,
> Against the frightful terror loathsome to all men,
> Against all evil, too, that may invade this land.[11]
> (trans. by Grendon 1909: 177)

The charm ends with a long catalogue naming the Holy Trinity, Mary and characters from the Old Testament, among others. Spells like this constitute an indication of a co-presence of traditions not only in metre and genre but also as regards the reality of the powerful word. As Heather Stuart argues, a 'charm can be viewed as a structure rather than a haphazard con-glomeration of magically necessary ingredients' (1985: 36).

A very special form of intentional use of the spoken word in order to achieve destruction is *níð*, referring to both verbal genre and ritual practice (Meulengracht Sørensen 1983, 1993; Hastrup 1990a: 200f.). It can be defined as ritual insulting and verbal defamation, very often with rough sex-ual allusions. There are hints of the concept in various texts and in Christian legal documents. A well-known example of this harsh form of poetic cre-ativity is found in *Egils saga Skalla-Grímssonar* (57). Already in the famous poet's genealogies there are comments about his ancestors which makes the reader realize that he is a person with extraordinary capabilities. Egill's grandfather's name is Kveld-Úlfr, literally 'Evening Wolf', which usually is interpreted to mean that he was thought to be a shapeshifter with the ability to take the temporal form of a wolf at night. Another relative of Egill's is noted to be 'half a troll', *hálftrǫll*, i.e. of demonic origin. Not surprisingly Egill is a man who knows how to use the spoken word and how to carve runes. At one point, as his conflicts with king Eiríkr of Norway (known as 'Eiríkr Blood-Axe') and his wife Gunnhildr reached their climax, Egill is said to have raised a hideous pole with carved runes, *níðstǫng*, against them.

> Egill went up onto the island. He took a hazel pole in his hand and went to the edge of a rock facing inland. Then he took a horse's head and put it on the end of the pole.
>
> Afterwards he made an invocation, saying 'Here I set up this scorn-pole [*níðstǫng*] and turn its scorn upon King Eiríkr and Queen Gunnhildr' – then turned the horse's head to face land – 'and I turn its scorn upon the nature spirits [*landvættir*] that inhabit this land, sending them astray so that none of them shall find its resting-place by chance or design until they have driven King Eiríkr and Queen Gunnhildr from this land'.
>
> Then he drove the pole into a cleft in the rock and left it to stand there. He turned the head towards the land and carved the whole invo-cation in runes on the pole.[12]

As in the poetical and mythological context of *Hávamál* there is no men-tion of what words are uttered, only a considerable stress on the act of speak-ing. To chase away the *landvættir* was obviously the best method of making the king and queen leave. When the spirits were displeased a place was thought to be left without protection and peace. Egill's *níð* is not left unan-swered, but follows a pattern of action and counteraction. Queen Gunnhildr is not without special abilities herself and the evil-minded woman sends back a spell against him. In a stressful situation further on in the text she keeps Egill awake the whole night by assuming the form of a twittering bird – since the malicious queen turns out to be a shapeshifter too (59).

Fate and Destiny

Most activities relating to *trolldómr*, positively or negatively, referred to conceptions of fate in one way or the other. The sagas tell of ceremonies and rituals that aim to reveal what the future holds. The task of conducting these ceremonies was limited to the knowledgeable.

In *Vatnsdæla saga* 10 a *vǫlva* is invited to tell fortunes at a grand feast. The knowledgeable woman is said to be from Lapland, a *Finna*. As will be discussed further down, Saami people are generally described in biased terms as specially skilled in cunning deeds. She has mainly positive things to forecast, but young Ingimundr does not want to hear about his future in advance and claims not to believe in prophecies. Then the *vǫlva*, unbidden, tells him that he will become a settler in Iceland and a lost token will be found as a sign of her trustworthiness. The scene is constructed as a confrontation between the attitudes towards one of the fundamental concepts in the Old Norse world view: an individual's given destiny. Ingimundr's companion repeatedly tells him how vain it is to struggle against his destiny. But as always in a good story the prediction comes true and the fight between the seeres and the recipient turns out to be an important narrative instrument.

A multitude of conceptions describing interhuman relations were linked to the ideas of fate and destiny. Power, control and domination were always more or less under the surface when different fortunes are told. Conceptions of *trolldómr* in relation to knowledge were also closely connected with conceptions of destiny (Hallberg 1973; Mundal 1974; Lönnroth 1976: 123ff.). The predicted destiny of individuals, families, gods and other mythological beings – even of the universe itself at *ragnarǫk* – is constantly referred to in various kinds of texts and all of these were, along with the material world, subject to the final fatal destruction. There is a strong relationship between conceptions of fate and Old Norse mythological narratives of creation and destruction.

The importance of destiny must not be understood to mean that the Norsemen held purely fatalistic beliefs. Rather it must be understood in terms of knowing the future, in order to keep it under some kind of control. Divination rituals and the performance of *seiðr*, either by Óðinn in myths or executed by invited specialists as in the example from *Vatnsdæla saga* above, were expressions of ways of finding the keys to hidden parts of reality and measuring what was given. The results of divination marked the limits of individual free will and after the divination ceremony strategies could be made for acting within these limits. Hence, prophecies, dreams and dream interpretations, and curses were treated with the greatest concern. Many of them also comprise reasonings on *trolldómr* and extraordinary knowledge. Relating to fate, or destiny, these ways of telling imply the limitations that have been staked out independently of human behaviour and choices. They reveal a tension between freedom and dependence. Nevertheless, there can seem to be a contradiction in terms: the conceptions of destiny could also be viewed as a definition of personal freedom. On the one hand, the limits are set and it lies within the human condition to identify them and act within the given space; on the other, choices and their consequences over a longer period of time is an important theme in the sagas. More than a general dependence on fate, it was used in the narratives when explaining something of utmost importance.

Destiny was in one sense given, but still there were opportunities for developing different strategies, as recently analysed by Margaret Clunies Ross (1994) in connection with the fundamental structure for the perception of time.

Prosperity and Envy

Abstract ideas about fate and destiny are found in Old Norse literature along with very concrete configurations of beings that are supposed to rule over success and failure. This inseparable blend flavours all the stories of *trólldomr*. Kirsten Hastrup and Orvar Löfgren have discussed what they call 'the economy of fortune' as a latent model in the social landscape of Scandinavia (1992). Such a model was a mode of explaining the hardships and the very different fortunes of life. Their article is based on much later folklore recordings, but their arguments can be applied to Old Norse society as well.

Linked to destiny, each individual and each family had their share of fortune, materially as well as in a more abstract sense. Fortune and the good things in life were considered a constant, i.e. when somebody gained prosperity, someone else necessarily lost it. Resources were limited. Conceptions of luck and fortune explained not only the current situation, but also social structures in general and why there were more and less prosperous families. Fortune was something given and only *trolldómr* could change what was settled. Not surprisingly, more attention was paid to bad luck than to success. There were many stories about destructive evil forces, personal ill-will, and greed. The notion of 'the economy of fortune' served as a repressive mechanism and offered explanations for economic inequality in rural Scandinavia. In this sense, it was also an instrument for social control in an oppressive system that concealed power relations (Hastrup and Löfgren 1992: 250; Hastrup 1992b). What little was left could always be taken away.

The notion of instability was not only an economic consideration; to a large extent it also concerned erotic affection. With *trolldómr*, love could be both aroused and stifled. Such notions created space for speculations about sinister manipulation. There was always a latent threat of insidious attack. A sudden mischief could be caused by an obscure enemy, acting himself/herself or through a cunning person's materialized will. In this moral economy emotions and social power intermingled to a great extent.

There are many references to destiny and fortune in Old Norse literature, either giving strength to an argument or for purely narrative purposes. There was also an abstract terminology of the subject (Hallberg 1973; Lönnroth 1976). Fate in general was called *auðna* or with positive connotations *gipta* and *gæfa*, and sometimes individual fate, *forlǫg*. Mostly, though, fate was discussed not in abstract exegesis but in stories, mythological or other.

There are many 'agents of fate', to use Lars Lönnroth's phrase – characters that appear in the sagas as personifications of destiny, luck or misfortune. The different mythological beings related to fate and destiny are hard to separate from each other and the texts interchange the different categories and names. Many times they have a double position of both forming individual destinies and having the ability to look into the future. The characters that represent the conceptions of fate are given female body, if not appearing in animal form.

The *fylgjur* are guardian spirits connected to individual persons or families (Mundal 1974, 1993b; Lindow 1987, 1993). The word derives from the Old Norse verb, *fylgja*, 'to follow', and is also associated with the noun for caul or afterbirth. They appear in the distinct visible shapes of animals or women and in a metaphorical sense follow their concerns. Else Mundal has shown that the different guises are accordingly used in two very different ways in the texts (Mundal 1974). 'These two types have little in common but the name', she writes (Mundal 1993b: 624). The animal *fylgja* was a symbolic image pointing at the inner qualities of its owner, a constant symbolic characterization. As metaphor the *fylgja* tells a lot about the person it follows. Strength, an evil mind, or social position was visualized in the image of a bear, a wolf, or an eagle. The animal shape was not supposed to vary over time and was therefore thought to be easy to identify. In the texts *fylgjur* bring warnings or advice. The animal *fylgja* is told of as appearing in front of its owner, often in dreams, and giving indications of events to come. As such it is a representation of the future itself, not the character of a person. Like a person's fate the *fylgja* is not changeable, nor can it improve or act on its own. The animal *fylgja* works, as Else Mundal puts it, like a mirror (Mundal 1974: 40). The identity of the two is absolute and therefore the death of a *fylgja* also predicts the death of its owner.

A *fylgja* in the shape of a woman is more of a guarding and helping spirit that protects not merely an individual but a whole family. This is a more abstract aspect closely related to the conceptions of *hamingja* (Mundal 1974: 86ff.). The two are hardly separable even for analysis. The *fylgja* in this latter aspect in not even always given a physical form, but spoken of more diffusely as standing behind the family. Sometimes the *fylgja* is called *spádís*, indicating that the character had a function as a diviner for the protection of the family. When appearing in a dream she could be called dream-woman, *draumkona*. These aspects of fate are very concrete in their bodily appearance, showing themselves for a short while, but leaving no room for alternative interpretations.

The norns, *nornir*, are perhaps the most well known in the group of mythological beings related to fate. They are spoken of as carving runes or weaving destinies and fortunes. In mythological narratives they are said to dwell at the foot of Yggdrasill, close to the well associated with insights and clandestine knowledge. In *Vǫluspá* they seem to control the destiny of the whole universe, doomed to destruction. The wise maidens, *meyiar, margs vitandi*, are in this text given individual symbolic names, Urðr, Verðandi, and Skuld, popularly interpreted as 'Past', 'Present' and 'Future'. Carolyne Larrington's translation is more faithful to the original text:

> I know that an ash-tree stands called Yggdrasill,
> a high tree, soaked with shining loam;
> from there come the dews which fall in the valley,
> ever green, it stands over the well of fate.
>
> From there come three girls, knowing a great deal,
> from the lake which stands under the tree;
> Fate one is called, Becoming another –
> they carved on wooden slips – Must-be the third;
> they set down laws, they chose lives,
> for the sons of men the fates of men.[13]
> (trans. by Larrington 1996: 6)

These two stanzas end the *Vǫluspá* version of the creation myth and it is hardly a coincidence that the 'I' that speaks – the *vǫlva* who is telling the fundamentals of the mythological universe – places the women by the trunk of Yggdrasill, the very symbol of the world of gods and men. When considering *trolldómr*, the etymology of the name is Yggr's [i.e. Óðinn's] horse indicates his ride to clandestine realms. Although mythical by definition, *nornir* briefly appear in sagas too. In *Norna-Gests þáttr* it is hard to differentiate between *nornir* establishing a destiny and the invited *vǫlur* reading the future. The text tells of a gathering at a wealthy farmhouse to which three invited and honoured women come. Of the three visiting women, one wants to punish Norna Gestr's mother for bad treatment by giving the boy a short life, while the other two save the situation. The variety and mixing of names of the agents indicate that not too much can be drawn from merely the use of a certain term. Focus is on the intention, action and consequence.

There are several other examples in the sagas of how female figures of more or less mythological character bring messages of times to come. *Darraðarljóð,* a long poem in *Njáls saga* 157, tells of a Good Friday shortly before an important battle when twelve women on horseback appear (Lönnroth 1976: 134; Darmsholt 1984; Kress 1993: 97f; Poole 1993). The women turn out to be valkyries and have come to give their support to the young king. They seem to have an important influence on the outcome of the coming battle and give a horrifying image of things to come. The metaphor of weaving is used in a monstrous mode. The introductory lines and the first two stanzas of this strong imagery read:

> Men's heads were used for weights, men's intestines for the weft and warp, a sword for the sword beater, and an arrow for the pin beater. The women spoke these verses:

> A wide warp
> warns of slaughter;
> blood rains
> from the beam's cloud.
> A spear-grey fabric
> is being spun,
> which the friends
> of Randvér's slayer
> will fill out
> with a red weft.
> The warp is woven
> with warriors' guts,
> and heavily weighted
> with the heads of men.
> Spears serve as heddle rods,
> spattered with blood;
> iron-bound is the shed rod,
> and arrows are the pin beaters;
> we will beat with swords
> out battle web.[14]
> (trans. by Cook 1997: 215)

Despite the gruesome images the poem ends with predictions of victory. It is the destiny of the enemies that is described. The *nornir* take an active part in the core conflict of the text and in some way they are mastering fate.

The *dísir* constitute another collective of female deities related to both fate and prosperity that are hard to distinguish from the *fylgjur.* A *vǫlva* in the sagas could also be given the name *spádís,* or female diviner. Conceptual figures and ritual activities become closely connected in the texts. The *dísir* are the only one of the three groups mentioned here that are recipients of any form of distinctive cult. The *dísablót* is mentioned in some texts as a form of sacrifice or feast in the winter time and shows similarities with other fertility rituals of a more private character. Popular surveys sometimes follow Snorri in a hierarchization of different mythological groups, calling them 'higher' or 'lower'. The *dísir* are often in such divisions proscribed to a lower dwelling – although they most certainly played a vital part in everyday ritual life and were not without connections to the major gods. Freyja is called *vanadís*, the *dís* of the Vanir. The function of the *dísir* has been interpreted as protecting the prosperity and good fortune of a certain place. They are more closely connected to the landscape and have a rather pronounced protective aspect than the more abstract *fylgjur*. The latter are related to an individual or family while the former are more connected to space. But some texts do not make any difference between *dísir* and *fylgjur*, since both are guardian spirits in some sense. As mentioned above, classifications and taxonomies are not in line with the tone of the texts.

There are other names for the spirits and deities of a certain place. The *landvættir* and the *alfar* seem to have their dwellings close to the farmhouse. The latter also received a cult, *alfablót*, according to some texts. As is obvious from their name, the *landvættir* are very closely connected to the land around the farm and the cultivated soil. In the quotation above from *Egils saga Skalla-Grímssonar* were noted the fatal consequences when the spirits abandoned a place. In this respect all these beings connected to a distinct place are part of the cosmological and social inside–outside conflict, as pointed out by Kirsten Hastrup (1981). As protectors these various beings formed a contrast to the clear-cut destructive forces from outside, like the trolls and their kind. Nevertheless, there are evil-minded *dísir* and the wrath of the *dísir* is mentioned in *Grímnismál* 53 and spoken of with fear: if the *dísir* are against a person or a family only destruction can follow. The valkyries are occasionally called Óðinn's *dísir* and associated with revenge and struggle.

When someone prospered, while others were troubled with setbacks, an explanation was needed. *Trolldómr* was an important cognitive category in an epistemological system where the very existence of such a knowledge produced an acceptable explanation for public and private incidents. The causal connections were obvious. Bad luck could be as perceptible: 'a kind of contagious moral disease, spreading from individual to individual throughout the saga', as Lars Lönnroth writes about the events in *Njáls saga* (1976: 130).

The Human Soul

The early Christian writers of Scandinavia did not adopt the Old Norse terminology for the inner qualities of humans, but introduced a new word soul, *sál*, from the Anglo-Saxon. This is quite understandable since the pre-

Christian conceptions of human mental capabilities were so radically different from the new religion's dogmas about the human soul. Indeed, they were not only different, but at some points decidedly heretical.

The most important discrepancy was the Old Norse belief that a person could leave the ordinary body and act in a temporary new shape. This is not only the most fundamental assumption for most *trolldómr* stories, but also essential to the conviction that the dead could act from the grave with their old personalities. A person's temporary split into body and soul is not a specifically Old Norse assumption. For centuries night riders, shapeshifters, and were-animals caused serious debates within the Church about how to relate to these phenomena and about their ontological status. For the Church Fathers, among them Augustine, the crucial question was whether the devil had such powers that he could appear in any tangible form, or help evil humans to transform themselves, only to draw Christians away from the true faith.

There are two terms fundamental to the semantic field of shapeshifting, *hugr* and *hamr*. The Old Norse term *hugr*, often translated just as soul, was much wider in meaning than the Christian concept (Alver 1971b; Raudvere 1993: 64ff.). The word connotes personhood, thought, wish and desire. Some people, with a strong *hugr*, had the capability to act over long distances without moving their bodies. In the tangible guise of an animal or an object, they could cause harm while their ordinary bodies lay as if sleeping. The shape adopted for the temporary appearance most often revealed the purpose or the moral status of the sender: a powerful bear, an aggressive wolf etc. *Hugr* was also applied metaphorically to describe a person's character or temper.

Hamr, literally 'skin', was the name of the temporary guise the *hugr* could take for its movements while performing *trolldómr*. The ability to change shape and act out of the ordinary body in a new guise was an inborn character or acquired through learning. The materialized will, power or lust is a common theme in many texts. A person who was called a *hamhleypa* could let the *hugr* leap into a *hamr* (see below).

No absolutely clear distinction can be made between a *fylgja* on a special mission, often in a guise characterizing the owner's intention, and a *hamr*. Technically it is the same kind of appearance. The former is more of a mythological character while the latter indicates a human. Furthermore, there is a relationship between the *hugr* and the *hamr*, that is quite different from that between the *fylgja* and its owner. The focus is on the personal will when *hamferð*, a travelling urge, is described. Different *hamfarir* and were-animals appear in several appearances, while the *fylgja* is a never-changing symbolic image of inner qualities or a guarding spirit.

Egill Skalla-Grímsson's grandfather Kveld-Úlfr was called *hamrammr*, which indicated that he was a *hamhleypa*. Apparently he was thought to be able to act in the shape of a wolf in the night when his own body was sleeping. Kveld-Úlfr's own father's name was Bjalfi, literally 'animal skin', which makes it easy to guess what abilities he was supposed to have. The genealogy of knowledge is a vital theme in both sagas and mythological texts. Svanr in *Njáls saga* 10ff. is also sleepy when it is time for him to conduct his shameful deeds. The implicit message of these characters' fatigue is that their strength and powers are far away from their bodies.

The *hamingja* was the shape of a person's fate and is also very hard to differentiate from *fylgja*. It can show itself to its owner and give hints about the future. The *hamingja* is closely connected to the notions of *gipta* (luck) and *gæfa* (personal qualities) and to destiny in terms of prosperity. Speaking of contact zones, ideas as well as practices must have been transformed over hundreds of years into hybrids acceptable in a local context: 'This Christian concept [divine grace] may also have influenced the use of hamingja in the sense of 'luck', for such usage is first attested in clerical sagas dealing with Christian kings blessed by God's grace. The impersonal hamingja, 'luck', which we find in the classical family sagas, may then be a further development of this concept', Lars Lönnroth writes (Lönnroth 1976: 126). 'Luck' is one of the most frequent abstract terms referred to in Scandinavian folkore collected in the nineteenth century. It was the basic prerequisite of the local 'economy of fortune'.

Shapeshifting

There were many names for persons with the capacity to change their shape and temporarily act outside the ordinary body. 'Shapeshifters' is used here as an umbrella term for a wide range of characters in Old Norse literature that were said to have the ability of letting their *hugr* leap into a temporary body or guise, *hamr*, i.e. of being a *hamleypa*, someone who leaps into a *hamr*. In many texts the materialized will's deeds are the principal basis for matters explained by *trolldómr*.

In both mythological narratives and the sagas individuals were given such capacities. It is quite impossible to distinguish categorically between metaphorical metamorphosis in poetry and mythology and assumed abilities of transformation. When *Egils saga Skalla-Grímssonar* was discussed above it was briefly mentioned that queen Gunnhildr was irritating Egill throughout the night in the shape of a bird. The term *hamhleypa* is used in this part of the text but it is both impossible to decide and uninteresting to speculate whether the queen was believed actually to change her shape or if this was just an easily accessible image of a strong-minded woman.

Ynglinga saga 7 states that Óðinn was the foremost shapeshifter, or *hamhleypa*. Snorri tells how Óðinn lay as if dead or asleep while his *hugr* was carrying out different deeds for himself or others in the shape of a bird, an animal, a fish or a serpent. His regular body was left behind, only his soul assumed temporary shapes. This is also the prevalent case in most Old Norse shapeshifting stories. No transformation with a complete disappearance of the ordinary body is told of; some part of the body is always left behind. It was thought to be a dangerous moment for the shapeshifter as it gave his or her enemies an opportunity either to steal or hurt the temporary body. An analogous stigma would immediately appear on the ordinary body. *Hávamál* refers to Óðinn's ability to hinder the souls of some night hags (*túnriður*) from getting back to their regular bodies when they are carrying out their nightly deeds (Schjødt 1990: 44ff.).

> I know a tenth one if I see witches
> playing up in the air;
> I can bring it about that they can't make their way back
> to their own shapes,
> to their own spirits.[15]
> (trans. by Larrington 1996: 36)

The stanza is cryptic, as is *Hávamál*, but we can recognize Óðinn's supreme power over the hags by means of spells, the spoken word. It is probable that the lines are hinting at how vulnerable the shapeshifter is when leaving the body behind for the new guise. This was also the moment to strike back against an attacking *hamhleypa*. A similarly interesting description of shapeshifting can be found in the introductory prose of *Vǫlundarkviða*, another poem of the *Poetic Edda*, where Vǫlundr and his two brothers steal the swan skins from three women who are said to be valkyries. Nothing more is said about the captured women or their origins. They are forced to remain in human shape and marry the brothers. The motif is well known from several international fairy tales as well as from later Scandinavian folk legends. Óðinn's aggression against knowledgeable women is also emphasized in *Hávamál* 113 where erotic relations with a *fiolkunnigri kono* are condemned. The mythological narratives seem to form models for history writing in the sagas where brute force and sexual dominion intermingle in male attempts to hinder female executions of *trolldómr*.

A comparable episode can be found in *Kormáks saga* chapter 18 where the actions of a shapeshifter, along with the counter actions taken against her, clearly illuminate some vital conditions of the human *hugr* and shapeshifting. The saga tells of how the cunning woman Þórveig has laid a curse on the young man Kormákr. It is her immediate revenge since he has caused the death of her two sons as a consequence of ongoing clan combats. The curse will make it impossible for Kormákr to have his beloved. Þórveig's curse and further actions are part of a larger pattern of conflicts, not isolated activities. The knowledgeable woman is using her abilities to protect her family honour. In this perspective her curse is the revenge on her sons' murderer. The conflicts escalate and Þórveig pursues Kormákr to the sea. The ship is attacked by a walrus that attempts to overturn it and Þórveig is recognized as acting out of her body by her eyes. The men on the ship press the animal down under the surface and at the same time Þórveig, at home, is said to be on her death bed. People around her later draw the conclusion that her death was caused by the events at sea. The link between the two bodies in this text, symbolized by Kormákr's recognition of her eyes, is so strong that the human body cannot ward off the injuries inflicted upon the walrus. A relationship of analogy exists between the woman and the animal – a recurring theme in many texts of shapeshifting. The link between them serves both as the tool of *trolldómr* and as a possible method of revenge. More than Þórveig's act of *trolldómr* itself, Kormákr's counteraction is the core of the episode. He makes use of his knowledge of shapeshifting and the analogous link – and so the originally evil action turns out to be the salvation of the attacked. This is a fundamental point where literary descriptions connect with ritual praxis. Apotropaic attacks against evil-minded shapeshifters, returning dead or assaulting demons are all based on the acceptance of such a connection between the bodies. Strategies of this kind are also apparent in later Scandinavian folk medicine as an obvious recurrent theme. In apotropaic rituals unfamiliar objects are cut, torn, or broken while waiting for an unveiling damage in the neighbourhood to appear, and the cause of affliction is thereby found.

The idea of the analogous links was vital to the Old Norse conceptions of *trolldómr*. It provided a theory of how the *hugr* of certain persons could work over such long distances and also formed the strategy for a possible way of averting the attack. Seemingly ordinary and harmless objects could be identified as carriers of 'insidious harm', to use Mary Douglas's term for the invisible and contagious peril (Douglas 1992). The attacking object was not a spectacular object but something so familiar that it was sometimes hard to observe and thereby served as a narrative surprise.

An expressive term of some frequency is *sendingar*, i.e. the figures sent by people with access to a strong *hamr*, *hamrammr*. The term explicitly emphasizes the performative aspect and ritual practices of *trolldómr*, the active performances of the sender of a distinct desire. Eddic poetry mentions different night-riders, apparently women, moving through the air. These *riður* should be interpreted as night hags acting in a temporary body. Their names associate them with darkness and the night, *myrkriður* and *kveldriður*. They are attacked by Óðinn as if he had the right to punish them. There are sexual overtones in the way the god is addressing them. It can be noted that the woman in *Eyrbyggja saga* mentioned above, who is accused of using her knowledge to take revenge on the young man who rejects her, is called *kveldriða*. Most likely she was assumed to haunt the man during the night and cause him severe damage. When she is summoned it is for being a night hag, *mara*. The end of this particular story is that it turns out to be another knowledgeable woman who is guilty and has misused her capabilities.

Closely connected to the shapeshifters are the many categories of returning dead, *draugar* and *aptrgangur* (Ellis Davidson 1981; Aðalsteinsson 1987; Clunies Ross 1994: 247ff.). These could be evil minded persons who could not obtain peace in the grave and appeared hostile and revengeful. The more friendly dead, still close to their families, come with a mission to fulfil among the living. Like the *fylgjur* they give warnings or reveal hidden truths. It was important to obey the advice and hints from the friendly dead. Messages from them were treated like replies to divination were. Against the evil dead, actions were often taken that can be compared to the punishments for *trolldómr* deaths among the living. Returning dead trouble makers were told to be reburied far away and dead associated with *trolldómr* could not rest near the living. The gaze of the returning dead was feared as much as the gaze of the evil-minded living.

The treatment of the dead gives a perspective on the concept ancestor. All these activities of the dead indicate that, at least for a time after death, they were thought of as having insight and interest in the world of the living, and having opinions about what was going on. The realms of the dead are described rather obscurely and most attention in mythological narratives is paid to the afterlife of the fallen warriors in Óðinn's dwellings. Returning dead are always encountered and related to in the perspective of the living. As long as they were remembered they were thought of as acting members of the family with legitimate reasons to take action.

Once again it must be stated that it is difficult and not meaningful to distinguish between 'beings' that appear in Old Norse texts, the activities of the returning dead and the deeds of people supposed to performing *trolldómr*. Classification does not take the various textual contexts into consideration.

Eyrbyggja saga provides us with several interesting stories of the dead turning back for different reasons. Þorgunna in chapters 50f. shares many characteristics with a *trollkona*. In her lifetime she was feared. Foreign and mysterious, she stands outside the network of family relations. When dead, she returns naked to ensure that her pall-bearers receive proper hospitality. When not obeyed she makes her will known from the other side of the grave.

Þórólfr bægifótr ('twist foot') in chapter 34 of *Eyrbyggja saga* becomes when most troublesome dead. At the time of his death he was deeply involved in conflicts and it is no wonder that he began to return as a *draugr*. In contrast to a *hamhleypa, mara*, or any kind of were-animal a returning dead is immediately identified as an individual. Þórólfr attacks humans and cattle. Like the *riður* he rides the oxen and the farmhouse. Finally, almost like a *mara*, he kills a shepherd. The bones of the shepherd are crushed and the man is strangled to death. The only way to stop the assaults is to dig the corpse out of the grave with great difficulty and burn it (ch. 59). Reburying accompanied with cremation was a way to stop the troublesome dead from returning. By this means an evident barrier (in some cases as concrete as a heap of stones) was constructed that marked the border between the living and the dead.

Knowledge and Destiny: Trolldómr Beliefs in the Old Norse World View

The literature of the Norsemen holds a special position in relation to the texts preserved from other Germanic peoples. In particular, the Old Norse sagas provide a social background for *trolldómr* narratives that is mostly lacking in texts from the Continent. The texts function as social memories; even if biased and imaginative they most often refer to historical persons and events.

When summing up the conceptual base for *trolldómr* beliefs it must be stressed once more that, even if odd and conspicuous in details, these assumptions were part of a consistent world view. Socially they were interwoven with a network of political and social conflicts among the settlers and their followers in Iceland.

In mythological narratives, as well as history writing, *trolldómr* was a reasonable cause for events past and present. These stories were founded on basic assumptions about human nature and man's relation to history and destiny. The ability to accomplish benefits outside the ordinary body required special knowledge. These extraordinary insights were inborn or learnt skills, quite different from the ideology introduced into Scandinavia during the epidemic 'witch craze' of the sixteenth and seventeenth centuries. The early modern Continental 'witch beliefs' was a hybrid of popular beliefs and learned tradition. The system was introduced by jurists and clergymen and associated with the legal administration rather than rural maintenance. Supported by the dogmas of Lutheran ortodoxy it heightened the dualism between the realm of God and that of the devil. The latter became a potentate of a magnitude he hardly held during the Middle Ages.

Nevertheless, persistence can be observed over a long time, despite dramatic social changes, for many of the vital conceptions. There are striking similarities between Old Norse modes of expressing *trolldómr* conceptions and folklore recordings made at the end of the nineteenth century and the beginning of the twentieth. With its cunning people, curses, and 'arrows of destruction' it also shows the positive aspects of this belief system: healing practices and protection. When discussing the confrontation between the old religion and the new, Kirsten Hastrup writes: 'But I would argue that even if the heathen faith is depicted through a learned Christian's concepts of right and wrong, we can legitimately compare the structures of the two thought systems, as these are thought to be more persistent than surface phenomena, such as the conversion to Christianity' (1981: 68). Scandinavian *trolldómr* conceptions were deeply embedded in a rural world dependent on farming, fishing and hunting. *Trolldómr* and its domains were a form of ritualization of the constant threat of famine and crop failure.

As we will see in the following chapter, however, the emphasis in Old Norse stories about *trolldómr* was not so much on conceptions, as on concrete acts, *gerningar*.

CHAPTER 2

Trolldómr *Rituals: Practice and Performance*

Religion is by no means only a cognitive category. Religion is to most people, past and present, a lived experience acted out in physical motion. Faith is expressed in actions and attitudes that cannot be defined as either exclusively sacred or solely profane. Religion is not limited to any distinguishable realm of holiness. Many religious activities may appear trivial and common, yet express concepts that are vital for how individuals understand their world.

In Old Norse one single word, *siðr*, comprised the wide field of religion, faith, moral, custom and tradition. It included both what were supposed to be traditional conceptions and also the way things were thought to be done. The multitude of meanings gave this term a wide range of possible usage: cognitive and practical as well as juridical and religious. The term certainly had a semantic field of great variety. Actions done, planned or omitted in connection with *trolldómr* are sometimes commented on in the texts as being opposed to *siðr*, which is then the appropriate mode. *Siðr* is almost always used as something positive, with a certain accentuation on what is directly expressed. The concept is thoroughly based in the old lore and customs, and therefore reliable. The word often appears in contexts where the question of Icelandic identity is crucial, with positive references to the old days. However, the term was adopted by Christian authors in Scandinavia during the processes of Christianization and here the religious aspect was exclusively stressed.

As discussed in the previous chapter, even if a strictly structuralist interpretation is highly debatable, there is a certain conflict between the social and the antisocial, order and chaos, inside and outside, as an apparent theme in *trolldómr* myths, sagas, texts, and even in early Christian laws. Likewise, in rituals *trolldómr* and extraordinary knowledge function symbolically as a link between chaos and structure. This image of the struggle for knowledge can correspondingly be noted in the descriptions of ritual practice. When considering rituals a simple model can be applied, which regards them basically as a communication in two different directions, like two axes: horizontal and vertical. The vertical direction is perhaps the most obvious one: here rituals can be seen as man's desire to communicate with suprahuman realms in expectation of some kind of response. But rituals are in most cases important social events as well. They work horizontally and establish human hierarchies and identities based on the social order, *siðr*. On the other hand, an

exclusively communicative approach to rituals limits the possible interpretations of them when it comes to the construction of meaning. In a ritual
powers are let loose that the human society must keep in control.

A ritual, as discussed by Paul Connerton, can be defined as a 'rule–governed activity of a symbolic character which draws the attention of its
participants to objects of thought and feeling which they hold to be of special significance' (Connerton 1989: 44). It is a wide definition where other
than solely religious dimensions of ritual life also have a given place.
Political, juridical and economical conditions are inseparably linked to pre-
Christian rituals. There were no rules in a formal sense for rituals, but a certain established practice seems to be at hand in Old Norse literature. We can
read how power relations were established and socially maintained at local
gatherings and feasts. The political and religious leader, *goði*, invited his men
to perform a *blót* (offering) of vital importance to the local community. In
saga texts the *blót* is often represented in a royal or aristocratic context and is
emphasized as being the most important ritual event. Despite the narrative
grandeur, the *blót* offerings seem to have been strongly related to the basic
needs of a rural community and to have followed the cycle of the seasons.
On the same occasions *þing*s were held where oaths were sworn, conflicts
were solved, and economic transactions were established. Within this context it was the responsibility of a *goði* to arrange for a public *blót* ritual. But
there were other important rituals even closer to agricultural living conditions, focusing on future prosperity and fertility. These activities have not
always been defined as rituals, but as we shall see from some examples they
certainly fulfil the criteria of Connerton's definition. Nor do the texts give
any clear distinction between actions related to divination, healing, dream
interpretation or curses and other destructive deeds.

The descriptions of *trolldómr* as ritual practice cover a wide range of different text types, from rather elaborate descriptions of performances in the
saga literature to simple and bald activities like single words uttered. These
ceremonies do not seem to confirm any social hierarchy in the same sense
that *blót* rituals did; rituals relating to hidden knowledge had a much more
ambivalent character and sometimes openly contested prevalent authority.
When divination was performed the outcome of the ceremony was in
most cases in the hands of the performer. Yet prominent landowners appear
to have been obliged to arrange formalized fortune-telling events, and the
result was not always in tune with his intentions.

Performing Seiðr: *For Better or Worse*

Seiðr is one of many words used for custom and praxis in connection with
persons of extraordinary knowledge. It is perhaps the most central ritual,

when trying to understand the different aspects of *trolldómr*. The term appears in many divergent contexts, although the corpus of texts related to *seiðr* is quite limited (Strömbäck 1935; Dillmann 1992; DuBois 1999).[16] In the broadest sense *seiðr* is a technique for gaining knowledge about the future or trying to change the options for events to come. The intention of the act could therefore be malevolent as well as beneficial. Thus, the use of the term *seiðr* does not per se give any indication of which was the case. Since the sagas always tell a highly subjective story it is not possible to draw any sharp distinction between what was regarded as good or evil from different points of view. A *seiðr* act to protect a member of one's family is viewed as an outrage by his or her opponents. Calling antagonists and enemies names like *seiðmaðr*, *seiðkona* had an ominous tone and was an effective form of defamation.

Some themes in the descriptions of *seiðr* are recurrent, though in some vital aspects they are very contradictory. A major difference concerns whether the texts express any Christian opposition to the ritual activities or not. In some sagas the pagan-Christian conflict is emphasized as a major theme, while in other sagas *seiðr* is regarded more as a communal local tradition, as the *siðr* of old times. It is a crucial question whether to regard the *seiðr* ceremony as occasional and sporadic or as a ritual practice profoundly ingrained in the rural living conditions of pre-Christian times. The texts might suggest that the performance of *seiðr*, as a recurrent ritual, was essential for the welfare of local communities. Many of the texts set the performer in an atmosphere of exoticism, which of course affects the interpretation. Was this a way for the saga authors to accentuate the pagan character of the rituals, or are the exoticisms to be read as if the rituals never took place, or were products of pure fantasy, or the conventional literary motifs of the time?

Seiðr is a complex term used in many contexts in Old Norse literature, referring to a multitude of practices performed in an attempt to intervene in the events of the near future. Judging from the way the term is represented in several texts, the ceremony seems to have been a ritual event of some importance. It is described as an act of divination, predicting the future and the fate, not only of individuals, but of a whole local community. It also included foretelling the weather and prosperity for the coming season. The ceremony was conducted by a person with special skills and knowledge, and in many cases by the request of an individual or a group. *Seiðr* could be performed for the protection of a family member, to damage an enemy, or as a remunerative fortune-telling. *Seiðr* was a full ceremony of some length, with one or more performers who acted to a great extent in front of an audience, and according to certain sagas various kinds of equipment were used. In contrast to *blót* rituals, *seiðr* was semi-public and its effect the concern of a smaller group. Conceptions of *trolldómr* formed the basis of the *seiðr* rituals in the sense that they assumed certain persons' extraordinary knowledge and ability to pass the limits of ordinary perception.

The Mythical Origin of Seiðr

Seiðr is performed both in the mythological narratives and in the sagas as a process for gaining knowledge from outside the balanced structure and order. No details of the ritual processes are described in the myths. The mythological genealogy of *seiðr* and its performers among the gods is an intriguing correlate to the narratives of the sagas. *Seiðr* is given a position as an institution within an ideological framework. A more complicated issue is whether there exists a mythical model for the social order expressed in the rituals; or if there is any obvious relation between myth and ritual at all. When it comes to *trolldómr* this is a fundamental question.

Vǫluspá, the most complex of all Eddic poems, reveals the history of the universe from creation to apocalypse in 66 stanzas. The poet has put the words in the mouth of a *vǫlva*, a prophetess claiming to have access to clandestine knowledge older than the universe itself. The *vǫlva* is speaking off and on in the first person addressing men and gods. Obviously she has the insight into how to *spá*, to disclose what is concealed in the past and the present. In the text *seiðr* is said to be performed at different significant phases of the progress and decline of the universe. In the very first stanzas of the poem, i.e. the *vǫlva*'s invocation, the wise woman is claiming authority by knowledge from before time, when she was raised and nurtured by the giants. Without this connection to the demonic forces the creation myth cannot be told. Order is established to distinguish Miðgarðr from the chaotic otherworld. Time, days and seasons are structured along with a model for the good life, including *blót* rituals. Then, suddenly, in the middle of the creation myth three maidens from the realm of the giants appear. Nothing is told of their message or mission, and maybe the narrative purpose of their appearance is to remind the listener/reader that Miðgarðr is surrounded by destructive forces. Immediately after the *vǫlva*'s version of the creation myth, another two females with fatal ambitions are introduced. The appearance of Gullveig and Heiðr (the latter a name commonly given in Old Norse literature to women conducting destructive deeds, 'witches') leads to an escalation of the conflicts and the text indicates a conflict between the gods themselves, 'the first war in the world' (Clunies Ross 1994: 203ff.). The mythological position and status of these two characters is a topic for discussion. Heiðr is also called *vǫlva* and her technique *seiðr*; apparently she is willing to teach vicious women how to predict the future, *spá,* in order to make bad things worse. Her name, 'the bright one', is related to Freyja, the matron of the Vanir, who, Snorri claims, was the one that originally taught the art of *seiðr* to the Æsir. The same source tells that *seiðr* was customary among the Vanir. Margaret Clunies Ross has discussed at length the position of Gullveig within 'two major semantic fields with the dominant operative metaphors of masculinity and femininity' (1994: 187).

The middle part of the poem refers to a war among the gods, between two groups named Æsir and Vanir. The text in this passage is obscure, probably corrupt. The origin of the rivalry is unclear, but broken oaths and fraud are designated. The conflict turns out to be the beginning of the end, *ragnarǫk*, and *seiðr* is said to be used successfully by the Vanir in the struggle against the Æsir, and with their powerful *galdr* songs they turn out to be undefeatable. Although Óðinn, the leader of the Æsir, is usually acknowledged as the master of *seiðr*, these stanzas indicate that this art originated among the Vanir. Further on in the complex structure of conflicts *seiðr* is used again. Once dissension is there, the successive devastation of harmony and order is inevitable.

Óðinn is seeking the assistance of a *vǫlva* before the final battle, i.e. the destruction of the world, *ragnarǫk*. Apparently he is paying the *vǫlva* for her divination with jewellery. A similar situation opens another Eddic poem, *Baldrs draumar*, where Óðinn wakens a *vǫlva* from the grave to question her. A *vǫlva* giving valuable advice to the living from her grave is also at hand in the opening of *Grógaldr*. *Vǫluspá* gives a hint of the knowledgeable woman's technique: it is stated that she is sitting out in the wilderness,[17] probably making an *útiseta*, seeking solitude to obtain visions. Her vision is lucid, although frightening. All she can see is valkyries and destruction. The *vǫlva* is briefly telling of the death of Baldr, the final sign of the coming end. The following stanzas, 31–2, describe the beginning of *ragnarǫk*, extended in Snorri's prose text *Gylfaginning* (33–5). It must be noted, as Clunies Ross does in her extensive analysis, that when destruction comes into the arena of the history of the universe, it is also the introduction of active feminine agents (Clunies Ross 1994, esp. 187ff.). The way *seiðr* is described in *Vǫluspá* accentuates not only the conflict between Útgarðr and Miðgarðr but also the one within the category of gods; and the quest for knowledge as vital for the balance of cosmos. The gods are dependent on the knowledge from the world of giants and trolls as a necessity for development, and still its origin is the seed of the end. Nevertheless, the evaluation of *seiðr* throughout *Vǫluspá* is more or less positive. Even though the future as seen by the *vǫlva* is dark it is emphasized as a powerful method of divination, not primarily a technique for destruction. This apparent ambiguity between necessity and destruction is prevalent throughout the *trolldómr* narratives of the sagas too.

Freyja: The Prime Seiðkona

The process of passing on the knowledge of *seiðr* appears to be of particular interest in some texts. Snorri refers to the mythological origin of *seiðr* in his *Ynglinga saga*, the mythical history of the Swedish kings, tracing their genealogy back to Óðinn himself. The source of his knowledge is said to be the gods of fertility. When connected with the Vanir *seiðr* is not associated with poetry or old-time wisdom. Freyja taught the art of *seiðr* to the Æsir.[18] In this part of the text nothing about technique or what constitutes *seiðr* is mentioned; if anything the focus is on the interplay between the Æsir and the Vanir. Clunies Ross has emphasized the similarities in mythological function between Gullveig in *Vǫluspá* and Freyja in *Ynglinga saga* (1994: 203f.). Both texts indicate that *seiðr* is a skill lacking among the Æsir and it must be captured from the Vanir or the giants. Although desired, it is obviously referred to with strongly negative connotations. Other texts concisely call Freyja *spádís* or *Vanadís*. By giving her these names the connection between Vanir, fertility and different aspects of *trolldómr* rituals is accentuated (Näsström 1995). This is a reasonable connection since the divinatory aspects of *seiðr* are strongly connected to future prosperity.

Yet clandestine knowledge and divination abilities were not assumed to be inborn qualities among the Vanir either. In the Eddic poem *Hyndluljóð* a conflict between Freyja and the *vǫlva* Hyndla is referred to. The goddess is addressing Hyndla as if awakening her, calling her 'sister' and thus claiming some kind of affinity (*Hyndluljóð* 1). But the *vǫlva*'s answers are quite aggressive. Hyndla gives a long genealogy of various mythological beings and in stanza 33 she mentions the origin of *vǫlur*, and classifies them among knowledgeable people, *seiðr* performers and giants. There is no mention of gods, but instead Freyja's helper is related to the destructive inhabitants of the outside world.

In Snorri's *Ynglinga saga* 10 Freyja is said to be the last surviving of the old gods and the last to keep up the old form of sacrifices. This comment could be compared to the image of the age-old *vǫlva* in *Vǫluspá*, and elsewhere, being the last with knowledge of the old lore. *Ynglinga saga* is not primarily a collection of myths, but a historical narrative in which Snorri places the gods as agents in the dawn of time. As will be noted further on in this chapter, it is not unusual that *seiðr* performers are said to be the last of their kind. In many texts the prototype of the *vǫlva* seems to be a very old woman, as a personification of age-old *siðr*.

Óðinn: Mythical Chieftain and Master of Seiðr

Óðinn is the most complex of the Scandinavian gods, contradictory in appearance and ambiguous in character (Lindow 1985; Mitchell 1993).[19] The god plays an important part in the mythical history of the universe, a position that is especially emphasized in the account of the creation of the world in the *Poetic Edda* as well as in Snorri's *Edda*. Óðinn is described as having an active part in the creation of the world and is repeatedly called father or lord of the other gods. He is presented as aristocratic, called 'the highest', and acts as a ruler, with a special relation to the warriors and valkyries at Valhǫll; he is referred to as the chieftain of men and gods and his dwellings in Miðgarðr seem to be the middle of the world. On the darker side of the representations of Óðinn are death, dying and the realm of the dead. These various aspects are amalgamated with the image of Óðinn as the god of poetry and wisdom. The supreme god is said to be the master of the spoken word and as such in control of ultimate knowledge. Death and poetry tend to intermingle in the image of the wise Óðinn. The god's harsh quest for knowledge is symbolically shown in different stories of Óðinn's self-sacrifices, when parts of his own body are sacrificed in exchange for knowledge and runes. In these texts the god of death is tasting death himself.

The most well-known scene is perhaps when Óðinn is hanging in the windswept tree, usually interpreted as Yggdrasill, sacrificing himself to himself, being both subject and object of the act (Schjødt 1993). Óðinn hangs for nine days and nine nights, without food or water. According to *Hávamál* 138–44, he fasts and suffers, in a form of *útiseta* in the wilderness one can assume, tormenting his body as a preparation to receive knowledge. This and other poems strongly stress that the prize for wisdom is a high one. A certain emphasis on direction is also apparent; knowledge is called up from below. Wounded by a spear, he is receptive to powerful runes that he is able to bring up. From these Óðinn becomes wise, *fróðr*, with acquired abilities to heal and to curse. In the opening section of *Grímnismál* the god, disguised as the wanderer Grímnir, is sitting between two fires to prepare himself for the wisdom duel with the *jǫtunn* king Geirrøðr.

Óðinn's offering of his eye in another variant of the wisdom-quest theme is related to the myth about the wise Mímir and takes us back to the conflict between Æsir and Vanir. *Ynglinga saga* 7 recounts that Óðinn brings Mímir's head with him and that it has told him about events in other worlds. There are different versions of the myth of Mímir, but it is always related to the war between the gods and the exchange of hostages. According to Snorri's account in *Ynglinga saga* 4 the Vanir felt betrayed by the peace agreement. Mímir was decapitated and his head was sent back to the Æsir from the Vanir where he had been kept hostage. Óðinn is said to have embalmed it with herbs and *galdr* songs, and spoken with the head in times of danger. The head is used technically in two ways according to the myths: as a tool for divination when Óðinn speaks with Mímir's head shortly before *ragnarǫk* (*Vǫluspá* 46; *Ynglinga saga* 4, 7), or in scenes where Óðinn is drinking from Mímir's well to acquire knowledge (*Vǫluspá* 28; *Gylfaginning* 8). Mímir, or rather the representation of his wisdom, and his liminal position as a hostage and as a giant among the gods, symbolize the point of connection between order and destruction.

Like *Vǫluspá*, *Ynglinga saga* stresses that *seiðr* originates from the Vanir and that Mímir has an important position in the process. But it is Óðinn who is hailed as the master of *seiðr* in the following chapters of the saga. By performing *seiðr* Óðinn can make his enemies blind and deaf in battles, or paralysed with fear and their weapons useless, while his own men, filled with fury and strength, can take part in the battle without armour. This state of wild rage among the mythical warriors is called *berserksgangr*. Seemingly it is related to the shapeshifting theme: the conception that certain people and mythological creatures can maintain temporary operations in the guise of an animal.

Snorri tells that 'Óðinn shifted shape and lay as if sleeping or dead, appearing as bird, or animal, fish or snake, and in a moment he could go to to remote places on his own or other's business'. And he 'could put out fire, calm, the sea, and turn the wind with his words'.[20] Further on in *Ynglinga saga* Óðinn's abilities due to access to knowledge achieve what is impossible for others.

Moreover, Óðinn is said to be the foremost shapeshifter and to have the ability to appear in different guises. Shapeshifting is a weighty theme in Old Norse *trolldómr* stories and also a continuous theme in later Scandinavian folklore. The myths of self-sacrifice and the journeys symbolically confirm that essential knowledge is to be gained outside Miðgarðr and that the border to the realm of the giants must be crossed. In mythological geography the border in between is symbolically marked by an imposing sea and a serpent. Few myths lack the conflict between the two opposing realms. Journeys into the other world or visits to its borderland are essential to achieve the advantages sought. Assisting himself or others is also the theme of the final part of *Hávamál*, the so called 'Ljóðatal', where Óðinn in eighteen *galdr* songs praises his own abilities (Larrington 1993: 62ff.). The god of poetry and knowledge speaks in the first person, giving a long catalogue of powerful skills. *Ljóð*, the songs Óðinn is in charge of, is far from the suffering depicted in *Hávamál* 138ff. and *Grímnismál* 1. The perspective is that of helping and assisting and a crafty god appears who has access to healing wounds, protection against enemies' attacks, putting out fire, calming the sea, raising the dead, making persons invulnerable and manipulating through love magic. *Hávamál* tells of very much the same abilities as does *Ynglinga saga* 6 and 7. The utmost aim of the skills is gaining power over other individuals. The same assisting purpose is stressed when *trolldómr* rituals are reported in sagas as being executed by humans. The genealogy of *seiðr* continues from the gods to the world of humans. Snorri tells in *Ynglinga saga* 7 of how Óðinn taught most of his skills to the sacrificial priests, *blótgoðar*. They were second to him in knowledge, *fróðleikr*, and insights, *fjǫlkynngi*. Many others learned from this and the practice of *trolldómr* became widespread and continued for a long time.

One of the heroic poems of the *Poetic Edda, Sigrdrífumál*, provides a catalogue of gnomic poetry close to the elaboration in *Hávamál* (Larrington 1993; Raudvere 1998). The wise Sigrdrífa, categorized as a valkyria, instructs the young hero Sigurðr by means of powerful charms. Victory, healing and wisdom is promised if her advice, *ráð*, is kept. The stanzas given in the poem are hardly formulas as such, rather sententious phrases, even though the mode of formulating the advice has a distinct ritualized character. Words are always followed by acting: what is verbally expressed is configured in motion. The poem is no manual, but a poetic application of the *rúnar* genre. The last group of *rúnar* mentioned in this catalogue is 'mind-runes' (*hugrúnar*), described in the cryptic style of the Eddic lays:

> Hroptr [Óðinn] interpreted them,
> cut them, thought them out,
> from that liquid which had leaked
> from the skull of Heiddraupnir ['Bright Dropper']
> and from Hoddrofnir's ['Hoard-tearer'] horn.[21]
> (trans. by Larrington 1996: 168)

Gender and the Performance of Seiðr in Mythological Narratives

Undoubtedly most Icelandic skalds were men, their audience was to a great extent male, and it was men who copied the manuscripts when written and kept them – even if there are examples of learned nuns in the Icelandic (and other Scandinavian) monasteries. Sigrdrífa hardly speaks on behalf of women or expresses any particular female wisdom, and the receiver of her advice is a man. The way she is portrayed in the poem, she hardly mirrors human females, but rather wisdom beyond everyday life, and she is depicted as one of the valkyries, the maidens serving close to Óðinn.

The question whether the performance of *seiðr* in Old Norse texts is a gender-specific activity has received many different answers. The relation between the mythological texts and the more realistic sagas is another complicated question in this context. Do the texts form a prototype or paradigm of the *seiðr* performer with relevance to actually performed rituals? The implications of the stated mythological genealogy of *seiðr* are hard to specify when trying to come to terms with this complicated matter.

As seen above, *seiðr* is described in some texts as originating from the Vanir, but Óðinn is represented as the master of *seiðr* in many others. Whether this mirrors a social conflict about the ritual responsibilities of men and women in the Old Norse world is highly questionable. As François-Xavier Dillmann has shown, when counted in the sources, men and women appear equally often as practitioners of *trolldómr* (1986). *Ynglinga saga* 7 comments on Óðinn's interest in and practice of *seiðr* as *ergi*, a term often translated as an indication of 'unmanliness' and also given the sexual interpretation, 'homosexual'. To perform *seiðr* was supposed to be shameful for men and the art was taught to the priestesses.[22] In fact this statement points in the opposite direction to the emphasis sometimes laid upon *seiðr* as a specifically female knowledge overpowered by the principal male god (Kress 1993). In Snorri's genealogy of *seiðr* the knowledge and skills seem to have been mastered by the supreme god and later handed over to vaguely described female ritual performers.

Interestingly enough a paragraph some lines further on keeps up the themes of power, knowledge and *trolldómr*, and states that these beneficial skills were passed on to the *blót* (sacrifice) priests. The priests were second to Óðinn in foresight and knowledge.[23] Instead of making negative remarks on *seiðr* this part of the text connects the important social position of a *blótgoði* with Óðinn and his extraordinary abilities. The passage has not received half as much attention as the *ergi* part, but there is nothing that indicates any inferior relevance. These two very different statements in the same text can serve as an indication of the ambiguous attitude with regard to *seiðr* expressed throughout Old Norse literature, and not necessarily as mirrors of ritual practices. Nevertheless, it is the former paragraph that is referred to and discussed in most handbooks and surveys.

Lokasenna ('Loki's Quarrel') 24 in the *Poetic Edda* also uses the terminology *ergi/argr* (noun/adjective) in relation to Óðinn and *seiðr*. When read out of its context it must be remembered that the stanza belongs to a longer catalogue of verbal defamation pronounced by Loki towards the other gods. One accusation more embarrassing than the other comes over Loki's sneering lips to many of them with erotic allusions. To Óðinn he says:

> 'But you once practised *seiðr* on Sámsey,
> and you beat on the drum as witches do,
> in the likeness of a wizard you journeyed among mankind,
> and that I thought the hallmark of a pervert.'[24]
> (trans. by Larrington 1996: 89)

Óðinn is compared to a *vǫlva* who, like Saami or Siberian shamans, uses a drum (*vétt*) and is called both *argr* and *vitki*, i.e. performer of *trolldómr*. Other Eddic poems give the image of the seeker of wisdom as afflicted, and because of that – not despite it – as the greatest of *seiðr* performers. Most other texts on *seiðr* do not mention *ergi/argr* at all, but emphasize Óðinn as the wisest of gods and the master of poetry without any hint of sexual defamation.

There is no sexual activity or erotic symbolism expressed in the *seiðr* narratives. It is debatable to what extent the connection between homosexuality and *ergi/argr* should be taken (Meulengracht Sørensen 1983; Kress 1990, 1993; Sayers 1992). Instead Carol Clover has stressed the moral aspect of the term: cowardliness (Clover 1993). She raises the question to what extent categories like woman, man, female and male are relevant for analyses of interhuman actions in the Old Norse world, loaded as they are with our own understandings of the terms. Instead, she points to 'a sex-gender system rather different from our own, and indeed rather different from that of the Christian Middle Ages' (Clover 1993: 364). Thereby she opens up a more fundamental discussion about gender as an analytic tool in Old Norse studies. To attract their audience the sagas and the Eddic lays had to be good and entertaining narratives.[25] As verbal art they were stuctured around 'a system based to an extraordinary extent on winnable and losable attributes' Clover 1993: 379). The tension between normative discourse and social reality was obviously a narrative possibility. What could be more effective than calling the aristocratic lord of the gods and warriors unmanly? As part of social interaction a certain negotiation with the definitions of male and female and the construction of gender-specific qualities was at hand. There is an apparent gender system expressed in the texts, with norms and rules. But it cannot be read apart from other systems of hierarchy to do with social status and age. Positioning norms within hierarchies was a basic way of describing persons as well as a tool of social manipulation. Movable categories, attributed to men and women, were one of many ways for a writer to heighten the temperature of the plot and make surprising turns more plausible (Clover 1993: 372). The gender roles in Old Norse texts are closely connected to the narrative structure and the creation of interesting fiction. Dreams, visions, sudden bad luck, *seiðr* divination and the like must also be seen from the perspective of the narrative rules of the respective genre.

Helga Kress holds a radically different opinion. She has several times argued that a pre-Christian female oral culture, in which women's arts and literature flourished, was crushed by the male literate Christian Latin culture (Kress 1990, 1993). To her the texts of *seiðr* and *trolldómr* bear witness to a battle between the sexes, where women are the representatives of a regressing culture. Despite the objections raised against a simplistic model of the relation between textual imagery in mythological narratives and existing social conflicts, a certain pattern is visible in the texts concerning the genealogy of *seiðr*. In various narratives gender does play a vital part in the construction of conflicts, along with other significant markers of 'otherness'. The *seiðr* performer was an outsider in one way or the other. But the fringed position of the performer was not exclusively marked by gender.

As we shall see in the examples from the sagas, the otherness of the *seiðr* performer was marked in various ways, among them a quite complicated interplay between gender roles and social status. Characters were given a marginal position when described as connected to *trolldómr* and *seiðr*. Being a woman is surely not a marginal position as such, but certain scenes in the sagas focus on women acting in a way they usually did not, that is, outside the conventional limits of supposed female behaviour.

The Tradition of Seiðr *as a Divination Ritual in the Saga Literature*

Pre-Christian Scandinavian mythology reveals a great interest in questions of fate and destiny. In urgent situations there is often, even among the gods, a desire to control the future, or at least to have knowledge of it. Accounts of *seiðr* in the sagas express the same interest in future events and reflect a social background to the ceremonies and a dependence on farming, fishing, and hunting. At the same time, divination and *trolldómr* are always part of a narrative strategy contructed by the author. *Seiðr* is said to be conducted either for the benefit of the acting person herself, but more frequently it was a ceremony offered by a more or less professional performer to assist a recipient in need of support. It served as an act of divination to be conducted by a person who was conceived to be 'of great knowledge', which was the most common phrase of all in relation to *trolldómr*.

The scholarly interest concerning rituals has, to a large extent, been focused on the communal sacrifices, *blót*, whereas *seiðr* has been classified as socially more marginal. On the contrary, *seiðr* could be put in the centre, emphasizing the ritual as an important act of divination and therefore of vital importance to maintain. *Seiðr* was not only an occasional act for solving immediate problems. It also seems to have been a periodically recurring ritual of considerable length; some texts state that it lasted several days. According to what can be gathered from the texts, such a ceremony had a certain formal structure that recurs as a customary pattern in the different sagas. In this respect *seiðr* was closely linked to rural life. The predictions made at a *seiðr* ceremony did not only concern personal destiny. They also had a vital social importance and indicated the future for a local area. In the literary context a prediction or a curse gave a hint about events further on in the text, or functioned as a revelation of conflicts.

There are obvious destructive aspects of *seiðr*, not only because dangers were always associated with the ceremony itself, but also due to the ambiguous intentions of the performer who, although respected, was apparently also feared. It must be remembered that in most cases when *seiðr* is mentioned in the sagas it is not in connection with any clear-cut ritual of a fertility character, but as an explanation of mishaps, as performed malevolence, often expressed in a short line rather than an elaborate narrative.

Some texts that tell of an invited honoured *vǫlva* also give her a flavour of danger. Through her knowledge and performance she held the destiny of many people in her hands and obviously she had potential to manipulate a given fate. The person who conducted the *seiðr* served as a mediator for the different avenues of communication. The *vǫlva* had the capability both to predict, *at spá*, and to give advice, *at ráða*. In contrast to various conceptions of shapeshifting, the performance of *seiðr* was not only a matter of the inner qualities of the acting person. To a great extent it was a question of instruction and learned skill, transmitted from an experienced performer to a disciple. In *Eyrbyggja saga* young Gunnlaugr frequently visits the middle aged woman Geirríðr. His eagerness to learn puts him in the forcefield between two knowledgeable women, with disastrous consequences for him.

What can be gathered from the texts is that *seiðr* was conceived as part of *siðr*, customary behaviour, but there were no dogmas, no written rules, only established custom. The traditions of those experienced in performing *seiðr* are emphasized in the sagas. The inner qualities of the performer, good or bad, are key points in the narratives, as well as knowledge of tradition. To become knowledgeable, *fjǫlkunnigr* or *margkunnigr*, was a development, a training, and a struggle to gain insights about what was hidden to others. The ritual showed the importance of being connected to ancient tradition, and the central character was a person who had access to long-forgotten knowledge. Many texts emphasize this ancient knowledge, not only in relation to *trolldómr* and *seiðr*, but as something valuable and desirable as such.

The Roman historian Tacitus noted in his descriptions of the Germanic tribes (*c.*98 CE) that certain women were thought to have a sacred and prophetic quality (*Germania* 8). they are said to deliver advice and forecasts and to be honoured for these skills. Tacitus points out a certain woman, Veleda, as specially well-known in this respect. Although he builds his account on hearsay and previous historians, the similarities with the recordings from Iceland from more than a thousand years later can be noted.

Þorbjǫrg Lítil-Vǫlva's Performance of Seiðr at Herjólfsnes

The most extensive and detailed account of a *seiðr* ceremony is found in the fourth chapter of *Eiríks saga rauða*, one of the Vinland sagas.[26] The saga deals with the Icelandic settlement on Greenland and the Norsemen's voyages to Vinland/America. The text was most likely written in the middle of the thirteenth century (Conroy 1980; Wahlgren 1993). In the centre of this early chapter stands a travelling father Þorbjǫrn and his daughter Guðríðr, temporarily staying on Greenland at Þorkell of the Herjólfsnes farm.

It is with some hesitation that I choose this text for a more detailed discussion, although it has many striking similarities to other Old Norse texts dealing with *seiðr* and divination. But too many times this particular account of the ceremony has been read as an accurate anthropological description of a *vǫlva*'s performance. Questions must also be raised concerning the purpose of the conspicuous image of the *seiðkona* and what was narratively gained from it. The significance of difference always seems to be at the core when *seiðr* performers are described.

The chapter opens with a description of the conditions at Herjólfsnes before the *seiðr* was performed. The area had had a harsh period of famine, and a change was urgently desired. The invitation to the *vǫlva* was a plea for alteration; her help was badly needed. As the most important farmer of the area it was Þorkell's responsibility to arrange for a divination ceremony. According to the explicitly claimed custom, *siðr*, he invites the *vǫlva* to his farm to predict the forthcoming period, a matter of concern for the whole local community. When the farmer admits the *vǫlva* into his house, social space is created for the ritual. He is in charge of the preparations, and the event as a whole is his responsibility. The invited woman is called *spákona* and given the nickname *lítil-vǫlva*, 'little seeress'. She is said to be the last surviving of nine sisters, and one manuscript of the saga states that all of them had been *spákonur*.[27] With this specification the text stresses her being part of an old tradition. It should be noted that the number nine occurs again, as it does on other occasions when Óðinn's capabilities are mentioned in mythological narratives.

The *seiðr* performance was part of a special event, a feast, *veizla*, but there was nothing spectacular about the situation. It is a time of crisis, but there is no 'gothic' atmosphere. The fortune-telling was obviously a social tradition of the area and it was also part of a local ritual pattern to invite the *vǫlva* to perform divination at the farm. The outfit and the utensils of the *vǫlva* are described as spectacular, i.e. her role as a performer is stressed. The text states that at the end of the winter season she wandered between the farms. Hopefully springtime would be more prosperous, which was a vital question for everybody. Different preparations were undertaken to honour the arrival of the *vǫlva* and a man was sent to call for her. She arrived at night escorted by the man. During his absence the farm people had made various arrangements. A comfortable high seat, *hásæti*, was arrayed for her and a feather bed was put under her. The status of the *vǫlva* in this text is apparently emphasized as being high. However, in other texts a rather ambiguous status can be expressed. This equivocality is obviously used by the saga authors to create intriguing plots. It is noticeable how well Þorbjǫrg *lítil-vǫlva* was received at the farm, in line with the local convention. It was the custom, *siðr*, to receive a *vǫlva* with reverence. The importance of holding her in great respect is explicitly stated three times in the chapter. Honouring her with an escort contradicts the image of the *vǫlva* wandering alone from farm to farm that is stressed elsewhere in other saga texts.

The text gives a colourful description at length of the outfit of the *vǫlva*. She differs from everything commonplace; her marginality is emphasized by her costume. This description by the Christian saga author can certainly not be read as 'the general costume of a *vǫlva*'. Rather it is in line with the saga's scenery of a remote place where pagan customs are still practised.

> She was wearing a black mantle with a strap, which was adorned with precious stones right down to the hem. About her neck she wore a string of glass beads and on her head a hood of black lambskin lined with white catskin. She bore a staff with a knob at the top, adorned with brass set with stones on the top. About her she had a linked charm belt with a large purse. In it she kept the charms which she needed for her predictions. She wore calfskin boots lined with fur with long, sturdy laces and large pewter knobs on the ends. On her hands she wore gloves of catskin, white and lined with fur.

Some details in her clothing are of special interest. It is complicated to make out what is in her purse, *tǫfr*, and whether and how the *vǫlva* was making use of it, *til fróðleiks at hafa*. The terminology only indicates that she is gaining knowledge with help from the substance. The wand and the hood are mentioned in other *trolldómr* stories, although the latter usually functioned as a protection from the evil eye. No estimation is expressed, or any hint of what was thought of this costume, or what feelings it challenged. Nothing is said about the looks of the woman, or if she was considered beautiful or ugly. Likewise, nothing is said directly about her age, but since she is the last of nine sisters it is very likely that she was supposed to be an aged woman. It is of course interesting to note that certain symbols recur when *seiðmenn* and *seiðkonur* are described and to observe that *seiðr* performers are said to use a special kind of equipment. But it must be remembered that all such characters are made to stand out from the rest. The literary uses of *trolldómr* symbolism do not represent the ritual practice or social interaction step by step. As a performer the *vǫlva* was the manifestation of old-time lore.

Eiríks saga rauða tells of a long ritual lasting two days, or more precisely two nights. The people of the farm considered it to be their duty to greet the *vǫlva* with great respect, although Þorbjǫrg *lítil-vǫlva*'s answers were according to her estimation of each person. The first night Þorkell, the master of the farm, took her hand and led her to the prepared high seat, which once more stresses the importance of honouring the important guest. A most intriguing scene is when the *vǫlva* is asked to look all over the place, *renna þar augum*, to set her eyes on people and livestock, and over the whole settlement. The eyes of the knowledgeable is a recurring theme in Old Norse literature, but it is the fear of their gaze that is emphasized in other texts. In this sequence the gaze is asked for as something favourable, but it could as well be hazardous. Once again we are confronted with the ambiguity of the capacities of *seiðr* performers. Every character in the text is dependent on the intention of the *spákona*. However, this first night Þorbjǫrg is somewhat reluctant and mostly silent, *fámálugr*. After the greeting ceremony and an introduction to the farm people, a special meal was prepared for the *vǫlva*; first she was served a porridge of goat's milk and then a stew of hearts from all animals. No comment on the food is offered in the text. The *vǫlva* had brought her own cutlery, which was as remarkable as her clothing: 'She had a spoon of brass and a knife with an ivory shaft, its two halves clasped with a bronze bands, and the point of which had broken off'.[29] As with the cloths, no comment is given on the cutlery either.

After the meal Þorkell, the farmer, approached the *vǫlva* and asked her what she thought about the place and its people. He also made an attempt to bring up subjects everybody was anxious to inquire about. But the *vǫlva* rejected his questions and said that she could not answer until the next morning after having slept. The text does not give us any indication whether or not there is a connection between the meal and her dreams. Before going to sleep the *vǫlva* is asked if she is content, but she keeps her silence.

Not until the next evening do the preparations start again, and for the first time the expression *seiðr* is used in the text. Arrangements to promote the *seiðr* are said to be made, but no details are offered. Before the *seiðr* could begin the *vǫlva* asked for a woman who knew the song that was essential for the ceremony. But no such woman was available. After a while Guðríðr, the guest, said: 'I have neither magical powers [*fjǫlkunnigr*] nor the gift of prophecy [i.e. I am not a wisewoman, *vísindakona*], but in Iceland my foster-mother Halldís taught me chants she called ward songs [*varðlokkur*].'[30] But she refuses to take part in the actual ritual since she is a Christian woman. Her father has left the farm and stays away as long as such pagan ceremonies are performed. With the exception of Guðríðr's rather gentle protests at the beginning and her father's absence, the conflict between the old religion and the new is not explicitly emphasized in this particular text. Þorkell is by no means represented as a pagan; nevertheless he is the one who persuades the young woman to perform the song required for the ceremony. Although nothing is said in the text about his reasons to procure her, it is plausible to think that he invites her out of concern for his farm. As the leading man of the area he knows that the period of famine must be broken.

In contrast to the preparations, the ritual itself is hardly described at all. The women formed a ring around the *hjallr* and Þorbjǫrg sat upon it. Neither the activities of Þorbjǫrg *lítil vǫlva*, nor the *hjallr* is explained, nor if she makes use of her wand or anything else in her equipment. Guðríðr's song, *kvæði*, is said to be the most beautiful ever heard. Considering the details already given in the text it is hard to agree with Strömbäck in his interpretation of the meaning of the *varðlokka* song. He argues that there is an obvious trace of shamanistic trance in the ritual.[31] But nothing is mentioned in the text about the *vǫlva's* soul or any journey of the soul, either in ecstasy or with the body lying down in any kind of altered state of consciousness. The song is just said to be sung and there are no comments on the effect on the participants. Direct influences on the Old Norse world view from circumpolar areas is still a little-investigated field, though most possibly interesting parallels are to be found. To label the performance of *seiðr* as shamanism in a post-Eliade manner seems an all too phenomenological and simplistic approach. In contrast to phenomenological argumentation, Thomas DuBois has recently offered linguistic evidence for Sami and/or Balto-Finnic influence on the Norse practice of *seiðr* (1999).

It is unclear how long it takes to perform the *seiðr*. After the actual ritual Guðríðr is first of all thanked for her achievement. Then the *vǫlva* tells that the spirits, *náttúrur*, are pleased with her beautiful singing. The name of the spirits is not known from mythological narratives either. The *vǫlva* is able to tell that they are pleased to hear the singing. Suggestions have been made that they should be interpreted as *landvættir*. 'Help in exploiting animal wealth is normally credited to *landvættir*, or "guardian spirits" of the country / … . *Landvættir* is grammatically a feminine noun, but when the creatures are represented, they appear either as animals or men' (Jochens 1993: 310). *Dísir* and *alfar* are other beings associated with the household, and as recipients of offerings and as the objects of rituals they could plausibly influence future prosperity. They were all collective beings living under family-like conditions and could in some respects be said to mirror the people of the farm. The well-being of the farmer was the prerequisite of the latter. Ancestors who are concerned about the farm and fertility spirits are spoken of in the same mode. Chasing away the *landvættir* was the goal for Egill Skalla-Grímsson when he was performing his gruesome *níð*.

After the singing the *vǫlva's* important predictions are to be made. The only forecast told at length is about Guðríðr's splendid future – dramatic but prosperous. The prophecy serves the same narrative purpose as foretelling, curses and dreams often do in Icelandic sagas; it outlines the forth-coming text (Conroy 1980: 119f.). The atmosphere is amicable and the *vǫlva* bids Guðríðr farewell and calls her 'my daughter'. This intimacy could be compared to the scene at the beginning when the *vǫlva* greets the peo-ple of the farm according to her opinions about them. The underlying tone is that the performer of the ritual, the *vǫlva*, has some distinct influence over the near future. Not only should the spirits be pleased to assure a flourish-ing summer season, but the *vǫlva* as well. Aggression against a diviner never pays off. Then the scene is settled for the last part of the long ritual and per-haps the most important for the common people – the opportunity for other people from the farm to ask the *vǫlva* what is on their minds. She was quite talkative and the saga states that most of what she said turned out to come true. When the ceremony was all over Þorbjǫrn, Guðríðr's father, was sent for, since he had left the farm while paganism was practised.

What was the author's purpose in providing us with this circumstantial picture of pagan rituals? The episode certainly stands out among other nar-ratives of individual persons in Old Norse literature. One plausible reason could be the wish to formulate a powerful contrast between the old and the new religion, with the two females as icons for old and new *siðr*. *Eiríks saga rauða* as a whole could be read as a glorification of Guðríðr as a favourable character, thus emphasizing the saga as a Christian text. As many scholars have argued, the main character in the saga is the young woman Guðríðr but her dominant position in the text has been interpreted in different ways. Since she is to become the female ancestor of several bishops, some observers note that the young woman's virtues and merits are emphasized throughout the text (Strömbäck 1935: 56ff.). Yet her role as main character can be interpreted from two very different points of view. As there are two prominent female characters important to the *seiðr* – the *vǫlva* and Guðríðr – one could focus on the women's different religious faiths. To begin with, claiming her Christian faith, Guðríðr refuses to take part in the ritual. But after some persuasion she agrees to sing the song necessary for the ritual. A more concealed conflict in the text, between the old traditions and the new, could therefore be stressed. On the other hand, the ritual is never con-demned in the text. Quite the opposite; the *seiðr* ceremony is said to obtain the effect desired. The divination does not seem to be necessarily contradic-tory to the Christian faith, no aggression towards the new religion is expressed. As in other texts, turning back to the old lore seems to be a solu-tion in difficult situations. The vivid scene could be the result of the histori-cal interests of an antiquarian author, who wishes to give a grandiose picture of times passed. The 'exotic' image is of Greenland as something more pagan and wild, a land of settlers, only slowly conquered by Christianity, in contrast to the Christian civilization of Iceland. According to the saga text the only ones who protest against the ceremony are Þorbjǫrn and his daughter, who

had recently arrived from Iceland. The Greenlanders seem to take the ceremony for granted, in all its phases and possibilities.

Instead of pointing to the contrast between Guðríðr and Þorbjǫrg one
could stress the fact that the ritual described is almost exclusively dominated by women and that it is the collaboration between the women that
makes it a success. Without doubt both women are needed for the fulfil-
ment of the ritual. Whether or not the conflict or the collaboration theme
is stressed, *Eiríks saga rauða* is nevertheless a text filled with more details
concerning *seiðr* than any other. Even so, unanswerable questions remain
regarding the actual practice and its meaning.

Several different agents appear on the ritual arena at Heriólfsnes, each of
them adding a perspective to the complexity; the farmer, who has the
social responsibility; the performer, alternately called *spákona* and *vǫlva*; the
singer, the main assistant of the performer; and the other women from the
farm that assemble around the *vǫlva* on the *hjallr* during her performance
and form a circle, co-assisting in some way. There is also an anonymous
'audience' to the ceremony which intermingles with 'the other women' in
a dual role; on the one hand they are co-performers, on the other they
are receivers of the benefits from the ritual. Indirectly, we can surmise a
gender-division of the farm people where the women seem to take a more
active part in the fertility ritual than the men.

The reason given for the promised turn of fortune is that the spirits are
now pleased when Guðríðr has sung the *varðlokka* song, and indirectly we
are led to believe that they have caused the famine. Throughout the chapter the *vǫlva* is the acting and dominant subject of all events and the object
is the people of the farm who have actually asked her to perform the *seiðr*.
There is no tendency to reverse subject and object as is the method for
altering the balance of power in some *trolldómr* stories.

With Connerton's definition in mind we can assume that divinatory
seiðr was a rule-governed social convention. I specially want to emphasize
his statement that a ritual 'draws the attention of its participants to objects
of thought and feeling which they hold to be of special significance'
(Connerton 1989: 44). Divination satisfied both intellect and emotions
since it gave insights into what had caused the famine as well as an impression of security as regards the future. As a semi-public event it was open to
the participation of women who – at least the most prominent among
them – could establish some social authority.

Frequent Themes in Accounts of Seiðr

Eiríks saga rauða is a unique full-length *seiðr* narrative of the whole ritual event, whereas other accounts only give parts or details that never-

theless follow a certain pattern. There were no settled rules for *seiðr* rituals, but some of the saga authors stressed in their texts some symbols
that seemingly must have been associated with such performances. Most
saga writers, in one way or the other, give *seiðr* performers and characters associated with *trolldómr* a marginal position in the text. As there
were reservations about *Eiríks saga rauða*, other accounts of *seiðr* are
likewise questionable as ethnographic sources.

Although the conditions and contexts of the texts may alter, there is
always a distinct purpose for performing *seiðr*. It is never said to be executed accidentally, but always by will. There was always a problem to be
solved, a condition to be changed, or a prediction to be made for the coming season, and for this reason a person with extraordinary knowledge was
called upon. Both the divinatory aspects of *seiðr* and the performed malevolence share this basic feature. When *seiðr* is conceived as a communal divinatory ceremony in sagas this is frequently expressed with an invitation to
the *vǫlva* to perform at quite a grand feast. As *Norna-Gests þáttr* states about
'the old days':

> At that time [Norna-Gest's childhood] wise women [*vǫlur*] used to go
> about the country. They were called 'spae-wives' [*spákonur*], and they
> foretold people's futures. For this reason people used to invite them to
> their houses and gave them hospitality and bestowed gifts on them at
> parting. [32]

The formal organization around the *vǫlva*'s visit hints at an understanding of the ceremony as an established social institution. But as with the
exotic surroundings for the *seiðr* ceremonies many explanations are plausible. The *vǫlur* are said to walk from one farm to another and be invited to
perform at larger gatherings arranged by a host who invites all his people
at the farm to a *seiðr* ceremony and to join the feast. The term *veizla* is
often used for these occasions. *Qrvar Odds saga* tells the following about
the *vǫlva* Heiðr: 'She would go to feasts, telling people about their destinies
and forecasting the weather for the coming winter.'[33] In almost all texts
personal fate and future prosperity are at the centre of interest. In *Vatnsdœla
saga* Ingjaldr and his people invited a Saami woman to *spá*. 'The Lapp
woman, splendidly attired, sat on a high seat. Men left their benches and
went forward to ask about their destinies. For each of them she predicted
that which eventually came to pass.'[34]

Some texts tell of preparations made for the honoured guest. In *Víga-
Glúms saga* we read: 'It was thought very important that housewives in the
area should give her [the *vǫlva*] a good welcome, for what she said was
rather influenced by the hospitality offered her.'[35] Interestingly, the text
goes on to tell about a conflict between the hostess and the *vǫlva*. The former is not content with what she hears and shouts: 'I should have thought

good hospitality deserved something better, and you'll be driven away if you go round predicting evil.'[36] Payment and gifts to the *spákona* are mentioned several times elsewhere and in this case a flavour of dissatisfaction with the result of the divination seems to be at hand. As mentioned above, even Óðinn pays the *vǫlva* with jewellery for advice before *ragnarǫk*.

Quite different from the stories when *seiðr* is performed to cause damage is divinatory *seiðr*, which seems to demand two things: the ceremony both as a joint effort by the community and also as a gathering of a semi-public character. There are no secrecies or hidden activities, just the performance of an expert, sometimes with the assistance of people from the farm. In *Ǫrvar Odds saga* the *seiðkona* comes to the feast with a group of young assistants who form a kind of choir for the nightly performances. It is obvious in *Eiríks saga rauða* how important the joint singing of the *varðlokka* song was to please the spirits. The ritual seemed to be completed with the circle of women around the *vǫlva*. In the exceptional ritual referred to in the *Vǫlsa þáttr* all the people from the farm come together to sing to and praise the cult object, Vǫlsi.

One text of great interest – although it does not mention any of the usual *trolldómr* terminology – is the observations made by the Arabic writer Ibn Fadlan, who encountered Vikings sailing down the Volga at the beginning of the tenth century. In a context utterly different from that of the sagas, he describes parts of a funeral ceremony that lasted for several days. Vital elements recognizable from texts in an Icelandic setting appear also in the Muslim writer's chronicle. Before the chieftain is burnt on his ship a kind of divination ritual is said to be performed by his company with the whole crew participating. Songs are mentioned and there is a woman at the centre of the performances.

An old woman, called 'the angel of death', and her two daughters assist in the long preparations for the chieftain's last journey. A young slave woman is selected to accompany him and she plays an essential role in the different parts of the ritual. In the final ceremony she is lifted over a wooden gate or frame construction and is thereby able to look into other dimensions of reality. As a kind of mediator the slave girl tells that she can see the realm of the dead and leaves messages for the other participants. The similarities with *seiðr* and the ceremony conducted by the farmer's wife in *Vǫlsa þáttr* have caught the attention of several scholars who point at the climbing or lifting up as essential to the diviner (Steinsland and Vogt 1981; Andrén 1993).

Incantation and the importance of singing are very much stressed in both Eddic poetry and the historical chronicles of the sagas. In the moment of vocalization the loud utterance made the words an absolute and concrete reality. Spells cast could not be removed with less than equally strong words. The climbing of the *hjallr* and the use of other equipment could either be textual markers of otherness or tools necessary for successful rituals. Undoubtedly the most intricate description of special clothing is Þorbjǫrg lítil-vǫlva in *Eiríks saga rauða*. No other *seiðr* performer is given such an outstanding outfit. Their outward appearance is in most cases not mentioned at all. A few other texts mention the wand, *stafr*, but we have no description of its ritual use. Hoods like Þorbjǫg's do also appear in relation to performers, but more to protect against the gaze of a knowledgeable person who performs destructive *seiðr* when captured and punished.

The *seiðr* performer was obviously not conceived of as an ordinary person and this discrepancy had to be marked in the text. But the variation between the individual sagas is so great that no fixed pattern can be established. For the saga writer a choice of different possibilities was available. As we have seen, the executor was a temporary guest and the performance was at night. Old age was one way to represent the old lore, i.e. the ancient traditions.

Along with age, ethnicity is the strongest marker of otherness, as when the Celtic Kotkell family performs *seiðr* in *Laxdœla saga* 35ff. (Sayers 1992: 133). When *finnir*, i.e. Finns and Saami people, appear they often serve as a warning in saga texts. Trouble is bound to come since these people were believed to be more skilled in *trolldómr* than others (Page 1964; Mundal and Steinsland 1989: 108). In *Hálfdanar saga svarta* a Saami man is captured and tortured in order to make him reveal clandestine things to the king. However, violence is not the way to make the Saami speak, whose spiritual strength lasts longer than brute force. The Latin chronicle *Historia Norwegiae*, an anonymous text from the latter part of the twelfth century, dedicates a whole chapter to the Saami and their extraordinary physical and spiritual abilities. Their use of *gandr*, their ability to achieve temporary guise, is especially stressed and conceived of as a terrible threat. Marriages to Saami women in Old Norse texts always turn out to be disastrous. In *Vatnsdœla saga* 10 a Saami woman is invited to tell fortunes according to the old traditions since such women did not always give bad prophecies, if treated well. Like the *vǫlva* in mythological narratives she is both feared and needed, and clearly defined to be of another kind – in *Vǫluspá* as raised by *jǫtnar*, in the sagas by ethnicity. Along with some more ethnographic notions on their nomadic life, skills in hunting and use of snow shoes and skies, Saxo tells of how Saamis are known to be able to deceive the sight of victims by illusion (V: 138).

King Haraldr of Norway in *Haralds saga ins hárfagra* is in raptures over the beauty of Snjófriðr, daughter of a Saami king. The young woman serves the king a cup of mead and when he takes her hand the text assures us that he feels as if fire burns his skin. Spellbound he marries the beautiful Snjófriðr and forgets his royal duties. Ordinary people's pleas are not sufficient to free the king's mind from what Snjófríðr has done to bind him. When she dies the king mourns inconsolably for three years and her body does not decompose – until the king is advised by a knowledgeable person to change the cloth under the corpse. Her body immediately begins to change. When burnt the truth is revealed; snakes, lizards, and other foul animals come out of her body. The imagery is significant for the hybridity of the Viking age: local conceptions about ethnic neighbours meet Christian themes of rejection. Since the early days of Christianity demons and devils – and persons associated with such creatures – were linked to foul animals. Physical contact in this case seems to be the solution to revealing the true nature of the Saami wife.

The performer of *trolldómr* was given a marginal status. Nevertheless, she or he was an important person, whom people depended upon. This ambiguity runs more or less constantly throughout the *seiðr* corpus. A clear example is in *Norna-Gests þáttr* 11 where three *spákonur* tell the fortune of young Gestr. The performing women are interchangeably called *spákonur*, *vǫlur* and *nornir*. One of them, who does not gain the estimation required, announces an ominous fortune for the little boy: he will not live longer than the candle beside him lasts. He is rescued by one of the other *spákonur* who blows the candle out and gives it to Gestr's mother. The account is skilfully placed at the end of the story so that in the following chapter Gestr can finally light the candle when he concludes that, at the age of 300, he has lived a full life.

The Cult of the Vǫlsi *and Other Private Rituals*

One of the few examples of private religious ceremonies in Old Norse literature can be read in the so called *Vǫlsa þattr*, an insertion of prose and poetry in the longer *Ólafs saga hins helga*. It is a story of conversion and describes King Ólafr's incognito visit to a remote farm in the far north of Norway. The disguised king and his company witness a remarkable ritual, in which the *vǫlsi*, a preserved horse phallus, is worshipped as a god. The text states that these people have no knowledge about the true faith. The local fertility ceremony is performed by the people from the farm and, according to the text, the ritual is first introduced, and then continously led, by the farmer's wife. The private character and the female activity makes it a unique description. The *þáttr* refers to an old *kvæði* (poem) as the origin of the story and through the thirteen stanzas the agents in the text are given individual voices in their relation to the cult of the *vǫlsi*.

Various aspects of this text have been analyzed by Gro Steinsland and Kari Vogt (1981). They make several new suggestions, stressing the text as a possible source for our knowledge of everyday religion. However, it is not my intention to take part in the discussion about the character of the ceremony and what it is aimed at, but only to notice their interpretation of the farmer's wife as a local *vǫlva* with the ability not only to foresee the future, but also to make it prosperous.

Actually two rituals are described. First, there is a preservation ceremony during which the horse phallus is embalmed in a piece of linen-cloth with onions and herbs. Secondly, there is the daily evening ritual when the farmer's wife takes the *vǫlsi* out of its coffin and brings it to the farm people. They sit together, they all take the *vǫlsi* in their hands, and each member of the household sings an individual verse, *kvæði*, to it. The phallus is simultaneously worshipped as a deity and sacrificed. The cult object is spoken to in terms of an offering and the receiver(s) are named *mǫrnir*. The identity of these powers is disputable and has caused debate. Fertility powers like *dísir* have been suggested, as well as the fertility god Freyr, and Steinsland and Vogt argue for giantesses. The first one to address the *vǫlsi* is the farmer's wife. She greets it and praises its size and strength – and calls it a 'gift' to the *mǫrnir*.

Disgusted by witnessing this pagan ceremony, the Christian king throws the *vǫlsi* to the farm dog, which swallows it immediately. King Ólafr reveals his identity and, since the saga is the story of a saint, he converts the whole farm and the *þáttr* ends.

Of special interest to the present discussion on *trolldómr* is the question whether the farmer's wife could be regarded as a performing *vǫlva* or not. Steinsland and Vogt offer two arguments which relate the farmer's wife to the activities of a *vǫlva* (1981: 103f.). The first one is the etymological connection between *vǫlr* (wand), *vǫlva* and *vǫlsi*. They suggest that the *vǫlsi* might be the equivalent of the wand in the cultic activities of the woman. But there are few examples of wands ritually used by *vǫlur* and, therefore, the second argument must be regarded as the stronger, which concerns the following points. Certainly a most interesting detail is that the ritual seems not to end when the *vǫlsi* is thrown away by the king. The farmer's wife, although very upset, can complete her ritual with a formula. In stanza 13 she asks to be raised over the door-frame so that she can rescue the offering that has been destroyed. The lifting up can be plausibly connected to the ability *at spá*, of foreseeing, with the door serving as a metaphor for seeing into 'another side'. Like Þorbjǫrg lítil-vǫlva and the slave girl, the woman climbs the tree construction as a part of the ritual performance. When the farmer's wife's worship is violently interrupted, her ability to use her gaze helps her to fulfil the ceremony in the way the knowledgeable always can, since they see what is clandestine to others. The divinatory aspect is what Steinsland and Vogt call 'the real and the immaterial aspects of the ritual' (1981: 104). For comparative reasons it can be added that in Tacitus' account of Germanic devination, the seeress Veleda is said to be kept in a high tower from which she answers questions (*Historiae* 4.65).

A third argument could be added to Steinsland and Voigt's in order to establish such a connection between the farmer's wife and *volur* is the close link to fertility and good living conditions. Future prosperity is also present in many activities performed by a *volva*. There is nothing in the text indicating any divination of individual futures, which – as we have seen in other texts – is a vital element in most *seiðr*-rituals. But collective prosperity is saved by the actions undertaken by the woman in charge of the rituals.

When trying to analyse *Volsa þáttr* many of the same problems occur as when discussing the *seiðr* ceremony in *Eíriks saga rauða*. In both cases an elaborate ritual is described and in the conversion story an exotic and heathen context is constructed in the text, as wild and remote as Greenland. Nevertheless the ceremony can be connected to a certain pattern of ritual practices, as stressed before. Two radically different positions can be argued for: either the *volsi* ritual is a burlesque of the hideous manners of the pagans of the far north, or it is a plausible model of local religious life.

It is told that only the daughter of the farm recognizes the guest at once as the king, but she does not reveal his true identity. Since the text is on the whole very well structured it is very tempting to read this detail as an image of the young generation's attitude regarding the new religion in contrast to the older generation's and the old religion. In this perspective, it can be noted that the farmer's wife is looked upon as stubbornly holding on to the heathen faith. At the beginning of the text she is said to be dominant and determined and at the end to be the most reluctant towards the new religion. Old women in other texts also serve as representatives of ancient lore. Those two features – age and gender – were, on the other hand, not the most important when trying to gain public authority to speak. What remained was 'corrosive discourse' (Lincoln 1994).

The famous *Buslubæan* that appears in the fifth chapter of *Bósa saga ok Herrauðs* is a poem that emphasizes the power of the spoken word to a greater extent than many other Old Norse texts (Kress 1993: 57ff.; Naumann 1993). The text is divided into three parts; the first seven stanzas follow each other, while the two last are anticipated by prose insertions. With its nine verses the text constitutes a unique example in Old Norse literature of how a saga writer has made use of the poetic form of spells and the supposed power of far-reaching strong words. Poetry appears with some frequency in the prose texts, but to my knowledge this is the longest use of the spell form in any saga. With its strong words the spell adds intensity to the conflict in the chapter. The narrative focuses on a dispute between King Hringr and an old woman, Busla, known for her wisdom. Her prayer is a petition to release the two imprisoned heroes of the saga, one of them the king's own son, the other her foster son. But what begins as a plea ends as a curse. The introductory prose gives some interesting details about the character of Busla. No really negative words are used, but her skills are apparently conceived of as ambiguous old-time lore, *tǫfr*.

The knowledgeable woman's monologue identifies itself by name in the second stanza, *Buslubœn*, 'Busla's prayer'. It is specifically called *bœn*, prayer, a word common in Christian terminology, and not *galdr*, *kvæði* or anything else we could easily translate as spell or charm. Still the poem is emphasized as pagan and 'wicked'.

> Busla appeared in the king's bedroom and recited a prayer which has been known as 'Busla's Prayer' ever since. It has become famous everywhere, and contains many wicked words unfit for Christian mouths.[37]

In this text the recurring motif of the performer of *trolldómr* as an old person with access to ancient lore and almost lost knowledge, *tǫfr*, appears again. Both before and after the poem explicit references are made to the new religion, as in *Grettis saga* discussed above. Nevertheless, Busla is asked to assist in a problematic situation and the text reveals at this point an ambiguous attitude towards the old religion.

Busla is not at all presented as an evil person and, from the saga author's point of view, she is supportive and loyal to her fosterson. Even so, what she threatens King Hringr with must fall under the category of performed malevolence. The use of the spoken word in an attempt to break fetters and release prisoners is not exclusively an Old Norse tradition. Release is the theme of the first Merseburg Charm and Bede's *Historia Ecclesiastica* 4: 22 as well as the Christian legend of St Paul's visit to and imprisonment in Rome.

The first part of *Buslubœn* constitutes a kind of invocation to listen to Busla. The king must realize her capacity when she threatens to make her words known all over the world, which will disgrace the man who is prepared to kill his own son. Busla's speech is necessarily 'corrosive' since she is neither the right person to command a king, nor does she choose the right time or place (the king's bedroom). There is force and confidence in her words and from the third verse she lets her powers loose. In the following verse Busla gives a catalogue of the bad things that will happen to the king if her plea is not obeyed. King Hringr will experience physical pain, and snakes and demons will attack him. Busla will raise storms and turn all nature against him; ships and horses will fail him and he will be an easy target for all trolls. Stanzas 3 to 7 express common views about what knowledgeable persons are supposed to be able to inflict on their opponents and show similarities to the catalogues of *trolldómr* abilities in Eddic poetry.

> Soon I shall dart
> Close to your heart
> With poison snakes
>   to gnaw your breast:
> Deafen your ears,
> Blind you with tears.[38]
> (trans. by Pálsson and Edwards 1985: 206)

Neither the place nor the mode is proper in addressing a king. Busla ends her threats with a hint about king Hringr's impotence and lost manliness; thereby she challenges him both as a man and as a ruler:

> And what a shame
> When you play the game,
> When she's on her back
> But you've lost the knack:
> Would you like to hear some more[39]
> (trans. by Pálsson and Edwards 1985: 206f.)

In the following prose the king is very upset and attempts to attack Busla with physical violence, to silence her, to cut her off, calling her *vánd vættr*, 'evil demon' or 'spirit'. But Busla has bound him with her spell. He cannot rise from his bed to attack her and the servants around him are put to sleep. We recognize from other sagas the aggressive attempt to stop the knowledgeable when unfavourable words are uttered. Thus, in this case nothing can hinder the forceful words uttered by Busla. She continues and her threats escalate. All kinds of supernatural beings are let loose according to her curse, all the beings that will attack if King Hringr does not obey Busla's plea to release the prisoners. They are called trolls, elves (*alfar*), knowledgeable norns (*tǫfranornir*), and different names for giants and demonic beings: *búar, bergrisar, hrímþursar* – beings presented as stronger than the power of the king.

After this cascade the king meets Busla's petition half-way and agrees to release one of the prisoners, his own son, but not her fosterson.

> 'In that case, I'll have to deal with you further,' said Busla. Then she started reciting the so-called 'Syrpa verses' which hold the most power-ful magic, and which nobody is allowed to sing after sunset.[40]

The final stanza is supposedly the strongest and if her plea is not fulfilled the king must either solve a riddle of six names or the worst of Busla's pre-dictions will come true. After the verse a line with runic letters is inserted, which is supposed to be the riddle. Facing this predominance the king gives up. Next day the prisoners are released and the following chapter recounts that the two men always followed Busla's advice in their future business. Neither equipment nor symbols are mentioned in *Buslubœn*. The text concentrates entirely on the spoken word. It is most likely that the poem existed as an individual text which the saga author made use of in a new context.

Spells were thought of as useful for distinct purposes, such as attempts to manipulate weather and love, and at hindering an opponent, and they are in that sense close to the catalogues of *Hávamál*, *Sigdrífumál* and other Eddic poems. A comparison could be made between *Buslubœn* and the second Old High German Merseburg Charm. Both texts are constructed in terms of a direct confrontation. The speakers are directly addressing the source of trouble. There seems to be a certain psychology in the conviction that there are benefits in facing a complicated situation with direct speech as a counteraction. Busla is threatening and plays with the double nature of *trolldómr*. With its divergent possibilities she cannot only release the prisoners, but must also put a curse on the reluctant king.

Performed Malevolence

Sinister characters, who operate on behalf of themselves or others, are far more frequent in the sagas than actual divination rituals. A certain pattern appears in connection with these actions of performed malevolence. There is always a sender, i.e. the person who performs or acts, who has the knowledge needed. This character is not always visible from the beginning. The act can be performed in great secrecy, and it can be part of the plot and the narrative strategy not to reveal the cause of the misfortune until much later in the text. The sender always makes use of an instrument to ahieve the goal. It can be the spoken word: a song, a formula or some kind of spell. Most often it involves an act, elaborate or simple, or even a full ritual. Some texts mention the use of concrete objects, like blood or a piece of wood. Signs and symbols like runes can be included. The intricate question of the use of the runes must be discussed in this context. The sender's use of the instrument(s) aims at a result. Something must be changed in favour of the person who initiates the performance, not necessarily the sender. However, it must be remembered that similar rituals were used for gaining prosperity, healing, and protection.

It is therefore important to ask: malevolence – from whose perspective? The sagas, as any other texts, are never neutral. Most explicitly they tell of a survey of events from a certain family's point of view, amalgamated with all the loyalties, animosities, and tensions of the group. *Trolldómr* rituals are often supposed to be executed among the enemies as an indication of how bad they really are. Everything else in a saga text may be obscure, but the conflicts are always lucid in the plot.

Þorbjǫrn and his Fostermother Fighting the Outlaw Grettir

An elaborate story of performed malevolence can be read in *Grettis saga* 78 and onwards. One of Grettir's enemies, Þorbjǫrn ǫngull, wants revenge and the reward for killing the outlaw Grettir. Despite the fact that Grettir is an outlaw the reader's sympathies are with him. He has caused a great deal of trouble but is certainly not characterized as an evil person. And Þorbjǫrn is also fully aware of the fact that he cannot overcome Grettir's greater strength with ordinary means. He needs old-time knowledge. Grettir's mother has previously warned her son, when interpreting an ominous dream, that he will never leave the island where he has entrenched himself, and she has also given him the advice to keep away from knowledgeable persons (ch. 69). Her words are also a hint that her son cannot escape his destiny. Knowing that Grettir is forceful, Þorbjǫrn asks his fostermother Þuríðr to support him. The old woman is said to have been of great knowledge in her younger days, and described as *fjǫlkunnig mjǫk og margkunnig mjǫk*, perhaps the most frequent terms to characterize knowledgeable people. Her age makes her a representative of ancient traditions and lore. The text relates her explicitly to the old religion, in contrast to the new customs. Þorbjǫrn is making use of his foster-mother's knowledge and once again the question can be raised whether a purely negative characterization of what is done in the name of *trolldómr* is really appropriate. From Þuríðr's perspective she is only supporting her own kinsfolk against their mutual enemies.

The knowledgeable woman's strategy towards such a strong opponent is action in several stages. She asks Þorbjǫrn repeatedly to follow her instructions, *ráð*, precisely.[41] A process of careful consideration slowly begins, nothing is done hastily, and over and over again it is repeated that Þorbjǫrn must follow the old woman's advice exactly. After a long time Þuríðr requests him to go to Grettir on Drangey. She wants to accompany him, hidden in the boat so that she can make her important calculations of the *hamingja* of the victims – then she can decide what words are suitable against them. She makes a prognosis about how much luck they have,[43] and tells Þorbjǫrn of the difficulties he will have to struggle against. It will not be an easy victory, the fostermother can foresee, and he must be prepared for adversity to begin with. And of utmost importance – he must depend on her and her decisions completely. Þuríðr follows the company onto the island to have a look at Grettir and his men. Apparently, she has the capacity to conduct a form of mental X-ray. After her observations she can state that they are strong, but without luck, *hamingjalausir*, i.e. without *hamingja*. Thereafter she is prepared to confront them. With all this power-ful information she lays Grettir under a curse that works as a prediction of how the balance of power will change:

'Now I curse you, Grettir, to be deprived of all favour, all endowments and fortune, all defence and wisdom, the more so the longer you live. I trust that you will have fewer days of happiness in the future than you have had until now.'[43]

With her uttered words she takes away not only his luck and fortune, *gipt ok gæfa*, but also all possibilities of help and wisdom. From Grettir's answer we can gather that he knows that he has lost: 'No words have ever unsettled me more than those that she spoke.'[44] His reaction against the old woman is very violent, not because she represents paganism, but because she is threatening him with her knowledge. Most of all he is afraid of her spoken words, being well aware of his mother's predictions. He throws a large stone at her and her leg breaks. Helga Kress has noted the similarity between Grettir's behaviour against Þuríð and the custom of stoning persons accused of *trolldómr* to death. The conflict with the knowledgeable turns out to be a vital part of this plot too, only it must be noted that this time there is no Christian opposition as in other scenes of the sagas.

Þorbjǫrn is very disappointed with the trip to Drangey, but Þuríðr can comfort him; this is only the beginning of Grettir's hard times. Þorbjǫrn still thinks he has made a fool of himself, eager as he is for immediate results. Nevertheless, a long time passes before the old woman makes her second move – the ritual. Since she is severely injured in her leg she is carried down to the beach, where her actions are carefully described:

He did as she requested, and when she reached the shore she hobbled along by the sea as if following directions, until she came to a tree lying there, a stub with the roots on, big enough to have to be carried on a man's shoulders. She looked at the tree and asked the men to turn it over for her. The underside looked burnt and rubbed down. She made them scrape a flat surface where the tree had been rubbed, then took her knife and carved runes into the root, smeared them with her blood and recited spells. Then she walked backwards and withershins around it, and spoke many mighty pronouncements upon it. After that she had the tree put to sea, pronouncing that it should drift out to Drangey, 'and may it harm Grettir in every way.'[45]

The old woman is consistently obeyed and the young man is loyally giving her assistance. Clandestine forces are guiding the fostermother. Her movements in walking backwards, counter-clockwise, make the ritual appear strange, as ancient and exotic as the clothing of the *vǫlva* in *Eiríks saga rauða*. The use of the wood and the carving of runes might be compared to *tréníð*, ritual defamation (when destructive runes are carved into a tree). Again there are reasonable narrative purposes for the conspicuous scenery; the author's intention is apparently to make the story seem odd and old.

Distant 'powers' seem to guide Þorbjǫrg. She is well prepared and can perform an elaborate ritual. Was the smearing of blood something spectacular to the saga audience, as it is to a modern reader? Was it a way of making the Christian audience understand how cruel the pagan rituals were?

It is an elaborate performance, well prepared in several stages. Þuríðr is probably operating with a piece of wood that has previously been used for *trolldómr*. The fostermother uses her sensitivity, and makes no over-hasty moves. Her instruments are the wood and her own blood, the carving of runes and her spell, the spoken word. She sends a tangible object against the victim. She is the performer, the medium, through which the wishes of the assigner are sent, although Þorbjǫrn is ignorant of how and why he has to rely on her. Some texts stress the importance of physical contact when *trolldómr* is performed, such as *Vatnsdæla saga* 44 where Þorkell can make his enemy speechless at the *þing* by touching him with a *spákona*'s wand. In the text discussed the moment of touch seems to be the turning point for events to go in a new direction.

Powerful forces are let loose and the results are bound to be quickly evident. Grettir twice tries to avoid contact with the piece of wood, having a sense of danger, but the third time it is brought to the house by the thrall. When chopping it up for firewood Grettir is wounded and is thereafter a weak and vulnerable target for his enemies. Þuríðr's deeds have fulfilled what Grettir's mother had foreseen in her dreams and warned her son about.

There are both similarities and differences when Þuríðr's deeds are compared to the *seiðr* performed by Þorbjǫrg *lítil-vǫlva* on Greenland. The same terminology is used for their capacities. Divination is performed, calculations and predictions are made, but the intention behind the act differs completely. *Grettis saga* tells of an exclusive private ritual where the goal is only to harm and eliminate the enemy. Þuríðr's ritual is a private ceremony for the benefit of an individual and her kin, an affair of interpersonal and interfamily conflict, not an event shared by a local community.

Kotkell Performs Seiðr Twice with his Family

Another story of some length about performed malevolence comes from *Laxdæla saga* (ch. 35ff.). It differs from the account in *Eiríks saga rauða* in several interesting matters. The *trolldómr* is performed by male practitioners for entirely destructive reasons and the activities are strongly condemned. The same kind of society forms the background, but in *Laxdæla saga* other themes are in focus. It tells of how Kotkell and his family – his wife and two grown-up sons – perform ceremonies causing death and disaster in the local community. It is interesting to note how the family acts together in these rituals and how they are treated as a group, not primarily as individuals. The succession of knowledge is evidently conceived of as kept within the family, to give a flavour of uninterrupted transmission. In some sense Kotkell himself takes the lead as head of the family, but there is no obvious gender division in the performances expressed in the text. No action is commented on as unmanly or with any equivalent term, but rather as immoral and, above all, foreign. The family is said to be from the Hebrides and to be newcomers to Iceland. When introduced, these people are given a description with negative connotations: 'all of them skilled in witchcraft [*mjǫk fjǫlkunnig*] and accomplished magicians [*mestu seiðmenn*]'.[46] Their foreign origin is emphasized in the episode and ethnicity serves here very clearly as a marker of otherness (Sayers 1992: 133ff.). Soon they are involved in local conflicts and Kotkell is offering the family's skills as a way of establishing allegiances in the new place. The family is said not to work particularly hard to support itself, which might indicate that they were also suspected of using their abilities and *trolldómr* knowledge to gain prosperity without hard labour. Such abilities are labelled 'magical milk theft' in later Scandinavian folklore and were literary and iconographic motifs on the Continent during the Middle Ages. In the Christian context both theological discourse and more didactic ambitions to explain the origins of evil were focused on the devil as a character. Such a figure could be used to visualize the sum and substance of the message existentially and ontologically as well as mythologically. The very existence of devils and demons was constantly confirmed by the Church in sermons, ceremonies and iconography. The attributes of these creatures that were impressed during the process of Christianization and further on during the Middle Ages have their origin in ancient Greece and the Near East. All over Europe the Christian mission could identify the demonized gods with the devils and fiends with cloven hoofs, tails and horns. Many stories, motifs and themes in the Old Norse literature are adaptations from a widespread Continental corpus of texts and pictures.

The *Laxdœla* text does not give any details of the ceremonies, but rather a striking and detailed picture of the conflict pattern behind them. First, the family members are accused of theft and of being knowledgeable, *þjófnaðr ok fjǫlkynig*, and are condemned to outlawry. However, there is never a formal trial at the *Alþingi*, since Kotkell and his family immediately take up the struggle against the accusation by performing *seiðr* with dramatic consequences. Kotkell raises a *seiðhjallr* and the whole family gets up to sing *galdr* songs. As a result a storm arises and causes the death of Kotkell's antagonists at sea. The family uses the *seiðhjallr*, an object of obscure construction that is also mentioned in *Eiríks saga rauða*, as their collective equipment. The text stresses that this object is climbed by the performers, the direction being clearly upwards, but no technical explanation is given. The core of the ceremony seems instead to be the use of the spoken word, in the form of powerful songs.[47] The ceremony is a joint effort by the whole family with a direct and fatal effect.

This *trolldómr* action leads to an escalation of the conflict and people in the area want the Kotkell family killed (ch. 36). Once again the family make use of local conflicts just as they are used themselves by people in the neighbourhood – in transactions between the families:

> Þorleikr then approached his tenants, Kotkell and Gríma, to ask them to take some action to discredit Hrútr [Þorleikr's enemy]. They agreed readily and promised to get right to work.[48]

For the second time the family performs a *seiðr* ceremony together. The song is said to be very beautiful but also strange. It is directed towards a certain person, who understands the purpose and therefore forbids his people to leave the house during the night. But to the young son of the house the sounds of the *seiðr* are irresistible and he walks out of the house only to fall dead immediately. This is quite similar to what happened to Þiðrandi in *Þiðranda þáttr*, who was enticed out of the house and killed by the *dísir*. In *Laxdæla saga* nothing is said about which powers or beings actually kill the boy – just that the sounds of the song from the Kotkells overpower him. The scene – with the foreign family singing outdoors in the night, while the local people have entrenched themselves inside the farmhouse – is a powerful image of the contrast between outside and inside, of being part of society and in a double meaning standing outside it (ch. 37). This situation corresponds more than in any other description of *seiðr* to the mythological struggle between aggressive destruction and cosmological order, between the misfits and the settled.

After the death of the boy, full revenge is inevitable. Kotkell and his wife are soon found and stoned to death. That place is thereafter called Skrattavarði, a derivation from *skratti* and *seiðrskratti*, other related terms for people of knowledge and destructive powers. The burial-mounds of such persons could be dangerous, as the *Laxdæla saga* tells further on in another context (ch. 76). A very pious Christian woman is disturbed during her nightly prayers and when the floor is opened on the recommendation of a returning dead:

> Under the ground they found bones, which were blackened and horrible, along with a chest pendant and a large magician's staff [*seiðstafr mikill*]. People then decided that a prophetess must have been buried here [*vǫluleiði*, a prophetess's grave]. The bones were moved to a remote place little frequented by men.[49]

Apparently the power of the old bones could not be overcome. The remains of the *vǫlva* could be moved, but their power could not be completely destroyed.

The *trolldómr* and *seiðr* story in *Laxdœla saga* is skilfully woven around a series of actions and counteractions. The accusations of theft and extraordinary knowledge lead to a spiral of conflicts with violent deaths and great anger among the local people. The final revenge and the punishments of the Kotkel family are undertaken by the local people without any formal trial.

No general classification of *seiðr* can be made according to the terminology in use, since only a vague distinction as to the intention of the rituals is adopted as a narrative tool by the saga authors. Still, compared to *Eiríks saga rauða* 4 there are some similarities of interest, even if the purpose of the acts are entirely different. In both texts the scenes of the *seiðr* ceremonies are focused on the singing on the *hjallr*, but there is no technical information. Obviously the equipment is of less interest than the power and effect of the spoken word. In both texts the *trolldómr* knowledge is considered to be of old times and associated with geographical fringes, Greenland and the Hebrides.

Apotropaic Acts and Rituals

Although the introduction to this section speaks of '*seiðr* for better or worse' I find it reasonable to deal with the positive aspects of *trolldómr* and *seiðr* in a briefer part at the end. There are fewer Old Norse texts focusing on healing (DuBois 1999: 93ff.), but on the other hand there is more comparable material from the Continent. Among these protective practices we will not find any descriptions of grand rituals or elaborate ceremonies, merely modest acts of protection against what were conceived as *trolldómr* assaults. In this category of rejecting diffuse negative influence I also include different attempts to achieve relief from physical and mental disease. Seeking to arouse or subdue love follows basically the same pattern.

Stories of *trolldómr* attacks do not always end with the person aimed at being harmed; they are in most cases followed by apotropaic acts and rituals concerned with revealing the sender and the source of the assault. These counteractions were based on the same methods and theories as the primary attack. One way was to attempt to harm the attacker's temporary body in order to accomplish an analogous injury on his or her ordinary body. This visible mark had a triple function. It was a punishment, it revealed the guilty party to the public and finally the counteraction served as a cure and the *trolldómr* attack was obstructed (Raudvere 1993: 173ff., 1995). Illness and mischief were conceived to be sent from outside, following the conceptual framework of the conflict between inside and outside. Following this pattern, knowledge of how to battle against misfortune also comes from contact with destructive powers.

Some lyrical catalogues were previously discussed, predominantly in Eddic poetry, with advice, threats and possibilities – the 'gnomic discourse type' as Margaret Clunies Ross calls them (1990: 221). They form long lists of capabilities and of knowledge attainable after training and struggle. *Hávamál* tempts with the knowledge and understanding of many clandestine matters:

> Do you know how to carve, do you know how to interpret,
> do you know how to stain, do you know how to test out,
> do you know how to ask, do you know how to sacrifice,
> do you know how to dispatch, do you know how to slaughter?[50]
> (trans. by Larrington 1996: 35)

In a healing perspective, parts of *Hávamál* and *Sigdrífumál* of the *Poetic Edda* are of special interest, as in both poems the metre of spells is used. *Sigdrífumál* is an excursus from the heroic Sigurðr cycle (known in Old High German versions as well) and the better part of the poem consists of stanzas on the knowledge of runes and the art of carving and chanting them (Andersson 1980: 81ff., 101ff.). The introductory prose tells of how the hero Sigurðr finds a sleeping person surrounded by a wall of shields. When Sigurðr slits the clothes with his sword what first seems to be a man, this 'he', turns out to be a woman. She presents herself as a valkyrie, and thanks the hero for rescuing her from her deep sleep by giving him the long catalogue of useful runes, that is healing songs. According to Anne Heinrich, 'Sigurð's encounter with her can be viewed as the final episode of his youthful education' (1986: 115). Two of the stanzas (4, 11) refer directly to healing practices, while the others are either more general or speak of victory, revenge etc. Before chanting the runes the woman offers Sigurðr a horn of mead, which gives strength to his memory, *minnisveig*, and promises wisdom, mighty spells and healing hands.[51] Then he is ready to learn:

> 'Limb-runes you must know if you want to be a healer
> and know how to see to wounds;
> on bark they must be cut and of the tree of the wood,
> on those whose branches bend east.'[52]
> (trans. by Larrington 1996: 168)

In Old Norse literature many things harmful to the individual body, to luck or prosperity or to the family or kingroup, were conceived of as projectiles. Therefore, powerful words and rituals were used to stop a threat often visualized as an arrow, a missile aimed at a certain target by a distinctive sender. A verbal projection could be as effective an answer as physical strength. The sagas tell of different ways of making weapons powerful, of deceiving of sight and of wonderful helmets of invisibility.

Not only humans could be supported, but also cattle and other farm animals. The same type of verses and spells are found in large numbers in later Scandinavian folklore. The Anglo Saxon charms also give many examples of spells against physical illness caused by elves and demons: elf-shot, elven race, dwarfs, etc. (Grendon 1909: 208; Page 1964; Gay 1988).

Healing physical and mental pain or even raising the dead is the explicit aim of some Eddic *galdr* songs. Not only Óðinn but also Freyja can be associated with curative processes. Probably it is Freyja who speaks in *Fjǫlsvinnsmál* 49 where an interesting intermingling of healing and sexual longing emerges:

> Long I waited
> on Lyfjaberg
> day on day I waited for you;
> now it has happened,
> that I anticipated,
> my lover, you have come to my halls.[53]
> (trans. by Robertson 1991: 84)

The verb *lyfja* is not very common in Old Norse, but in later Scandinavian languages it is quite frequent and forms several compounds like *lifja* and *lövja* in association with *trolldómr* and healing. The latter form is used by Christian writers before and after the Reformation as a broad term for all kinds of paganism and superstition. In Old Norse the nouns *taufr* and *lyf* can refer to knowledge of healing, but are mostly used in their negative meaning of damage or destruction.

Egils saga Skalla-Grímssonar 72 gives a lucid example of the process of action and counteraction in a healing procedure performed by Egill himself. A young woman is laid up in bed, weak and feeble, due to runes cut against her. She is described as the victim of a rejected suitor, who had failed in his attempt to handle the runes. Instead of raising love he had caused her illness. Apparently the knowledge of rune carving was not easily accessible. Due to his sufficient knowledge, Egill finds the runes, cut on a fish-bone, in the woman's bed and immediately burns it. Thereafter, as a confirmation of the failure of the unskilled carver, Egill sings:

> No man should carve runes
> unless he can read them well;
> many a man goes astray
> around those dark letters.
> On the whalebone I saw
> ten secret letters carved,
> from them the linden tree [i.e. woman]
> took her long hair.[54]
> (trans. by Scudder 1997: 143)

New runes, apparently more powerful, are cut by Egill and the young woman is freed from her paralysing weakness. Egill is said to be generously rewarded by the family, in the same manner as the direct payment or reward given to the *seiðr* performers.

A particular aspect of healing through spells is the aid given to women at childbirth (Mundal and Steinsland 1989: 104f.; Morris 1993: 78ff.). *Sigdrífumál* 9 mentions what are called *bjargrúnar*, runes that can help at delivery. It is interesting to note that Sigrdrífa's advice in the long catalogue of charms is directed to a man. The stanza relates to help, healing and strength in general.

> 'Helping-runes you must know if you want to assist
> and release children from women;
> they shall be cut on the palms and clasped on the joints,
> and then the *dísir* asked for help.'[53]
> (trans. by Larrington 1996: 168)

There is a distinct physical contact between the helper and the woman in need. The runes on the hand serve as mediators for the healing power. Nothing is said here about whether any special ritual was needed to get help from the dísir, but it seems that the powerful spoken word could be accompanied by some kind of ceremony in favour of these protective fertility deities. Not only the female dísir were challenged. In Oddrúnargrátr other mythological beings are addressed by Oddrún when trying to help with delivery pains. It can be noted that the Old Norse text mentions the vættir. Like the dísir this is a group of a collective character, living nearby the farmhouse under family-like conditions, but not exclusively female. In later Scandinavian folklore there is a great number of legends telling of females from the 'little people' coming to help women in childbed. Along with the vættir Oddrún asks the goddesses Frigg and Freyja for help:

> 'May all the kindly beings help you,
> Frigg and Freyja and more of the gods,
> as you warded away that dangerous illness from me.'[56]
> (trans. by Larrington 1996: 206)

The Anglo Saxon charms also offer help at delivery with ceremonies that combine the spoken word with prescribed bodily movements:

For delayed birth

Let the woman who cannot bring forth her child go to the grave of a wise man, and step three times over the grave, and then say these words three times:

> This be my cure for the loathsome late-birth,
> This be my cure for the grievous swart-birth,
> This be my cure for the loathsome lame-birth.[57]
> (trans. by Grendon 1909: 207)

As in many spells, words and ritual gestures are combined, in this case along with frequent triads of repetition. The visit to the grave of the helper is, as discussed above, a metaphor used in Eddic poetry. When it comes to the ritual aspects of the Anglo-Saxon charm quoted above, it could be interpreted in two ways – either as genuinely descriptive, indicating that people actually went to such a grave, or in terms of the introductory line telling of the wise woman's grave functioning as a form of invocation giving legitimacy to the following three lines. The latter way of reading the text would indicate a rather obvious similarity with the formulaic elements of Eddic song tradition.

Trolldómr *and Love*

Texts dealing with the amorous aspects of *trolldómr* are much more scarce than those concerned with the destructive. Interestingly they mirror the same attitudes and methods as the descriptions of performed malevolence (Ellis Davidson 1973: 33; Holtsmark 1980; Møller-Christensen 1980; Mundal and Steinsland 1989; Sayers 1992; Damico 1993; Morris 1993: 77ff.). The theme of arousing love in Old Norse literature is not so much a question of stories of affection and tenderness, but has to do with the process of gaining power over another person; the conflict pattern is as apparent as ever.

Skírnismál in the *Poetic Edda* can serve as a good example (Larrington 1992). Skírnir, the servant of Freyr, is sent to propose to a giant woman, Gerðr. Since she is unwilling and rejects him from the beginning, *trolldómr* and runes are used to weaken her:

> ' "Giant" I carve on you and three runes:
> lewdness and frenzy
> and unbearable desire;
> thus I can rub that off, as I carved that on,
> if there is need of this.'[58]
> (trans. by Larrington 1996: 67)

Gerðr cannot resist the powerful runes from the suitor and gives up her resistance. A tone of cruelty and violence is present throughout the poem. The young woman is exposed to the caprice of a superior force. Actually it is not a question of arousing love, but of breaking down the other person's will. As in the later medieval ballads with their abducted brides and *Zauberberg* motif this is more or less a metaphoric image for rape. Saxo tells of how Óðinn punishes a reluctant young mistress by touching her with a piece of bark inscribed with spells (III: 71).

The harsh *trolldómr* against reluctant lovers is used by both men and women. When the *mara* appears in Þjóðolfr's poem *Ynglingatal* it is the first supernatural category to be given a name in Old Norse literature. The term is etymologically related to the Indo-European root **mr*, 'to crush', which is most interesting considering the actions ascribed to it in some texts. The *mara* is a transformed and disguised human being and, in contrast to other more 'collective' beings, acts purposefully as an individual, often with erotic implications. The story of king Vanlandi's painful death is told in three different early texts, all part of the legendary history of the Yngling family. The kings all suffer mysterious deaths, each one more astounding than the previous. (Krag 1991:102f., 193f.; Rausing 1993). The third stanza in *Ynglingatal* is the shortest and earliest version of the events, focusing on the moment of death, when a demon tramples on and stifles Vanlandi. No reason is given in this text for the conflict between Vanlandi and the demon. The being attacking the king is spoken of in the feminine and given three significant names: 'she' is called 'creature of *trolldómr*', (*vitta vættr*), 'night struggle' (*grímhildr*) and *mara*, and her demonic origin, *troll-kund*, is emphasized. Her purpose, however, is clear-cut – killing the king.

Snorri's prose adaptation of the poem, *Ynglinga saga*, gives a more detailed account of the cause of the king's death. According to Snorri Vanlandi abandoned his wife Drífa and did not keep his promise of a prompt return to her in Finland. Therefore, Drífa asked the *seiðkona* Huldr to perform *seiðr* to make Vanlandi come back or die.[59] Drífa is, according to Snorri, a *finnkona* (Page 1963). Such liaisons are always dangerous in Old Norse texts, and when Vanlandi in Sweden feels a sudden urge to go to Finland his company try to stop him. They immediately suspect the Finns.[60] But king Vanlandi falls asleep paralysed, calling out that a *mara* is pressing him, *at mara trað hann*. Snorri gives a forceful image of the helpless king and of how the *mara* crushes the deceitful king's legs and finally stifles him to death.

The Latin chronicle *Historia Norvegiæ* is as short as *Ynglingatal* when it comes to telling of the painful death of king Vanlandi. But all three texts mention the name *mara*, which in later Scandinavian folklore is also a name for a being associated with lustful women taking revenge on reluctant men (Raudvere 1993, 1995). Components vital to *mara* texts over hundreds of years are already manifest in the story of king Vanlandi, including not only a suffocating victim, but also a jealous or evil person, often a woman, who uses the power of transformation to gain advantages in temporary guise. Seemingly from the beginning, sex and violence are at the core of the Scandinavian supernatural revenge stories.

Trolldómr could serve as an effective weapon in love conflicts and be the cause of impotence and disturbed emotional relations. In *Kormáks saga* young Kormákr is the target of Þórveig's curse; he will never have his girl (Davidson 1973; Mundal and Steinsland 1989: 114ff.; Sayer 1992: 141ff.). As discussed in the first chapter, the knowledgeable woman can attack Kormákr from a far distance and in a temporary guise. The saga has a complicated plot of conflicts, power, loyalties – and love. When Þórveig utters the harsh words that the young man will never enjoy his beloved Steingerðr,[61] Kormákr immediately strikes back verbally: 'You will have no say whatever in that, you evil woman.'[62] The verb *ráða* is used with the same significance here in the context of a curse as it is in connection with divination rituals. He cannot change what is once uttered and he does not have the ability to compete with Þórveig's extraordinary insights. And as the following chapter in the saga recounts, Kormákr wins Steingerðr's hand, but fails to appear at the marriage, and she marries another man.

In *Buslubœn* we noticed that a strong threat from the knowledgeable woman was her power over the king's sexual abilities. Several stanzas in the Eddic poetry also refer to Óðinn's power over love and lust. The 'Ljóðatal' at the end of *Hávamál* stresses the god's abilities to turn the minds of young maidens and make himself attractive (161ff.). Arousing love perhaps sounds sweet, but when Óðinn is praising his own seductive power it is in a harsh and rough tone:

> I know a sixteenth if I want to have all
> a clever woman's heart and love-play:
> I can turn the thoughts of the white-armed woman
> and change her mind entirely.
> I know a seventeenth, so that scarcely any
> young girl will want to shun me.[63]
> (trans. by Larrington 1996: 37)

Sexual desire is also a vital part of Óðinn's relation to supernatural women. In *Hárbarðsljóð*'s dialogue Hárbarðr (Óðinn) boasts about his influence over night riding hags, *myrkriður*, claiming his potency, *miklar manvélar* (Mundal and Steinsland 1989):

> 'Mighty love-spells I used on the witches,
> those whom I seduced from their men.'[64]
> (trans. by Larrington 1996: 72)

Manvélar and *manrúnar* are both terms with erotic connotations hinting at the ability to arouse love by the force of *trolldómr* insights (Pálsson 1990: 175ff.). The same aggressive atmosphere surrounds the heroic poem *Helgakviða Hjǫrvarðssonar* 15 where the hero Atli is involved in a verbal duel with the giantess Hrímgerðr. The tone is very aggressive and we can note that the metre is the same as in *Hávamál*'s catalogue of spells. He is praising himself for haunting night riding hags, *kveldriður*:

> 'Atli I'm called, atrocious I shall be to you,
> I am most hostile to ogresses;
> I've often stayed at the dew-washed prow
> and tormented night-riding witches [*kveldriður*]'.[65]
> (trans. by Larrington: 126)

Knowledgeable women and sexuality was a theme that recurred in later Christian literature. 'When female sexuality comes to the fore, it is usually in a demonic or "Otherworld" context, explicitly or implicitly connected to the pagan past', Margaret Cormak writes in her discussion of sex and the supernatural in Icelandic saints' lives (1992: 228). Cunning women and their abilities became an image of the seductive power of the devil. The combination of unrestrained lust and *trolldómr* in the writings of witch-hunters centuries later, as well as of clergymen, continued to some extent in Scandinavia into the catechisms of the Reformation.

Heal or Destroy: The Ambiguity of Performing Trolldómr

As this chapter has indicated, both mythological narratives and sagas give descriptions of more or less elaborate rituals performed in an attempt to achieve knowledge of otherwise hidden matters. To some extent the deeds of the gods seem to have formed a prototype for the understanding of the origin and effect of *trolldómr*. In sagas some historical and contemporary individuals were conceived to have the extraordinary skills to conduct such *trolldómr* rituals. Knowledge was sought from the outside, from sources that could be destructive of the social order. The demonic beings of the realm of the giants are often involved, as if knowledge could not be with harmony only or be fully operative unless also in contact with disharmony.

The juridical and political decisions of the *þing* meetings were accompanied by *blót* offerings performed according to the established custom of society, *siðr*. While *blót* was conducted among influential men, that is, by the *goði* in local society, *seiðr* seems to have taken place less formally at farms. It was also a ritual of a highly ambiguous character. The performers are described as odd and significantly different in one way or another, according to age, ethnicity or social position. Among the performers women play a more active role than otherwise in Old Norse literature. Whether this indicates that women took a more direct part in *seiðr* and divination rituals outside the texts is a matter for debate. Some texts situate the rituals in remote places, presumably to stress the image of practices from days gone by. Many rituals are performed in order to destroy and harm, sometimes on behalf of a person other than the performer. On the other hand, from time to time the saga texts stress that the knowledgeable were invited to perform divination rituals, *seiðr*. Insight into the conditions of the forthcoming year was a form of knowledge that was eagerly sought after. *Seiðr* and related ceremonies could also be seen as private fertility rituals in accordance with the needs of a rural society.

Vital pre-Christian conceptions can be observed in much later documentation of Scandinavian folk beliefs and folk medicine as regards both form and content. The authority of skilled persons' use of the spoken word for destruction or healing is apparent over a long period of time. In popular discourse this was not explicitly expressed as an opposition against the Church (although clergymen after the Reformation definitely regarded it as such) but as a way of handling more or less clandestine powers.

Compared to the world of the Norsemen very little is known about the ritual practices of other Germanic peoples on the Continent. When it comes to *trolldómr*, there are no texts comparable to the Eddas or the sagas. However, correspondences can be observed with Old High German and Anglo-Saxon poetry, especially in the use of charms and spells. Not only in metrics and form, but also in content and ideology, this corpus shows striking similarities with different Old Norse modes of expressing trust in the power of the spoken word. Many of the Continental spells combine uttering with bodily movements in a way that is familiar from Scandinavian traditions.

The knowledgeable could also use their special knowledge to perform ceremonies to bring injury and misery to others. In this perspective *trolldómr* was malevolent performance as a strategy of handling difficult situations. Most protective actions taken to avert trolls and illness follow the same pattern: both actions and speech directly face the source of *trolldómr* using parallel motions. Aiming back was the only way of defence.

As expressed in the literature, *trolldómr* was acted out in rituals and formalized speech as well as in paradigmatic mythological narratives. A third mode of expressing the complex conceptions of knowledge, destruction and healing was the interplay between accusations and trials.

CHAPTER 3

The Legal Code: Law and Trial

As social memory the sagas dealt much with the administration of justice, including accusations of *trolldómr*. In Iceland time and social space were explicitly allotted for trials. The rules for these events represent a circumstantial process of formalization, when a local conflict was to be solved in public. Any accusation or other issue should always be brought to public knowledge in due time before negotiations could start. Since the code of honour is so visible as an important matter in the saga texts, it is interesting to speculate on what was thought of people who took the law into their own hands. The killing of a person connected with *trolldómr* was not always followed by revenge or legal proceedings; rather, the spontaneous revenge was in some cases conceived to be a praiseworthy deed.

The Old Norse texts reveal several different strategies regarding people who were supposed to perform *trolldómr* and cunning deeds. Some of them were dealt with directly, while others faced formal trials. The cases were then treated like any other criminal case and followed an established set of rules. Compared to other aspects of social organization the sources provide the modern reader with quite a lot of useful information.

The Oral Law Tadition

In contrast to *trolldómr*, the concept of law was a commonly accepted and used abstract term. Tradition recounts that law was brought to Iceland from Norway with some of the first settlers, *landnámsmenn* (Fix 1993b). The early laws of the Norsemen were orally transmitted and are only known as echoes in the first written legal documentation, *Grágás*, and in the sagas (Dennis, Foote and Perkins 1980). However, names of institutions and positions used long after the introduction of Christianity give hints about the organization of the oral law. It is generally assumed that the laws were among the first texts in Scandinavia to be written down. *Grágás*, literally 'Grey Goose' because of the grey cover to one of the manuscripts, is a mixed collection of legal manuscripts of the so-called Icelandic commonwealth (Fix 1993a). The texts were brought together in a first compounded form perhaps as early as the late twelfth century, and express the legal code from the time of the sagas. However, the latter aim at days past while the former mirror the morals of contemporary time, and in between there is more than one drastic shift in social life. In contrast to the sagas, the laws were explicitly Christian texts that based their authority on the new religion. No obvious distinction was made between *trolldómr* deeds, divination, healing or *blót* offerings. These acts were all condemned as pagan.

There was a reciprocal relationship between the introduction of written culture and other important social and cultural changes in Scandinavia. The development of kingdoms and territorial states was parallel to that of state authority and the establishment of national legal codes. This process went along with an acceleration in the establishment of the first urban communities and the introduction of a monetary economy. All these changes during the thirteenth and fourteenth centuries strengthened Scandinavia's links to Continental Europe even more. In many respects these radical changes led to processes of institutionalization of public life, among these the organization of legal matters. Due to the political and cultural conflicts, Iceland did not take part in this development to the same extent as did the newly established kingdoms of Norway, Sweden and Denmark.

The ambition of the saga writers was to link their contemporary time to the world before these changes. Before the submission to the Norwegian king in 1262–4 there was no state or general state authority in Iceland. A certain idealizing romanticism flavours the accounts of time past, but based on the conviction that a social order existed from the beginning. Regions were ruled by local chieftains, *goðar*. The relationship between the ruler and the local inhabitants formed the basis of a social network that included both law and religion, among other social activities. Free men could make a treaty of mutual loyalty with a *goði* that both parties could annul. The possibilities of local variation must, therefore, always colour any reconstruction of the Icelandic judicature.

The Social Organization of the Law

When the sagas speak of law it is not a national code for Iceland that is referred to – as was the case with the Scandinavian codes of the later Middle Ages – but local agreements with a more or less explicit connection with a general assembly for the whole island. Despite other major changes, the social organization of the law remained to a large extent and for a long time unchanged and the development of more formal legal institutions was a later process. Power relations were always very visible in the social operations surrounding crime and punishment. In the legal system of the oral culture the lawspeaker, *lǫgsǫgumaðr*, memorized and recited the law at joint meetings of the *goðar*. Elected for a period of three years, the lawspeaker held a special position with responsibility for the proper preservation and transmission of the law and tradition.

The Alþingi, the general annual assembly, was the foremost unifying political factor in the absence of state authority. According to tradition the institution was founded in 930 and meetings were held for a few weeks every summer. The legendary history of the foundation of the Alþingi gives the original number of chieftains as thirty-six. A special area with no permanent buildings was reserved for the assembly. It was a clearly defined social space for the leading members of society, as well as a gendered space since women could generally not speak before the Alþingi. The meetings were certainly not of a purely legal character, but of religious, social and economic importance too. The Alþingi was an important opportunity for trading. It was also a time when political power was negotiated and agreements of different kinds were made. Long after the establishment of the Church and national legal codes, this kind of multipurpose meeting kept its relevance for local social life all over Scandinavia. A legislative assembly also met on these occasions, constituted by the most prominent *goðar*. This group also elected the *lǫgsǫgumaðr*, a most honourable position.

There were also regional assemblies in the spring and in the autumn. The *þing*, the assembly of the local free men, was an occasion for negotiations, decisions and trials (Sandvik 1993). It was an opportunity to solve local conflicts and disputes and a time when agreements were confirmed by oaths. Very few conflicts involved only individuals. At the *þing* the male head of a family spoke on behalf of his household. The proceedings of a *þing* were led by a *goði*, who was also responsible for the *blót* offerings of the neighbourhood. The etymology of the title of the leader *goði* (from *goð*, 'god') hints at an original religious interpretation of a position that in the days of the sagas and *Grágás* was mainly a political office. The *goði* obviously held a position of power and great influence that was traditionally inherited within the family. The stationary system led to the petrification of conflicts between the stronger families. A *goðorð* was not as such a distinct geographical area, but referred to the authority that the *goði* had in relation to his *þingmenn*. It was a relationship of a contractual character that both parties could give up. A *goðorð*, like any item of property, could be dealt with in different ways; it could be bought and sold, inherited, given away etc. Due to elaborate commerce and other political and social processes, power was consolidated in the thirteenth century into the hands of a few families. Snorri Sturluson's life and death is a good example of this development. Born as he was into the ruling elite he could achieve more wealth and influence through marriage, but was at the same time also involved in new conflicts. His contacts with the Norwegian king caused suspicion about his loyalties and an escalation of the conflict led to Snorri's murder in 1241. During this period the *goðorð* were ruled by only a few members of the dominant families. This was the harsh reality, far from the idealized accounts of the *landnám* period when the thirty-six *goðorð* were supposed to have been settled.

Trial and Ritual

Trials and rituals are in many respects very similar social events. When a trial is analysed in terms of a ritual the legal process becomes a lucid example of the indisputable interconnection between law and religion. In Old Norse texts distinctions between these two areas were not made. Both law and religion were regarded as part of *siðr*, traditional custom. Through the trial a social conflict was ritualized and a process of formalization – from the private to the public arena – was made visible.

Paul Connerton's wide definition of a ritual, discussed above, has proved to be helpful in the discussion of Old Norse *trolldómr* trials. An advantage of the wide definition is that the difference between religious, political and social activities in many ways becomes irrelevant. At what point, then, should the distinctions between the religious, social, legal and economic characteristics of the *þing* be made? If rituals are not limited to specific belief systems the definition could also cover major upheavals like Christianization or the introduction of Latin written culture.

The Old Norse trials seem to have been rule-governed acitivities where certain steps were stipulated. The proceedings of the trial had a symbolic character and the situation was clearly limited in time and space. Both rituals and trials are necessarily occasional, although mostly regular. They are defined by their relation to everyday life and to the mainstream, in comparison to which they stand out as events of special importance. The roles for participants in rituals and trials were commonly known and easy to recognize.

In the sagas, accusations of *trolldómr* are spoken of much more often than actual trials and penalties. Suspicious speech was often used as defamation or threat and did not necessarily lead to any legal proceedings in the texts. William Ian Miller writes: 'Sorcery accusations in the sagas frequently appear as reactions to untimely death or illness', and continues further on: 'The neat thing about the sorcery accusation was that it foreshortened the causal chain that led to the misfortune' (1986: 110f.). It can be noted that when *trolldómr* performers were dealt with and punished this could be done in two separate ways. Either the punishment was the result of negotiations at a *þing* or the people involved took the law into their own hands. The two reactions to assumed *trolldómr* deeds described in the sagas lead to a distinction between accounts of formal trials and accounts of the more informal ones. The latter are much more common than the former and sometimes consist of only a few sentences, being part of a web of gossip and slander.

Something Has Happened

The most elaborate narrative in the sagas of a formal trial against a person suspected of performing *trolldómr* can be read in *Eyrbyggja saga* 16. In relation to the rest of the corpus this text must be regarded as an exception because of its length and details. The sequence is focused around guilt, responsibility and punishment. It suggests a given set of legal rules and a social organization in which *trolldómr* crimes could be punished and disputes settled.

Eyrbyggja saga 16 opens at the heart of a conflict. Further events lead to a severe accident that is considered in the neighbourhood to be caused by *trolldómr* and one woman is under suspicion. The erotic implications of the *trolldómr* practices in chapters 15 and 16 that cause young Gunnlaugr bodily harm have been discussed above. The intrigue focuses around the struggle between two women with contradictory attitudes towards their *trolldómr* skills. These two knowledgeable women do not act exclusively on their own but on the periphery of other major family conflicts. This confirms the idea that a *trolldómr* conflict never appears on its own. There are many layers of dispute and much more violence will occur before the saga comes to its end. Still, these two chapters on *trolldómr* can be read as a complete story in its own right.

Both women are old enough to have grown-up sons. Katla is still good-looking but not very much liked by the local people and her son Oddr is given an entirely negative characterization: 'boisterous and very talkative, a trouble maker and a slanderer'.[66] Geirríðr on the other hand is just said to be *margkunnig*, 'knowing a lot', and is shown to be willing to pass on her insights generously to the younger generation.

Katla keeps repeating her invitation to the young man to stay overnight, but she is always rejected. Her sneering and insinuating words to Gunnlaugr when he refuses to stay the fatal night reveal her coarse manners and lack of qualities: 'She asked him whether he was going to Mávahlíð [Geirríðr's place] again "to stroke the old woman's groin" '.[67]

For the young man the antagonism between the women leads to disaster; he is found unconscious and severely wounded in the morning, after trying to travel on his own during the night. From a legal point of view there is an incident and a victim, and behind him a whole family. The local interpretation is that Gunnlaugr is hurt by *trolldómr*. But there are no witnesses, only rumours, and an intricate conflict to be solved.

Oddr, acting on behalf of his mother, puts the blame on Geirríðr, telling people that she has attacked Gunnlaugr as a night hag, *riðit honum*. The relatives of the injured therefore want to bring the case before the *þing* and they act in a given sequence in accordance with custom: 'Þorbjǫrn rode to Mávahlíð and summonsed Geirríðr, accusing her of being a night-rider [*kveldriða*] and having caused injury to Gunnlaug'.[68] The serving of the summons, when representatives of the prosecutors visited the house of the accused to announce their intentions, was a highly significant moment. The announcement of the accusation was a performative act; after this the conflict was a public matter and continued to be so until a decision was made. What we can gather from the text is that the meeting described was probably a local *þing*. The term for the charge, *kvelriða*, shows that Geirríðr was accused of being a shapeshifter, a night-riding hag. From the characterization of the two women the reader already knows that the accusation is false. On the contrary, Geirríðr has tried to warn the young man against the dangers she could foresee. But the social customs of gender and speech made the situation even more complicated.

Although innocent, as a woman Geirríðr cannot speak before the *þing*. Therefore, her brother Arnkell represents her in the public arena. The proceedings of the *þing* are not fully described, but we can see how specific actions were made. In this case there were no proofs, the accusation was entirely based on rumours, and hence a *tylftarkviðr*, a jury of twelve, was appointed to solve the case. For serious crimes such a panel was needed: 'It was a means of proof chiefly used in cases where a greater degree of public interest was involved (e.g. sorcery, theft, and perjury)' (Dennis, Foote and Perkins 1980b: 253). Apparently there were also elaborate rules about who was suitable for such a commitment and not immediately involved in the conflict, since the saga states 'neither Snorri nor/Arnkell could give a decision in the case because of their kinship with the plaintiff and the defendant'.[69] The *tylftarkviðr* freed Geirríðr and the question of her guilt was ritually closed as the twelve members of the jury swore an oath by the *stallahringr*, the altar ring, to testify to the knowledgeable woman's innocence. After such a procedure the accusation could not be raised in public again. Words uttered aloud like accusations, testimonies, oaths and announcements were surrounded with ritual activities. The conflict was solved for ever.

Spreading gossip concerning serious matters was certainly not an honourable thing to do and the chapter closes with a harsh remark: 'Snorri and Þorbjǫrn's case was quashed, which brought them dishonour.'[70] The misuse of the spoken word was considered a major crime and only dishonour could come from such behaviour.

All the actions of the formal trial took place in well-defined public space and were, as such, clearly observable activities. The informal trial had more of the character of an act of revenge and often took place in the vicinity of domestic areas. The informal settlement was not surrounded by the institutionalized procedures of the negotiations at the *þing*. In both cases the question of guilt was the focus and all activities were aimed at finding out the identity of the guilty party. Revenge was not only a question of stating a righteous punishment; the revealed guilt also threw light on a whole chain of events. But social space for operations in both formal and informal trials was based on conceptions of honour and tradition (*siðr*); any form of solution, therefore, involved whole families.

Guilt and Responsibilities

The formal trial in *Eyrbyggja saga* 16 did not solve the question of who had caused young Gunnlaugr's injuries; it only freed the wrongly accused party. It was the responsibility of the relatives to find the guilty party. The search for the night hag leads to an informal trial against Katla at Holt in chapter 20. The false rumours had turned out to be a failure, and instead had added shame to an already disliked family. Katla's son Oddr was involved in other despicable conflicts in the area. When his antagonists come to take revenge, his mother makes use of her extraordinary knowledge and makes him invisible. These tricks of hers are the beginning of her surrender. The enemies only see a distaff, a goat, and the third time they come, a hog, and the revengers become suspicious that Katla is manipulating their sight with her cunning abilities. At this point in the escalating conflict only a person with equal insight and capacities can help them. Geirríðr is called for and from a long distance Katla can see that the company searching for Oddr has increased by one person: ' "That will be the *troll*, Geirríðr, coming with them,' said Katla, 'and simple illusions [*sjónhverfing*, i.e. deceiving of sight] will not be enough now." '[71] Knowledgeable and sensitive as she is, Katla feels that this time things might go in a direction unfavourable to her.

When Geirríðr and the men enter the room they immediately put a skin bag over Katla's head as protection against her evil eye. They find Oddr and hang him at once. As he is recalcitrant it is commented by the revengers that all his trouble is due to his evil-minded mother. The response comes immediately: ' "Maybe he doesn't have a good mother," said Katla, "but I never wished him to get such an evil end because of me. It's my will that you all get an evil end because of me, and I expect that will be the case." '[72] As always in the sagas the curse will later turn out to be effective.

Katla makes a confession that she was the one causing Gunnlaugr damage and the question of guilt is thereby settled. Apparently, the revengers fill the same role as the witnesses in a formal trial. But before she is killed she lays yet another curse, *ákvæði*; this time on Arnkell. Even if her gaze is

2 test

Witchcraft and Magic in Europe: The Middle Ages

rendered harmless by the skin bag there are still powerful words to be used and until the last moment the knowledgeable fights back against her enemies. Katla is stoned to death and the chapter ends: 'The news quickly travelled everywhere, but no one thought it was sad. And so the winter passed by'.[73] The sagas may be laconic, but they are certainly not neutral in their ways of telling.

The foreign Kotkell family's malevolent *seiðr* performances in *Laxdæla saga* chapters 35ff. were discussed in the previous section; and there is also a legal aftermath to their activities (Miller 1986: 110ff.). The Hebredian family was accused of theft and *fjǫlkyngi* because they gained prosperity without any seeming effort, which implied the use of *trolldómr*. The episode starts as if a formal trial is going to take place. An old woman stands behind the accusation but it is her son who is the formal actor. As a man he can summon the Kotkells in public:

> Þórðr rode to Kotkell's farm with nine other men. Kotkell's sons were not at home. Before witnesses, Þórðr charged Kotkell and his wife and sons with theft and sorcery [*fjǫlkyngi*], an offence punishable by outlawry for life [*skóggangr*].[74]

Skóggangr figuratively speaking meant that the person was doomed to walk the woodlands and not stay in populated areas. It distinctly meant that the condemned was outside the law, as the English 'outlaw' suggests. Apparently outlawry is the only thinkable punishment since such a very serious crime as *trolldómr* is suspected, a feature which agrees with the later Christian codes. But before the proper time for the Alþingi comes there is a new *trolldómr* incident that clearly links the family to clandestine deeds. No formal trial ever takes place.

By means of *trolldómr* the Kotkells cause a storm in which the accuser Þórðr dies. The event arouses the anger of the local people even more. The fatal storm is followed by the incident when Hrútr's young son is killed by *seiðr* and incantations. The relatives of the victim now act on their own – although, as the saga states, it is too late – and they immediately go for the Kotkell family. Altogether, seventeen men leave to find the *seiðmenn* and to get rid of them for good. The revenge on the family comes in three phases.

The first one found is Hallbjǫrn and he is caught so that he can be drowned. When he is captured a skin bag is immediately put over his head, as was done in the case above. Kotkell and Gríma are stoned to death as previously noted and a cairn of stones is constructed over their bones. No comments are made on this except that the place is named after the incident. Thereafter Hallbjǫrn is to be drowned and while he is in the boat, 'they removed the sack and tied a stone about his neck. As they did so, Hallbjǫrn turned a gaze that was anything but gentle towards land.'[75] He also takes the opportunity to lay a curse, *atkvæði*, on his enemies. 'Events are thought to have proved how effective was his curse' is the short comment in the saga.[76] Hallbjǫrn's destructive gaze and the powerful words in his mouth show him fighting not only to the end, but even later still. He is, as planned, drowned by the revengers. However, the sea does not keep his body and washes the corpse ashore. Hallbjǫrn has no peace and shows himself to the living and causes trouble as a revenant. The conflict goes on from the other side of the grave. As noted before, no sharp distinction can be made between the living and the dead when it comes to action and counteraction in *trolldómr* cases.

The last surviving member of the Kotkell family, Stígandi, remains free for some time. He is condemned in public as an outlaw, but manages to keep away. The saga calls him *útilegumaðr*, which has associations in two different directions – socially with outlawry, and ritually with being thought of as a performer of *útilega/útiseta* and *seiðr*. In both meanings he belongs to the wilderness outside society. In either aspect he had no expectations of protection from anyone. A *seiðr* performer and an outlaw could be killed like an animal.

Stígandi is captured through crafty trickery (ch. 38). Somehow it is known that he is meeting a woman sent out to watch the cows while they graze. She is forced by means of violence to betray Stígandi: Þórðr had her threatened to try and find out the truth. When suitably frightened, the woman revealed that a man came to her, "a large man, and handsome, he seemed to me." '[77] The harshness of the conflicts is shown in these few sentences and when Stígandi is finally captured, while resting with his woman. The same procedure takes place as with the execution of his relatives. The revengers are afraid that Stígandi will cause the same damage with his fatal gaze as did his brother, and are very careful when they put the skin bag over his head. But this time there is a small slot in the head bag and the gaze of the *seiðmaðr* causes the surrounding land to languish as if a whirlwind has passed:

> There was a tear in the sack through which Stígandi could see the slope opposite. It was a fertile bit of land, green with grass, but suddenly it was as if a tornado struck it. The land was transformed and never again did grass grow there. It is now called 'the Fire-Site'.[78]

Here we find another example of a place given its name after *trolldómr* incidents; naming the landscape preserved memory. The place name here functions in the same way as a monument of stone. Stígandi is finally stoned to death. An outlaw had no more protection, either socially or legally, than a wild beast. Killing an outlaw was even rewarded.

So, what do the two informal trials have in common and what makes them differ from the formal? The informal trials had a clear character as acts of private revenge. It can be noted that in the private arena during the informal trial against Katla, she takes part in a debate with her accusers ending with her cursing them while the innocent Geirríðr remains silent throughout the negotiations. Secondly, there are no indications in the texts that the informal disputes are made public. It does not seem to have been considered dishonourable to execute persons proved to be associated with *trolldómr*. The latter is a critical point since the formal trial demanded evidence or at least a trustable jury to pronounce a sentence.

In the narratives the theme of trial could be used almost in a mocking way, or at least jocularly, and even the disobedient dead could face a trial. The recently departed retained a strong relationship to the living, a bond that the latter sometimes wanted to cut. In *Eyrbyggja saga* chapters 54–5 a group of drowned people start to return in the evenings in their wet clothes. Each night they draw closer and closer to the fire. The closer they come, the more problems arise and the people of the farm fall ill and some die. 'Six people died this time, and some people fled because of the hauntings and the ghosts.'[79] The situation becomes more and more chaotic and desperate. A man known for his wisdom advises the people to have 'all the revenants prosecuted at a door court. Then the priest should say mass, consecrate water and hear everybody's confession.'[80] This is done and finally there is peace and the sick start to improve. Evidently the methods of both the new and the old faith could help in critical situations.

The descriptions of the drowning and stoning of people found guilty of *trolldómr* agree with what is written in *Grágás* and other later legal texts. Katla is stoned to death and in *Haralds saga hárfagra* some eighty *seiðmenn* are burnt to death. These methods of execution also appear in Christian laws.

Grettis saga 82 can serve as an illuminating example of how the question of guilt was conceived in a *trolldómr* case. The old woman who carved runes against Grettir was commissioned by his enemies. Like many other knowledgeable women she was acting out of loyalty against her family, not on her own. She served as a mediator due to her access to the methods of *trolldómr* and she was not held personally responsible for the consequences of her acting. The fostermother was herself never taken to court, but the man who gave her the mission was. 'The many foster mothers in the sagas who were adept at magic and lore seldom suffered sorcery accusations. They apparently were well protected in the *bóndi*'s household and of little interest to those competing with that household' (Miller 1986: 115). Individual guilt and responsibility is much more strongly emphasized in the Christian laws.

The present text indicates a tense situation. As Grettir is seriously hurt due to the old woman's rituals, he becomes vulnerable and an easy victim. His enemy Ǫngull claims that it was Christ who led him the Grettir the outlaw, but is afterwards looked upon as a coward: 'looked upon as a coward and "greatly despised for his deed when people realised that he had overcome Grettir with sorcery [gørningar]" '.[81] It is not the killing of Grettir that has brought the case before the Alþingi, but the use of *gerningar*. Not even against an outlaw is *trolldómr* regarded as acceptable behaviour.

The proceedings of the Alþingi are described in chapter 84. Qngull claimed a reward for killing an outlaw, as custom stipulated. Instead, it was decided that he was responsible for killing by means of *trolldómr*. It is also stated in *Grágás* 7 that it is considered a crime to pay a person to perform *trolldómr*. As a consequence, Qngull was now deemed an outlaw himself and had to leave the same summer, never to return to Iceland. At the same meeting a new law is said to have been made that outlawed all knowledge-able men, *forneskjumenn*.

Several of the episodes referred to above imply a 'contact zone' where old and new norms were amalgamated. The trial constituted a 'spatial and temporal copresence', as discussed by Mary Louise Pratt (1992: 7). The introduction of written Christian laws into the early Scandinavian king-doms in one way marks the end of this essay. The Continental Christian legal traditions brought changes to the procedures of law and justice along with the influence of Mosaic and canonic law. Local traditions of legal administration became less relevant. Nevertheless, the world view behind certain kinds of accusations shows striking similarities with the sagas. *Trolldómr* was apparently considered a serious crime in Christian times. The radical changes and differences must have worked together for a long time in a form of hybridization. We can recognize a stress on the spoken word, the talk of cunning deeds, and an apparent awareness that an accusation of *trolldómr* could serve as serious defamation. The victims of *trolldómr* could be people and cattle, as well as material goods. The early Christian legal texts state that spreading superstition should be punished by fine, but it is not very clear what superstition was conceived as. The laws vary in giving different forms of penalties and as in the saga texts the terminology varies in a way that indicates a variation in degrees of *trolldómr*. It is spoken of in very general terms as a threat to the true Christian belief. The Swedish *Dalalagen* mentions women's use of nails and hair as instruments for evil deeds, and the older Borgarþing's law from Norway speaks of men sitting out in the wilderness to seek visions and raising the trolls.[82]

Gísli Pálsson suggests that the decline of accusations of *trolldómr* as a motif in saga texts was not connected to the introduction of Christianity, but came 'as a result of increased social distance, that is, with the develop-ment of increasingly asymmetrical power relations', and (he continues at the end of his essay) 'was a consequence of changes in the political organi-sation of the Commonwealth, these changes being the result of inherent contradictions in relations among chieftains and followers' (1991: 157, 168). It is a discerning observation since there are so many similarities between saga texts and Christian laws. The old gods were transformed into demons, but many vital conceptions obviously remained the same. Shapeshifters, the power of spells and destruction by means of *trolldómr* were treated by Christian authors for centuries as if they objectively existed – they were evil but real. But now a new theological entity was added; the devil.

Bibliographical Note

The most recent general introduction to Old Norse mythology and religion in English are Margaret Clunies Ross's two volumes *Prolonged Echoes* (1994, 1998). These thorough monographs give an analytical survey along with commentaries on the sources and a useful bibliography. Thomas A. DuBois, *Nordic religions in the Viking Age* (1999) covers a wider area than the conventional 'Scandinavian' including materials from Saami and Balto-Finnic sources. Several chapters touch discussions related to *trolldómr*. Jenny Jochens' *Old Norse Images of Women* (1996) discusses several of the female agents taken up by the present study. *Old Norse-Icelandic Literature: A Critical Guide*, edited by Carol Clover and John Lindow (1985), presents six major essays on myths, Eddic and skaldic poety and sagas, each with an extensive bibliogaphy. *Medieval Scandinavia*, edited by Philipp Pulsiano (1993), is a one volume dictionary with very informative and detailed articles on texts, persons and different aspects of society and religion, as well as material culture and places. All articles have bibliographies and references to editions and translations of relevant texts. *Kulturhistorisk leksikon för nordisk middelålder* (2nd edn 1981–8 in 18 volumes) goes more into detail, but the articles are written in Scandinavian languages. *Medieval folklore: an encyclopedia of myths, legends, tales, beliefs, and customs* (2000) edited by Carl Lindahl *et al.* in two volumes give a detailed overview over popular culture and popular religion of the European Middle Ages. John Lindow's bibliography *Scandinavian Mythology* (1988) covers articles and monographs published world wide and in most languages.

Some periodicals that publish essays relevant to the Old Norse field can be mentioned: *Scandinavian Studies, Arkiv för nordisk filologi, Maal og minne,* and *Arv.* To these well established journals two new ones can be added: *Alvíssmál* and *Skáldskaparmál*.

Most of the saga texts used in this study are to be found in critical editions with commentaries and introductury essays in *Islenzk fornrit*. The original texts of the *Poetical Edda* are edited by Gustav Neckel and Hans Kuhn in *Edda: die Lieder des Codex Regius* (5th edn, 1983). The majority of the translations used in the present study are taken from Carolyne Larrington's translation of *The Poetic Edda* (1996), Anthony Faulke's of Snorris *Edda*, and most saga text from *The Complete Sagas of Icelanders*, vol 1–5 (1997). All of these translations are rich in commentaries and references to further reading.

Notes

Chapter 1

1. Trans. Scudder, The Complete Sagas of the Icelanders II: 158. Grettis saga 69: Gætið ykkar vel við gørningum; fátt er rammara en forneskjan. All translations of sagas are taken from The Complete Sagas of the Icelanders (henceforth CSI), and of Eddic verse from the translation of Larrington (see under Poetic Edda), unless noted otherwise. To avoid confusion, however, forms of names are standardized in the translations. Original texts are referred to by chapter number (sagas) or stanzas (verse). It should be noted that manuscript or editorial differences from the originals of texts quoted here may be reflected in the translations cited; the general aim has been to use the most readily available and up-to-date texts and translations.

2. Attempts to establish such a distinction have been made. For Katherine Morris (1993) this difference constitutes the basis for her study.

3. Cohn 1975; Levack 1987; Flint 1991; Mary Douglas writes when discussing the Continental witch craze (1992: 86): 'The medieval witch was also thought to be given to unnatural vice and to an insatiable sexual appetite. Charges of secret sexual deviance, spite, heresy, and occult dangerous powers were combined. Everything significant about the European witch was occult, hidden, unknowable by ordinary means.'

4. *Hávamál* 142:

    > Rúnar munt pú finna oc rádna stafi,
    > miǫc stóra stafi,
    > miǫc stinna stafi,
    > er fáði fimbulþulr
    > oc gorðo ginregin
    > oc reist hroptr rǫgna.

5. For general overviews on Scandinavian folk beliefs accompanied by texts translated to English see Lindow 1978; Kvideland and Sehmsdorf 1988; Simpson 1988, and with special emphasis on *trolldómr*: Alver 1971a, b; Alver and Selberg 1990; Raudvere 1993, 1995.

6. *Hávamál* 151:

    > Þat kann ec it sétta, ef mic særir þegn
    > á rótom rás viðar:
    > oc þann hal, er mic heipta qveðr,
    > þann eta mein heldr enn mic.

7. Trans. and ed. Robinson. *Grógaldr* 15–16:
   Far þú nú æva
   þar er forað þykkir;
   ok standit þér mein fyr munum!
   á jarðfǫstom steini
   stóð ek innan dura,
   meðan ek þér galdra gól.

   Móður orð
   ber þú, mǫgr, heðan,
   ok lát þér í brjósti búa;
   iðgnóga heill
   skaltu of aldr hafa,
   meðan þú mín orð of mant.

8. Trans. and cited (from Braune and Ebbinghaus 1969: 89) by Simek 1993: 278.
   Phol ende uuodan uuorun zi holza.
   du uuart demo balderes uolon sin uuoz birenkit.
   thu biguol en sin*th*gunt, sunna era suister;
   thu biguol en friia, uolla era suister;
   thu biguol en uuodan, so he uuola conda:
   sose benrenki, sose bluotrenki,
   sose lidirenki:
   ben zi bena, bluot zi bluoda,
   lid zi geliden, sose gelimida sin.

9. There are different opinions as to whether 'baldr' refers to the name of the
   god or should be interpreted as 'lord, master' and refer to Óðinn.

10. *Hávamál* 149:
    Þat kann ec it fiórða, ef mér fyrðar bera
    bǫnd at boglimom:
    svá ec gel, at ec ganga má,
    sprettr mér af fótom fioturr,
    enn af hǫndom hapt.

11. Trans. and ed. Grendon 1909: 177, A14:
    Ic mē on þisse gyrde belūce, and on godes helde bebēode
    wið þane sāra stice, wið þane sāra slege,
    wið ðane grymman gryre,
    wið ðane micelan egsan, þe bið ēghwām lāð,
    and wið eal þæt lāð, þe intō land fare.

12. Trans. Scudder, *CSI* I: 113f. *Egils saga Skalla-Grímssonar* 57: Gekk Egill upp í
    eyna. Hann tók í hǫnd sér heslistǫng ok gekk á bergsnǫs nǫkkura, þá er vissi
    til lands inn; þá tók hann hrosshǫfuð ok setti upp á stǫngina. Siðan veitti hann
    formála ok mælti svá: 'Hér set ek upp níðstǫng, ok sný ek þessu níði á hǫnd

Eiríki konungi ok Gunnhildi dróttningu,' hann sneri hrosshǫfðinu inn á land
– 'sný ek þessu níði á landvættir þær, er land þetta byggva, svá at allar fari þær
villar vega, engi hendi né hitti sitt inni, fyrr en þær reka Eirík konung ok
Gunnhildi ór landi.' Síðan skýtr hann stǫnginni niðr í bjargrifu ok lét þar
standa; hann sneri ok hǫfðinu inn á land, en hann reist rúnar á stǫnginni, ok
segja þær formála þenna allan.

13. *Vǫluspá* 19–20:

    Asc veit ec standa, heitir Yggdrasill,
    hár baðmr, ausinn hvítaauri;
    þaðan koma dǫggvar, þærs í dala falla,
    stendr æ yfir, grœnn, Urðar brunni.

    Þaðan koma meyiar, margs vitandi,
    þriár, ór þeim sæ, er und þolli stendr;
    Urð héto eina, aðra Verðandi
    – scáro á scíði –, Sculd ina þriðio;
    þær lǫg lǫgðo, þær líf kuro
    alda bornom, ørlǫg seggia.

14. Trans. Cook, *CSI* III: 215. *Njáls saga* 157:

    Mannahǫfuð váru fyrir kljána, en þarmar ór mǫnnum fyrir viptu ok garn,
    sverð var fyrir skeið, en ǫr fyrir hræl. Þær kváðu þá vísur nǫkkurar:

    Vítt er orpit
    fyrir valfalli
    rifs reiðiský,
    rignir blóði;
    nú er fyrir geirum
    grár upp kominn
    vefr verþjóðar,
    er þær vinur fylla
    rauðum vepti
    Randvés bana.

    Sjá er orpinn vefr
    ýta þǫrmum
    ok harðkléaðr
    hǫfðum manna;
    eru dreyrrekin
    dǫrr at skǫptum,
    járnvarðr yllir,
    en ǫrum hrælaðr;
    skulum slá sverðum
    sigrvef þenna.

15. *Hávamál* 155:
> Þat kann ec iþ tíunda, ef ec sé túnriðor
> leica lopti á:
> ec svá vinnc, at þeir villir fara
> sinna heim hama,
> sinna heim huga.

Chapter 2

16. The most detailed narrations describing the ritual performances of *seiðr* are: *Eiríks saga rauða* 4; *Vatnsdœla saga* 10; *Laxdœla saga* 35ff.; *Ǫrvar Odds saga* 2; *Hrólfs saga kraka* 3; *Víga-Glums saga* 12. Several other texts are of interest and some of them will be discussed in what follows. For a more or less complete catalogue of texts relevant to *seiðr* see Dillmann 1987. General discussions on *seiðr*: Strömbäck 1935; Dillmann 1982, 1987; Mundal and Steinsland 1989; Hastrup 1990a: 197ff; Clunies Ross 1998: 32f.; DuBois 1999: 121ff.

17. *Vǫluspá* 28: Ein sat hon úti.

18. Snorri, *Ynglinga saga* 4: Hon kenndi fyrst með Ásum seið, sem Vǫnum var títt.

19. Some Old Norse texts are of special interest: In the *Poetic Edda*: *Vǫluspá*, *Hávamál* and *Grímnismál*; and Snorri's *Edda* and the first chapters of his *Ynglinga saga*. Especially the latter deals at length with these more clandestine but severe aspects of the god.

20. Snorri, *Ynglinga saga* 7: Óðinn skipti hǫmum. Lá þá búkrinn sem sofinn eða dauðr, en hann var þá fugl eða dýr, fiskr eða ormr ok fór á einni svipstund á fjarlæg lǫnd at sínum ørendum eða annarra manna. Þat kunni hann enn at gera með orðum einum at sløkkva eld ok kyrra sjá ok snúa vindum hverja leið, er han vildi.

21. *Sigrdrífumál* 13:
> Hugrúnar scaltu kunna, ef þú vilt hveriom vera
> geðsvinnari guma;
> þær of réð, þær of reist,
> þær um hugði Hroptr,
> af þeim legi, er lekið hafði
> ór hausi Heiddraupnis
> oc ór horni Hoddrofnis.'

22. Snorri, *Ynglinga saga* 7: at eigi þótti karlmǫnnum skammlaust við at fara, ok var gyðjunum kennd sú íþrótt.

23. Snorri, *Ynglinga saga* 7: Váru þeir næst honum um allan fróðleik ok fjǫlkynngi.

24. *Lokasenna* 24:
> 'Enn þic síða kóðo Sámseyo í,
> oc draptu á vétt sem vǫlor;
> vitca líki fórtu verþióð yfir,
> oc hugða ec þat args aðal.'

25. 'Certainly between women's de jure status and de facto status (as it is represented in literary and even historical texts) there appears to have been a very

large playing field, and the woman (especially the divorced or widowed woman) sufficiently ambitious and sufficiently endowed with money and power seems not to have been especially hindered by notions of male and female nature' (Clover 1993: 369).

26. The chapter has been interpreted from many points of view. For some important studies of the various approaches, see Strömbäck 1935; Pálsson 1991: 164f. (with emphasis on Guðríðr); Dillmann 1992: 25ff.; Mundal and Steinsland 1989: 99 (divination as healing) DuBois 1999: 121ff.

27. The Háuksbók manuscript gives this information.

28. Trans. Kunz, *CSI* I: 6. *Eiríks saga rauða* 4: Þá var hon svá búin, at hon hafði yfir sér tuglamǫttul blán, ok var settr steinum allt í skaut ofan; hon hafði á hálsi sér glertǫlur, lambskinnskofra svartan á hǫfði ok við innan kattskinn hvít; ok hon hafði staf í hendi, ok var á knappr; hann var búinn með messingu ok settr steinum ofan um knappinn; hon hafði um sik hnjóskulinda, ok var þar á skjóðupungr mikill, ok varðveitti hon þar í tǫfr sín, þau er hon þurfti til fróðleiks at hafa. Hon hafði á fótum kálfskinnsskúa loðna ok í þvengi langa, ok á tinknappar miklir á endunum. Hon hafði á hǫndum sér kattskinnsglófa, ok váru hvítir innan ok loðnir.

29. Trans. Kunz, *CSI* I: 6. *Eiríks saga rauða* 4: Hon hafði messingarspón ok kníf tannskeptan, tvíhólkaðan af eiri, ok var brotinn af oddrinn.

30. Trans. Kunz, *CSI* I: 6. *Eiríks saga rauða* 4: Hvárki em ek fjǫlkunnig né vísindakona, en þó kenndi Halldís, fóstra mín, mér á Íslandi þat kvæði, er hon kallaði Varðlokur. (Manuscripts vary between *varðlokkur* and *varðlokur.*)

31. Dag Strömbäck writes: 'Varðlokkur syftar på den speciella sång, som användes för att återkalla den schamanerandes själ till den i extatisk utmattning liggande kroppen' (Strömbäck 1935: 139: '*Varðlokkur* refers to the special song used to recall the soul of the one shamanizing to the body lying in a state of ecstatic exhaustion').

32. Trans. Kershaw 35–6. *Norna-Gests þáttr* 11: Þar fór þá um landit völur, er kallaðar váru spákonur ok spáðu mönnum aldr. Því buðu menn þeim ok gerðu þeim veizlur ok gáfu þeim gjafir at skilnaði.

33. Trans. Pálsson and Edwards 28. *Ǫrvar Odds saga* 2: Hún fór á veizlur ok sagði mönnum fyrir um vetrarfar ok forlög sín.

34. Trans. Wawn, *CSI* IV: 14. *Vatnsdæla saga* 10: Finnan var sett hátt ok búit um hana vegliga; þangat gengu menn til frétta, hverr ór sínu rúmi, ok spurðu at ørlǫgum sínum.

35. Trans. McKinnell, *CSI* II: 285. *Víga Glúms saga* 12: Þótti mikit undir, at húsfreyjur fagnaði henni vel um heraðit; sagði nǫkkut vilhalt, sem henni var beini veittr.

36. Trans. McKinnell, *CSI* II: 286. *Víga Glúms saga* 12: 'Eigi ætla ek þér nú allgóðan þykkja beinann fyrir skútu þessa.'

37. Trans. Pálsson and Edwards 205. *Bósa saga ok Herrauðs* 5: Þetta kveld it sama kom Busla í þat herbergi, sem Hringr konungr svaf í, ok hóf upp bæn þá, er síðan er kölluð Buslubæn, ok hefir hún víðfræg orðit síðan, ok eru þar í mörg orð ok ill, þau sem kristnum mönnum er þarfleysa í munni at hafa.

38. Trans. Pálsson and Edwards 206. *Bósa saga ok Herrauðs* 5, st. 4:
    Svá skal ek þjarma
    þér at brjósti,
    at hjarta þitt
    höggormar gnagi,
    en eyru þín
    aldregi heyri
    ok augu þín
    úthverf snúist.

39. Trans. Pálsson and Edwards 206f. *Bósa saga ok Herrauðs* 5, st. 7:
    Sé þér í hvílu
    sem í hálmeldi,
    en í hásæti
    sem á hafbáru;
    þó skal þér seinna
    sýnu verra,
    en ef þú vilt við meyjar
    manns gamman hafa,
    villist þú þá vegarins;
    eða viltu þulu lengri?

40. Trans. Pálsson and Edwards 207. *Bósa saga ok Herrauðs* 5: 'Þá skal taka þér fram betr,' segir Busla. Hóf hún þá upp þat vers, Syrpuvers er kallat ok mestr galdr er í fólginn ok eigi er lofat at kveða eftir dagsetr.

41. *Grettis saga* 78: Ef þú vill mín ráð hafa, þá vil ek ráða, hversu með er farit. Trans. Scudder, *CSI* II: 168: 'If you want my advice, I must also decide how you should employ it.'

42. *Grettis saga* 78: hversu heilladrjúgir þeir munu vera. Trans. Scudder, *CSI* II: 168: 'how providence favours them'.

43. Trans. Scudder, *CSI* II: 169. *Grettis saga* 78: Nú mæli ek þat um við þik, Grettir, at þú sér heillum horfinn, allri gipt ok gæfu ok allri vǫrn ok vizku, æ því meir, sem þú lifir lengr.

44. Trans. Scudder, *CSI* II: 169. *Grettis saga* 78: ok við engi orð hefir mér meir brugðit en þessi.

45. Trans. Scudder, *CSI* II: 170. *Grettis saga* 78: Nú var svá gǫrt, sem hon beiddi, ok er hon kom til strandar, haltraði hon fram með sænum, svá sem henni væri vísat til. Þar lá fyrir henni rótartré svá mikit sem axlbyrðr. Hon leit á tréit ok bað þá snúa fyrir sér; þat var sem sviðit ok gniðat ǫðrum megin. Hon lét telgja á lítinn flatveg, þar gniðat var; síðan tók hon kníf sinn ok reist rúnar á rótinni ok rauð í blóði sínu ok kvað yfir galdra. Hon gekk ǫfug andsœlis um tréit ok hafði þar yfir mǫrg rǫmm ummæli. Eptir þat lætr hon hrinda trénu á sjá ok mælti svá fyrir, at þat skyldi reka út til Drangeyjar, ok verði Gretti allt mein at.

46. Trans. Kunz, *CSI* 5: 47. *Laxdœla saga* 35: ǫll varú þau mjǫk fjǫlkunnig ok inir mestu seiðmenn.

47. *Laxdæla saga* 35: kváðu þar harðsnúin frœði; þat váru galdrar. Trans. Kunz, *CSI* 5: 50: 'Then they chanted powerful incantations; they were sorcery.'

48. Trans. Kunz, *CSI* 5: 53. *Laxdæla saga* 36: Fór Þorleikr nú á fund landseta sinna, Kotkels ok Grímu, ok bað þau gera nǫkkurn hlut, þann er Hrúti væri svívirðing at. Þau tóku undir þetta léttliga ok kváðusk þess vera albúin.

49. Trans. Kunz, *CSI* 5: 117. *Laxdæla saga* 76: Þar fundusk undir bein; þau váru blá ok illilig; þar fannsk ok kinga ok seiðstafr mikill. Þóttusk menn þá vita, at þar mundi verit hafa vǫluleiði nǫkkut. Váru þau bein fœrð langt í brott, þar sem sízt var manna vegr.

50. *Hávamál* 144:

>   Veiztu, hvé rísta scal, veiztu, hvé ráða scal?
>   veiztu, hvé fá scal, veiztu, hvé freista scal?
>   veiztu, hvé biðia scal, veiztu, hvé blóta scal?
>   veiztu, hvé senda scal, veiztu, hvé sóa scal?

51. *Sigrdrífumál* 4:

>   'mál oc manvit gefit ocr mærom tveim
>   oc læcnishendr, meðan lifom!'

52. *Sigrdrífumál* 11:

>   'Limrúnar scaltu kunna, ef þú vilt læcnir vera
>   oc kunna sár at sía;
>   á berki scal þær rísta oc á baðmi viðar,
>   þeim er lúta austr lima.'

53. Trans. and ed. Robinson. *Fjǫlsvinnsmál* 49:

>   Lengi ek sat
>   Lyfjabergi á,
>   beið ek þín dœgr ok daga:
>   nú þat varð,
>   er ek vætt hefi,
>   at þú ert kominn, mǫgr, til minna sala.

54. Trans. Scudder, *CSI* I: 143. *Egils saga Skalla-Grímssonar* 72:

>   Skalat maðr rúnar rista,
>   nema ráða vel kunni, þat verðr mǫrgum manni,
>   es of myrkvan staf villisk;
>   sák á telgðu talkni
>   tíu launstafi ristna,
>   þat hefr lauka lindi
>   langs ofrtrega fengit.

55. *Sigrdrífumál* 9:

>   'Biargrúnar scaltu kunna, ef þú biarga vilt
>   oc leysa kind frá konom;
>   á lófa þær scal rísta oc of liðo spenna
>   oc biðia þá dísir duga.'

56. *Oddrúnargrátr* 9:
    'Svá hiálpi þér hollar vættir,
    Frigg oc Freyia oc fleiri goð,
    sem þú feldir mér fár af hǫndom.'
57. Trans. and ed. Grendon 1909: 207:

    Wið lætbyrde.

    Sê wîfman, sê hire cild âfêdan ne mæg, gange tô gewîtenes mannes bir-
    genne, and stæppe þonne þriwa þâ byrgenne, and cweþe þonne þriwa þâs
    word:
        Þis mê tô bôte þère lâþan lætbyrde,
        Þis mê tô bôte þère swèran swærtbyrde,
        Þis mê tô bôte þère lâðan lambyrde.
58. *Skírnismál* 36:
    'Þurs ríst ec þér oc þría stafi,
    ergi oc œði oc óþola;
    svá ec þat af ríst, sem ec þat á reist,
    ef goraz þarfar þess.'
59. Huldr also appears in chapter 14 and is then called a *vǫlva*.
60. Snorri, *Ynglinga saga* 13: at vera myndi fjǫlkynngi Finna í fýsi hans.
61. *Kormáks saga* 5: þú skalt Steingerðar aldri njóta. Trans. McTurk, *CSI* I: 187:
    'you will never enjoy Steingerðr's love.'
62. Trans. McTurk, *CSI* I: 187. *Kormáks saga* 5: Því mantu ekki ráða, in vánda ker-
    ling.
63. *Hávamál* 161:
    Þat kann ec iþ sextánda, ef ec vil ins svinna mans
    hafa geð alt oc gaman:
    hugi ec hverfi hvítarmri kono
    oc sný ec hennar ǫllom sefa.

    Þat kann ec iþ siautiánda, at mic mun seint firraz
    iþ manunga man.
64. *Hárbarðsljóð* 20:
    'Miclar manvélar ec hafða við myrcriðor
    þá er ec vélta þær frá verom.'
65. *Helgakviða Hjǫrvarðssonar* 15:
    'Atli ec heiti, atall scal ec þér vera,
    miǫk em ec gífrom gramastr;
    úrgan stafn ec hefi opt búit
    ok qvalðar qveldriðor.'

Chapter 3
66. Trans. Quinn, *CSI* V: 142. *Eyrbyggja saga* 16: hávaðamaðr mikill ok málugr,
    slysinn ok rógsamr.

67. Trans. Quinn, *CSI* V: 142. *Eyrbyggja saga* 16: en hon spurði, hvárt hann ætlar þá enn í Mávahlið – 'ok klappa um kerlingar nárann?'

68. Trans. Quinn, *CSI* V: 143. *Eyrbyggja saga* 16: Þetta vár um stefnudaga reið Þorbjorn í Mávahlíð ok stefndi Geirríði um þat, hon væri kveldriða ok hon hefði valdit meini Gunnlaugs.

69. Trans. Quinn, *CSI* V: 143. *Eyrbyggja saga* 16: en hvárrgi þeira Snorra né Arnkels þótti bera mega kviðinn fyrir hleyta sakar við sœkjanda ok varnaraðilja.

70. Trans. Quinn, *CSI* V: 143. *Eyrbyggja saga* 16: ónýttisk málit fyrir þeim Snorra ok Þorbirni, ok fengu þeir af þessu óvirðing.

71. Trans. Quinn, *CSI* V: 154. *Eyrbyggja saga* 20: Mun Geirríðr trollit þar komin, ok mun þá eigi sjónhverfingum einum mega við koma.

72. Trans. Quinn, *CSI* V: 154. *Eyrbyggja saga* 20: Vera má víst, at hann eigi eigi góða móður, en eigi hlýtr hann af því illt af mér, at ek vilda þat; en þat væri vili minn, at þér hlytið allir illit af mér; vænti ek ok, at þat mun svá vera.

73. Trans. Quinn, *CSI* V: 154. *Eyrbyggja saga* 20: spurðusk nú þessi tíðendi oll jafn-saman ok var engum harmsaga í. Líðr nú svá vetrinn.

74. Trans. Kunz, *CSI* V: 50. *Laxdœla saga* 35: Þórðr kom til bœjar Kotkels með tíunda mann; synir þeira Kotkels váru eigi heima. Síðan stefndi hann þeim Kotkatli ok Grímu ok sonum þeira um þjófnað ok fjolkynngi ok lét varða skóggang; hann stefndi sokum þeim til alþingis ok fór til skips eptir þat.

75. Trans. Kunz, *CSI* V: 54. *Laxdœla saga* 37: síðan tóku þeir belg af hofði honum, en bundu stein við hálsinn. Hallbjorn rak þá skyggnur á landit, ok var aug-nalag hans ekki gott.

76. Trans. Kunz, *CSI* V: 54. *Laxdœla saga* 37: Mjok þykkir þetta atkvæði á hafa hrinit.

77. Trans. Kunz, *CSI* V: 55. *Laxdœla saga* 38: lætr henni nauðga til sagna, ok er hon verðr hrædd, þá segir hon, at maðr kemr til fundar við hana, – 'sá er mikill,' segir hon, 'ok sýnisk mér vænligr.'

78. Trans. Kunz, *CSI* V: 55. *Laxdœla saga* 38: ok getr Stígandi sét oðrum megin í hlíðina; þar var fagrt landsleg ok grasloðit; en því var líkast, sem hvirfilvindr komi at; sneri um jorðunni, svá at aldregi síðan kom þar gras upp. Þar heitir nú á Brennu.

79. Trans. Quinn, *CSI* V: 202. *Eyrbyggja saga* 54: létusk þá enn sex menn í hríðinni; en sumt fólk flýði fyrir reimleikum ok aptrgongum.

80. Trans. Quinn, *CSI* V: 202. *Eyrbyggja saga* 55: en sœkja þá menn alla í duradómi, er aptr gengu; bað prest veita þar tíðir, vígja vatn ok skripta monnum.

81. Trans. Scudder, *CSI* II: 178. *Grettis saga* 82: Ongull var óþokkaðr mjok af þes-sum verkum, þegar at menn vissu, at Grettir hafði með gørningum unninn verit.

82. The 'Christenret' of the older Borgaþing's law, *Norges gamle love* I: 372: maðr sittær uti, oc vækkir troll up; Dalalageu, *Kyrkobalken* 11: maðr sittær uti, och væckir troll up.

PART 3

The Medieval Church and State on Superstition, Magic and Witchcraft: From Augustine to the Sixteenth Century

Edward Peters

The roots of the attitudes of medieval ecclesiastical and secular authorities towards superstition, magic and witchcraft – as well as their definitions of these terms – may be found in a number of originally diverse sources from late antiquity that were drawn together in the thought world of the Mediterranean around the turn of the Common Era (Flint and others, in *Witchcraft and Magic in Europe* II; Markus 1974; Bernstein 1993; Russell 1977, 1981, 1984; Brashear 1992; Fox 1986; Pagels 1995; Beard and North 1990; Beard, North, Price 1998). Among these are the texts of Jewish scripture included in the canon of the Christian Bible (particularly Exodus 7: 8–13, 22: 18; Leviticus 20: 6, 20: 27; Numbers 22: 7, 23: 23; Deuteronomy 13: 18: 9–14; 26: 10–12; 1 Samuel 15: 23; 1 Samuel 28: 3–25; Isaiah 28: 15; Daniel 2: 1–13) and texts from Christian Scripture itself (Matthew 2: 1–12, 10: 8; Luke 8: 26–39; Acts 8: 9–24, 18: 19–20; 1 Corinthians 10: 20; 2 Thessalonians 2; 1 Timothy 4: 1; Nock, 1972a). Many of the themes of Scripture were expanded and elaborated in much of the Jewish and Christian apocryphal literature and the early Christian romances (especially the *Book of Enoch* (de Jonge 1985: 26–55), *The Clementine Recognitions* (esp. IV, 27–9; Elliott 1993: 431–8), and the later *Apostolic History of Abdias* (Elliott 1993: 525–31)).

They were further elaborated in the writings of the Church Fathers, most effectively in the writings of those Fathers whose work exerted a continuous influence through the entire period, from late antiquity to the sixteenth century, chiefly the complex thought in the voluminous works of Augustine (354–430, especially *The City of God*, books IX-X, and *On Christian Teaching* (*De Doctrina Christiana*) book II, 19–25) and the *Etymologies* (especially Book VIII) of Isidore of Seville (560–636; Harmening 1979: 332–9).

In terms of formal law there is also the legislation of the Roman emperors, particularly the Christian emperors of Rome from the fourth century on (especially in the *Theodosian Code*, book IX, and Justinian's legal compilations in the sixth century, both of which long influenced European learned law). There is also a variety of other texts ranging from Christian readings of Latin poets – particularly Vergil, Horace, Ovid, and Lucan on magic and sorcery, the literary reworking of classical myths, notably those of Circe and Medea (for Circe, see Yarnall 1994; Roberts 1996), the sections of the *Natural History* of Pliny the Elder that dealt with magic, especially book 30, and the interest of Roman writers like Apuleius in sorcery and shapeshifting – to historical accounts, saints' lives, sermons, collections of penitential literature and the literature of ancient magic, pagan or Christian (for pagan, Jewish, Near Eastern and Christian antiquity, see Thee 1984; Luck 1985; Neusner-Frerichs-Flesher 1989; Faraone and Obbink 1991; Gager 1992; Daxelmüller 1993; Meyer and Mirecki 1995; Graf 1997). These were supplemented after the fifth century by the law collections of the new Christian Germanic kingdoms of Europe, by the texts of early canon law and by later royal and ecclesiastical law-making from the age of Charlemagne (768–814) on, initially in the works known as penitentials and in the canons issued by Church synods and councils but later including more elaborate works of canon and secular law. These ideas guided later spiritual and temporal authorities as they encountered and became part of the still pagan peoples of late Iron-Age northern Europe and began the slow process of their conversion to a new normative Latin Christianity (Hillgarth 1986; Flint 1991; Hen 1995; Muldoon 1997; MacMullen 1997; Fletcher 1997; Milis 1998).

But not all of these ideas were readily available to all individual writers and law-makers on these subjects, nor were superstition, magic and witch-craft always matters of great concern to authorities or always clear or iden-tified as heresy. Even in the fourteenth and fifteenth centuries when the problem of sorcery and witchcraft attracted more attention, the laws and theoretical literature concerning them remained a very small part of an immense devotional, legal and theological literature that was chiefly devoted to other aspects of the social and spiritual lives of Christian Europeans (Duffy 1992; Swanson 1995; Van Engen 1994). By focusing only on superstition, magic and witchcraft, there is a danger of overrating their importance in a much larger literature, for they are difficult to understand without their devotional and legal contexts. Definitions and the under-standing of all of these terms also changed from the fourth century to the sixteenth. So did readings of Greek, Roman and biblical history. In the thirteenth, fourteenth and fifteenth centuries, many writers on magic and witchcraft read the literature of the remote past as if it spoke of contempo-rary concerns and meant the same things by its terminology as later thinkers did. Our concern in this chapter is with the nature of activities generally then designated as 'superstition', 'magic' and 'witchcraft' that could – or were thought to – be triable in ecclesiastical or temporal crimi-nal courts and be subject to specific disciplinary measures such as penances or punishments. From the twelfth century on, discussions of superstition, magic and witchcraft occur in a widening variety of sources, many of which also influenced the policies of ecclesiastical and temporal justice.

This chapter will treat its subject in seven sections: (I) Superstition and Magic in the Mediterranean World from Augustine to Isidore of Seville; (II) Superstition and Magic in the Early Germanic Law Collections; (III) The Development of Early Canon Law and Carolingian Legislation to Burchard of Worms, who died in 1025; (IV) The Legal and Theological Literature of the Twelfth and Thirteenth Centuries; (V) The Outburst of Accusations of Magic and Witchcraft in High Political Circles at the Turn of the Fourteenth Century; (VI) The Sorcerer and the Witch; (VII) Superstition, Magic and Witchcraft on the Eve of the Reformation. The focus of the chapter is less upon the very wide range of practices considered to be superstitious or magical than upon the formally conceived ideas of churchmen and temporal rulers that shaped legislation and directed the operation of judicial institutions. Our focus is Latin Christian Europe rather than the Greek East (Maguire 1995, 1997), late antique or medieval and early modern Judaism (Blau 1898, 1970, 1974; Trachtenberg 1970; Goldin 1976; Schäfer 1990; Faraone and Obbink 1991; Meyer and Mirecki 1995: 111–208; and earlier works in the present series) or the Islamic world (Burnett 1996). I have cited English translations where these are available and reliable; where not, I have translated some texts myself, and I have translated all titles of literary works into English.

Although the terms *superstitio* and *magia* were regularly used throughout the period, since most of the literature was written in Latin, the term 'witchcraft' as a translation of either of these is not always appropriate before the late twelfth century, perhaps even later. There is considerable good sense in remembering that for many centuries particular terms in Greek, Latin and vernacular European vocabularies did not translate each other precisely and exactly, and that some terms – 'witch' and 'vampire' are good examples, the former better described by the Latin terms of *stria* or *striga* and the latter by *lamia* – did not appear in any language until much later than early Christianity (Burris 1936; Wagner 1939; Lecouteux 1983, 1985; Klaniczay 1990; Harmening 1990a, b; Caro Baroja 1990; Murray 1992: 189; Behringer 1998; Griffiths 1996). In fact, the Latin language maintained a particular set of terms for the subjects of this chapter that in many cases shaped the vernacular languages of Europe and imposed at least a linguistic and conceptual identity on a set of originally very diverse phenomena. Latin terms will be retained throughout this chapter where appropriate, but they will be explained at their first use. These problems are not pedantic – this chapter must take these uses and linguistic differences, and the matters that they are thought to describe, regularly into account.

CHAPTER 1

Superstition and Magic from Augustine to Isidore of Seville

Christian writers first encountered the Latin words *superstitio* and *magia* when Greek and Roman writers and rulers applied them to Christianity itself in their combined senses of divination, magic, secret and forbidden practices, and excessive religious fear (MacMullen 1966; Achtemeier 1976; Harmening 1979: 14–32; Fox 1986: 37; Graf 1997). Christians in turn reversed the usage: for them, superstition referred to what they considered to be the irrational and false beliefs – that is, the 'religions' – of all others besides Christians and, to a limited extent, Jews, although Christian scripture portrayed some Jews as magicians (Acts 13: 6–12; 19: 13–20; Nock 1972b: II: 308–30; Fox 1986: 143) and the poisonous image of the Jew as sorcerer survived for a long time in later European thought (Trachtenberg 1943). Christians captured for themselves the old and respected Latin word *religio* – which originally designated the bond between humans and the gods – and restricted its application to Christianity alone (Graf 1997: 254, n. 76; Beard and North 1990; Beard, North and Price 1998). To the late second-century Christian apologist Tertullian, all pagan religious practice was 'Roman superstition'. Early Christian teachers like Ignatius of Antioch also pointed out that although the Magi had used their skills as magician-astrologers to find the Christ-child, once they had found their destination, their skills ceased, since they were no longer needed after the fact of the Incarnation and Nativity (Flint 1991: 364–75; Veenstra 1998: 104). To the fourth-century Christian polemicist Lactantius the definitions were crisp and simple: 'religion is the true cult paid to God – superstition is the false' (La Roche 1957; Grodzynski 1974; Cardini 1979; Harmening 1979: 14–40; Salzman 1987; MacMullen 1997: 74–102; for a later period, Clark 1997: 472–88). In the late sixth century Martin of Braga, strongly under the influence of Augustine in his work *On the Correction of Rustics*, explained how demons had made themselves into pagan gods in order to deceive humans and receive their worship (Psalm 95 [96]: 5; Barlow 1969: 71–85). In Martin's work, Jove was described as a magician and a sexual corrupter of his wife and daughters (Hillgarth 1986: 58–60; Barlow 1969: 81–2). Shortly after Martin, Gregory of Tours in Gaul repeated the theme in his *Histories* (Hillgarth 1986: 81; de Nie 1995).

Roman religion was one thing for Christians, and although they often called it both superstition and magic, magic generally was quite another. Christians knew that Roman law had condemned magic, especially magic worked by private practitioners for their own or their clients' private and usually harmful ends, often as profoundly as Christians themselves did. Pliny the Elder had dismissed much magic in the Roman world as 'magical vanities'. The magicians' techniques included the use of incantations, inscribed amulets, images, texts, and the use of magical substances. The emperor Augustus was said to have burned the books of the diviners; the third-century emperor Septimius Severus was said to have buried all the magic books his agents could collect in the tomb of Alexander the Great; an imperial law of 297 condemned sorcerers because of the private and secret nature of their activities and their destructive powers. The Christian historian Eusebius (260–340) accused Maxentius, the opponent of the Christian-favouring imperial claimant Constantine, of using magicians to defend Rome against Constantine's legitimate invasion. Several panegyrics of Constantine and other early Christian emperors contrasted the 'divine teachings' that guided them to the 'superstitious magic' to which their pagan rivals resorted. In these instances, 'magic' seems to have meant to Christians something distinct from pagan religion in general, and the enemies of the Christian emperors were thus doubly condemned – for superstitious paganism and for the use of magic.

Richard Kieckhefer has said of these attitudes, 'While "magic" obviously served as a polemical term, even its polemical usage presupposed a shared understanding of magic as a cluster of countercultural rituals worked privately for the magicians' personal ends or those of his clients. The term "magic" was sometimes used for the rituals of insiders (even members of elites) as well as outsiders or for the rites of people who became defined as outsiders only because they used magic. To brand a Christian, a pagan, or a Jew as a magician was to use a word with a prior and independent meaning and to give it abusive, polemical application' (Kieckhefer 1994a: 815).

These attitudes and ideas were not without consequences in Roman law (MacMullen 1966; Pharr 1932). In a law of 319/320 the emperor Constantine prohibited the private consultation of diviners, but he also permitted the public practice of divination, an old and respected component of Roman religion, although he also noted that Christians could not legally be compelled to participate in public sacrifices. Constantine also prohibited any *haruspex* from entering a private house. Constantius II dealt savagely with those accused of any form of magic outside those permitted by Roman religion and custom (Barb 1963: 109). The emperor Julian, formerly a Christian, was accused by Christian critics of favouring magicians. In 371 the Christian emperor Valentinian I could still label the benevolent public divinatory practice known as the *haruspicina* as *religio*, rather than as *superstitio* or the criminal category *maleficium* (Beard and North 1990).

But Valentinian's law was issued towards the end of a period when Christian emperors were attempting to preserve some of the most cherished and otherwise respectable religious components of a Rome that was still largely pagan. With the discovery of a plot that employed sorcerers against the life of the emperor Valens in 374, the full force of Roman criminal law was brought against all magicians and those who employed them; imperial officials searched libraries for books of magic of all kinds, and the books – and sometimes whole libraries – were burned (Speyer 1992; MacMullen 1997; Bologne 1993: 18–19; Beard and North 1990). By charging the defendants with high treason, the most serious crime Roman law recognized, the emperor also automatically subjected them to torture and the most ferocious forms of public execution that the empire employed (Callu 1984; Funke 1967; Ammianus Marcellinus 1952–6: III: 215; Matthews 1989, 258–62; Cameron 1983: 163–4). Late Roman law continued to deal harshly with all those accused of magical practices. Even possession of magic books was sufficient to send a high-ranking Roman into exile and entail the loss of his property, while a lower-ranking person convicted of the same offence was to be executed. The emperors of the early fifth century, however, permitted those who owned magic books simply to purge themselves if they converted to Christianity and did not become recidivists (Barb 1963: 114). Anyone using predictive magic concerning the emperor or the future of the Roman state was to be sent to the beasts in the arena or to crucifixion, while anyone convicted of being a *magus* was to be burned alive (Pharr 1932; Lear 1965: 117). Enough cases survive from the fourth and fifth centuries to indicate that these laws were regularly used. Sorcerers were exiled from Rome in 409 (Pharr 1952: 9.16.2; MacMullen 1966: 132–4). Around the year 500, sorcerers appear to have been exiled from Rome once again, and when one of them, Basilius, returned, he was burned to death at the order of the Ostrogothic king in Italy, Theoderic (Cassiodorus 1992: 77–8).

The increasing degree of Christianization of the Roman Empire led to the ultimate prohibition of all forms of pagan religion, both public and private, by the end of the fourth century. In this context, a number of Christian thinkers reviewed the earlier ideas of superstition and magic, and a number of Christian emperors issued stiffer laws defining and condemning both. For example, several imperial laws of the fourth and early fifth centuries that were later included in the *Theodosian Code* , published in 438, prohibited all subjects of the emperors from consulting soothsayers, diviners, astrologers, augurs and seers (Pharr 1952: 9.16.1–3). The older imperial toleration for the beneficial public aspects of some of these practices had now disappeared: 'The Chaldeans and wizards, and all the rest whom the common people call *malefici*' will use their arts no more (Pharr 1952: 9.16.4; Pharr 1932; Burriss 1936; Hunt 1993). It is important to note that the terms *maleficus* and *maleficium*, which conventionally meant 'criminal' and 'criminal act', and continued to do so in law until much later, appear from this text to be now also applied 'by the common people' especially to magicians of various kinds. The term *maleficium* designated what we term some kinds of 'magic' and all kinds of 'witchcraft' down to the end of the eighteenth century (Rousseau 1979; Flint 1991: 17). The *Theodosian Code* and several abbreviated versions of it constituted what most Europeans knew of Roman law until the rediscovery of Justinian's *Digest* in the late eleventh and early twelfth century. The work of Justinian and his legal advisers in the 530s, however, preserved many of the strictures on magic and superstition in the *Theodosian Code*, especially in *Code* IX.18 and *Digest* XLVIII.8 (Pharr 1932), so that the transition from one Roman law text to another in the twelfth century did little to change later Europeans' notions of the place of magic in Roman and later European learned law.

With the late fourth-century emperors, Church leaders, too, took a sharper and more precise position regarding superstition and magic. Assemblies of clergy in synods and councils began to lay down rules for the governance and disciplining of Christian communities. A synod at Elvira in 306 prohibited the last rites to those who had killed others by *maleficium*; a synod at Ancyra of 314 condemned to a long period of penance those who had used divination; the council of Laodicaea in the mid to late Fourth century prohibited the use of magic by the clergy, as did the fourth Council of Carthage in 398 and later councils. These rules adopted by synods and councils were collected and preserved, most importantly in the canon law collection of Dionysius Exiguus of around 500, and from Dionysius they were cited much later, since they had come to constitute a large part of the most widely known and used collection of canon law, particularly the version of Dionysius' collection augmented by Pope Hadrian I (772–95) and known as the Dionysio-Hadriana (Brundage 1995: 27–8), which was sent by Hadrian to Charlemagne (768–814) for his guidance in ecclesiastical affairs.

The work of synods and councils could also have immediate consequences. The Synod of Saragossa in 380 condemned the scholar Priscillian as a heretic, and in 385 a later relentless imperial investigation found Priscillian guilty of magical practices and sentenced him to death. The execution of Priscillian was the first one of a convicted heretic, and it is important to note both that the trial and execution were carried out by imperial officials, even against the protests of Christian bishops, and that the actual capital charges were those of magic (Chadwick 1976).

A second source in early ecclesiastical legislation for attitudes toward magic and superstition is the *indiculi superstitionum*, lists of widespread beliefs and practices that were condemned by synods, councils and individual churchmen, one of the earliest being the list drawn up by Martin of Braga mentioned above, and appended to the legislation of the Second Council of Braga in 572 (Homann, 1965). Martin's list and later lists continued to be made, copied and repeated down to the beginning of the twelfth century (McNeill and Gamer 1938; Flint 1991: 41; Russell 1972: 45–62; Harmening 1979: 53–5; Dierkens 1984; Milis 1998).

Individual Christian leaders and thinkers, too, wrote vehemently against all forms of what they considered to be superstition and magic, from Tertullian and Irenaeus of Lyons in the late second and third centuries to Augustine and Jerome in the late fourth and early fifth (Thorndike 1923–58: I: 337–503). One of the most influential of Christian thinkers was Augustine, whose voluminous writings addressed subjects of all kinds that concerned Christians and exerted an enormous influence on all later Christian thought.

Augustine was a provincial from Roman north Africa whose skills as a teacher of rhetoric led him into the highest aristocratic and scholarly circles of Rome and later Milan, the effective capital of the western Roman Empire. Converted to Christianity in Milan, Augustine left the city to return home to north Africa, where he was made a priest and later bishop of Hippo Regius. He spent the rest of his life as bishop and as the most prolific and respected Christian theologian of the Latin-speaking world. One of Augustine's considerable achievements in dealing with magic was his ability to reshape the categories that included magic and to fit them into a comprehensive Christian position on all aspects of demonology, magic and superstition (Harmening 1979: 33–40; Thorndike 1923–58: I: 504–22). Magic did not figure prominently in his early thought, but as Augustine's confidence in human capacities grew less after his re-reading of the Epistles of Paul in the 390s, and his sense of human vulnerability to the temptations of the world and to demons grew greater, magic began to figure more and more prominently (Markus 1990: 47–62). It is after this period that he wrote his most important discussions of superstition and magic.

In his treatise *On Christian Doctrine* (II.20.30 Kors and Peters 2001) Augustine lists as superstition virtually all forms of pagan religion, including the making of idols and the worship of creatures. Taking up and greatly articulating the increasingly familiar Christian idea that 'the gods of the pagans are demons in disguise', Augustine then condemns the making and worship of idols, consultations and pacts made with demons, as well as soothsaying, augury, amulets, consulting books of haruspicy and augury and medical charms (Psalm 95: 5; Harmening 1979, 1989; Russell 1981; Kelly 1985). He sums up his argument in II.23, when he says:

For it is brought about as if by a certain secret judgement of God that men who desire evil things are subjected to illusion and deception as a reward for their desire, being mocked and deceived by those fallen angels to whom, according to the most beautiful ordering of things, the lowest part of this world is subjected by Divine Providence.

The twin themes of divine permission to demons to tempt humans and the active role of demons in that process were part of Augustine's comprehensive approach to the problems of fallen human nature and the consequent vulnerability of humans to demonically inspired magic and illusion (Kelly 1968; Peters 1978; Russell 1981). To strengthen his point, Augustine draws into his discussion not only pagan practices, but several scriptural episodes, including that of King Saul and the witch of Endor (1 Kings [1 Samuel] 28: 15–19) and Paul's driving a prophetic spirit out of a woman (Acts 16: 16–18) to make his interpretation of scripture consistent with his views on pagan practices (Smelik 1977). In the first instance, Augustine states flatly that either God permitted the devil to bring back the dead prophet Samuel, or that the ghost was not Samuel at all, but a demon in Samuel's likeness, an approach that dates among Christians from the writings of Hippolytus in the early third century. Augustine prefers the latter opinion, consistent with his view of the vulnerabilty of fallen human sense perception to the illusions of demons, whose spiritual nature allowed them to operate in realms of nature that humans could not perceive. In any case his views of the episode are consistent with his views on magic generally. Augustine's views on the witch of Endor were later included in the great collection of canon law compiled by Master Gratian in the twelfth century. In the case of the prophetic woman, Paul drove out the demon that inhabited her. Here, too, illegitimate prophecy and necromancy are nothing but expressions of the power of the demons, acting with God's permission to delude and thereby test weak human nature. And for Augustine superstition is firmly linked to pacts and contracts with demons (II.22.34), an assertion that had a long and very influential history.

Augustine took up the problem of superstition and magic again in his massive work *The City of God*, a vast meditation on human history and the ultimate purpose of human existence. In book IV.30–1, Augustine condemns all of earlier Roman religion as superstition. In book VII the gods of the pagans are identified as demons. In book X.9, Augustine dismisses the pretensions of learned pagans that theirs was a purer and higher art than lowly necromancy or everyday private consultation of magicians, identifying both 'high' and 'low' magic as 'engaged in the fraudulent rites of demons'. Although Augustine acknowledged both legitimate Christian prophecy and legitimate wonder-working (which he termed 'miracle' in contrast with the Latin term *mira*, which he and other Christians understood to mean 'wonders'), he distinguished so sharply between the two categories as to separate them in most Christian minds forever (Ward 1982; Flint 1991: 31–5; Kee 1983).

In Augustine's view – and under his considerable influence – hitherto discrete magical beliefs and practices are now grouped entirely under the category of *superstitio* and condemned emphatically, their existence being blamed on the deceit of demons and the insatiable curiosity of ignorant and weak humans. In one of his later works, Augustine attributed both conditions to God's anger at human transgressions. He cited Psalm 77 [78]: '[God] has sent upon them the anger of his indignation, rage and tribulation, and possession by evil spirits' (cited in Brown 1970, 1972: 132–3). This citation effectively conveys Augustine's conviction of the power of the devil in this world and the role of superstition and magic as manifestations of that power. By reducing both pagan religion and all manifestations of magic to the category of superstition, Augustine created a Christian perspective on both past and present that had great impact in his own day and exerted an enormous influence on all later Christian thought.

Augustine was one of the most influential, but certainly not the only Church Father to deal with the themes of demonology and magic. Paul himself had identified idolatry with the worship of demons (1 Corinthians 10: 20). Justin Martyr, the second-century Christian apologist, had earlier emphasized the demons' use of magic to bind humanity to their service (Kelly 1968: 30–1). Ambrose of Milan, Augustine's older contemporary, developed the theme of the figure of Antichrist, the great apocalyptic deceiver of humanity who was to use magicians to gain power over the world (McHugh 1972). The concerns of Ambrose and Augustine were echoed by Pope Leo I in the mid-fifth century, who argued that magic was one of the many tricks of the devil through which he gains control of the greater part of humanity by means of *superstitiones*. Caesarius (469/70–542), bishop of Arles from 503 to 542, also contributed substantially to disseminating the views of Augustine, Ambrose, and other early Christian writers on the subjects of superstition and magic. Caesarius' sermons against magic and surviving pagan practices circulated widely, sometimes because of their attribution to Augustine and sometimes because they were quoted in the work of later writers, including those of the popular genre of saints' lives (Caesarius 1956; Blum 1936: 31; Harmening 1979: 49–64; Markus 1992; Klingshirn 1994; Flint 1991; 42–3; Kors and Peters 2001).

The work of Roman imperial legislators, Church synods and councils, the letters and other literary works of popes like Leo I (440–61) and Gregory I (590–604), the *indiculi superstitionum* and the writings of such figures as Augustine and others elaborated a fully developed Christian view of the role of demons and fallen human nature in the context of superstitious and magical practices. That work had depended upon the formation of an organized Christian Roman church and empire in the Mediterranean world and upon the learning and extensive means of communication available to individual thinkers. By the end of the sixth century that world slowly became subsumed in the larger and equally complex world of late Iron-Age migrating peoples who merged it into the culture of northern Europe. As the Roman world gradually folded into a sub-Roman Germanic culture in western Europe, much of the work of organized Roman law and Christian ecclesiology was preserved in summarized versions of laws, rules, and ecclesiastical legislation. Of these summaries, the most influential was that of Isidore of Seville (570–636).

Isidore's twenty books of *Etymologies* constituted a vast, but compressed, storehouse of ancient pagan and Christian learning (Flint 1991: 50–5; Kors and Peters 2001). It is important to note the context in which Isidore treats superstition and magic. Book VIII of the *Etymologies* deals with 'The Church and the Sects'. After a brief account of the Church and its difference from the Synagogue (VIII.1–2), Isidore treats heresy and schism among Christians and Jews (VIII.3–5), pagan philosophy and poetry (VIII.6–7) and pagan prophecy in the figure of the Sibyl (VIII.8). Isidore then turns to *magi* (VIII.9), beginning with a fanciful historical account of the invention of the magical arts by the Persian king (*sic*) Zoroaster and their transmission throughout the ancient world, including to the magicians of Pharaoh whom Moses defeated, and the figure of Circe, who tempted Odysseus.

Isidore then states that *magi* are called 'by the common people' (echoing the *Theodosian Code*) *malefici* and enchanters. They disturb both the elements of nature and the minds of humans. Supported by demons, they make use of blood and sacrificial victims as well as the dead. Necromancers revive the dead and make them speak. Isidore allows for a considerably greater degree of reality in these practices rather than demonic illusion in his discussion. He then lists other types of magicians: hydromancers, geomancers, aeromancers, pyromancers and a long list of others, including oracles and 'mathematicians' (whose knowledge of the stars gives them their power). In the case of the latter, God permitted their skills to survive (in the Magi of the Gospels) until they predicted the birth of Jesus, after which they were forbidden. All these arts come from demons, however, 'from a pestiferous association of men and evil angels, and they are therefore to be avoided by Christians and to be repudiated and condemned savagely', because 'the demon is in all these arts' of magic and divination (VIII.9.31). But Isidore is not finished with magic in VIII.9. He goes on to conclude book VIII by discussing pagans (VIII.10) and pagan gods (VIII.11). Pagan gods were humans whom other demons persuaded later humans had been deities, thus inventing idolatry. Isidore then discusses *daemones* and their relation to fallen angels, followers of the devil, whose name and origins are also discussed, as is Antichrist and other demons in the sevice of the devil. Isidore concludes with a discussion of *lamiae* and *incubae*.

The great appeal of Isidore's work was its compact and categorical character, and hence its convenience. Not only did Isidore provide an exhaustive summary of both Roman and Christian doctrines on superstition and magic from both scripture and pagan literature, but he located those doctrines in the context of a Christian culture and the forces that challenged and disturbed it, including schism and heresy, pagan philosophy, poetry, oracles and prophecies and pagan religion, thus providing his later readers with a picture of pagan, Jewish and Christian antiquity within which superstition and magic are firmly and categorically defined and located. The legacy of Isidore proved to be as great in this respect as that of Augustine, and it shaped the transmission of much of the knowledge of the pagan and early Christian worlds to the new world of the Germanic Mediterranean and northern Europe. That knowledge became the basis, not only of the process of the Christianization of northern Europe, but of the Christian understanding of the religious practices and beliefs of the late Iron-Age northern world.

CHAPTER 2

Superstition and Magic in the Germanic Law Collections

The earliest Christian attitudes toward superstition and magic had been shaped in a specific Mediterranean and Graeco-Roman context. From the sixth century on, that context was adapted to characterize the beliefs and practices of northern European peoples as the process of Christianization moved north and west, ultimately to Ireland, Scandinavia, Iceland and to the lands east of the Elbe and north of the Danube. The process of Christianization is a long and complex story and cannot be told here. But the process also contains some structural elements that are important for this subject. The Germanic peoples who established kingdoms in the old western parts of the Roman Empire – the Visigoths in Spain, the Franks in Gaul and the Ostrogoths and later Lombards in Italy – encountered a Christian Roman population and became Christians themselves, first through their kings and their families and advisers. Germanic Christian rulers usually cooperated with Roman Christian churchmen in prohibiting earlier religious practices now deemed idolatrous, magical, or both, and in absorbing into their own legal systems some of the constraints of Christian belief, as did Theoderic the Ostrogoth in the case of Basilius the sorcerer around 500. Elsewhere in Europe the conversion process either took place in areas where little memory of Rome survived – as in Anglo-Saxon England – or where Rome (and hence Christianity) had never come – Ireland, the northern Low Countries, the German lands generally east of the Rhine and north of the Danube, Scandinavia and Slavic and Baltic eastern and northeastern Europe.

Three related ideas prevailed everywhere, however: the gods of the pagans were still demons in disguise, pagan religious practices were superstition, and some pagan religious practices were magical.

Such views are found also in narrative accounts of the history of various peoples – in his account of the origins of the Huns in his *History of the Goths*, Jordanes states that the king of the Getae discovered 'witches' among his people and expelled them, but the witches were discovered by unclean spirits who begat the race of the Huns upon them (Mierow 1915, XXIV; Wolfram 1988: 107). In a number of other origin-narratives the presence of women with magical powers at the very moment of the formation of a distinctive and named people is a prominent feature, as it is in the legends of Libussa and the origins of the Czechs (Graus 1975: 89–108; Demetz 1997: 16–29). In northern Europe the Lapps were considered a race of sorcerers, much as Thessalians had been in the anthropological literature of earlier Greece (Christiansen 1997: 9). However different the culture of late Iron-Age northern Europe was from that of Mediterranean antiquity, Christian missionaries and Christianized rulers conceptualized it in a common set of Latin terms that had been worked out in Mediterranean Christianity and the Roman empire since the first century of the Common Era. The Germanic laws themselves suggest that they fall into two periods, before and after the late eighth century.

The first written collection of laws for the subjects of Germanic kings was composed in Latin in the kingdom of the Burgundians at the end of the fifth century. The laws of the Burgundians, the Visigoths in Spain and other early Germanic law codes often reflect Roman, rather than uniquely Germanic ideas. Thus, in *The Burgundian Code* (34.3), a husband is allowed to put away his wife only if he can prove one of three crimes against her: adultery, *maleficium*, or the violation of graves (Drew 1949: 45). This seems distinctly Roman and echoes earlier Roman law.

Another example is found in Visigothic Spain at the beginning of the sixth century in the *Lex Romana Visigothorum* (*The Roman Law of the Visigoths*), or the *Breviarium Alarici* (*The Breviary of Alaric*) of 506, a reworking of the *Theodosian Code* for the Roman subjects of the king, Alaric. In the *Breviarium* 9.13.3, the punishment for worshipping demons is death, another Christian-Roman echo. Later Visigothic law added further strictures. In the *Visigothic Code* 6.1.4, the rule that no slave or servant can be tortured in a case involving a master or mistress is excepted in the special cases of adultery, treason, counterfeiting, homicide or *maleficium*. This, too, seems to echo earlier Roman law (Lear 1965: 150). Later Visigothic law prohibited those convicted of *maleficium* and divination from giving testimony in legal cases; still later laws condemned those who invoked demons or caused damage to property or to other humans by means of magic to be publicly whipped and subsequently imprisoned (*Visigothic Code* 6.2.1–5; Hillgarth 1980, 1986; King 1972: 145–9). The influence of Roman law is strong throughout these rules, although the extreme harshness of Roman punishments is often reduced to public whipping and confinement.

These echoes of Roman law raise the question whether the Visigothic and later written laws and accounts of superstitious practices were simply repetitions of those of earlier Rome without concern for Visigothic and other contemporary Germanic practices, or whether they were deliberately adapted to deal with Germanic beliefs and practices. The problem of what Janet Nelson has astutely termed 'the artificiality, in a sense, of the written tradition' has plagued historians, anthropologists and folklorists for more than a century (Nelson, in Markus 1992: 169). Briefly, the problem asks whether any of the early medieval written laws and even the penitentials and the *indiculi superstitionum* deal with activities that were contemporary with the texts that describe and denounce them or simply conventionally repeat earlier material.

The list of known Germanic practices is long. Not only does it include the worship of deities of the sky and the earth, but also the figure of Diana-Herla, or Holda, or Herodias, the female leader of the 'wild ride', a particularly problematic case, since the earliest references to women believing that they ride with the goddess Diana (under one or another Latin or Germanic name) are few and scattered until the late ninth century, but from the thirteenth century on constitute one element of the later 'witches' sabbat' (Bonomo 1959; Russell 1972: 74–82; Flint 1991; Ginzburg 1991; Jacques-Chaquin and Préaud 1993). The practices and beliefs condemned in the laws also include a large number of charms, and the practice of ritual blessing and cursing (some of these are preserved in runic writing: Flowers 1986; Harmening 1979), healing (usually said to be done by a *hariolus* or *incantator*), divining (done by *aruspices*, *divini* or *vaticinatores*), lot-casting (done by *sortilegi*), fortune-telling, storm-raising, herblore, and the use of amulets and talismans (Russell 1972; Kieckhefer 1990; Flint 1991; Milis 1998). Some of these were said to have used occult powers that might be natural, others powers that required ritual. Other terms like *malefici* and *venefici* are less specific. The latter might mean 'poisoner', but the former may generically mean anyone using a mixture of *materia medica* and *materia magica*. Some Visigothic laws reflect these practices: the destruction of vineyards by magically caused hailstorms (Hillgarth 1986: 109; Dutton 1995), divination in general, the use of charms either for the purpose of erotic compulsion or to injure humans or animals or to destroy the harvest, the use of ligatures to cause sexual impotence, and other offences, including seeking to know the health of the king by divination, are all named as crimes and punished severely, although again not as severely as earlier Roman law would have allowed. This combination of Roman and distinctively Visigothic law suvived into the laws of the medieval Spanish kingdoms. It was also strengthened by the provisions of the Visigothic and later Christian churches in Spain and elsewhere, considered in the next section of this chapter.

The laws of the Franks display less Roman influence, although they echo some of the concerns of the Romans and Visigoths. The *Pactus Legis Salicae* (*The Agreement of the Salic Law*), issued around 510, contains several criminal provisions that may indicate the chief concerns of the Frankish authorities (Drew 1991). Section 19 of the *Pactus* sentences to an enormous fine anyone proved to have cast a magical spell over another human (so that he dies), or of having given someone a (presumably magical) herbal potion that kills him. If either action injures, but fails to kill, the fine is reduced. Since Germanic law focused largely on a calculus of degree of injury and appropriate compensation – that is, restitutive rather than retributive justice – the amounts of the fines can measure the severity of the offence. Section 19.4 condemns a woman who has cast a spell over another woman so that she cannot bear children to a fine of the same amount as the fine for magic that causes injury but not death. Section 64 of the *Pactus* illustrates the seriousness of such charges: anyone who calls another person a sorcerer ('that is, a *strioportio* or one who is said to carry a brass cauldron in which witches brew') and is not able to prove it is sentenced to the same amount of fine as one who uses spells without causing death (Drew 1991: 125). But anyone who calls a free woman a witch (*stria* or *meretrica* in the Latin) and cannot prove it is sentenced to a fine three times as great as for calling a man a sorcerer without proving it. But the last law of the section also states that 'if a witch eats a man and it is proved against him, he must pay two hundred *solidi*', the same amount stated in Section 19. Later revisions of the *Pactus* under Charlemagne in the late eighth and early ninth centuries continued to note the criminal character of these offences and sentences (Drew 1991: 197–9), as did later Carolingian Frankish legislation, considered below.

The language of Frankish and other Germanic law raises another problem, that of the terminology used to designate the magician and the witch. Such terms as *stria*, *strioportio* and other terms here replace or sometimes join the older Latin terms *magus*, *maleficus* and *malefica*. Lombard law will contribute the variant *striga* and the term *masca*. These seem to designate different functions from the terms in older Latin. The grandiose male and female magicians of Greek and Latin literature and law appear to have given way to individuals using occult powers for more limited, if no less lethal ends, using such powers as they are believed to possess for the injury of persons and property. Whatever learning they may be thought to have possessed does not resemble the learned magic of antiquity; it is rather the technical magic of the knowledge of herbs and charms, as well as the powers of divination and weather-making, but on a personal rather than a political level. In language as well as law, legal and ecclesiastical authorities are dealing with specific actions that they assumed were practised by their contemporaries and are not simply repeating conventional Roman legal wisdom.

The laws of the Lombards, issued in written form from the middle of the seventh to the middle of the eighth centuries under a series of kings, were, like Frankish law, less influenced by Roman usage than were the laws of the Visigoths (Drew 1973). Rothair's *Edict*, chapter 197, the earliest Lombard law concerning magic, focuses on the damage to the reputation of a woman unjustly accused (presumably by a guardian or a husband) of being a witch (*striga*) or enchantress (*masca*). If the accusation against the man is true, he must lose his right to protect and rule her, and the woman may then choose to return to the protection of her family or to that of the king. If the man denies that he has made such an accusation, he may clear himself by taking an oath and may retain her guardianship. C.198 expands upon this case. If a man admits that he called a woman a harlot or a witch in a state of uncontrolled anger, he may take an oath that he spoke in anger and not with any knowledge of whether the woman was a harlot or a witch. But if the man does not claim the defence of uncontrolled anger and repeats the charge, he must prove it in a duel, and if he succeeds, the woman must be punished. If he fails in his proof, he must pay the woman her life-value (*wergeld*). C. 368 specifies that no one fighting a duel may carry charmed herbs or 'similar prohibited things' secreted upon his person.

C. 376 of Rothair's edict, however, puts these laws into a different perspective:

> No one may presume to kill another man's *aldia* [dependent servant] or woman slave as if she were a vampire (*striga*), which the people call witch (*masca*), because it is in no wise to be believed by Christian minds that it is possible that a woman can eat a living man from within.

Rothair's terminology offers two distinctive terms and differentiates between them, although the term 'vampire' is not technically appropriate (*lamia* would seem to be more appropriate here than *striga*), nor is the term 'witch', but there are really no better English equivalents. The accuser must pay the accused woman acccording to her status, and he must also pay a fine to her master and to the king. This law reflects that of the graded ranks, cited above, and suggests that 'eating a man from within', however incompatible with Christian belief in Lombard thought, nevertheless was an accusation made among both the Franks and the Lombards. The laws of King Liutprand, of 727 (84.I), add yet another perspective to Lombard ideas of magic. Liutprand prohibits the consultation of sorcerers or witches for purposes of divination, and he also prohibits worshipping trees or springs. He condemns those who know of sorcerers or witches and do not reveal them and their clients. Nor may a Lombard send slaves to consult sorcerers, nor can slaves themselves consult sorcerers on their own (Drew 1973). Chapter 85.II condemns public officials who fail to prosecute sorcerers and witches and regulates the rewards each official shall receive for reporting such activities to his superiors. Public officials are also ordered to announce that all who have practised magic in the past must cease and desist. Thus, from Lombard law, as from Frankish, it is possible to observe at least the formal expression of areas in which public concerns over the practice of magic operated.

The earliest Alamanic laws, the *Pactus Legis Alamannorum* (*The Agreement of the Laws of the Alemans*), date from the first quarter of the seventh century (Rivers 1977). Law XIII repeats the Frankish law against calling another woman a witch or a poisoner. Law XIV prohibits the private punishment of a woman accused of witchcraft. The laws of the Bavarians, compiled around 750, punish the use of magic to damage the crops of another (Rivers 1977).

The laws tell what was prohibited and what actions were feared and designated as magic, but they do not always indicate the context of the forbidden acts (Kieckhefer 1990: 43–55), nor do they address the important and irritatingly vague question of shamanism (Ginzburg 1991; Klaniczay 1990 ; Behringer 1998). Narrative souces, however, histories and hagiography (saints' lives), offer occasionally more detailed accounts of what may have been actual practice. Many accounts of medical cures achieved by saintly intervention often indicate that sick people had first consulted a *hariolus* before they consulted the saint, suggesting that some form of what was designated magic was often the first resort of people in cases of illness. The *Histories* written by Gregory of Tours in the early seventh century describe a number of episodes in which we find similar detail (de Nie 1995). In book IV.29, Gregory notes that the entire people of the Huns was 'skilled at necromancy'. In book V.38, the use of magical arts by a servant of Queen Fredegund encompasses the deaths of the queen's sons, an accusation that elicits a terrible punishment from the queen in VI.35. In book IX.6 Gregory tells the story of Desiderius, a wandering magician who professed to be in contact with the Apostles Peter and Paul and to perform healing miracles, when in fact he was a *maleficus*. The chapter also tells of an unnamed man who professed to carry precious relics with him, and, when his belongings were searched, produced, 'the roots of various plants, moles' teeth, the bones of mice, bears' claws, and bears' fat. The Bishop [of Paris] had all this thrown into the river, for he recognized it as "witchcraft" '.

These sources indicate something of the extent and character of the practices and the society in which the laws operated. Although both figures described by Gregory appear to have professed some quasi-clerical status, it is also clear that clerics themselves were not above resorting to similar practices, particularly since they knew at least some Latin and also knew the powerful protective rituals of baptism and exorcism. An early ninth-century Bavarian synod denounced such activities on the part of clerics: 'If any presbyter or cleric observes auguries or divinations or dreams or lots or phylacteries, that is [magical] writings, let him be prepared to undergo the penalties of the canons' (McNeill and Gamer 1938: 399). Valerie Flint has argued that these sources, together with the laws, reveal a widespread set of beliefs and practices that provide much of the context of the Christianization of Europe from the fourth century on (Flint 1991; Markus 1992; Mordek and Glathaar 1993; de Nie 1995). A good example of the identification of magic with pagan practices is found in the early eighth-century *Life of Wilfrid* by Eddius Stephanus. In describing Wilfrid's return to England from a journey to Gaul, Eddius depicts the returning pilgrims as threatened by a large pagan army which Eddius compares to that of Pharaoh, of which the high priest, 'standing on a high mound, like Balaam, attempted to curse the people of God and to bind their hands by his magical arts [*magicis artibus*]' (Eddius, 1925: 29, 160; Little 1993).

From the laws imitative of the *Theodosian Code* to the more limited and specific concerns of Lombard, Frankish, Alamannic and Bavarian laws it is possible to see the changing idea and concern with magical practices on the part of European rulers of the sixth, seventh and eighth centuries. From 800 on, however, both the revival of earlier Christian and Roman thought concerning magic and a new sense of responsibility on the part of rulers for the spiritual and temporal status of their subjects led to a broader, more encompassing idea of magic. This new sense is best reflected in the legislation of early canon law and its susequent influence on Charlemagne and his successors.

CHAPTER 3

Early Canon Law and Carolingian Legislation to 1100

The early legislation of Germanic peoples did not always take ecclesiastical policies directly into account. But from the fifth century on, collections of conciliar and synodal canons, statements of prominent individuals and popes and selected texts from the Church Fathers were collected and transmitted in most parts of western Europe, as were the handbooks of penance, the penitentials (McNeill and Gamer 1938; Reynolds 1986; Gurevich 1988; Flint 1991; Milis 1998)). By the late eighth century these attained great influence in the Frankish kingdom of Charlemagne (768–814) and his successors, and they endured until the development of a more scientific theology and ecclesiastical legal science in the course of the twelfth century.

From the Council of Nicaea in 325, the practice of holding both general Church councils and local diocesan synods throughout the Roman world was instituted by the Christian emperors and cooperative ecclesiastical leaders. The canons, or rulings, of these councils shaped both the entire body of Christian doctrine and the rules of Christian discipline. A synod held at Laodicaea around the middle of the fourth century decreed that clerics who practised magic or astrology, or made amulets were to be deposed. A Frankish church council at Orleans in 511 (c. 30) repeated the condemnation (Hillgarth 1986: 103). Although councils and synods met in Gaul from the Council of Orleans in 507 through most of the sixth century under the direction of Clovis and his successors (later Frankish councils at Orleans in 549, at Eauze in 551 (c. 3), and at Auxerre in 561–605 (c. 4) (Hillgarth 1986: 103) dealt particularly with magic and superstition), Frankish councils fell into disuse in the seventh and early eighth centuries, and the most important conciliar legislation is that of the Visigothic kingdom in Spain. Councils at Braga held by Martin of Braga in 572 and the seventeen councils held at Toledo in the seventh century echoed Roman law in their condemnation of magical practices and superstitions of all kinds, but their aim was to achieve the penitence of the offender, and their method was ecclesiastical discipline, usually performed in public (Harmening 1979: 225; Hillgarth 1986: 53–64; Markus 1992). The list of superstitious practices compiled and issued by Martin of Braga remained influential down to the fifteenth century. In the Visigothic kingdom the high degree of cooperation between king and ecclesiastical leaders led to a more thorough discussion of such offences as magic and a greater likelihood that those who practised it would be subject to both ecclesiastical discipline and royal justice.

Some of the characteristics of this legislation is reflected in the rich literature of saints' lives (Brown 1981; Stancliffe 1992; McNamara and Halborg 1992; Smith 1992; Van Dam 1993; Head and Noble 1995). The life of St Martin of Tours offers vivid pictures of pagan practices rooted out by the saint (Head and Noble 1995: 14–16), as do the lives of St Eligius (Harmening 1989: 435; Banniard 1992) and other saints, originally and primarily on the Continent, but also in Britain and Ireland as well (Stancliffe 1992). The continuing influence of the literature of saints' lives was signalled in the late thirteenth century by Jacobus de Voragine's vast collection, *The Golden Legend*, and its role in refamiliarizing Christian Europe with its ancient and later saints and, among many other things, the world of magic, superstition and sorcery that they defeated (Jacobus de Voragine 1993; and see below).

From around 500 on, synodal canons and a rich penitential literature began to appear in Ireland. A synodal canon attributed to St Patrick prescribed a year's penance for anyone who consulted a diviner and condemned anyone who professed to believe that there were such things as witches or who accused someone else of being a witch (McNeill and Gamer 1938). But the penitential literature is much more substantial, since it brought the decisions of many councils and synods into the hands of the individual confessor as a guide to assigning appropriate penances to specific offences. In one of the earliest examples of the genre, the early sixth-century penitential of Finnian, any cleric or woman who practises deceptive magic commits a monstrous sin, but may purge it by six years of penance, chiefly fasting. Those who make love potions must repent for a year, and those who interfere with the birth of a child by magical means must undergo the same penance. The early seventh-century penitential of Columban required six years of penance for the destruction of anyone by magic (Hillgarth 1986: 133–4; McNeill and Gamer 1938: 252–3).

Irish and Welsh penitentials also influenced the practice of ecclesiastical discipline in early England. In the late seventh-century penitential of Theodore, for example, a woman who puts her daughter in an oven or on a roof in order to cure a fever must do penance for seven years. Further, women or men who perform incantations or divination, or perform auguries from omens or dreams, must do penance for five years. If the man is a cleric, he is to be degraded. Anyone possessed by a demon may keep stones and herbs whose natural properties are therapeutic, but these cannot be used with incantations (McNeill and Gamer 1938; Frantzen 1983). An eighth-century penitential attributed to Bede forbids the random consultation of scripture in order to predict the future (the practice known as *sors*), divinations, the placing of a young girl on a roof or in an oven to cure a fever or the employment of illusionists, diviners or makers of amulets. The tenth-century confessional of Egbert condemns any woman who has used witchcraft, enchantment or potions to a year's penance, but to seven years if her arts have killed anyone, and repeats the prohibition of placing a daughter in an oven or on a roof to cure a fever.

Both Irish and English penitentials influenced those later produced on the Continent. The early eighth-century Burgundian penitential prescribes seven years of penance for anyone who kills another by magic and a shorter term for those who do not injure, but practise erotic magic instead (McNeill and Gamer 1938: 273–7). Those who conjure storms must also do penance for seven years. The early ninth-century penitential of Silos (McNeill and Gamer 1938: 285–90) offers a useful summary of the penitential literature:

> If any Christian pays respect to diviners, enchanters, or fortune tellers to observe auguries, omens or elements, or if they busy themselves with and seek after consultations of writings, dreams, woollen work [the offering of wool to local spirits] or magical practices, he shall do penance for five years.

Further, anyone who uses incantations while bathing himself in reverse must do penance for a year, but if he does not use incantations, for forty days: 'Those who in the dance wear women's clothes and strangely devise them and employ jawbones and a bow and a spade and things like these shall do penance for one year' (McNeill and Gamer 1938).

The practices that the penitentials condemn can often be cross-checked with the lists of superstitions, such as the eighth-century list printed by McNeill and Gamer (1938: 419–21; cf. Blöcker 1981; Dierkens 1984), although these lists do not distinguish between what can be called superstition and the practice of magic or witchcraft. The list condemns religious rites held in forests, amulets, magical knots, incantations, auguries, divining and sorcerers, and a broad range of other practices that seem less magical than religious but are grouped here with magic under the general category of 'superstition'. There is evidence that pagan groups borrowed Christian signs and ceremonies because of their assumed power and effectiveness, and in one case a sorceress in Bavaria gave several animals to the local church in order to thank its patron saint for the success of her incantations (Brown 1996: 258). And in the eyes of Anglo-Saxon missionary-reformers, at least, the Franks appear to have seemed most susceptible to these vices. As Boniface or one of his followers wrote around the middle of the eighth century:

No Christian people in the entire world commits such grave sins and wickedness against the Church of God and the monastery as the people of the Franks – not in Greece, nor in Italy, nor in Britain, nor in Africa, nor in any other Christian people. (Mordek and Glatthaar 1993: 35; Coupland 1991)

By the middle of the eighth century a substantial conciliar, synodal and penitential literature circulated widely on the Continent and in Britain and Ireland. With the reform of the Frankish church in the councils of 742 and 743 and later, and with the new and vigorous political and religious reforms of Charlemagne (768–814), this literature and the beliefs it reflected began to be systematized and circulated throughout Charlemagne's vast empire (McKitterick 1977; Wallace-Hadrill 1983; Imbert 1996: 198–202). Gradually the penitentials came under criticism for being too locally based, informally used and unauthoritative. In their place there emerged a much better organized and royally sponsored systematic canon law.

The reforms of the eighth and ninth centuries offer a considerably fuller picture of Carolingian ideas of superstition and magic, first by reviving and disseminating much of the earlier Christian literature concerning these topics, and second by recording a number of specific instances of accusations and prosecutions for magic and related offences.

The reform synod of 742 prohibited strongly 'the casting of lots, divinations, amulets and auguries, [and] incantations'. A list of superstitions appended to the only surviving manuscript of the canons of the Council of Leptinnes of about 743 reflects the beginnings of Frankish church reform. The thirty practices condemned include a mixture of erroneous religious practices (particularly pagan rites performed under the guise of Christianity), and a number of practices that are clearly considered as magical: the use of amulets and ligatures, incantations, auguries, divining and sorcery, weather-magic and the belief that women control the moon and the hearts of men (McNeill and Gamer 1938: 419–21; Dutton 1995; MacMullen 1997: 139–44). At about the same time, the *Scarapsus*, a book of moral guidance based on the Bible, written by Pirmin, a monk at Reichenau, drew heavily on the writings of the earlier churchmen Martin of Braga and Caesarius of Arles, and from both reiterated the earlier strictures of Augustine. The general tendency of ecclesiastical and other legal literature from the mid-eighth century on was to restore a rigid and categorical condemnation of both superstitious and magical practices in Frankish Christianity. The increasingly close alliance between Frankish churchmen and Frankish kings, especially after the establishment of the Carolingian dynasty on the Frankish throne in 751, lent the power of the kings to the reform-minded clerics, in cases of superstition and magic as well as in other areas of devotional life (McKitterick 1977; Wallace-Hadrill 1983; Angenendt 1992).

Charlemagne's *Admonitio Generalis* (*General Admonition*) of 789 took up these reforming measures and prohibited magical practices throughout his kingdom. Drawing upon the increasingly severe strictures of the mid-eighth century and echoing the powerful language of the condemnation of magic in Leviticus and Deuteronomy, the *Admonitio Generalis* is the first of a long line of Carolingian legislation to condemn magical practices systematically, not only among the Franks, but among other peoples whom Charlemagne brought under his rule, particularly the Saxons. The danger of reverting to pagan practices and hence to what was considered blasphemy and magic is illustrated in the revolt of 841–2 by the Saxon *Stellinga* (Goldberg 1995). The *Admonitio* (ch.18) states explicitly that no one is permitted to become a sorcerer, magician, enchanter or enchantress. C.65 prohibits the use of augury and all forms of magic (citing Deuteronomy 18: 10–11) and states that those who perform them are to correct their ways or be condemned to death. The Capitulary of Paderborn, issued to regulate the conquered and converted Saxons in 785, ordered that

> If anyone is deceived by the devil, and believes after the manner of pagans that some man or woman is a witch and eats people, and if because of this he burns her or gives her flesh to someone to eat or eats it himself, let him pay the penalty of death.

Charlemagne's instructions in 802 to his travelling inspectors of government, the *missi*, insist that his counts should not conceal 'any thieves, robbers or murderers, adulterers, evil-doers and performers of incantations and auguries, and all other sacrilegious people', but rather bring them to public justice in order to cleanse the kingdom from their pollution.

A text from a council held around 800 in the area of Freising and Salzburg elaborates considerably on earlier injunctions:

> Concerning incantations, auguries and divination, and those things done by people who conjure up tempests and commit other similar crimes, it is pleasing to the holy council that, wherever they may be found, the archpriest of their diocese shall examine what they do and constrain them by the most careful examination and make them confess to their evils. But he should subject them to moderation in punishment so that they do not lose their lives, but should be confined in prison for their own salvation, until by the inspiration of God they spontaneously mend the ways of sinners. (Mordek and Glatthaar 1993: 42)

If any royal official overlooks such offences or conceals them or hears them in secret, either because he is related to the sinners or has been bribed by them, the archpriest must act in his place. Around 804 Alcuin wrote to Arn, Archbishop of Salzburg, urging him to prohibit in his province all auguries and the interpretation of birdsongs, which are believed only by the credulous. Around the beginning of the ninth century, then, a considerably more rigorous jurisdiction was established by Frankish councils and rulers in identifying these offences as specifically criminal (Mordek and Glatthaar 1993: 61, citing Trusen 1989; Blum 1936; Riché 1978b: 181–6; Wallace-Hadrill 1983: 248–9, 404–6; Imbert 1996). The diocesan statutes of Gerbald, bishop of Liège, issued around the turn of the ninth century after having been considered at a diocesan synod at the command of Charlemagne, offer a concise summary of Carolingian concerns:

> Those who perform *sortilegium* should be inquired about, as should *aruspices* and those who observe months and seasons, who interpret dreams and wear certain phylacteries around their necks, with [strange] words written on them. Women should be inquired about who give out potions to other women [in order to kill a fetus] and perform other divinations so that their husbands may have more love for them. All *malefici* who are denounced for any of these things are to be brought to us so that their cases may be discussed before us. (de Clercq I, 1936: 360)

In the years immediately following 802, a number of documents from both the Carolingian clergy and the king expanded on this early vigorous attack. In 813, for example, bishops announced that priests must inform their people that sorcery, enchantments and ligatures have absolutely no therapeutic effect on men or animals and are only inventions of the devil. The practices, however, appear to have continued, because in 813 the council of Tours re-emphasized that all magic was a delusion of the devil. The *Penitential* of Halitgar, written at Cambrai in the 820s, treated many of the practices considered here under the headings of 'magic' and 'sacrilege', the latter heading including what other writers called 'superstition' (McNeill and Gamer 1938: 297–314; Kors and Peters 2001). In 829 a Council of Paris issued a substantial and even stronger condemnation:

> Certain very pernicious evils are assuredly remnants of paganism, such as magic, judicial astrology, sorcery, witchcraft, or poisoning, divination, charms and belief in the guidance of dreams. These evils should be very severely punished according to the Law of God. For there can be no doubt that people exist, and we know of several, who through prestidigitation and diabolic illusions so imbue human spirits with a taste for their philtres, flesh and phylacteries that they are apparently rendered stupid and insensible to the evils brought upon them. It is also said that their *maleficia* can trouble the air, bring down showers of hail, predict

things to come, steal the fruit and milk of some folk to bestow it on others, and do an infinity of such things. If any people of this sort, men or women, are discovered, they should be punished all the more rigorously in that they have the malice and temerity not to flinch from the public service of the demon. (Riché 1978b: 183–4)

By the end of the first quarter of the ninth century, Carolingian hostility to the practice of magic had been systematically articulated by the highest authorities in the kingdom, condemned to the strictest sanctions known to Carolingian law and its identification with the deceptions of the devil conclusively established. If anything, the strictures had grown stronger than they had been a century earlier, and it is likely that more systematic investigation on the part of both clerical and lay officials had found more of it than they had expected. It is also clear that legislation and active enforcement of the laws did not stop it, since in the years following 829 such practices were found at the royal court itself and brought down the wrath of yet later canon lawyers, theologians and Carolingian and post-Carolingian kings.

The first charge of magic in use at the royal court itself is found in the biography of Wala, an adviser of Charlemagne who skillfully survived in the complex political divisions during the reign of Louis the Pious (814–40). Following Louis's marriage to Judith, an able, intelligent and influential noblewoman, and the birth of a son to them in 823, the sons of Louis's first marriage, especially Lothar, the eldest, launched a campaign of slander and innuendo against Judith and Louis's most influential counsellor, Bernard of Septimania (Ward, 1990). A number of scholars have pointed out that ninth-century Frankish queens, particularly Judith, assumed a new political prominence and that the charges of illicit sexual activity and sorcery against them derived from their new role (Stafford 1993: 145). Among the charges that Lothar and Wala made against Judith and Bernard was that of using magic to influence the king. The somewhat uncritical author of the biography of Wala, Paschasius Radbertus, thus characterized the court of Louis under the influence of Judith and Bernard as a 'sty where shame ruled, adultery reigned, where felonies, sorcery and all manner of prohibited black arts abounded':

> There was witchcraft everywhere. Policy was based not on sound judgement, but on auspices, and forward planning on auguries. … Lot casters, seers, interpreters of omens, mimers, dream mediums, consulters of entrails and a whole crowd of other initiates in the malefic arts were driven out of the palace. (Flint 1991: 63; Murray 1992; Ward 1990)

In 830 Lothar, Wala, Pippin of Aquitaine and others forced Louis to lay down the government and confined Judith in the convent of St Radegund in Poitiers. By autumn of 830, however, Louis had begun to recover his power, and in February 831, at an assembly at Aachen, Louis was formally restored, Judith freed, and Lothar pardoned and sent to Italy. In 833 Lothar revolted again and had Louis deposed. But in 834, Louis was restored yet again, and Lothar was forced to flee south, where he managed to capture the city of Chalons. There, he accused the nun Gerberga, a sister of Bernard of Septimania, of having been one of Bernard's and Judith's assistants in their magical practices, and he had her drowned in the Saone river, 'after the manner of sorcerers', and ordered that two other women accomplices be beheaded. This case, of course, deriving as it does from a complex political conflict, proves little about actual practices, but it is important because it indicates that such charges were at least plausible in the second quarter of the ninth century, and that they could be made against the highest ranking people in the realm. The charges against Judith, Bernard and Gerberga were one of the earliest, but certainly not the last instances of the political use of charges of sorcery. It is not likely that they would have been made if not for the heightened Carolingian awareness of the imminent danger posed by magicians and sorcerers in the century preceding the 830s.

The same first half of the ninth century saw two treatises by Carolingian churchmen that attacked the efficacy of magic and the belief in that efficacy. Agobard of Lyons's 'Against the erroneous opinions of the people regarding hail and thunder' condemned the belief that people from a mysterious land called Magonia could fly over fields, causing hail, thunder and the destruction of crops (Dutton, 1995; Blöcker, 1981). Hrabanus Maurus, Abbot of Fulda, wrote several attacks, including 'On the magical arts', much of which was derived from Isidore of Seville, on those who believed that magicians and sorcerers could accomplish anything that depended upon their powers alone. On the other hand, Charles the Bald at Metz in 859 and again at Quierzy in 873 stated that sorcerers indeed injured and killed people and they must be hunted down and punished (Harmening 1979: 269–70). But the best-known case was that of the divorce of Lothar II from his barren wife Theutberga in 855 and his marriage to his mistress, Waldrada. Hincmar, Archbishop of Rheims, a learned churchman who opposed the divorce and remarriage, charged Waldrada with using magical arts to prevent Theutberga from having children, and in his treatise 'On the divorce of Lothar and Theutberga' brought together many of the strongest arguments from Augustine and Isidore in an elaborate catalogue of magical practices that he condemns categorically. Hincmar was arguing strongly in favour of the reality of witches' activities, and he added considerably to Isidore's list of magical activities, including accounts of measuring magic, divination from the inspection of animals' bones and the use of diabolical skills to disturb human sense-perception (Brundage 1987: 143–5).

The cases of Judith and Gerberga and that of Waldrada were the most conspicuous ninth-century instances of the new political trials for magic or witchcraft, but they were not the last. In 899 two people were executed because it was thought that they had used a magical poison to kill the emperor Arnulf (Kieckhefer 1990: 187). In 1028 several women were tried and executed for having used magic to kill William, Count of Angoulême. The champion of one of them in a trial by battle was said to have drunk magic potions in order to win the duel. The political context of this case resembles strongly the earlier ninth-century cases and suggests some continuity in the idea that political conflict might employ the techniques of magic to achieve its ends, or at least that accusations of magic remained potent elements in political disputes (Blöcker 1979).

Between Carolingian scepticism about the actuality of magic and Carolingian condemnations of apparently successful, but sinful, instances of the use of magic, the rulers and ecclesiastical writers of the ninth century created a legacy that one historian has called 'the point of departure in the history of European sorcery' (Riché 1973: 135). By the end of the ninth century there had occurred a consensus throughout most of Latin and Germanic Europe that magic generically could not be accomplished by natural means without the aid of (and hence the invocation of and homage to) demons. What was not revealed by God in dreams, visions, signs, portents or legitimate protective rituals and prophecies could only be provided by demons, and recourse to demons thus became a normative explanation of all other similar phenomena (Fichtenau 1991: 319–24).

The laws issued by the kings of England from the late seventh to the ninth and tenth centuries echoed much of the Continental Carolingian concern with magic and witchcraft, and they introduced the Old English terminology of witchcraft. The late seventh-century laws of Wihtred of Kent describe all surviving pagan practices as sacrifice to devils (Whitelock 1955: 363), as do the laws of Cnut in the early eleventh century, which also specify that witchcraft and divination are to be considered heathen practices. The late ninth-century laws of Alfred condemn women who receive wizards, sorcerers and magicians to the literal penalty of Exodus 22: 18: 'Thou shalt not suffer a witch to live', and the later laws of Edward the Elder and Guthrum identify witches and diviners with perjurers, murderers and prostitutes, condemning them to exile, execution or fines unless they repent (Jolly 1996: 71–95; Griffiths 1996: 89–111).

The Old English laws, written (unlike Continental laws, which remained in Latin) in the vernacular, give several sets of terms, only one of which has remained – much transformed from its original meaning – in the modern English vocabulary. The practices condemned in many of these laws are termed *scinnlac* and *scinncræft*, both of which mean any generic magical action or ability, *galdorcræft* – enchantment – as well as *lyblac*, whose practitioners were termed either a *lyblæca* (m.) or a *lybbestre* (f.). This group of terms, with *lybcræft* (m.), seem to designate primarily poisoning (presumably with the use of charmed *materia magica*) and correspond roughly to the Latin *veneficium*. A fourth set of terms deals primarily with divination, *wiccaræd* (m.). Its practitioners are a *wicca* (m.), that is a wizard or diviner, or a *wicce* (f.), that is, a female wizard or diviner. The practice is *wiccecræft* (m.), *wiccedom* (m.) or *wiccung* (f.), all meaning what later came to be termed 'witchcraft'. Thus, in spite of its distinctive vernacular forms, the Old English terminology roughly approximates to that of Continental Latin from the seventh to the early eleventh century (Griffiths 1996; for Scandinavian terms and views, not considered here, see Jochens 1993, 1996).

At the end of the ninth century Regino of Prüm (d. 915) compiled a handbook of canon law, 'On synodal cases', which was dedicated to the archbishop of Mainz and designed to help a bishop making the pastoral rounds of his diocese. In book II Regino addressed such questions as whether magicians, diviners and enchanters existed, whether magical herbs and ligatures were used to cure humans and animals, whether women, by magical arts, could induce love or hate in men, and whether some women professed to ride out at night with demons who were transformed into the shapes of women:

> Wicked women who have given themselves back to Satan and have been seduced by the phantasm and illusions of demons believe and declare that they can ride with Diana the pagan goddess and a huge throng of women on chosen beasts in the hours of the night. They say that in the silence of the night they can traverse great stretches of territory, that they obey Diana as though she were their mistress and that on certain nights she calls them to her special service. (Kors and Peters 1972, 2001; Flint 1991: 122)

In order to help the bishop in his investigations, Regino provided an abundance of texts from early Church councils, material from Carolingian penitentials, and Carolingian legislation (Bonomo 1959: 15–37; Flint 1991: 122–6).

Regino's collection was learned, thorough and very influential. It became a principal source for later and more fully developed collections of canon law, and it effectively summed up the long Carolingian concern with magic and witchcraft. In particular, the text cited above became a widely copied and collected rule. In book II of Regino's collection, the text, generally known as the canon *Episcopi*, follows a canon of the fourth-century Council of Ancyra, and a careless reading of Regino led subsequent collectors to assume that it also was a fourth-century text, and hence particularly authoritative. In fact, at least part of the text probably came from a ninth-century capitulary that is now lost (Russell 1972: 75–81, 291–3). The canon says two quite different things about practitioners of magic. First, following what might be called the stronger line of Carolingian thought, the canon states that the art of sorcery and malefice was invented by the devil and that if bishops find men or women practising it they must expel them from their dioceses. The second part, however, denounces as an illusion the claim that some women ride out at night with Diana. Priests much teach that this is merely a phantasm imposed upon human minds by demons. The devil deceives 'miserable women' into thinking that that which happens in their imagination happens in reality. Thus, although some assertions about magic are merely the result of the devil's deceptions, other magical practices really do take place, and those who peform them must be punished with exile. Regino's collection thus preserved and summed up much of the Carolingian concern with magic, and it did so efficiently, in a single, apparently ancient and authoritative text. That text became the basis of virtually all subsequent discussions of the problem. Although it echoes earlier discussions of the 'wild ride' with Diana, it may also illustrate a continuing belief, because at the end of the tenth century Rather of Verona echoed a similar concern (Rather 1991: 26–34). The later history of theories of prosecution for magic and witchcraft may be considered virtually as a long set of changing interpretations of the canon *Episcopi* and the problem of diabolically caused flight and sacrilegious assembly.

In some respects, however, the cautious use of magic may also have contributed to the northern European assimilation of the Gospel story. In the tenth-century Old Saxon epic retelling of the Gospel, *Heliand*, the poet appears to have used the terminology of magic subtly in order to characterize for his northern hearers the nature of Christ's powers as distinct from those of conventional deities (Murphy 1992: 205–20).

One feature of earlier ecclesiastical and secular legislation that Regino's collection helped to overcome was its sheer volume, diversity and lack of single authoritative voice in the fragmented Europe of the tenth and early eleventh centuries. By the early eleventh century, many of the penitentials, for example, came under criticism precisely because they had originated locally and had no general claim to authority; Carolingian and Old English legislation was not widely known or observed; the texts of the canons of Carolingian church councils were not collected or systematically arranged. All of these survived only when they were included in later collections, but most later collectors had access only to a limited number of earlier texts. By 1100, there emerged the demand for rational, authoritative, universally applicable collections of both ecclesiastical and secular law. The way to that law lay through individual collections of laws and rules whose intellectual prestige transmitted their contents to the new schools of the twelfth century.

After Regino's collection, the most important of these in the case of magic and witchcraft (as in ecclesiastical law generally) was that of Burchard, bishop of Worms (d. 1025), who compiled his great collection of canon law, the *Decretum*, between 1008 and 1012. Although Burchard's collection was limited in its authority only to the diocese of Worms, its immense scope, degree of thoroughness, and intellectual attractiveness broadened its appeal well beyond the boundaries of the diocese proper. Books X and XIX of Burchard's *Decretum* (book XIX is itself a systematic penitential, popularly called the *Corrector, sive Medicus* (*The Corrector, or the Physician*) sum up a great deal of earlier literature, including the canon *Episcopi* from the collection of Regino. Book X of the *Decretum* consists of a systematic attack on all prohibited pagan practices, preserves the longer of the two versions of the canon *Episcopi* found in Regino and sums up the redefinition of paganism that had begun centuries before in the literature of the early Church. Book XIX offers a spectrum of forbidden beliefs and practices that merged superstition and magic (Vogel 1994; Gurevich 1988; McNeill and Gamer 1938: 321–45; Shinners 1997: 441–56; Milis 1998; Kors and Peters 2001).

In one well-known instance, a problem dealt with by Burchard is corroborated by a different text. In chapter V, c. 186, Burchard notes that mistresses sometimes use magical means to impose sexual impotence upon their lovers who wish to take wives (McNeill and Gamer 1938: 340). Such a case is recounted in the memoirs of the monk Guibert of Nogent (*c.*1064–*c.*1125), who noted not only that his own father had been made impotent through the use of magic, but that 'a certain old woman' had been able to remove the spell (Benton 1970: 64–7; Archambault 1996)). Guibert's memoirs also illustrate other alleged uses of magic and sorcery in late eleventh and early twelfth-century northern France.

So does the history of the formation of the legend concerning Gerbert of Aurillac, later Pope Sylvester II (999–1003). Gerbert, a learned monk who studied widely and had a long career in royal and imperial service, was the subject of a complex set of legends that attributed to him the study of Arabic magic in Spain, the working of magic on various occasions throughout much of southern Europe, and even practising magic during his brief papacy (Oldoni 1987; Riché 1987; Guyotjeannin and Poulle 1996). The myth of Gerbert the magician echoed the older story of the clerk Theophilus, who, in disappointment on not having been elected bishop, sold his soul to the devil in exchange for magical powers (Flint 1991: 344–7), an early version of what later became the Faust story. Later discussions of learned magic well into the sixteenth and seventeenth centuries returned again and again to both legends.

Burchard's penitential in book XIX was also nearly the last in the tradition of lists of superstitions considered thus far. From the eleventh century on, the concern of churchmen, whether theologians or canon lawyers, turned to the internal regulation of a society that seemed to have been virtually entirely Christianized. When beliefs of ordinary lay people next came to be considered in matters of ecclesiastical discipline after the eleventh century, the chief concern of churchmen was heresy, or rather practices and forms of devotional or dogmatic expression and dissent that came to be categorized as heresy, not primarily superstition, magic or witchcraft (Russell 1972: 63–166; Schmitt 1983). By the middle of the eleventh century the vast and scattered literature dealing with superstition, magic and witchcraft had been ordered and precisely located in the context of ecclesiastical law, first by Regino and then by Burchard about a century later. The work of theologians and jurists after that period derived largely from the transmission of Burchard and its re-reading in a late eleventh and early twelfth-century context.

CHAPTER 4

The Legal and Theological Literature of the Twelfth and Thirteenth Centuries

The collection of canon law of Burchard of Worms was, like most of its predecessors, individually made and hence applicable only in the diocese of Worms. But Burchard's immense industry in discovering and collecting authoritative texts made his collection a convenient repository of material that appealed to later collectors, whose work took on a distinctively scholarly character. In the case of the canon *Episcopi*, for example, Burchard's text was taken up into the more influential collections made by Ivo, Bishop of Chartres, at the beginning of the twelfth century, and from Ivo's collections it was taken up into the work that became the most important collection of classical canon law, the *Concordia Discordantium Canonum (The Concord of Discordant Canons)*, or *Decretum*, of Master Gratian of Bologna around 1140 (Brundage 1995; Kors and Peters 2001).

Gratian's treatment of magic and the simultaneous regularizing of the study of theology both mark a new focus in ecclesiology. But it must be noted that they were produced at a time when a great deal of literary consideration was also being given to magic, not always consistently, but reflecting nevertheless an increasing interest on the part of learned writers. Anselm of Besate in the early eleventh century and William of Malmesbury in the mid-twelfth both drew upon earlier literary tradition and local anecdote to describe in vivid terms the operations of magicians and witches who had given themselves to the devil in return for preternatural powers (Peters 1978: 21–57; Kors and Peters 2001). Not surprisingly, these subjects offered ample scope for writers to exercise their literary imaginations and rhetorical skills – much in the same way as the later visual depiction of magic and witchcraft gave similar oportunities to artists in the sixteenth and seventeenth centuries (Hoak 1985; Zika 1998). Such narratives were not intended to provoke prosecution, but rather to serve as moral reminders of the powers of the devil, the fragility of fallen human nature, and the depiction of unusual and grotesque activities as a means of morally entertaining the leisure time of nobles and rulers. In monastic circles they also served to depict the external world as temptation-filled and dangerous, hence reinforcing the monastic vocation to flee the world and its dangers.

In addition to literary adventurism, entertainment and moral exhortation, discussions of magic also occurred in considerations of the organization of knowledge in the twelfth century. The recovery of much earlier Latin literature, the absorption of Arabic learning, and the translation of Greek scientific literature at the end of the twelfth century raised serious questions about natural magic – the theory that with appropriate learning and intellectual discipline humans might acquire knowledge about the natural world that was hidden from ordinary people (occult) but was not inherently demonic in itself. But theologians also observed that demons had particular expertise in natural matters, both because of their spiritual essence and their long experience, and that even 'natural' magic could be dangerous in this regard. Peter Abelard, for example, noted that Pharaoh's priests in Exodus 7 acted against Moses because the demons gave them some of their own natural knowledge (Abelard 1971: 37). There was considerable moral, ethical and philosophical debate in the twelfth and thirteenth centuries over these questions, and it forms the background for the work of theologians and canon lawyers.

By the late twelfth century the Christian cosmology of Europe regarded human nature as innately weak, sinful and vulnerable to demonic temptation and deception (with divine permission) as a consequence of the fall of Adam and Eve, the subsequent human capacity for sin and the loss of the human ability to perceive the full spectrum of the natural world. Although human reason, to the extent that it received divine grace and was properly instructed, could distinguish right from wrong, human will might not always choose what was right. Not only could humans reason badly and misdirect their wills, but they were also unable to perceive the created world except in a limited and incomplete way. The fall of Adam and Eve also diminished the human capacity to understand fully the natural world. Those operations of nature that humans could not perceive or understand could, however, be manipulated by demons, who were believed to operate in realms of nature that were not perceptible to humans and to be able with God's permission to deceive and tempt humans. The devil could intervene in the course of 'natural causation', thereby working what seemed to humans to be 'wonders', tempt humans to pay him homage of a kind due only to God and enter agreements with humans through which humans received powers over nature and human affairs not attainable by any other means – not miracles (*miracula*), but rather *mira*, wonders. The servants of the devil could, on their own or with the devil acting through them, perform acts that harmed or illicitly influenced others in their persons, families and servants or property by occult (= 'hidden from humans', not 'supernatural') means. Pacts with the devil presumed the sins/crimes of idolatry and apostasy, because they constituted a willful rejection of Christian baptism (both a contract with God and a spiritual bond to fellow Christians) and the paying of a kind of homage to the demon that should be paid only to God or the saints. This cosmology lay beneath the development of both theology and canon law.

The work of the theologians began with the explanation of the meaning of Scripture and by the end of the twelfth century had expanded to include detailed studies of particular theological questions and from there developed the discipline of speculative theology and moral theology as a distinct field, and the arts of preaching and hearing confession. In terms of scriptural exegesis – the actual teaching explanation of the meaning of the scriptural text – the conclusions of the biblical theologians are of particular interest. In explaining the meaning of Exodus 22: 18, 'Thou shalt not suffer a witch to live', for example, the most widely accepted explanation – and the standard text used for teaching students of theology – was that

> those who perform acts by the illusions of the magical arts and the figments of the devil are to be understood as heretics, who are to be excluded from consorting with the faithful, who may truly be said to live, so that their error may die in them.

That is, sorcerers are to be excommunicated and exiled, as are other heretics, not literally killed or otherwise punished. The gloss to Leviticus 20: 6 states that

> it is a great sin to consult magicians and diviners, because this is to depart from God. There are magicians who in the name of God prophesy falsely, and there are deceitful diviners who corrupt many with poisonous words and turn them away from truth.

The comments of the exegetes were repeated by twelfth-century theologians, most notably Hugh of St Victor, who sharply denounced both the practice of magic and its entire history and exclusion from all legitimate branches of knowledge (Hugh of St Victor 1961: 154; Kors and Peters 2001):

> Magic is not accepted as a part of philosophy, but stands with a false claim outside it: the mistress of every form of iniquity and malice, lying about the truth and truly infecting men's minds, it seduces them from divine religion, prompts them to the cult of demons, fosters corruption of morals and impels the minds of its devotees to every wicked and criminal indulgence.

Although the twelfth-century theologians routinely condemned magic as sinful, they insisted that no penalty stronger than excommunication or exile was appropriate for it. But these were also considered enormous spiritual and social penalties.

Theologians had a wealth of texts to work with, but canon lawyers worked with fewer. The canon *Episcopi* passed from Regino through Burchard and Ivo of Chartres to Master Gratian, who included it in his great and influential collection of canon law, the *Concordance of Discordant Canons*, or *Decretum*, around 1140. The text occurs in *Causa* 26, *quaestio* 5, *canon* 12 (Kors and Peters 1972: 28–31). The *Causae* were hypothetical cases, each of which was broken down into particular questions of relevant law. These in turn were answered by Gratian's assembling of apparently authoritative and sometimes apparently conflicting excerpts from older and more recent legal pronouncements, laid out and explained by Gratian's own commentary (Brundage 1995: 44–69). *Causa* 26 is located at the end of a series known as the *causae hereticorum*, 'the *causae* pertaining to heretics', and it describes the case of an unrepentant cleric who is a magician and diviner, excommunicated by his bishop, and reconciled to the Church at the point of death by another priest, without the bishop's knowledge. The various questions ask what *sortilegium* is (the answer comes from Isidore of Seville), whether it is a sin (the answer comes chiefly from Augustine), what is the nature of divination, and finally raises the question of whether magicians should be excommunicated. Gratian, following the tradition of misunderstanding Regino, attributed the canon *Episcopi* to the fourth-century Council of Ancyra and therefore allowed considerable authority to it.

Gratian also treated magic in *Causa* 33, one of a group of *causae* concerning marriage (Brundage 1987; Kors and Peters 2001). Here, Gratian was concerned with sexual impotence, and his key text is taken from Hincmar of Reims's treatise on the divorce of Lothar, which he found in the collection of Ivo of Chartres. The text, *Si per Sortiarias*, states that impotence caused by magic may indeed be an impediment to marriage and sometimes grounds for annulment. This text received greater attention from later commentators on Gratian, usually law professors, because it was a part of the rapidly developing marriage law of the Christian Church (Brundage 1987: 229–55).

Thus, like the theologians, canon lawyers by the twelfth century had a convenient location of authoritative texts and learned interpretations that identified magic as sinful, heretical (and thereby ecclesiastically criminal), and deserving of excommunication if it were not repented and penance for it performed. The actual working out of the procedures for confession and penitence took place in the work of late twelfth and early thirteenth-century theologians, canonists and writers of specialized handbooks for confessors (Peters 1978: 67–81), but these generally remained consistent with the work of Gratian and his contemporaries among the theologians.

Causa 26 and the other '*causae* of the heretics' were also central locations for Gratian's discussion of superstition as well as heresy, and the greatest influence in these sections is that of Augustine of Hippo. Augustine's bleak view of human nature and his initially reluctant insistence that the worst results of fallen human nature could legitimately be curbed by the administration of punishment in a spirit of charitable discipline were consistent with the view of the world adopted by many late eleventh and twelfth-century thinkers. In the great conflict between papacy and empire that had begun in the 1070s, as well as in the discussions of the justice of certain kinds of warfare that came out of them and were later reviewed in the context of the First Crusade of 1095–9, a new attitude toward physical coercion began to be articulated in the context of penitence and a sharpened idea of ecclesiastical sins that might be considered crimes as well. As a result, a new system of criminal law and jurisprudence emerged in both ecesiastical and secular courts around the turn of the thirteenth century. Both sets of courts were also related, since ecclesiastical courts were prohibited from shedding blood and capital punishment could only be carried out by secular courts to which convicted ecclesiastical criminals were turned over. Eventually the most important among the offences that both ecclesiastical and secular courts had to deal with was the category of heresy.

Churchmen had long known and condemned heresy, but before the twelfth century heretics were urged to repent, and the chief penalty if they did not was excommunication and exile, since these were understood to be biblically sanctioned and served to preserve the normative religious integrity of the individual community. During the eleventh and early twelfth centuries there are accounts of heretical behaviour that depict the heretics as demon-worshippers and committers of criminal acts, usually involving sexual and sacramental deviance and blasphemy (Russell 1972; Lambert 1992; Moore 1985, 1987; Peters 1980; Given 1997; Kors and Peters 2001). They were also considered to be sects – that is, anti-churches, with their own anti-equivalents of baptism, and other elements of the liturgy. By the time of Gratian, heresy loomed larger in the growing and diversifying population of western Europe and attracted public attention and concern. Increasingly, churchmen associated heretics with the service of demons, as they had earlier associated magicians, and the laws against consorting with demons had grown stiffer and carried more severe punishments. The identification of sorcery and magic with heresy and of both with diabolism increased from the mid-twelfth century on. Jeffrey Burton Russell has summarized the development by the end of the thirteenth century:

> Through its connection with heresy, witchcraft [we may add sorcery as well] in this period witnessed the addition of new elements and the further development and definition of older ones: the sex orgy, the feast, the secret meetings at night in caves, cannibalism, the murder of children, the express renunciation of God and adoration of demons, the desecration of the cross and the sacraments. All these had now become fixed elements in the composition of witchcraft. (Russell 1972: 100; cf. Moore 1987; Lambert 1992)

As penalties applied to unrepentant heretics became more harsh, including confiscation of property in 1184 and even stronger punishments for heretics and their supporters over the next several decades, accusations of sorcery began to resemble accusations of heresy, and they appear most prominently not at first in the work of the canon lawyers who commented on Gratian, but in the work of those theologians who composed the new genre of handbooks for confessors and preachers. In the great transformation of theology that occurred after the middle of the twelfth century a science that had once largely consisted of scriptural commentary and statements of dogma developed into speculative theology and moral theology, the latter of which guided confessors, preachers, and ecclesiastical lawyers. Confession was made mandatory for all Christians at least once a year at the Fourth Lateran Council of 1215, and the role of the confessor was one of the most important pastoral roles in the clergy. The *Summa Confessorum* (*Summa for Confessors*) of Thomas of Chobham, written around 1215, for example, emphasizes the vulnerability of humans to the temptations of demons and the central role of demons in all manifestations of magic, whether in the superstitions of the unlettered or the elaborate pretensions of learned magicians. Such views are echoed in other manuals for clergy, such as those of Bartholomew of Exeter and Robert of Flamborough (Peters 1978: 78–81). This movement toward an intensified pastoralism, of course, did not move uniformly across Europe, and it was often derailed by natural disasters and other circumstances. But it constitutes one aspect of that continuing ideal of reform that characterized Latin Christianity for centuries, and the heightened emphasis on pastoralism must always be considered when one encounters new classifications of sin and ecclesiastical crime (Harmening 1989; Paravy 1979; Duffy 1992: 53–87). Between 1320 and 1323 William of Pagula produced a very influential handbook for parish clergy called *The Pastoral Eye*. The work was often abbreviated and excerpted, and one such abbreviation, produced in 1385, succinctly stated that:

> [The parish priest] should instruct his parishoners that they should not practise the magical arts, incantations, or sorcery, since these things have no power to cure either man or beast and besides are utterly worthless and unlawful. Moreover clerics who do these things shall be degraded and lay people shall be excommunicated. (Shinners 1997: 19)

Both groups came more and more to the attention of ecclesiastical agents and officials during the thirteenth century. In the movement for pastoral reform that was marked by the Fourth Lateran Council, clergy were urged to provide better ecclesiastical care to Christians, whether in the growing cities or in the most remote rural areas. Clerics who travelled to these areas discovered some varieties of Christian belief that seemed to them to distort orthodoxy and verge on superstition (Schmitt 1983; Brooke 1984). In other instances, the world of the growing universities produced some enthusiastic defences of non-demonic learned magic that increasingly troubled ecclesiastical authorities. On 7 March, 1277, the bishop of Paris, Etienne Tempier, issued a formal condemnation of two hundred and nineteen propositions drawn from the work of Arabic, Greek and Latin thinkers. The condemnation also included a book of geomancy and

> books, scrolls, or sheets that contain details of necromancy or contain experiments of diviners, invocations of demons, or conjurations that place the soul in danger, or that in these or other similar works the orthodox faith and good morals are treated with hostility. (Peters 1980: 226; de Ridder-Symoens 1987; Kieckhefer 1997)

At the same universities and law schools at the same time, concepts of heresy, divination, magic, and sorcery were placed in consistent and clearly-defined categories of knowledge that made them easier to identify and deal with by both theologians and lawyers. In his great works of systematic theology, Thomas Aquinas (1225–74) clearly located demonic temptation and the demonic powers that humans could acquire within the context of Christian ontology and theological tradition (Kors and Peters 1972, 2001; Peters 1978: 95–8). Jurists, too, began to use other texts besides those of Gratian as new collections of canon law appeared in 1234, 1298 and 1317. The 1298 collection of canon law, the *Liber Sextus* of Pope Boniface VIII, contained a letter originally issued by Pope Alexander IV in 1258 and reissued in 1260 which stated that papally appointed inquisitors could prosecute those accused of sorcery only if their activities 'manifestly savoured of heresy':

> It is reasonable to assume that those charged with the affairs of the faith, which is the greatest of privileges, ought not thereby to intervene in other matters. The inquisitors of heretical depravity, commissioned by the apostolic see, ought not to intervene in cases of divination or sorcery unless these clearly savour of manifest heresy. Nor should they punish those who who are engaged in these things, but leave them to others for punishment.

Both Alexander IV and Boniface VIII appear to have considered sorcery an offence punishable either by ordinary ecclesiastical courts or lay courts – unless it appeared that the accused had invoked demons and committed other acts that clearly constituted heretical behaviour. Boniface himself echoed Alexander IV in a statement of 1298: 'The inquisitors of heretical depratity deputed by the apostolic see should not intrude themselves into cases of divination or *sortilegium* unless these savour of manifest heresy, nor should they punish those involved in these cases, but rather turn them over to their own judges for punishment' (Trusen, 1989: 442; Kors and Peters 2001).

One example of secular law that is roughly contemporaneous with Alexander IV is the law code called *Las siete partidas* (*The Seven Parts*),

designed by Alfonso X of Castile, whose text dates from the 1260s and
1270s. In the seventh *Partida*, the law states that there are two kinds of divination, one natural and connected to astronomy and hence acceptable, at
least to cultivated students. The other, however, depends on the reading of
omens, casting lots, making images or using forbidden means of divination
– such as the head of a dead man. The latter are condemned. Necromancy,
here the calling up of evil spirits and asking them for information or for
power over others, is also prohibited. The condemned forms of divination
and necromancy may be prosecuted by anyone in court, and those convicted
shall be put to death (*Las siete partidas*, 1931: VII: 1–3). But few secular jurisdictions had such detailed laws in the late thirteenth century, and inquisitors
of heretical depravity tended increasingly to take responsibility for prosecuting these offences as part of their charge against heresy generally.

By the end of the thirteenth century, of course, heresy itself had
acquired sharper and more precise definitions, one of the most concise of
which was that attributed to the thirteenth-century philosopher-theolo-
gian, and bishop of Lincoln, Robert Grosseteste: 'Heresy is an opinion that
is contrary to sacred scripture, arrived at by human powers, openly taught
and pertinaciously defended.' That is, heresy was no longer simply and
vaguely any erroneous belief, but erroneous belief that was contrary to
proclaimed dogma, publicly asserted (thereby giving rise to the serious
offence of scandal), even after the heretic had been corrected by legitimate
authorities (thereby committing the equally serious crime of contumacy,
or rebellious disobedience to legitimate religious authorities). Johannes
Andreae, the author of the standard teaching commentary on the *Liber
Sextus*, noted that the phrase 'clearly savour' in the text of Alexander IV
meant: 'as in praying at the altars of idols, to offer sacrifices, to consult
demons, to elicit responses from them … or if they associate themselves
publicly with heretics in order to predict the future by means of the body
and blood of Christ, etc.' (Kors and Peters 1972: 79, 2001: 118; Peters 1978:
99–100). The ready identification of superstition with violation of the First
Commandment against idolatry and the new learning of canon law are
reflected in the questions that inquisitors are told to ask of those accused
of magic and sorcery in the handbook for inquisitors written by Bernard
Gui around 1323:

> Also, inquire especially into those things which smack of any possible
> superstition, irreverence, or insult towards the Church's sacraments, most
> especially towards the sacrament of the Lord's Body, and also towards
> divine worship and sacred places. (Hansen 1901: 47–8; Shinners 1997:
> 458; Rubin 1991)

Gui's handbook represents one of the earliest treatments of the crime of
magic in inquisitorial literature. In the course of the fourteenth century,

Gui's questions were expanded into volumes of ecclesiastical learning concerning sorcery, superstition, magic, and demonology. The legal interpretation of Johannes Andreae was echoed in a brief of legal advice for two
inquisitors at the court of John XXII by the jurist Oldradus da Ponte
around 1325 (Hansen 1901: 55–9) and the inquisitor Zanchino di Ugolini
in 1330 (Hansen 1901: 59–63; *Bibliotheca Lamiarum* 1994: 95–6). The culmination of the inquisitorial and legal doctrine that many kinds of magic
constituted the sin of idolatry was reached in the *Directorium Inquisitorum* of
the inquisitor Nicolau Eymeric in 1376 (Hansen 1901: 66–71; Kors and
Peters 1972: 84–92, 2001: 120–127; Cohn 1975: 177–8; Peters 1978:
196–202; *Bibliotheca Lamiarum* 1994: 98–9). Eymeric's was the most comprehensive handbook of inquisitorial procedure ever produced, and it was
printed several times in the sixteenth century and remained influential into
the seventeenth. The literature of canon law and inquisitorial procedure
between the late thirteenth and the early fifteenth century thus laid down
both a substantive and procedural groundwork for trying both heretics and
sorcerers, particularly as it came to consider the latter guilty of idolatry and
in violation of the First Commandment.

Three examples from the many kinds of literature that reflected some, at
least, of the ideas of theologians and jurists may illuminate the distribution
of some of the ideas considered above. Towards the end of the twelfth century the learned poet Walter of Châtillon produced his long epic poem,
the *Alexandreis*, an account of the wars and ambitions of Alexander the
Great. Almost immediately after its appearance the poem received several
detailed commentaries, or glosses. It was also read and taught in the literary
schools of western Europe. In one of these sets of glosses, contained in a
manuscript now in Vienna and written in the second half of the thirteenth
century, the commentator extended his discussion of one of Alexander's
opponents in the poem, a magician-king named Zoroas of Memphis. In
his discussion the commentator offered a systematic survey of the magical
arts, one far more relevant to his own time than to the age of Alexander
(Colker 1978: 394–5; Townsend 1996: 193–4). Magic, the commentator
says, includes the five categories of prophecy, conjuring, mathematics,
witchcraft (*maleficium*) and fortune-telling. Prophecy contains five categories: pyromancy, aeromancy, hydromancy, geomancy and necromancy.
Conjuring includes making oneself invisible and shapeshifting.
Mathematics contains haruspicy, horospicy and auspicy – that is, with foretelling the future and divination. *Maleficium* entails finding out the future
by the aid of demons. Fortune-telling is the discovery of the future by
casting lots. The key element here is that while many of these forms may
be forbidden, it is specifically *maleficium* that requires the assistance of
demons, and hence would bring the *maleficus/a* under the jurisdiction of

the inquisitors of heretical depravity. King Zoroas of Memphis illustrates an important feature of thirteenth-century thought, the rediscovery (or discovery) of learned magic; that is, of magic performed without the aid of demons by skilfully exploiting occult (hidden) natural and spiritual powers. Such learned magic spread quickly throughout Europe from the late twelfth and thirteenth centuries to the sixteenth, and intermittently played an important role in general discussions of magic of all kinds (Thorndike 1923–58; Cohn 1975: 164–79; Peters 1978; Kieckhefer 1990: 116–50; Fanger 1998), often, especially after the fifteenth century, running the risk of being condemned as diabolical magic regardless of its practitioners' claims to innocence and spiritual purity. The material for the stories of Alexander the Great circulated widely through the sixteenth century, and they often emphasized their authors' interest in sorcery. In the Alexander romance written by Johannes Hartlieb in Bavaria between 1451 and 1454, the story found an author who was also widely known for his studies and books on various aspects of magic and sorcery, particularly the work known as 'The Book of All Forbidden Arts' (Fürbeth 1992; Lea 1957: 275; Hansen 1901: 130–3; Behringer 1998; Kors and Peters 2001: 170).

Another example, one that bridges learned and unlearned cultures, is the vast collection of materials concerning saints' lives and the ecclesiastical calendar compiled around 1260 by the Dominican friar Jacobus de Voragine (Jacobus de Voragine 1993). Here the preacher or confessor could find material on the Magi (Jacobus de Voragine 1993: I: 78–84), the identification of sorcery with demons (Voragine, 1993, I: 108–13, 129, 1512–13, 318–21, 340–50, II: 3–10, 106–8, 192–5, 260–5) and a late thirteenth-century perspective on the entire length of Church history and the festivals of the eccesiastical calendar that familiarized a wider public with the concerns of the early Church and tended to treat all of the lives and events that they considered as if they were contemporary with thirteenth and fourteenth-century western Europeans (Boureau 1984; Duffy 1992: 155–205; Swanson 1995: 142–71; Sticca 1996; Vauchez 1997; Kors and Peters 2001). Early Christian legends of sorcerers like the convert Cyprian and the magician Hermogenes and his contest with St James the Greater thus returned to wider familiarity in an age that understood them very differently from that in which they were first written. *The Golden Legend* and its adaptations were the main sources for hagiographical knowledge in the fourteenth, fifteenth and sixteenth centuries, and they were used as material for preachers and in the celebration of individual saints' cults, as well as for general edification. The stories of ancient and more recent conflicts between saints and demons and sorcerers had long been part of a Christian moral literature, and their periodical retellings kept them part of the narrative stock of preachers and moralists. Nearly a century before Jacobus de Voragine, the reformer and critic Gerald of Wales had included several of them in his work the *Gemma Ecclesiastica* of around 1190, including the story of St James and the magician Hermogenes as well as that of the sorcerer Cyprian (Gerald of Wales 1979: 51–4, 74–6). The career of Cyprian can thus be readily traced through Gerald of Wales, the encyclopedist Vincent of Beauvais, through Jacobus da Voragine into the demonological tract of Nicholas Jaquier in 1458 (see below).

Dante, whose great poem, the *Comedy*, was written in the second decade of the fourteenth century, treated heretics and diviners in two separate places in the *Inferno*, but his heretics in canto 10 were specifically only those who denied the immortality of the soul. In canto 20, however, his diviners ranged from classical seers and prophets to learned and well-known figures of the thirteenth century – his representative figure is Michael Scot, a scholar and ritual magician in the service of the emperor Frederick II, who had produced a large book on ritual magic for the emperor – to poor women who abandoned their families to make a living by telling fortunes. Although Dante was aware of the elaborate portraits of witches in classical literature – notably Lucan's portrayal of Erictho in the *Pharsalia* – and called the Siren an *antica strega*, 'an ancient witch,' in the *Purgatorio*, he did not elaborate further on the theme of contemporary sorcery. Dante, a lay theologian with an extensive knowledge of both Roman and canon law, and greatly concerned with human sinfulness, may thus be considered as representing some of the most important currents of twelfth and thirteenth-century thought on the nature of sorcery and divination in both their theological and legal contexts (Brucker 1963; Peters 1978; Harmening 1979: 217–58; Larner 1980: 16–18, 169–70). It is also worth noting that Dante himself, in a papal charge of magic against another figure, was suspected, because of his legendary learning and his reputation as a living man who had walked through hell, of having been solicited to perform magical injury against Pope John XXII (Kieckhefer 1997: 19).

CHAPTER 5

Political Sorcery at the Turn of the Fourteenth Century

The turn of the fourteenth century was marked by a group of political trials in France, at least one in Florence – that of Cecco d'Ascoli in 1322,
several in England and several at the papal court in Avignon, in which
charges of sorcery figured prominently. Accusations of sorcery had flared
up in political trials briefly in the ninth and the eleventh centuries, but the
cluster of trials in the early fourteenth century occurred toward the end of
a process in which a set of systematic, coherent and highly articulated
views of sorcery as both heresy and secular crime had been fully developed. In secular courts generally, jurists looked for damage actually caused
by sorcery; in ecclesiastical courts canonists looked for indications that sorcery was practised by means that clearly savoured of heresy, especially the
homage paid to demons in return for magical powers. As William R. Jones
put it, 'From the thirteenth century forward, at least on the continent, sorcery was becoming more visible as a matter of legal record' (Jones 1972:
670–1). The trials of the early fourteenth century are important for
another reason; most earlier instances of prosecution for magic, sorcery or
witchcraft were known mostly locally – individual cases were not widely
known unless they were taken up into a more widely circulated literature,
usually of a professional kind. The doctrines of heresy and sorcery, however, tended to be more widely known, particularly among those who
studied theology and canon law or became professional theologians and
canonists themselves. That is, a common professional literature grew up
after the late twelfth century that was used in schools and courts throughout western Europe. This literature, some of which has been considered
above, constituted a body of doctrine known to theologians, jurists, secular
magistrates and inquisitors and could be used as a standard for estimating
the character of charges of sorcery or witchcraft throughout western
Europe, even in local settings. Those who did not know it could learn its
contents through personal contacts at church councils, on diplomatic missions and from books and university scholars who did.

The sorcery accusations and trials of the fourteenth and fifteenth centuries occurred in the context of royal, princely, episcopal and papal courts –
that is, in formalized households that were in the process of transformation

from rudimentary itinerant households to centres of government. In these courts not only the ruler, but family members, the higher aristocracy, officers of state, princely favorites, attendants and domestic servants contended for access to power, wealth and security. Individuals might wield considerable influence, well beyond their official or domestic status, because of their friendship or proximity to the prince. Courtiers also knew that royal favour did not circulate in clearly marked channels, but instead was subject to obscure influences, the apparently inexplicable choice and rise to prominence of favorites, momentary passions, and the 'hissings and murmurings' not only of blood relatives, favourites, mistresses, friends, clerics and attendants, but also of astrologers and magicians. Skilful rulers manipulated both the explicit, official aspect of their courts and the more obscure dimensions of favouritism. At its fullest, the late thirteenth-century princely court was packed with people from virtually all social ranks and occupations, and since governance was the court's primary business, it was difficult to keep the different realms of courtly life separated (Peters 1978; Carey 1992).

Criticism of the court usually took its varied structure into account. The types of the wicked adviser, the overly influential favourite, the treacherous queen or mistress, the envious prince and the ambitious parvenu fill the literature on the courts, and in their train were to be found the poets, artists, physicians, astrologers, ladies and gentlemen in waiting, itinerant holy men, clerics and various kinds of entertainers, including illusionists. They served figures inside and outside the world of the court as formal or informal advisers, gossips, go-betweens, panders, agents and confidants. They might also use the services of ritual magicians – 'learned' practitioners who claimed to be able to manipulate the spirit world by means of gestures, words and songs contained in the increasingly available books of magical practices that proliferated from the late twelfth century on, some translated and adapted from Arabic or Greek and others concocted by local European practitioners (Cohn 1975: 164–79; Kieckhefer 1990; Peters 1978; Braekman 1997; Veenstra 1998).

In addition, precisely because of its domestic character the court was also the scene in which princely domestic dramas were played out – the inexplicable illness or death of the prince, his consort, or his heir apparent; dynastic turbulence in general, such as the arrival of a new queen with new favourites; the rise of obscure advisers of low social rank to great prominence at the expence of those claiming high position by virtue of birth, blood and high social status, and the playing out of dynastic and other rivalries, all allowed considerable leeway for charges of magic to be made. Rumours of deaths by poisoning – which usually carried a connotation of poisons created by magical means – circulated about the deaths of Louis, the heir of Philip III of France in 1276, of Philip IV in 1314, of

Louis X in 1316 and of Philip V in 1322. Similar rumours circulated about Hubert de Burgh, the justiciar of Henry III of England. Other English officials, notably Walter Langton, the treasurer of Edward I, and Adam Stratton, the chamberlain of the Exchequer under Edward II, were accused of using magic to gain considerable fortunes through the demonic manipulation of royal favour (Jones 1972; Beardwood 1964). In the great constitutional duel between Philip IV of France and Pope Boniface VIII around the turn of the fourteenth century, Philip's agents and the pope's own Italian enemies accused the pope himself of devil worship and of having a familiar demon in his service (Schmidt 1989; Coste 1995). Even after the death of Boniface in 1303, agents of the French king persisted in accusing the late pope of magic and insisting on his public condemnation by his successor, Clement V (Menache 1998; Schmidt 1989).

After the death of his young wife Jeanne de Navarre in 1305, Philip IV of France and a number of others charged Guichard, Bishop of Troyes, in 1308 with having murdered the queen of France and her mother by sorcery and poison, and others were charged along with Guichard and still others were charged with similar offences over the next several years , including Enguerrand de Marigny, the royal chamberlain and once favourite of Philip IV of France (Jones 1972; Russell 1972: 193–8; Cohn 1975: 185–92; Peters 1978: 110–37; Strayer 1980; Barber 1994: 299–300; Rigault 1896). The death of the young queen Jeanne of Navarre appears to have affected Philip IV deeply and helps to explain the king's fear that sorcery had killed her and threatened the rest of his family. Philip's fears of the prevalence of sorcery and the dangers that it raised of pollution to a Christian kingdom is also illustrated by his attack on the Order of Knights Templar in 1307, which led to the trials and destruction of hundreds of its members and the abolition of the Order by Pope Clement V in 1312. The destruction of the Order of the Knights Templar invoked charges of both blasphemy and magical practices (Barber 1978, 1994; Partner 1982). As the summons to the meeting of the Estates-General of France in 1308 asserted: 'Against so criminal a plague everything must rise up: laws and arms, every living thing, the four elements.'

The moral dynamics of royal courts were echoed in the papal court as well. Not only had Boniface VIII been accused of sorcery and demonolatry (accusations of sorcery on the part of popes, and indeed against clerics generally, came to correspond roughly to papal accusations of heresy against secular rulers), but Pope John XXII, elected in 1316, imagined himself the victim of a number of magical plots, including one to which the bishop of Cahors, Hugues Géraud, confessed in 1317, and John XXII wrote voluminously about the dangers to all of Christendom of the sorcerers and their activities, particularly in decretals of 1318, 1326 and 1331 (Hansen 1901: 2–4, 5–6, 7–8; Thorndike 1923–58: III: 18–38; Cohn 1975:

180–5; Kors and Peters 2001: 118–120), in which the sorcerers suspected were all clergy. Similar charges were made against Bernard Délicieux at around the same time (Eubel 1897; Maier 1952; Kors and Peters 1972: 80–4; Russell 1972: 173; Cohn 1975: 192–6; Partner 1982: 55–8; Friedlander 1996). It is important to note that in both kinds of political milieu – royal and papal courts – the accused were often clerics themselves, that is, the social group whose access to learning may have made them more likely than others, not only to be accused of performing sorcery, but of actually practising it. Such papal pronouncements circulated widely. The first quarter of the fourteenth century thus witnessed an outburst of charges and widespread discussions of maleficient sorcery in the highest ruling circles of Europe. Such sorcery was usually what was termed necromancy, or ritual magic – the use of secret rituals, words and substances to affect royal affairs, whether the health and life of the king and the royal family, love and marriage, or political misfortune (Kieckhefer 1990: 151–75; Cohn 1975: 163–79).

Nor did this sort of accusation and trial end after the first half of the fourteenth century. In 1358 Charles V of France accused Charles of Navarre of using ritual magical practices against him. In 1398 two Augustinian monks were executed in Paris after they had failed to cure the madness of Charles VI and then accused the king's brother, Louis of Orleans, of having bewitched him (Famiglietti 1986: 209–10, nn. 26, 52; Veenstra 1998: 64–72). Valentina Visconti, the wife of Louis, was also accused of the use of sorcery (Famiglietti 1986: 238–9; Veenstra 1998: 81–5) And charges of magic also circulated around the memory of the assassinated Louis of Orleans after his murder in 1407 (Vaughan 1979: 70–3; Veenstra 1998). In 1376 Alice Perrers, mistress of Edward III of England, was tried for injuring the king by magical arts, and in 1399 Henry IV of England charged some clerks of the late Richard II with having used the same arts (Kelly 1977: 215; Carey 1992). In 1419 Joan of Navarre, widow of King Henry IV, was imprisoned on a charge of having attempted to harm the king by sorcery and necromancy (Kelly 1977), and in 1441 Eleanor Cobham, wife of Humphrey, Duke of Gloucester, was tried for having plotted by magic against the life of King Henry VI (Kelly 1977; Jones 1972). In 1469 Jacquetta of Luxemburg was acquitted of trying to enchant Edward IV into marrrying her daughter (Jones 1972).

Nor was John XXII the last pope concerned with magic. Necromancers were accused at the court of Benedict XIII (1394–1423), as was that pope himself in 1409 (Harvey 1973), and in the next century Eugenius IV accused the antipope Felix V (1439–49) of protecting sorcerers in his duchy of Savoy (Hansen 1901: 18–19, and below). Charges of papal magic increased greatly, of course, especially in the protestant polemics that circulated widely during and after the Reformation of the sixteenth century

(Clark 1997: 361, 489–508; Cameron 1998). Although John XXII had also briefly removed sorcery from the purview of the inquisitors of heretical depravity, the offence was reinstated in their powers by Gregory XI in 1374. In short, besides large numbers of occasional local trials, the political trials from the end of the thirteenth century to the late fifteenth kept the reality of necromancy in the foreground of public attention. In 1398 the faculty of theology at the University of Paris issued a broad and unqualified condemnation of sorcery, arguing that lust, timidity, and proud curiosity drive men to idolatry, and that such cases have been found more often in recent times, the faculty listed twenty-eight articles that it condemned in the harshest possible terms (Thorndike 1944: 261–6; Kors and Peters 2001: 127–132). In 1466 the faculty of the University of Paris condemned a number of books of magic owned by a recently deceased astronomer (Thorndike 1944: 351–2). The conjunction of the Paris executions of 1398 and the condemnation of sorcery by the faculty of theology marks the beginning of collective and sustained attention on the part of the ruling and learned institutions of Europe to the problem of sorcery and its dangers (Lea 1955: 464–6; Veenstra 1998: 343–55). And if kings and their families as well as popes acknowledged their own terrible vulnerability to sorcery, could the rest of the population of Europe be any less vulnerable (Cohn 1975: 180–94)?

CHAPTER 6

Sorcerer and Witch

The political cases of sorcery were generally widely known, because they were extensively discussed and recorded. The many local trials that took place in the thirteenth and fourteenth centuries were neither well known nor often recorded, and it is pointless to try counting local cases until the fifteenth century, when the inquisitorial criminal procedure had come into more widespread use, written records were both made and preserved, and information concerning trials and convictions circulated more and more widely throughout western Europe (Hansen 1901: 445–613; Russell 1972: 209–18; Kieckhefer 1976: 106–47).

One of these early fourteenth-century cases, however, is both well documented and well worth consideration. In 1324 the bishop of Ossory in Ireland, Richard Ledrede, accused Alice Kyteler, a wealthy and prominent woman in Kilkenny, and several others, charging them with being a group of heretics and witches who held nocturnal meetings at which they made sacrifices to the devil and performed forbidden magical acts in order to injure others. Alice herself was also accused of having a familiar demon (Russell 1972: 189–93; Cohn 1975: 198–204; Davidson and Ward 1993). As its most recent historians have noted,

> the Kyteler witch trial is of great historical interest because it it the first witchcraft trial in European history to treat the accused as members of an organized sect of heretics, and the first to accuse a woman of having acquired the power of sorcery through sexual intercourse with a demon. It is also the first occasion on which a woman was burnt for heresy on charges deriving from witchcraft and occult practices rather than from the familiar sectarian heresies. (Davidson and Ward 1993: 1)

Richard Ledrede had been trained on the Continent and resided at the papal court at Avignon and had probably learned his views about witchcraft in the world of John XXII and brought them with him when he was appointed to the Irish diocese (Cohn 1975: 202–3; Davidson and Ward 1993: 2). If this is true, it supports the argument that the later fully developed concepts and prosecutions of sorcerers and witches were more the product of learned theology and jurisprudence, particularly of the conflicts between different kinds of laws, than the result of the discovery of popular, folkloric practices (Ginzburg 1991). But there is more to the problem than this stark contrast.

Ledrede ran afoul, not only of Alice Kyteler's local supporters, but also of the resistance of English judges. The society of Kilkenny abounded with local alliances and resentments, many of the latter directed against Alice Kyteler, both for her several marriages and for the considerable wealth she had acquired from them. Alice's good fortune sems to have excited her local enemies, including her stepchildren, to charge her before the new bishop and the new bishop himself to understand the charges in terms of his own background and the confession he wrung from the torture and burning in 1324 of Petronilla of Meath, one of Alice's servants. One of Alice's strongest supporters was Arnold le Poer, seneschal of Kilkenny and Carlow, whom Ledrede eventually imprisoned until le Poer died. But Ledrede never managed to obtain custody of Alice Kyteler, and he was later discredited in a number of political conflicts with local Irish and English rivals.

The trial of Alice Kyteler is an important early case, particularly well documented, that illustrates not only the conflict of canon and secular law in early fourteenth-century Ireland (and, by implication, elsewhere), but the battery of charges that it was thought possible to bring in a local conflict of this kind and the prominence of what appears to be a new kind of diabolical witchcraft among them. The case, however, is virtually unique, and it started no general hunt for sorcerers or witches in either Ireland or England. Continentally inspired, the concept of sorcery and witchcraft used in the Kyteler case developed more strongly and regularly on the Continent from the later fourteenth century.

At first glance, the fourteenth century seems to offer many explanations for the growth in the conceptualization and prosecution of magic and witchcraft, but the considerable number and varying degrees of scale in these explanations are of different orders of magnitude and cannot be cited simply in a direct causal way to explain the changes in conceptualization and prosecution that took place, after all, in very different regions at different times – and in many regions not at all (Briggs 1996: 287–316; Nirenberg 1996; Behringer 1998). It is necessary to consider the macro-conditions of the late fourteenth and fifteenth centuries at some length, because they have sometimes been used indiscriminately to 'explain' the new ideas about sorcery, magic and witchcraft that emerged at the time.

A vast series of large-scale natural disasters struck western Europe from 1315 until well into the fifteenth century, but their connection with ideas of sorcery and witchcraft has not been established. We must first consider the macro-scale. In 1315–17 a great famine occurred throughout most of western Europe (Jordan 1996). From 1348 on, the Black Death, a pandemic of bubonic, septicaemic and pneumonic plague followed (Ziegler 1969; Platt 1996). Throughout the century warfare devastated many areas,

and it was waged on a larger scale of destruction and injury to both com-
batants and non-combatants and with a high degree of mobilization of
state resources unheard of earlier. Finally a wave of financial collapse struck
both the great and small banking firms of northern Italy, causing economic
ruin and confusion throughout Europe. Certainly these disasters must have
affected Europeans' confidence in both material and spiritual protectors,
but in no case can a direct causal connection with ideas of magic and
witchcraft be established.

There is also the intellectual and legal tradition that had developed especially since the eleventh century, shaped by a growing body of criminal law
theory and a sharper and more precise concept of the offence and punishment of heresy. The new and comprehensive legal doctrines were not
exclusively those of the schools or of judicial theory generally, nor of
canon law exclusively, but they had begun to be applied in both ecclesiastical and secular courts from the late twelfth century on. They were part of
what has been called the *ius commune* of Continental Europe, a legal system
with an increasingly developed concept of both crime and criminal law
and the distinctive Romano-canonical legal procedure (Bellomo 1995;
Fraher 1989). From its origins in the schools of northern Italy and southern France, the new *ius commune* moved out irregularly across most of
western Europe, introducing both new rules of evidence and the romano-
canonical inquisitorial judicial procedure and giving to new and centraliz-
ing court systems and the magistrates who operated them a learned law
that could – and did – successfully challenge local and traditional legal systems. Romano-canonical procedure also used the inquisitorial method –
the control of a case by a single magistrate simultaneously as investigator,
prosecutor, and judge – and the use of torture as a legal incident; in the
presence of what is now called extensive circumstantial evidence, the
absence of the identical testimony of two eyewitnesses, or of a confession
by the accused, torture was permitted in order to obtain a confession when
significant other evidence indicated the probable guilt of the accused
(Peters 1996b; Pennington 1993: 132–64).

The best way to approach these elements on the macro-scale and use
them as evidence in particular instances – if they can be used as evidence
at all – is to look at specific regions in which new kinds of accusations and
trials appear to have taken place and to ask whether famine, plague, war or
social and economc disorder is particularly marked in them and what role
these might have played in conjunction with any other factors that may be
relevant. As a number of historians have pointed out, the particular mix of
the 'factor-bundle' will largely determine the resulting understanding and
explanation. Arno Borst has said, 'We have ... to attend to the dirty details
of the first witchcraft trials and put them into the historical context of
their specific locations, instead of spending time on religious and social

history at large' (Borst 1992: 104). Among the mid-level factors, for example, is the redesign of local economies or local legal structures: that is,
changing the forms of rural livelihood in ways that made many regions less
self-reliant and brought them into more contact with larger markets and
made them more vulnerable to their influence and fluctuations, hence los-
ing some sense of economic autonomy (and sensing more anxiously the
relative prosperity or economic misfortune that such changes entailed); or
the intrusion of new legal systems in the place of old, thereby making certain practices criminal that had earlier not been thought to be criminal.
There are also, finally, the particular circumstances and experience of individual jurisdictions in which the earliest trials were held. These 'middle-
scale' changes might then be considered in relation to particular outbreaks
of larger-scale troubles (Briggs 1996).

Finally, the fourteenth century also witnessed the long residence of the
papacy outside Rome, at Avignon, from 1305 to 1378, the return to
Rome, a bitterly contested papal election in 1378 that was followed by the
Great Schism, that is, by a period between 1378 and 1409 when two men
claimed to be the legitimate pope, and from the Council of Pisa in 1409 to
1415, when three men did so. Although the Schism was healed at the
Council of Constance in 1415–18, the Council of Basel in 1439 elected
Amadeus VIII, Duke of Savoy, pope as Felix V (1439–51) in place of the
living Eugenius IV (and thus 'Felix V' is conventionally recorded as an
antipope). Such disorder at the very top of the hierarchy of Latin
Christendom did little to calm the anxieties of Christians throughout
Europe, although as František Graus has shown, 'the most shattering crisis
for the people of the period was not the duplication of the papacy and the
college of cardinals, but the doubtful validity of the communion, the concern about the earthly and eternal salvation of every Christian, and the loss
of the community of living and dead in heaven and on earth' (Borst 1992:
121). One might add that such a sense of loss and uncertainty comple-
mented a heightened sense that the assaults of Satan were growing more
powerful, that defences against them were weaker, and that this awareness
was linked to ideas about the end of the world, especially those aspects of
it that dealt with the growth in strength of the assaults by Satan and the
coming of the Antichrist. Against these fears, the intensity of devotion
increased; the rise of all forms of devotionalism, as Richard Kieckhefer has
said, was 'perhaps the most significant development in late medieval
Christianity' (Kieckhefer 1987: 75).

In the wake of the Avignon papacy and the Great Schism, there were
many calls for reform, not only of the papacy, but of Christian life on all
levels, and one of the results was a series of Church councils that dealt with
a wide range of matters and the emergence of a number of religious
reform movements within particular dioceses and ecclesiastical provinces.

These brought to the attention of both learned scholars and political and legal authorities an entire panorama of local beliefs and practices that came to be reassessed in the light of the entire experience of fourteenth and fifteenth-century Europe and many of them condemned as superstitions. Some of these began in certain places to be condemned as sorcery and witchcraft, others as manifestations of regrettable superstition. Such ideas circulated effectively in fifteenth-century Europe among the mutual contacts on the part of university scholars, in treatises and handbooks, and among certain classes of officials, notably the Dominican and Franciscan inquisitors of heretical depravity and energetic lay magistrates, as well as groups of reform-minded prelates. Church councils also provided occasions for churchmen and laymen from all corners of Europe to meet and exchange ideas. Important councils were held at Pisa in 1409, at Constance in 1414–18, at Pavia-Siena in 1423–4, and at Basel in 1431–9. The Council of Basel in particular was one of the most important and influential occasions for such contacts and exchanges of ideas. At the council a number of new ideas concerning the diabolical character of sorcery, superstition and witchcraft circulated and spread outside the orbit of Basel itself as members of the Council and their companions and servants returned to their homes elsewhere, carrying ideas with them, and a number of treatises were written and discussed at the Council, one of them dealing with some of the earliest cases of prosecution for sorcery (see below).

Basel is an important example of the new role of communications in fifteenth-century Europe. As Margaret Aston has said of the Councils of Constance and Basel: 'They might in fact be regarded as a combined form of summit conference, trade fair and ecumenical council, with membership drawn from all parts of Europe, including both secular and ecclesiastical rulers, accompanied and provided for by all the enormous following of retainers, craftsmen, and traders who were deemed necessary for the wants of such numbers. Never before had people met together from so many parts on such a scale' (Aston 1968: 79). At these new-style assemblies, ideas, books, stories, and gossip moved easily and quickly. The assemblies became an entirely new source of information as well as an extremely efficient circulation system. Nor were Church councils the only such large-scale meetings in fifteenth-century Europe; the Congress of Arras in 1435, assembled to settle diplomatic differences among France, England and Burgundy, numbered around five thousand people (Dickinson 1955).

Of course other means of more rapid and extensive communications also appeared, print being perhaps the best known, but there were others as well. Messenger services among great and lesser powers, the regularizing of the post messengers carrying both public and private written communications, the internal communications systems of diplomatic missions, commercial corporations, religious orders, and the attendant sharing of information and ideas, including conversations and gossip that these systems inevitably permitted suggest the speed and extent of the ciculation of ideas and information across Europe after the late fourteenth century, even independently of the spread of printed matter (Aston 1968: 49–116).

In this milieu, news – and texts – travelled rapidly and widely. And when the news of new kinds of sorcery and superstition began to circulate in the late fourteenth and early fifteenth centuries, it circulated far more widely and more rapidly than had news of earlier cases, for example, that of Alice Kyteler. At the Council of Basel the theologian Johann Nider first learned of the trial and execution of Joan of Arc several years earlier, in 1431 (see below). These circumstances provide the context for the spread of ideas about sorcery and witchcraft that circulated from the early fifteenth century on.

The conciliarist movement was accompanied by a number of efforts to reform the beliefs and behaviour of ordinary Christians. The 1398 condemnation of sorcery by the faculty of theology of the University of Paris was one of the earliest, but larger and more ambitious projects soon followed (Veenstra, 1998: 343–55). Jean Gerson (1363–1429), chancellor of the University of Paris, preached a number of sermons and wrote several tracts against what he considered the superstitious religious practices of his own day, including one 'On errors concerning the magical art and the forbidden articles' (Thorndike 1923–58: IV: 114–31; Bonney 1971: 88–9; Hansen 1901: 86–7; Brown 1988: 159–60; Veenstra 1998: 142–3). Gerson's criticisms focused on the interpretation of particular events – the croaking of a crow above the roof, for example – as signs of impending disaster or bad luck, the fear of 'unlucky days', that is, days that were unpropitious, as well as on the use of incantations, images and certain herbs, and the misuse of astrology, a discipline that straddled both the world of learning and that of 'superstition.' Gerson also insisted that while it was permissible to have recourse to good angels when faced with illness or temptations, it was absolutely forbidden to have recourse to demons. Gerson also insisted that the moment one even considers entering into a pact with demons, he has already made such a pact. Shortly after Gerson's tract, in 1412, John of Frankfurt, professor of theology at the University of Heidelberg and an inquisitor at Wurzburg, condemned such beliefs as the supernatural powers of infants born with a caul (Hansen 1901: 71–82; Veenstra 1998: 147; Lorenz 1994a: 87), and tracts by Nicholas Jauer in 1405, the anonymous treatise *Tractatus de Daemonibus* (*Treatise Concerning Demons*) of 1415, and a treatise on superstitions by Henry of Gorkum in 1425 all regarded these and other superstitious practices as bringing humans closer to the power of demons (Thorndike 1923–58: IV: 274–307, 683–7; Bonney 1971; Hansen 1901: 82–6, 87–8; Paton 1992; Veenstra 1998: 138–53; Cameron 1998). In one case, that of Werner of Freiburg, an Augustinian friar tried at Speyer and Heidelberg in 1405 for maintaining superstitious beliefs, Nicholas Jauer perceived a link between superstitious beliefs and the performance of magic (Lerner 1991; Veenstra 1998: 151). During the late fourteenth and early fifteenth centuries a number of other sermons and treatises in Italy, England, France and the German lands both echoed and expanded the criticisms of Gerson, particularly the remarkable collection of sermons delivered at Siena in 1427 by Bernardino of Siena, a reader of Passavanti and one of the earliest theoreticians of the relations among superstition, sorcery, and witchcraft (Owst 1957; Bonney 1971; Paton 1992: 264–306; Swanson 1995: 182–99, 235–56, 267–310; Duffy 1992: 266–98; Bossy 1985; Veenstra 1998: 137–201; Kors and Peters 2001: 133–137; on Bernardino, Mormando 1998). As Duffy has said, what the reformers found when they looked at what they called 'superstitions' was 'not paganism, but lay Christianity' (Duffy 1992: 187; Segl 1990; Monter 1983: 6–22; Clark 1997: 473–88, and 821, s.v. superstition).

During the mid-fifteenth century Cardinal Nicholas of Cusa (1401–64) made a reforming journey throughout much of western Europe, and his agenda was remarkably similar to those of Gerson and his successors earlier in the century (Sullivan 1974). At the point at which the general criticism of superstitious practices blended into the specific topic of sorcery, the sermon by Bernardino of Siena of 1427 is a good example from Italy (Kieckhefer 1990: 194–5; Paton 1992; Shinners 1997: 242–5; Mormando 1998), and on the local level both handbooks for confessors and sermons, particularly sermons on the First Commandment, reinforced the connection between superstitious practices and sorcery by linking both to the sin of idolatry. A fifteenth-century English manual for confessors requires the confessor to ask the penitent, regarding the First Commandment, 'Have you had any belief, trust, and faith in witchcraft or sorcery, "necromancy" or in dreams, or in any conjurations, for theft or in any "other" writings or charms for sickness or for peril of bodily enemies, or for any other thing, "disease", for all of this is against the faith?' (Harmening 1988, 1989, 1990a, 1990b; Maggioni 1993: 54). John Bossy has persuasively argued that one of the major transformations in the characterization of sin in the later Middle Ages and especially in the sixteenth century was the shift in penitential emphasis from the seven deadly sins to the Ten Commandments (Bossy 1988; Harmening in Blauert 1990: 68–90; Clark 1997: 493–508, 562–3). In this shift, the sin of idolatry (now emphatically including magic and witchcraft) was committed against the First Commandment and thus became the greatest of all sins.

The power of demons to tempt humans with God's permission, said Gerson, had four causes: to achieve the damnation of the obstinate, the punishment of sinners, a testing of the faithful and to manifest God's glory. Such occasions of temptation were the constant material of sermons and confessional manuals, and they were often thought to employ rituals and materials analogous to normative Christian devotional practices and objects, always for personal benefit or the benefit of clients to the exclusion of the charitable and fraternal concern for the spiritual and material welfare of the entire local community.

Certain rites and certain objects were believed to possess innate power. Not only liturgical books, and bibles and the texts they contained, but books of magic or necromancy themselves were thought to possess such powers (Kieckhefer 1997). So did prayers. So did the consecrated host. So did the class of objects known as sacramentals: the water used in baptism, holy oil and blessed candles and palms. So might the bodies of the dead. These were material exchanges between the sacred liturgical order of reality and the desires of individuals to appropriate such power for themselves, sometimes in a socially harmless way – as protections against illness or other harm or – at somewhat greater risk – to find lost or stolen objects, but at other times in asocial ways – to curse rather than bless, to cause illness instead of curing it or to use them as techniques of sorcery exclusively for private, rather than socially beneficial purposes. Once such objects left the control of the clergy who administered them and normally regulated their proper use – and hosts, water, oil, candles, blessed palms, and the texts of prayers routinely did so – they became potentially dangerous in the hands of private individuals who hoped to use their innate or acquired power for personal gain, even when those who misused them might themselves be hermits, monks or other members of what Richard Kieckhefer has termed 'the clerical underworld' and Peters, following Peter Brown, the 'demimonde' (Peters 1978: 110–37; Carey 1992). The same problem existed in the case of prayers and liturgical rituals (Franz 1909; Harmening 1988: 191), particularly those rituals concerning exorcisms and blessings.

As the idea of heresy came to define the offence not only as a violation of the bonds between the individual and God but also between individuals in the Christian community, the image of heretical groups as anti-churches also developed. These counter-societies were then accused of possessing their own rites, perversions of the normative rites of the Christian liturgy: baptism was perverted by blasphemous initiation rites; benedictions and blessings were perverted into curses; worship due only to God was paid to the devil; sacramentals were perverted for blasphemous misuse, as were such rites as exorcism. The ideal of Christian chastity was perverted by accusations of indiscriminate sexual orgies, and the sanctity of the consecrated host was perverted in obscene sexual contact with demons and unholy banquets and collective, grotesque festivities. Some of these ideas had long been understood as signs indicating the increasing and despairing fury of Satan as the end of the world – and his own final defeat – drew near, doubling his onslaught against the people of God. Such eschatological ideas were widespread in the fifteenth century (Cohn 1975; Clark 1997: 321–74, with extensive references). Such anti-churches came to be considered the norm of heretical individual and social existence several centuries before the fifteenth. But with the larger changes in devotional and material life after the late fourteenth century, all of these features came to be brought to bear, no longer exclusively on heretical groups, but upon all enemies of God and man, however these may have been thought to be constituted.

Beginning in the early fifteenth century many of the different kinds of offences that had earlier constituted the separate offences of magic, sorcery, divination, necromancy and even learned natural magic began to be considered in some places by some theologians and magistrates, both ecclesiastical and civil, as a single type of crime whose essence was defined as a conspiratorial alliance with the devil whose purpose was to ruin human society. At its most comprehensive (and not all demonologists included all of the features that collectively came to distinguish it) individuals were believed to have made a pact with the devil, signed it with their blood, rendered homage and entered into sexual relations with him, travelled by flight to assemblies at which they participated in blasphemous rites and carried with them, usually on their bodies, a mark or sign of their membership in the diabolical conspiracy of witches and were sometimes accompanied by a familiar demon, often in the shape of an animal.

The novelty of this definition lay in the application to formerly individually accused magicians and others of the idea of conspiracy, that is, of collective enmity toward the human race, and of collective action that was undertaken to accomplish its destruction. The earlier separate categories and the distinctions reflected in the canon *Episcopi* between fantasy and actuality gave way to a new and inclusive understanding of both. As Paravy notes: 'It is this fundamental distinction [that of the canon *Episcopi* between fantasy and reality] that disappears. The diverse worlds of throwers and raisers of *sortes*, of men and women who cure illnesses, are uniformly included without mercy in a single condemnation, to the extent that every kind of magic, when investigated, reveals a member of the devil's sect. ... None of these elements is new, and all of them are attested in a complex intellectual and psychological heritage that unified pagan Mediterranean and [northern] Germanic traditions. What was new was the rigorous tie that bound and combined these elements to and with each other, coordinating them in a system that was at the same time fantastic and coherent' (Paravy 1981: 121, 124; Trusen 1989; Harmening 1988: 187). These elements may be seen in the 1405 *Treatise Concerning Superstitions* of Nicholas Jauer (Lorenz 1994a: 86; Veenstra 1998: 149–50).

Such a transformation of thought also permitted earlier accounts of magic and sorcery from many different periods and contexts to be reinterpreted according to the new theories. When monastic writers, for example, had depicted the world outside the monastery as filled with demonic temptation and power and weak human beings who regularly succumbed to these, such depictions reinforced the monk's original decision to leave the troubled world for the cloister and perhaps to transfer onto that world his own fears – what some psychologists now call cognitive dissonance. But when these texts were read in the late fourteenth and fifteenth centuries by a non-monastic audience outside the original cloister context, they confirmed the new beliefs about the alarming vulnerability of the world and its inhabitants to the powers of Satan and were added to the new literature of demonology, sorcery and witchcraft. As early as 1409 Pope Alexander V spoke of a 'new heresy', and by 1450 the Dominican inquisitor of Carcassone, Jean Vineti, in his *Tractatus contra Demonum Invocatores*, *Treatise against Those Who Invoke Demons*, argued that diabolical sorcery – witchcraft in its later classical meaning – was a new heresy (Lea 1957: 272–3; Hansen 1901: 124–30; *Bibliotheca Lamiarum* 1994: 100–1).

What was also new was the legal argument that the immediacy and imminent danger of this crime, its inherently monstrous character, made it one of those 'excepted crimes' for which there was to be no possible expiation short of death, since there was no way by which an accused person could adequately repent, and hence no justification for mercy in sentencing. Every individual manifestation of 'magic' became simply one of many tips of a gigantic iceberg – the 'new' conspiracy directed by Satan to destroy the human race (Larner 1984: 35–67). The spread of learned law gave great moral, as well as legal authority to the secular magistrate, and these, too, were expected to engage vigorously in prosecuting the enemies of the human race.

A heightened consciousness of the unified and irreparably grave character of the crime of witchcraft and news of actual instances of magic, sorcery and witchcraft seen as new crimes had to have a basis in both theory and practice. There needed to be actual prosecutions of the new crime, and accounts of these prosecutions had to circulate in order to attract the attention of devotional reformers and magistrates in other regions and thus constitute news that needed to be known by them. Although a number of isolated trials had been held in Italy in the last several decades of the fourteenth century (Bonomo 1959; Paton 1992; Brucker 1963), the key geographical areas in which such trials and reports of them first appear to have occurred are in the region from the lower Rhone valley east and northeast in the area of the Dauphiné, the Pays de Vaud, Piedmont, Savoy and the valley of Aosta, and in what is now western Switzerland – Lucerne, Fribourg, Bern and the dioceses of Geneva, Lausanne, Neuchâtel and Sion.

From these areas the new ideas and legal procedures concerning sorcery and witchcraft spread along familiar and heavily used communications routes into northern and northeastern Italy – Lombardy, including the region around Como, and into eastern Switzerland, the Tirol, Swabia, Bavaria and the upper and lower Rhineland. These are the earliest sites of what became the first significant movements of witchcraft prosecution in western Europe. But these were not remote mountain backwaters of residual folk paganism, as some historians once claimed. They were lively and fluid areas of contact between different linguistic regions and cultures and exchange points for the transmission of ideas, governed by ambitious state-building rulers and cities, and strategically placed in the view of the Council of Basel. In the light of the complexity of the late fourteenth and fifteenth centuries, it is certainly necessary to look initially at the earliest particular local instances of a new conception of sorcery and witchcraft before invoking the large-scale disasters and other macro-conditions as explanatory devices.

The key years appear to be 1430–40 (Blauert 1989: 26; Ostorero *et al.* 1999). Neither the records of episcopal visitations in the diocese of Geneva from 1412 to 1414, nor the five books of the *Decreta seu Statuta Sabaudiae* (*The Decrees or Statutes of Savoy*), a general law code for the duchy of Savoy issued by Amadeus VIII in 1430, reveal any concern for a new kind of sorcery. A single tract, the *Errores Gazariorum* (*The Errors of the Gazars [Cathars]*), written in the francophone section of western Switzerland and recently redated to the early 1430s, however, spoke for the first time since the Alice Kyteler trial of a sect, or 'synagogue', whose members paid homage to and entered a pact with the devil, bestowed the *osculum infame*, feasted on the dead bodies of infants, held sexual orgies and received ointments and powders to kill their enemies and destroy harvests. Although they pretended to be good Catholic Christians, they represented the most dangerous of all enemies of the human race and the Christian Church (Lea 1957: 273–5; Hansen 1901: 118–22; Lorenz 1994a: 85; Ostorero *et al.* 1999; Kors and Peters 2001: 159–162). The *Errores Gazariorum* also identified the heresies of Catharism and Waldensianism with one another and attributed to their members many of the features that later applied to sorcerers and witches.

Two narrative sources, both written in the same general area around 1437, attribute the appearance of a new kind of sorcery to the years beginning in the 1390s. At the Council of Basel between 1435 and 1437, the Dominican theologian and prior of the Dominican convent at Basel, Johann Nider, wrote his large, reform-minded theological work, the *Formicarius* (*The Antheap*; printed in 1479). In book V, Nider recounted conversations that he had had with a judge in the service of the city of Bern, Peter von Greyerz, concerning von Greyerz's cases tried in the

Simme Valley under the jurisdiction of the city of Bern between 1392 and 1406, when von Greyerz retired. Nider's account of von Greyerz's cases depicted them as dealing both with traditional individual acts of sorcery, and also with an association of sorcerers who adored the devil, caused damage to the property and persons of others and enriched themselves (Borst, 1992; Kors and Peters 2001: 155–159). The most recent student of these cases, Andreas Blauert, has argued that the cases that von Greyerz tried had been indeed conventional cases of individual sorcery, but that in Nider's understanding and retelling they became something different – the account of a new phenomenon, diabolical, collaborative sorcery (Blauert 1989: 56–9; *Bibliotheca Lamiarum* 1994: 100–1; Bailey 1998). The cases tried by Peter von Greyerz and retold by Nider at Basel and in the *Formicarius* were those of damage to persons (including infanticide) and possessions, including crops and animals, by individuals from the middling levels of communities, who, in a period of economic and social transformation, had achieved some measure of economic success, but had also behaved in an ambitious, self-dependent and unneighbourly way and were accused by jealous or at least suspicious neighbours. They seem also to have been people who were rising in social status by these methods, earning the resentment of a traditional set of elites.

A second source, also written around 1437, the chronicle of the Lucerne scribe Hans Fründ, told of earlier cases in which sworn testimony indicated that the devil approached people who were depressed and melancholic, promising them riches and revenge on their enemies, organizing them into a group dedicated to his service, demanding sacrifices from them, and teaching them flight and shape-shifting. Fründ, like Nider, also appears to have read back into these earlier localized instances ideas of diabolical temptation, the existence of sects and homage to the demon that had recently become current in his own day.

The most persuasive piece of evidence, however, is the remarkable treatise *Ut Magorum et Maleficorum Errores* (*In order that the Errors of Sorcerers and Witches*), written by the judge Claude Tholosan, who served for several years in the district of Briançon in the Dauphiné. Pierette Paravy, who edited the treatise, has dated it to 1437 (Paravy 1979; Ostorero *et al.* 1999; Kors and Peters 2001: 162–166). The Tholosan document is important for several reasons. First, it is the work of a lay judge, and second, it reveals that judge drawing upon all the learning available to him, including consultations with learned jurists at Aix-en-Provence, Avignon and elsewhere, in order to characterize a sect of diabolical sorcerers, identify and justify the punishment they deserve, assemble the juristic rationale for the crime and justify the legitimate power of the prince who had commissioned his magistrates to carry out the law. Tholosan used canon and Roman law extensively, as well as the opinions of Zanchino de Ugolini and other jurists from the early fourteenth century. The treatise is important, not only for its use and reinterpretation of substantial theological and legal learning and for its timing, but because the author was a working lay magistrate, not a hunter after superstitions like Jauer, an inquisitor like Eymeric, a theologian like Nider or a chronicler like Fründ and others. In these cases, the theologians, the chronicler and the magistrate alike could point to direct contact with actual prosecutions – which two of them understood to have been for conspiratorial and diabolical sorcery and during which the magistrate had actually tried, convicted and executed people for these offences – that had taken place within recent human memory and in readily identifiable nearby places.

All of these sources, as well as others written just after them, agreed that the origins of the 'new sect' of sorcerers and witches lay in the last half, and particularly in the last quarter of the fourteenth century. In these cases social memory recognized that the offences of sorcery and witchcraft that were being commited in the first quarter of the fifteenth century were relatively recent, but all sources located their origin at around the same time a generation or two before the present at the end of the first quarter of the fifteenth century.

The geography of these instances lies just to the west of the great mountain passes of Mont Cenis, Lesser St Bernard, Greater St Bernard and the Simplon. From Lucerne and Bern, the territory in which these cases and theoretical works took place extends southwest to Fribourg, Lausanne, Geneva and Chambéry, and from there southeast to Briançon. That is, these instances occurred in the territory of two newly formed and ambitious states: part of the Swiss Confederation, particularly the city of Bern, and in the territories of the ambitious, state-building dukes of Savoy, especially Amadeus VIII. Savoy was the principal overland route into Italy for French travellers and into France for Italians, and since the twelfth century its dukes had added a number of contiguous territories to the original duchy and exerted their influence over several more.

Nider wrote his book and circulated his narrative at the Council of Basel, at the time virtually the crossroads of Christian Europe and the point at which diverse regional ideas about sorcery – and other topics – could conveniently encounter and influence each other. It was at Basel, after all, where Nider himself heard for the first time of the prosecution and burning of Joan of Arc, informed by a fellow Dominican from the Sorbonne, another case which Nider understood as one of diabolical sorcery (Kay 1988: 304–5). The Council of Basel also had business with the duke of Savoy, Amadeus VIII (1391–1451). Amadeus VIII and his immediate predecessors had greatly increased the territory ruled or dominated by the dukes of Savoy, and their court patronized French artists, resembling in this aspect the contemporary lavish courts and patronage of the dukes of

Burgundy in Burgundy and the Low Countries, especially Flanders. Disillusioned with Pope Eugenius IV (1431–47), the members of the Council of Basel declared him deposed, and they elected the widowed duke Amadeus VIII of Savoy as pope in his place. Taking the papal name Felix V (1439–51), Amadeus/Felix proceeded to attempt to increase the number of areas that recognized him as pope and to hasten the reform of Christian society, especially in his own ducal territories.

No pope ever took deposition lightly, and one of the responses on the part of Eugenius IV against Amadeus/Felix V was the charge that both heresy and diabolical sorcery flourished widely in the lands of the duke of Savoy. Eugenius IV had written other letters in the same vein (Hansen 1901: 17–19; Kors and Peters 1972: 98–101; 2001: 153–155), revealing himself to be an austere and devout prelate with a strong fear of diabolical magic. One of Eugenius' correspondents on the matter of diabolical sorcery was the inquisitor Pontus Fougeyron, whose work in the early fifteenth century contributed substantially to the demonization of heretics (Blauert 1989: 27). The response of Amadeus/Felix V was to intensify the search for diabolical sorcerers and witches in his territories. It is in these circumstances that the work of Claude Tholosan and a number of contemporary inquisitors in the area exerted a strong influence.

But magistrates, inquisitors, theologians and chroniclers did not produce the only sources that make this period a key one. The canon of Lausanne and secretary of Amadeus/Felix at the Council of Basel, Martin le Franc, wrote a long and illustrated poem around 1440 called *Le champion des dames* (*The Defender of Ladies*), which was generally a poem in praise of womanhood, except for its section concerning women sorcerers. Here, le Franc described a group of old women going to the 'synagogue' – that is, the sabbat – and paying homage to the devil in the form of a goat. Le Franc's information appears to have come from the same region near Briançon as the cases of Claude Tholosan. Amadeus/Felix V later made le Franc provost of the cathedral chapter in Lausanne (Veenstra 1998: 152; Kors and Peters 2001: 166–169). Not only did le Franc's poem echo the concerns of both his own master and Eugenius IV, but in its illustrated margins the manuscript depicted for the first time witches riding on broomsticks to the sabbat. By 1440 all of the elements of the later theories of witchcraft had assembled in place and had even begun to acquire a distinctive visual imagery.

From 1440 on, a number of local trials and works on demonology – with a new insistence on the diabolical character of sorcery – took place and were produced in this region, although not on a large scale and not everywhere. But the occurrence of trials and convictions gave a new immediacy to the works of demonology, and the works of demonology framed the investigations and trials for diabolical sorcery. The results were conveyed in the words of preachers and chroniclers. From the core areas in which they began, both doctrines and trials influenced areas both adjacent and further away. These new trials and works of demonology became the province of both ecclesiastical (including ordinary episcopal jurisdiction and inquisitorial jurisdiction) and lay magistrates. It is also possible to correlate periods and places of prosecutions of diabolical sorcery in the mid to late fifteenth century with periods of severe social and economic crisis: 1447–56, 1457–66, the exceptional decade 1477–86 and the nearly as exceptional decade 1487–96 (Blauert 1989: 18; Behringer 1998). Rather than see the social and economic crises as causing the persecutions, however, it may be more advisable to consider diabolical sorcery as a crime particularly suited – because of its alleged rejection of God and its conspiratorial hostility and destructiveness to neighbours – to be invoked in periods of such crisis, at least from the fifteenth century on.

CHAPTER 7

Superstition, Magic and Witchcraft on the Eve of the Reformation

During the half-century after 1440 numerous trials, usually of individuals or relatively small groups were held in the Valais (Strobino 1996), and at Lausanne, Vevey (Ostorero 1995), Neuchâtel, Bern, Fribourg and Basel (Blauert 1989: 37–60). From these origins both works of demonology and trials spread east into Austria, south into Italy, and north into the Rhineland. At the same time, the number of treatises dealing with diabolical sorcery also increased. From being particular subjects treated in longer works – as in Nider's *Formicarius* or le Franc's *Champion des dames* – the new offence continued to be treated in this way, but it also soon became the subject of separate works of demonology in its own right. Among the former were the commentary on the Bible by Alfonso Tostado around 1440, which treated the problem of demonic transportation of human beings from one place to another (Lea 1957: 189–91; Hansen 1901: 105–9; *Bibliotheca Lamiarum* 1994: 101), and the *Fortalicium Fidei* (*The Fortification of Faith*) of Alfonso de Spina just after mid-century (Lea 1957: 285–92; Hansen 1901: 145–8; *Bibliotheca Lamiarum* 1994: 105–6; Clark 1997: 81). These works incorporated current demonological theory into the kind of literature read by preachers, confessors and academics – thus bringing these views into the awareness of clerics who normally might not have been aware of individual demonological treatises. Among the latter, however, such works as Jean Vineti's *Tractatus contra Daemonum Invocatores* of 1450 (Lea 1957: 272–3; Hansen 1901: 124–30), and Nicholas Jacquier's *Flagellum Haereticorum Fascinariorum* (*The Lash of Heretics who Fascinate* [*Enchant*]) of 1458 (Lea 1957: 276–80; Hansen 1901: 133–45; *Bibliotheca Lamiarum* 1994: 104–5; Ostorero *et al.* 1999; Kors and Peters 2001: 169–172), indicate the increasing importance of demonology and diabolical sorcery as subjects of separate and detailed investigation and analysis.

The most important and influential example of the latter, however, was the result of an inquisitorial career that differed from those of other inquisitors. Heinrich Krämer (Latinized: *Institoris*), a Dominican, worked during the 1470s in the area of Constance, concentrating chiefly on the heresy of diabolical sorcery (Segl 1988: 103–26, esp. 109, n. 35; Schnyder 1991, 1993). In 1485 Institoris received permission from Georg Golser, the bishop of Brixen, to investigate heresy in the bishop's domains, and he undertook his investigations in the city of Innsbruck. Institoris, a furious misogynist, questioned particularly the women who came before him in great detail concerning their sexual lives, dismaying his fellow inquisitors, incurring judicial irregularity, and bringing the inquisitorial investigation in Innsbruck to a halt. The bishop of Brixen said of him that 'because of his advanced age, Institoris had become senile (*propter senium gantz chindisch*)' – although Institoris was only fifty-nine at the time.

Aged, misogynist and senile Institoris may have been in 1485, but he had lost neither his zealous determination to combat diabolical sorcerers – particularly women – nor his literary energy (on the problem of witchcraft accusations and gender history, see Edith Ennen in Segl 1988: 7–21; Burghartz 1988: 57–74; Dienst 1990; review of the question and the scholarly literature in Purkiss 1996; extensive discussions in Briggs 1996: 257–86; Sharpe 1997: 169–99; Clark 1997: 106–33). In 1487 he published the most important of all demonological treatises, the *Hammer of Witches* (*Malleus Maleficarum*, literally *The Hammer of Women Who Commit Maleficia*: on the metaphor of the hammer, see Arbesmann 1945; later editions, which included other works of demonology along with the *Malleus*, were called the *Malleus Maleficorum*, expanding the gender definition by shifting to the masculine). The work appeared with what appeared to be a letter of approbation, *Summis desiderantes affectibus*, issued by Pope Innocent VIII in 1484, an endorsement from the faculty of theology at the University of Cologne, and with Jacob Sprenger, a Dominican inquisitor from Cologne with whom Institoris had often worked, identified as co-author, although Sprenger's role in the project is now generally doubted (Anglo 1977a; Segl 1988; *Bibliotheca Lamiarum* 1994: 107–10). But both the papal letter and the Cologne endorsement are problematic. The letter of Innocent VIII is not an approval of the book to which it was appended, but rather a charge to inquisitors to investigate diabolical sorcery and a warning to those who might impede them in this duty, that is, a papal letter in the by then conventional tradition established by John XXII and other popes through Eugenius IV and Nicholas V (1447–55). The approval of the theological faculty of Cologne was arranged through a complicated series of academic negotiations – it, too, does not address the remarkable qualities of the work itself. It is doubtful whether either Innocent VIII or the theological faculty of Cologne ever read the work. The work was essentially a defence of prosecutions for witchcraft written in the face of considerable scepticism – its arguments, especially in part III, are clearly aimed at reluctant lay magistrates.

The treatise itself is in three parts (Hansen 1901: 360–407; summary in Lea 1957: 306–36; English translation in Summers 1971; excerpts in Kors and Peters 1972: 105–89, 2001: 176–229; see also Schnyder in Segl 1988:

127–49; Clark 1997) in the form of scholastic questions. Part I insists on the reality of diabolical *maleficium*, part II deals with the kinds of witches and the nature of their activities, and part III consists of describing the legal procedures by which both ecclesiastical and civil magistrates should proceed against them. The scholastic question format allowed Institoris to draw upon the work of earlier inquisitors and demonologists such as Eymeric, Nider, Jacquier and Spina, as well as virtually all other sources that touched, however remotely, on the subject. The purpose of the treatise was thus to demonstrate the nature and ubiquity of the offence of witch-craft, to refute those who expressed even the slightest scepticism about its reality, to prove that witches were more often women than men, and to educate magistrates on the procedures that could find them out and con-vict them. The first two parts of the treatise prepare for the third – the urg-ing of more widespread and intense prosecutions, chiefly by lay magistrates, in spite of any theological or legal scepticism or opposition they might encounter – by arming them with apparently irrefutable argu-ments against such opposition. The *Malleus* strengthened its arguments from theology and law by providing copious detail about recent, actual cases and insisting upon the consistency of its arguments with daily life (Segl in Tanz 1993: 127–54).

The *Malleus* was not, however, all-inclusive of the features of witchcraft as these emerged in the sixteenth century. It makes 'no mention of familiar spirits, of the obscene kiss, or even of the feasting and orgies of the sabbat. Nor is there any reference to the witches' or Devil's mark. The *Malleus* defined witchcraft as the most abominable of all heresies, its four essential characteristics being the renunciation of the Christian faith, the sacrifice of unbaptized infants to Satan, the devotion of body and soul to evil, and sex-ual relationships with incubi' (Russell 1972: 232; there is a pictorial repre-sentation of the devil as a he-goat and the obscene kiss in a mid-fifteenth-century (about 1460) manuscript of Johannes Tinctoris' tract, *Contra Sectam Valdensium* (*Against the Sect of Waldensians*) reproduced in Cohn 1975: Plate 1, and below). Even with these features, the *Malleus* had a durable publication history. Thirteen editions appeared between 1487 and 1520 and sixteen more between 1574 and 1669. Although these editions did not necessarily have large print-runs (and the phenomenon of print played a considerable role in circulating these ideas), they were printed in various cities in Gemany, France and Italy, and they suggest the appeal and durability of the work until more elaborate and specific demonological treatises began to appear after 1580. Copies of the *Malleus* were in the libraries of the early sixteenth-century magician Johannes Trithemius as early as 1492 and slightly later in that of Gianfrancesco Pico della Mirandola. Moreover, some of the omissions in the *Malleus* were compensated for in other works of demonology, so that by 1500 a reading of the *Malleus* and a few other works provided a virtual encyclopedia for the investigation of diabolical sorcery and witchcraft. One such work was the 1524 treatise *Tractatus de Haereticis et Sortilegis* by Paulus Grillandus, which contributed substantially to the image of the witches' sabbat (Lea 1957: 395–412; Hansen 1901: 337–41; *Bibliotheca Lamiarum* 1994: 133–5; on the sabbat, see Bonomo 1959; Cohn 1975: 206–24; Ginzburg 1991; Jacques-Chaquin and Préaud 1993). Later editions of the *Malleus* often included editions of Grillandus's and other related and by then supplementary works.

Nor was the *Malleus* immediately regarded as a definitive work. Its appearance triggered no prosecutions in areas where there had been none earlier, and in some cases its claims encountered substantial scepticism (for Italy, Paton 1992: 264–306). In 1538 the Spanish Inquisition cautioned its members not to believe everything the *Malleus* said, even when it presented apparently firm evidence. Long before then, however, the *Malleus* was the subject of considerable debate among both clerics and lay thinkers (Caro Baroja 1990: 19–43). Indeed, the chief function of the work was to serve as a centrepiece in demonological theory whose arguments might be expanded and added to by such works as that of Grillandus, as well as a focus for arguments and debates concerning particular points it made, some of the latter reflecting traditional rivalry between religious orders and ecclesiastical schools of theology. For example, an attack on some of the central arguments of the *Malleus* was made by the Franciscan Samuel de Cassini in 1505 and answered in favour of the *Malleus* by the Dominican Vincente Dodo in 1507 (Max 1990: 55–62; Lea 1957: 366–8; Hansen 1901; 262–84; *Bibliotheca Lamiarum* 1994: 114–15; Clark 1997: 486–7, 538). A similar criticism by Gianfrancesco Ponzinibio of Florence in 1520 was countered by the support of the *Malleus* position by the Dominican Bartolommeo de Spina in 1523 (Caro Baroja 1990: 32; Max 1993: 55–62; Lea 1957: 385–95; Hansen 1901: 326–7; *Bibliotheca Lamiarum* 1994: 120–2). The cautionary advice of the Spanish Inquisition in 1538 was merely another instance of the kinds of interest, and objections, that the *Malleus* raised.

Ulrich Molitor, doctor of laws and advocate of Archduke Sigismund of Austria, published his treatise *Tractatus de Pythonicis Mulieribus* (*Treatise Concerning Women Who Prophesy*) in 1489. The treatise is important in several respects. The territories of the archduke were contiguous with those in which the trials for diabolical sorcery and witchcraft had begun in the mid-fifteenth century and included lands in which Institoris had worked as an inquisitor. The archduke of Austria had every reason to discover whether the crime occurred in his territories and evidently – like many others – had considerable doubts about the details depicted in the *Malleus*. Molitor's treatise was intended to dispel those archducal doubts. It is cast as a discussion among Molitor himself, the archduke and Conrad Schatz, the chief magistrate of the ducal city of Constance. In the dialogue, the archduke raises sceptical questions which Molitor and Schatz answer (Lea 1955: 542–3; Lea 1957: 348–53; Hansen 1901: 243–6; *Bibliotheca Lamiarum* 1994: 110–11). Another feature of Molitor's work is the series of woodcut illustrations that it included, depicting various forms of witchcraft and diabolical sorcery. Illustrations of witchcraft had occurred as early as the few in Martin le Franc's poem, in the work of Johannes Tinctoris, and in a 1487 treatise on the vices and virtues by Johannes Vintler. From Molitor on, however, the visual depiction of the witch became virtually a genre subject, inviting such artists as Baldung Grien, Cranach, Dürer, Bruegel and others, and adding an important and still perplexing art-historical dimension to the study of the subject (Jacques-Chaquin and Préaud 1993: 397–438; Muchembled 1994: 322; Kors and Peters 1972, 2001: 30–40; Clark 1997: 11–30; Hoak 1985; Davidson 1987; Levack 1992; Lorenz 1994a: 209–19; *Bibliotheca Lamiarum* 1994; Zika 1998).

Shortly after the middle of the fifteenth century similar accusations were made in trials at Evreux in Normandy and at Arras (Hansen 1901: 149–83; Cohn 1975: 230–2; Kieckhefer 1994b: 35–8). In the first, in 1453, Guillaume Adeline, a doctor of theology, was convicted of having made a pact with Satan, of being forced by that pact to preach against the reality of the sabbat, and to have attended sabbats himself. In the second, in 1459–60, known as the 'Vauderie of Arras', the trial of a hermit who was later executed as a witch elicited the names of several other people, who were arrested, named still others, and were themselves executed. In all, thirty-four people were arrested as witches and twelve were executed by burning. As the round of accusations and convictions grew wider still, the duke of Burgundy, Philip the Good, began an investigation that ultimately slowed the accusations and arrests, until the furore died down and the Parlement of Paris finally delivered its verdict on an appeal in 1491, which rehabilitated the memory of all those who had been executed. In his treatise on the Arras trials of 1460 the theologian Johannes Tinctoris provided an illustration of the performance of homage to the devil in the form of a goat (Cohn 1975, Plate 1; Veenstra 1998: 152). By the second half of the fifteenth century similar prosecutions had reached as far down the Rhine as Cologne, where two women were burned for witchcraft in 1456 – by then the Rhine valley and its vicinity had also come to serve as a conduit for the new conception of diabolical sorcery and witchcraft, as did southwestern Germany (Lorenz 1994a, b). With several trials in Dommartin in 1498 and Kriens in 1500, the initial outbreak of trials for the new crime of witchcraft and diabolical sorcery slowed dramatically, not to be resumed extensively until the Reformation was well under way, after the middle of the sixteenth century (Blauert 1989: 87–109), although individual trials were held in some parts of western Europe in the early sixteenth century, as was the trial at Orleans reported sharply in one of the letters of Erasmus in 1501 (Allen 1906: 334–41; Kors and Peters 2001: 231–236) .

Throughout the fifteenth century a temporarily distinctive set of material and psychological circumstances in a particular geographical and jurisdictional area had drawn together a number of perennial concerns of Latin Christianity into a single concept of collaborative, conspiratorial, diabolical sorcery, which became 'witchcraft' as the term was used during the later great wave of persecutions after the middle of the sixteenth century and as it is still generally understood. Those circumstances generated a profound mistrust in both certain kinds of neighbours, their attitudes, and their reputations, and in the ability of traditional devotional practices to protect ordinary people from the assaults of those neighbours and their master, the devil. Even the developing arguments on behalf of learned, 'natural' magic – a beneficent and benevolent practice that claimed to help humans by using the occult powers of the stars and celestial spirits as a high and pure learned art – came to be regarded by both theologians and inquisitors potentially at least as a learned variant of diabolical sorcery, even though its most eminent practitioners and defenders passionately attempted to distinguish it from the traditionally despised and feared necromancy, now incorporated into diabolical sorcery (Peters 1978, 1996b; Vickers 1984; Kieckhefer 1990, 1994b, 1997; Clark 1997: 214–32, 236–40).

After the beginning of the sixteenth century, trials for witchcraft declined in number quickly, even in those regions in which the trials had most quickly developed. In Lucerne, Lausanne, Fribourg, Bern and Neuchâtel, for example, where the number of trials had reached more than thirty in the decade between 1477 and 1486, and nearly twenty in the following decade, there were only ten trials in the decade 1497–1506, and none during the decade 1507–16 (Blauert 1989: 18). The cases cited in Dommartin in 1498 and Kriens in 1500 were among a very few until after the middle of the sixteenth century. Although the new doctrines – and the new crime – remained in place and were further considered in a substantial literature during these years, the particular circumstances that had led to the accusations, trials and executions between 1430 and 1500 no longer seem to have existed after the turn of the century. And western Europe had new and pressing devotional and ecclesiological concerns after 1519 that may have pushed sorcery and witchcraft temporarily into the background (Clark 1997: 488–545; Cameron 1998).

But they left a substantial legacy, not only in the literature of demonology and witchcraft produced in the last three-quarters of the fifteenth century, but in a series of new laws and legal and theological/pastoral works produced in the first decade of the sixteenth century. In 1507, for example, the bishop of Bamberg issued a new set of laws concerning capital offences, in which the crime of magic figured prominently and justified the use of torture and execution by burning and which were invoked later in the century during large-scale witchcraft persecutions in Bamberg and elsewhere (Hansen 1901: 278–9). In 1508 the Dominican Bernard of Como published his *Tractatus de Strigiis* (*Treatise concerning Witches*), an extensive discussion of witchcraft that was often reprinted during the next two centuries (Hansen 1901: 279–84; Lea 1957: 370–3; *Bibliotheca Lamiarum* 1994: 119–20; Clark 1997: 522). The popular sermons of the theologian Johann Geiler von Kaisersberg, preached in Strassburg in 1508, condemned not magic (*Zauberei*), but witches *(Von den Unholden oder von den Hexen)* (Hansen 1901: 284–91; Lea 1957: 358–9; *Bibliotheca Lamiarum* 1994: 115–19; Behringer 1998: 56–8, 79–80; Kors and Peters 2001: 236–239). The 1510 *Mirror for Layfolk* (*Layenspiegel*) by Ulrich Tengler identified witchcraft firmly with heresy, fortune-telling, the black art, and magic and included a woodcut depicting various kinds of these being performed (Hansen 1901: 296–306; Lea 1957: 374; Clark 1997: 588). In 1515 the fifteenth-century work of the Spanish theologian Martin of Arles was first printed as *Tractatus de Superstitionibus contra Maleficia seu Sortilegia, quam Hodie Vigent in Orbe Terrarum* (*A Treatise Concerning Superstitions and against Witchcraft and Sorcery which Today Flourish All over the World*) (Hansen 1901: 308–9; Lea 1957: 296–8; Clark 1997: 480, 486–7; *Bibliotheca Lamiarum* 1994: 104; Cameron 1998: 165).

Martin of Arles's title thus drew together the key terms with whose historical development in western Europe this chapter has been concerned – superstition, magic and witchcraft, the latter two now designated *sortilegium* and *maleficium*. These were certainly not synonymous with the kinds of concerns with 'magic' expressed in Greek and Latin antiquity and in early Christianity with which this chapter opened, and Martin of Arles's work appears to have been written primarily because of a problem of determining whether or not a particular religious practice was superstitious. But those who held ideas like those of Martin of Arles and others in the early sixteenth century could now read their contemporary concepts of diabolical sorcery and witchcraft back into the texts of antiquity, and earlier Latin Christianity and see their own concerns mirrored in them, as they could also read Jewish and Christian scripture. The earliest printed and illustrated editions of Ovid and Apuleius, for example, clearly indicate sixteenth-century interpretations of the magic described in them, and that magic is now diabolical sorcery and witchcraft as sixteenth-century thinkers understood it. Even the distant past now appeared to have had the same concerns and fears that plagued the sixteenth-century present. The trials had temporarily slowed and grown fewer; the literature continued to be produced and even increased as the sixteenth century wore on. The pictures kept appearing, now in the hands of gifted artists, now in those of hacks. The crimes, as defined, remained on the books and appeared in new ones. It only remained for the new concerns to continue, the pictures to be produced in greater numbers, and the books to be opened during the political and religious crises later in the sixteenth century.

Bibliography

Abelard, Peter (1971) *Peter Abelard's Ethics*, ed. D. E. Luscombe (Oxford).

Achtemeier, P. J. (1976) 'Jesus and the disciples as miracle workers in the Apocryphal New Testament', in Schüssler-Fiorenza (1976): 149–86.

Aðalsteinsson, Jón Hnefill (1987) 'Wrestling with a ghost in Icelandic popular belief', *Arv: Nordic Yearbook of Folklore*, 43: 7–20.

— (1994) 'Sæmundr fróði: a medieval master of magic', *Arv: Nordic Yearbook of Folklore*, 50: 117–32.

— (1996) 'Six Icelandic magicians after the time of Sæmundr fróði', *Arv: Nordic Yearbook of Folklore*, 52: 49–61.

Ælfric (1966) *Lives of Saints*, 2 vols., ed. W. Skeat (London).

Affeldt, W., ed. (1990) *Frauen in Spätantike und Frühmittelalter: Lebensbedingungen – Lebensnormen – Lebensformen* (Sigmaringen).

Albertus Magnus (1973) *The Book of Secrets of Albertus Magnus of the Virtues of Herbs, Stones, and Certain Beasts, also A Book of the Marvels of the World*, ed. M. R. Best and F. H. Brightman (Oxford).

Allen, P. S. (1906) *Opus Epistolarum Des. Erasmi Roterodami*, I (Oxford).

Alver, B. (1971a) *Heksetro og trolddom* (Oslo).

— (1971b) 'Conceptions of the living human soul in the Norwegian tradition', *Temenos*, 7: 7–33.

— and Selberg, T. (1990) *Det er mer mellom himmel og jord* (Bergen).

Ammianus Marcellinus (1952–6) *Res Gestae*, ed. J. C. Rolfe (Cambridge, MA).

Andersson, T. (1967) *The Icelandic Family Saga* (Harvard).

— (1980) *The Legend of Brynhild* (Ithaca).

Andrén, A. (1993) 'Doors to the other worlds', *Journal of European Archaeology*, 1: 33–56.

Angenendt, A. (1992) 'Libelli bene correcti. Der 'richtige Kult' als ein Motiv der karolingischen Reform', in Ganz (1992): 117–36.

Anglo, S. (1977a) 'Evident authority and authoritative evidence: the *Malleus Maleficarum*', in Anglo (1977b): 1–31.

— ed. (1977b) *The Damned Art: Essays in the Literature of Witchcraft* (London and Boston).

Ankarloo, B., and Henningsen, G., eds. (1990) *Early Modern European Witchcraft: Centres and Peripheries* (Oxford).

Arbesmann, R. (1945) 'The 'Malleus' metaphor in medieval civilization', *Traditio*, 3: 389–91.

Archambault, P. (1996) *A Monk's Confession: The Memoirs of Guibert de Nogent* (University Park, PA).

Aston, M. (1968) *The Fifteenth Century: The Prospect of Europe* (London and New York).

Augustine of Hippo (1995) *De Doctrina Christiana*, ed. and trans. R. P. H. Green (Oxford).

Aune, D. (1980) 'Magic in early Christianity', in Haase (1980): 1507–57.

Bailey, M. (1996) 'The medieval concept of the witches' sabbath', *Exemplaria*, 8: 419–39.

— (1998) 'Heresy, Witchcraft, and Reform: Johannes Nider and the Religious World of the Late Middle Ages', Ph.D. dissertation (Northwestern University).

Baker, D., ed. (1973) *Sanctity and Secularity: The Church and the World*, Studies in Church History, 10 (Oxford).

Bang, A. C. (1902) *Norske hexeformularer og magiske opskrifter*, Videnskabsselskabet i Christiania 1901, II. Historiskfilosofisk Klasse (Christiania).

Banniard, M. (1992) 'Latin et communication orale en Gaule franque: le témoinage de la *Vita Eligii*', in Fontaine and Hillgarth (1992): 58–86.

Barb, A. A. (1950) 'Birds and medical magic', *Journal of the Warburg and Courtauld Institutes*, 13: 316–22.

— (1963) 'The survival of the magic arts', in Momigliano (1963): 100–25.

Barber, M. (1978) *The Trial of the Templars* (Cambridge).

— (1994) *The New Knighthood: A History of the Order of the Temple* (Cambridge).

Barkley, H. (1997) 'Liturgical influences on the Anglo-Saxon charms against cattle theft', *Notes & Queries*, 44: 450–2.

Barlow, C., ed. and trans. (1969) *The Iberian Fathers*, I (Washington, DC).

Barry, J., Hester, M., and Roberts, G., eds. (1996) *Witchcraft in Early Modern Europe* (Cambridge).

Bartsch, K., ed. (1873) 'Alt- und mittelhochdeutsches aus Engelberg', *Germania*, 18: 45–72.

Bayerschmidt, C. F., (1965) 'The element of the supernatural in the sagas of Icelanders', *Scandinavian Studies: Essays Presented to Dr. Henry Goddard Leach on the Occasion of his Eighty-Fifth Birthday*, ed. C. F. Bayerschmidt and E. J. Friis (Seattle): 39–53.

Beard, M., and North, J., eds. (1990) *Pagan Priests: Religion and Power in the Ancient World* (Ithaca).

—— , with Price, S. (1998) *Religions of Rome*, 2 vols. (Cambridge).

Beardwood, A. (1964) 'The trial of Walter Langton, Bishop of Lichfield, 1307–1312', *Transactions of the American Philosophical Society*, n.s. 54, pt. 3 (Philadelphia).

Bede (1994) *The Ecclesiastical History of the English People*, trans. B. Colgrave, ed. J. McClure and R. Collins (Oxford).

Behringer, W. (1996) 'Witchcraft studies in Austria, Germany and Switzerland', in Barry, Hester and Roberts (1996): 1–17.

— (1998) *Witchcraft Persecutions in Bavaria: Popular Magic, Religious Zealotry and Reason of State in Early Modern Europe*, trans. J. C. Grayson and D. Lederer (Cambridge).

Bellomo, M. (1995) *The Common Legal Past of Europe 1000–1800* (Washington, DC).

Benson, R. L., and Constable, G., eds. (1982) *Renaissance and Renewal in the Twelfth Century* (Cambridge, MA).

Benton, J. F. (1970) *Self and Society in Medieval France: The Memoirs of Abbot Guibert of Nogent (1064? – c. 1125)* (New York).

Bernstein, A. E. (1993) *The Formation of Hell: Death and Retribution in the Ancient and Early Christian Worlds* (Ithaca and London).

Bertrand-Rousseau, P. (1978) *Île de Corse et magie blanche* (Paris).

Bibliotheca Lamiarum: documenti e immagini della stregoneria dal medioevo all'età moderna (1994) (Pisa).

Blau, L. (1898, repr. 1970, 1974) *Das altjüdische Zauberwesen* (Budapest, Westmead and Graz).

Blauert, A. (1989) *Frühe Hexenvefolgung. Ketzer-, Zauberei- und Hexenprozessen des 15. Jahrhunderts* (Hamburg).

— ed. (1990) *Ketzer, Zauberer, Hexen. Die Anfänge der europäischen Hexenverfolgung* (Frankfurt).

Blöcker, M. (1979) 'Ein Zaubereiprozess im Jahre 1028', *Schweizerische Zeitschrift für Geschichte*, 29: 533–55.

— (1981) 'Wetterzauber. Zu einem Glaubenskomplex des frühen Mittelalters', *Francia*, 9: 117–31.

Blum, E. (1936) *Das staatliche und kirchliche Recht des Frankenreichs in seiner Stellung zu Dämonen-, Zauber- und Hexenwesen* (Paderborn).

Boglioni, P., ed. (1979) *La culture populaire au moyen âge* (Montreal and Paris).

Bologne, J. C. (1993) *Du flambeau au bûcher: magie et superstition au Moyen Age* (Paris).

Bonney, F. (1971) 'Autour de Jean Gerson. Opinions de théologiens sur les superstitions et la sorcellerie au début du Xve siècle', *Le Moyen Age*, 77: 85–98.

Bonomo, G. (1959, repr. 1986) *Caccia alle streghe: la credenza nelle streghe dal sec. XIII al XIX connparticolare referimento all'Italia* (Palermo).

Borst, A. (1992) 'The Origins of the Witch-craze in the Alps', in Borst, *Medieval Worlds: Barbarians, Heretics, and Artists* (Chicago): 101–22; original German version in Blauert (1990): 43–67.

Bósa saga ok Herrauðs (1830), ed. C. C. Rafn, Fornaldar Sǫgur Norðrlanda, 3 (Copenhagen); *Bosi and Herraud* in *Seven Viking Romances*, trans. Hermann Pálsson and P. Edwards (Harmondsworth, 1985).

Bossy, J. (1985) *Christianity in the West 1400–1700* (Oxford and New York).

— (1988) 'Moral arithmetic: Seven Sins into Ten Commandments', in Leites (1988): 214–34.

Boureau, A. (1984) *La légende dorée. Le système narratif de Jacques de Voragine* (Paris).

Boyer, R. (1986) *Le monde du double* (Paris).

Bozóky, E. (1992) 'Mythic Mediation in Healing Incantations', in Campbell, Hall and Klausner (1992): 84–92.

— (1994) 'From matter of devotion to amulets', *Medieval Folklore*, 3: 91–107.

Brady, T., Oberman, H., and Tracy, J., eds. (1994) *Handbook of European History 1400–1600. Late Middle Ages, Renaissance, Reformation*, I (Leiden, New York and Cologne).

Braekman, W. L. (1980) 'Fortune-telling by the casting of dice: a Middle English poem and its background', *Studia Neophilologica*, 52: 3–29.

— (1991) 'Prolegomena bij een compendium van de verboden kunsten', in *Een school spierinkjes: kleine opstellen over middelnederlandse artes-literatuur*, ed. W. P. Gerritsen *et al.* (Hilversum): 21–3; translated in the *Newsletter of the Societas Magica*, 2 (1996), available at http://skinner-69.umd.edu/socmag/index. html.

— (1997) *Middeleeuwse witte en zwarte magie in het nederlands taalgebied* (Gent).

Brand, J. (1870) *Popular Antiquities of Great Britain*, III, ed. W. Carew Hazlitt (London).

Brashear, W. (1992) 'Magical papyri: magic in bookform', in Ganz (1992): 25–58.

Braune, W., and Ebbinghaus, E. A. (1969) *Althochdeutsches Lesebuch*, 15th edn (Tübingen).

Briggs, R. (1996) *Witches and Neighbours: The Social and Cultural Context of European Witchcraft* (London).

Brooke, R., and Brooke, C. (1984) *Popular Religion in the Middle Ages: Western Europe 1000–1300* (London).

Browe, P. (1930) 'Die Euchariste als Zaubermittel im Mittelalter', *Archiv für Kulturgeschichte*, 20: 134–54.

Brown, D. C. (1988) *Pastor and Laity in the Theology of Jean Gerson* (Cambridge).

Brown, P. (1970) 'Sorcery, demons and the rise of Christianity: from Late Antiquity to the Middle Ages', in *Witchcraft Confessions and Accusations*, Association of Social Anthropologists Monographs, 9: 17–45, repr. in Brown (1972a): 119–46.

— (1972a) *Religion and Society in the Age of Saint Augustine* (London and New York).

— (1972b) = (1970) as repr. in (1972a).

— (1981) *The Cult of the Saints: Its Rise and Function in Late Antiquity* (Chicago).

— (1995) *Authority and the Sacred: Aspects of the Christianisation of the Roman World* (Cambridge).

— (1996) *The Rise of Western Christendom: Triumph and Diversity AD 200–1000* (Oxford).

Brucker, G. A. (1963) 'Sorcery in early Renaissance Florence', *Studies in the Renaissance*, 10: 7–24.

Brundage, J. A. (1987) *Law, Sex, and Christian Society in Medieval Europe* (Chicago and London).

Brundage, J. A. (1995) *Medieval Canon Law* (London and New York).

Budge, E. A. W. (1913) *Syriac Anatomy, Pathology and Therapeutic* (London).

Bühler, C. F. (1964) 'Prayers and charms in certain Middle English scrolls', *Speculum*, 39: 270–8.

Bullough, V. L. (1966) *The Development of Medicine as a Profession: The Contribution of the Medieval University to Modern Medicine* (New York).

Burghartz, S. (1988) 'The equation of women and witches: a case study of witchcraft trials in Lucerne and Lausanne in the fifteenth and sixteenth centuries', in Evans (1988): 57–74.

Burke, P. (1992a) *History and Social History* (Ithaca).

— ed. (1992b) *New Perspectives on Historical Writing* (London).

Burnett, C. (1996) *Magic and Divination in the Middle Ages: Texts and Techniques in the Islamic and Christian Worlds* (Aldershot).

Burriss, E. E. (1936) 'The terminology of witchcraft', *Classical Philology*, 31: 137–45.

Caciola, N. (1996) 'Wraiths, revenants, and ritual', *Past and Present*, 152: 3–45.

Caesarius of Arles (1956) *Saint Caesarius of Arles: Sermons*, I, ed. M. M. Mueller (Washington, DC).

— (1973) *Saint Caesarius of Arles: Sermons*, III, ed. M. M. Mueller (Washington, DC).

Caesarius of Heisterbach (1929) *The Dialogue on Miracles*, 2 vols., trans. H. von E. Scott and C. C. Swinton Bland (New York).

Callu, J.–P. (1984) 'Le jardin des supplices au Bas-Empire', in *Du châtiment dans la cité*, 313–57.

Cameron, A. (1983) *The Later Roman Empire* (Cambridge, MA).

Cameron, E. (1998) 'For reasoned faith or embattled creed? Religion for the people in early modern Europe', *Transactions of the Royal Historical Society*, Sixth Series, VIII: 165–87.

Campbell, S., Hall, B., and Klausner, D., eds. (1992) *Health, Disease and Healing in Medieval Culture* (New York).

Caquot, A., and Leibovici, M. (1968) *La divination*, 2 vols. (Paris).

Cardini, F. (1979) *Magia, stregoneria, superstizioni nell'occidente medievale* (Florence).

Carey, H. M. (1992) *Courting Disaster: Astrology at the English Court and University in the Later Middle Ages* (London).

Carey, J. (1998) *King of Mysteries: Early Irish Religious Writings* (Dublin).

Caro Baroja, J. (1990) 'Witchcraft and Catholic theology', in Ankarloo and Henningsen (1990): 19–43.

Carse, J. P. (1987) 'Shape shifting', in *Encyclopedia of Religion*, XIII: 225–9 (New York).

Cary, G. (1956) *The Medieval Alexander*, ed. D. J. A. Ross (Cambridge).

Cassiodorus (1992) *Variae*, trans. S. J. B. Barnish (Liverpool and Philadelphia).

Castelli, P. (1994) ''Donnaiole, amiche de li sogni': ovvero i sogni delle streghe', in *Bibliotheca Lamiarum*, 35–85.

Chadwick, H. (1976) *Priscillian of Avila* (Oxford).

Du châtiment dans la cité: supplices corporels et peine de mort dans le monde antique (1984), Collection de l'École française de Rome, 79 (Rome).

Chélini, J. (1991) *Aube du Moyen Age* (Paris).

Cholmeley, H. P. (1912) *John of Gaddesden and the Rosa Medicinae* (Oxford).

Christiansen, E. (1980, repr. 1997) *The Northern Crusades* (London and New York).

Clark, S. (1997) *Thinking with Demons: The Idea of Witchcraft in Early Modern Europe* (Oxford).

Clercq, C. de (1936 (I), 1958 (II)) *La législation religieuse franque*, 2 vols. (Louvain and Paris, Antwerp).

Clover, C. (1985) 'Icelandic family sagas', in Clover and Lindow (1985): 239–315.

—— (1986a) 'Maiden warriors and other sons', *Journal of English and Germanic Philology*, 85: 35–49.

—— (1986b) 'Hildigunnr's lament', in Lindow, Lönnrot and Weber (1986): 141–83.

—— (1988) 'The politics of scarcity', *Scandinavian Studies*, 60: 147–88.

—— (1993) 'Regardless of sex', *Speculum*, 68: 363–87.

—— and Lindow, J., eds. (1985) *Old Norse–Icelandic Literature: A Critical Guide* (Ithaca).

Clunies Ross, M. (1990) 'Voice and voices in eddic poetry', in Pároli (1990): 219–30.

—— (1994) *Prolonged Echoes Old Norse Myths in Northern Society* vol 1 *The Myths* (Odense).

—— (1998) *Prolonged Echoes Old Norse Myths in Northern Society* vol 2 *The Reception of Norse Myths in Medieval Iceland* (Odense).

Cockayne, O., ed. and trans. (1864–6, repr. 1961) *Leechdoms, Wortcunning, and Starcraft of Early England*, 3 vols., Rolls Series (London).

Cohn, N. (1975) *Europe's Inner Demons: An Enquiry Inspired by the Great Witch-Hunt* (London and New York).

Colker, M. (1978): see under Walter of Châtillon.

Collins, M. (1999) *Medieval Herbals: The Illustrative Tradition* (Toronto).

Comparetti, D. (1885, repr. 1997) *Vergil in the Middle Ages*, trans. E. F. M. Benecke (Princeton).

The Complete Sagas of the Icelanders: Including 49 Tales (1997), 5 vols., general ed. Viðar Hreinsson, ed. team Robert Cook *et al.*, intro. Robert Kellogg (Reykjavík).

Connerton, P. (1989) *How Societies Remember* (London).

Conroy, P. (1980) '*Laxdæla saga* and *Eiríks saga rauða*', *Arkiv för nordisk filologi* 95: 116–25.

Cormak, M. (1992) '"Fjǫlkunnigri kono scallatu í faðmi sofa': sex and the supernatural in Icelandic saints' lives', *Skáldskaparmál*, 2: 221–8.

Corpus Iuris Sueo-Gotorum Antiqui: Samling af Sweriges gamla lagar (1827–77), 13 vols., ed. H. S. Collin and C. J. Schlyter (Stockholm).

Coste, J. (1995) *Boniface VIII en procès: Articles d'accusation et dépositions des témoins 1303–1311: édition critique, introductions et notes* (Rome).

Coulton, G. G., trans., (1928) *Life in the Middle Ages*, I (Cambridge).

Coupland, S. (1991) 'The Rod of God's Wrath or the People of God's Wrath? The Carolingian Theology of the Viking Invasions', *Journal of Ecclesiastical History*, 41: 535–54.

Damico, H. (1993) 'Women in eddic poetry', in Pulsiano (1993): 721–3.

Danmarks gamle landskabslove med kirkelovene (1933–61), 8 vols., ed. J. Brøndum and P. J. Jørgensen (Copenhagen).

Darmsholt, N. (1984) 'The role of Icelandic women in the sagas', *Scandinavian Journal of History*, 9: 75–90.

Davidson, J. P. (1987) *The Witch in Northern European Art, 1470–1750* (Freven).

Davidson, L. S., and Ward, J. O. (1993) *The Sorcery Trial of Alice Kyteler* (Binghamton).

Davies, J. C., ed. (1957) *Studies Presented to Sir Hilary Jenkinson* (London).

Davis, N. Z. (1983) *The Return of Martin Guerre* (Cambridge).

Dawson, W. R., ed. and trans. (1934) *A Leechbook or Collection of Medical Recipes of the Fifteenth Century* (London).

Daxelmüller, C. (1993) *Zauberpraktiken: eine Ideengeschichte der Magie* (Zurich).

Demetz, P. (1997) *Prague in Black and Gold: Scenes from the Life of a European City* (New York).

Dennis, A., Foote, P., and Perkins, R. (1980) *Laws of Early Iceland* (Winnipeg).

Dickinson, J. G. (1955, repr. 1972) *The Congress of Arras 1435: A Study in Medieval Diplomacy* (Oxford, New York).

Dictionary of the Middle Ages (1982–9), 13 vols., ed. in chief J. R. Strayer (New York).

Dienst, H. (1990) 'Zur Rolle von Frauen im magischen Vorstellungen und Praktiken – nachausgewählten mittelalterlichen Quellen', in Affeldt (1990): 173–94.

Dierkens, A. (1984) 'Superstitions, christianisme et paganisme à la fin de l'époque mérovingienne: à propos de l'Indiculus superstitionum et paganiarum', in Hasquin (1984): 9–26.

Dillmann, F. (1986) *Les magiciens dans l'Islande ancienne* (Caen).

—— (1992) 'Seiður og shamanismi í Íslendingasögum', *Skáldskaparmál*, 2: 20–33.

Dinzelbacher, P., with Bauer, D. R., eds. (1990) *Volksreligion im hohen und späten Mittelalter* (Paderborn and Munich).

Dobbie, E. van Kirk, ed. (1942) *The Anglo-Saxon Minor Poems*, Anglo-Saxon Poetic Records, VI (New York).

Douglas, M. (1992) *Risk and Blame* (London).

Drew, K. Fischer (1949) *The Burgundian Code* (Philadelphia).

—— (1973) *The Lombard Laws* (Philadelphia).

—— (1991) *The Laws of the Salian Franks* (Philadelphia).

DuBois, T. A. (1999). *Nordic Religions in the Viking Age* (Philadelphia).

Duffy, E. (1992) *The Stripping of the Altars: Traditional Religion in England c. 1400 – c. 1580* (New Haven).

Dupont-Bouchat, S., ed. (1987) *La sorcellerie dans les Pays-Bàs sous l'Ancien Régime: aspects juridiques, institutionnels et sociaux* (Courtrai).

Durham Collectar (1992), ed. A. Corrêa (London).

Durham Ritual. Rituale Ecclesiae Dunelmensis:The Durham Collectar (1840, rev. 1927), ed. J. Stevenson (London).

Dutton, P. E., ed. (1993) *Carolingian Civilization:A Reader* (Peterborough, Ontario).

— (1995) 'Thunder and Hail over the Carolingian Countryside', in *Agriculture in the Middle Ages: Technology, Practice, and Representation*, ed. D. Sweeney (Philadelphia): 111–37.

The Eadwine Psalter: Text, Image, and Monastic Culture in Twelfth-Century Canterbury (1992), ed. M. Gibson,T. A. Heslop and R. Pfaff (University Park, PA).

Eamon,W. (1983),'Technology as magic in the late Middle Ages and Renaissance', *Janus*, 70: 171–212

Edel, D. (1995) *Cultural Identity and Cultural Integration: Ireland and Europe in the Early Middle Ages* (Dublin).

Eddius (1925) *The Life of Bishop Wilfrid by Eddius Stephanus*, ed. and trans. B. D. Colgrave (Cambridge).

Egils saga Skalla-Grímssonar (1933), ed. Sigurður Nordal, Íslenzk fornrit, 2 (Reykjavík); *Egil's Saga*, trans. B. Scudder in *The Complete Sagas of the Icelanders*, I.

Eichberger, D., and Zika, C., eds. (1998) *Dürer and His Culture* (Cambridge).

Eiríks saga rauða (1935), ed. Einar Ól. Sveinsson and Matthias Þórðarson, Íslenzk fornrit, 4 (Reykjavík); *Eirik the Red's Saga*, trans. K. Kunz in *The Complete Sagas of the Icelanders*, I.

Elliott, J. K. (1993) *The Apocryphal New Testament* (Oxford).

Ellis, H. (1844) 'Extracts in prose and verse from an old English medical manuscript, preserved in the Royal Library at Stockholm', *Archaeologia*, 30: 397.

Ellis Davidson, H. (1973) 'Hostile magic in the Icelandic sagas', in *The Witch Figure*, ed.V. Newall (London): 20–41.

— (1981) 'The restless dead', in *The Folklore of Ghosts*, ed. H. Ellis Davidson and W. Russell (London): 155–75.

Elsakkers, M. (1987) 'The Beekeeper's Magic: Taking a Closer Look at the Old Germanic Bee Charms', *Mankind Quarterly*, 27: 447–61.

Eubel, K. (1897) 'Vom Zaubereiwesen anfangs des 14. Jahrhunderts', *Historisches Jahrbuch*, 18: 608–31.

Evans, J. (1922) *Magical Jewels of the Middle Ages and Renaissance, Particularly in England* (Oxford).

— and Serjeantson, M. S. (1933) *English Medieval Lapidaries*, Early English Text Society, 190 (London).

Evans, R. J., ed. (1988) *The German Underworld: Deviants and Outcasts in German History* (London and NewYork).

Evans-Pritchard, E. E. (1937) *Witchcraft, Oracles, and Magic among the Azande* (Oxford).

Eyrbyggja saga (1935) ed. Einar Ól. Sveinsson and Matthias Þórðarson, Íslenzk fornrit 4 (Reykjavík); *The Saga of the People of Eyri*, trans. J. Quinn in *The Complete Sagas of the Icelanders*, V.

Fahd, T. (1966) *La divination arabe* (Leiden).

Faire Croire: Modalités de la diffusion et de la réception des messages religieux du XIIe au Xve siècle (1981), Collection de l'École française de Rome, 51 (Rome).

Famiglietti, R. C. (1986) *Royal Intrigue: Crisis at the Court of Charles V, 1392–1420* (New York).

Fanger, C., ed. (1998) *Conjuring Spirits: Texts and Traditions of Late Medieval Ritual Magic* (University Park, PA).

Faraone, C. A., Obbink, D., eds. (1991) *Magika Hiera: Ancient Greek Magic and Religion* (New York).

Faulkes, A. (1987) 'Introduction' to Snorri's *Edda*, vii–xix (Oxford).

Fentress, J., and Wickham, C. (1992) *Social Memory* (Oxford).

Ferreiro, A. (1996) 'Simon Magus: The Patristic-Medieval Traditions and Historiography', *Apocrypha*, 7: 147–65.

— ed. (1998) *The Devil, Heresy and Witchcraft in the Middle Ages: Essays in Honor of Jeffrey B. Russell* (Leiden).

Fichtenau, H. (1991) *Living in the Tenth Century*, trans. P. J. Geary (Chicago).

Finnegan, R. (1992) *Oral Traditions and the Verbal Arts* (London).

Fix, H. (1993a) '*Grágás*', in Pulsiano (1993): 234–5.

— (1993b) 'Laws: Iceland', in Pulsiano (1993): 384–5.

Fjǫlsvinnsmál: in the *Poetic Edda*; ed. and trans. P. Robinson (1991) 'An Edition of *Svipdagsmál*', D.Phil. dissertation (Oxford University).

Fletcher, R. (1997) *The Barbarian Conversion from Paganism to Christianity* (Berkeley and Los Angeles).

Flint, V. I. J. (1991) *The Rise of Magic in Early Medieval Europe* (Princeton).

Flowers, S. E. (1986) *Runes and Magic: Magical Formulaic Elements in the Older Runic Tradition* (New York).

— (1993) 'Magic', in Pulsiano (1993): 399–400.

Fontaine, J., and Hillgarth, J. N., eds. (1992) *The Seventh Century: Change and Continuity* (London).

Forbes, T. R. (1966) *The Midwife and the Witch* (New Haven).

Foucault, M. (1970) *The Order of Things: An Archaeology of the Human Sciences* (New York), translation of *Les mots et les choses* (Paris, 1966).

Fox, R. L. (1986) *Pagans and Christians* (Cambridge and New York).

Fraher, R. M. (1989) 'Conviction according to conscience: the medieval jurists' debate concerning judicial discretion and the law of proof', *Law and History Review*, 7: 23–88.

Frantzen, A. J. (1983) *The Literature of Penance in Anglo-Saxon England* (New Brunswick, NJ).

Franz, A. (1909) *Die kirchlichen Benediktionen im deutschen Mittelalter*, 2 vols. (Freiburg im Breisgau, Graz).

Frazer, J. G. (1911) *The Golden Bough: A Study in Magic and Religion*, 3rd edn (London).

Freedman, P., and Spiegel, G. M. (1998) 'Medievalisms Old and New: the Rediscovery of Alterity in North American Medieval Studies', *American Historical Review*, 103: 677–704.

Friedlander, A. (1996) *Processus Bernardi Delitiosi: The Trial of Fr. Bernard Délicieux, 3 September – 8 December 1319* (Philadelphia).

Fuller, S. D. (1980) 'Pagan Charms in Tenth-Century Saxony?', *Monatshefte*, 72: 162–70.

Funke, H. (1967) 'Majestäts- und Magieprozesse bei Ammianus Marcellinus', *Jahrbuch für Antike und Christentum*, 10: 145–75.

Fürbeth, F. (1992) *Johannes Hartlieb. Leben und Werk* (Tübingen).

Gager, J. (1992) *Curse Tablets and Binding Spells in the Ancient World* (New York).

Gallée, J. H. (1887) 'Segensprüche', *Germania*, 32: 452–60.

Ganz, P., ed. (1992) *Das Buch als magisches und als Repräsentationsobjekt* (Wiesbaden).

Gaster, M. (1925–8, repr. 1971) *Studies and Texts in Folklore, Magic, Mediaeval Romance, Hebrew Apocrypha and Samaritan Archaeology* (London; New York).

Sir Gawain and the Green Knight (1967) ed. J. R. R. Tolkien and E. V. Gordon, 2nd edn rev. N. Davis (Oxford).

— (1991) *Sir Gawain and the Green Knight: A Dual-language Version*, ed. and trans. W. Vantuono (New York).

Gay, D. (1988) 'Anglo-Saxon metrical charm 3 against dwarf', *Folklore*, 99: 174–7.

Geary, P. (1994) *Phantoms of Remembrance: Memory and Oblivion at the End of the First Millenium* (Princeton).

Geertz, H. (1975) 'An Anthropology of Religion and Magic, I', *Journal of Interdisciplinary History*, 6: 71–89.

— and Thomas, K. (1975) 'An Anthropology of Religion and Magic, II', *Journal of Interdisciplinary History*, 6: 91–109.

Geoffrey of Monmouth (1966) *The History of the Kings of Britain*, trans. L. Thorpe (New York).

Gerald of Wales (1979) *The Jewel of the Church: A Translation of 'Gemma Ecclesiastica' by Giraldus Cambrensis*, trans. J. J. Hagen (Leiden).

Gesta Romanorum, or Entertaining Moral Stories (1876, repr. 1959), ed. and trans. C. Swan and W. Hooper (New York).

Gijswijt-Hofstra, M. (1992) 'Recent witchcraft research in the Low Countries', in van Sas and Witte (1992): 23–34.

Ginzburg, C. (1991) *Ecstasies: Deciphering the Witches' Sabbath*, trans. R. Rosenthal (New York).

Gísla saga Súrssonar (1943), ed. Björn Þórólfsson and Guðni Jónsson, Íslenzk fornrit, 6 (Reykjavík); *Gisli Sursson's Saga*, trans. M. S. Regal in *The Complete Sagas of the Icelanders*, II.

Given, J. B. (1997) *Inquisition and Medieval Society: Power, Discipline, and Resistance in Languedoc* (Ithaca and London).

Glosecki, S. (1989), *Shamanism and Old English Poetry* (New York).

Godman, P., and Collins, R., eds. (1990) *Charlemagne's Heir: New Perspectives on the Reign of Louis the Pious (814–840)* (Oxford).

Goldberg, E. J. (1995) 'Popular revolt, dynastic politics, and aristocratic factionalism in the early Middle Ages: the Saxon *stellinga* reconsidered', *Speculum*, 70: 467–501.

Goldin, J. (1976) 'The magic of magic and superstition', in Schüssler-Fiorenza (1976): 115–47.

Gǫngu-Hrólfs saga (1954), ed. Guðni Jónsson, Fornaldar sögur Norðurlanda (Reykjavík); *Göngu-Hrolfs Saga*, trans. Hermann Pálsson and P. Edwards (Toronto, 1976).

Gottfried von Strassburg (1960, rev. 1967), *Tristan*, trans. A. T. Hatto (New York).

Graf, F. (1997) *Magic in the Ancient World* (Cambridge, MA).

Grambo, R. (1990) 'Folkebiologisk taksonomi: formler mot orm', *Nord nytt*, 41: 64–77.

Grant, R. (1979) *Cambridge, Corpus Christi College 41: The Loricas and the Missal* (Amsterdam).

Grattan, J. H. G., and Singer, C. (1952, repr. 1971) *Anglo-Saxon Magic and Medicine, Illustrated Specially from the Semi-Pagan Text 'Lacnunc'* (Oxford).

Graus, F. (1975) *Lebendige Vergangenheit. Überlieferung im Mittelalter und in den Vorstelungen vom Mittelalter* (Cologne and Vienna).

Greenblatt, S. (1991) *Marvelous Possessions: The Wonder of the New World* (Chicago).

Greenfield, R. P. H. (1988) *Traditions of Belief in Late Byzantine Demonology* (Amsterdam).

Gregg, J. Young (1997) *Devils, Women, and Jews: Reflections of the Other in Medieval Sermon Stories* (Ithaca).

Gregory of Tours (1974) *The History of the Franks*, trans. L. Thorpe (New York).

— (1988) *Glory of the Confessors*, trans. R. van Dam (Liverpool).

Gregory the Great (1959) *Dialogues*, trans. O. J. Zimmerman, OSB (New York).

Grendon, F. (1909) *The Anglo-Saxon Charms* (New York).

Grettis saga (1936), ed. Guðni Jónsson, Íslenzk fornrit, 7 (Reykjavík); *The Saga of Grettir the Strong*, trans. B. Scudder in *The Complete Sagas of the Icelanders*, II.

Griffiths, B. (1996) *Aspects of Anglo-Saxon Magic* (Hockwold-cum-Wilton).

Grímnismál: in the *Poetic Edda*.

Grodzynski, D. (1974) 'Superstitio', *Revue des études anciennes*, 76: 36–60.

Grógaldr: in the *Poetic Edda*; ed. and trans. P. Robinson (1991) 'An Edition of *Svipdagsmál*', D.Phil. dissertation (Oxford University).

Guibert of Nogent (1996) *A Monk's Confession: The Memoirs of Guibert of Nogent*, trans. P. J. Archambault (University Park, PA).

Gurevich, A. (1988) *Medieval Popular Culture: Problems of Belief and Perception*, trans. J. M. Bak and P. A. Hollingsworth (Cambridge and Paris).

Guyotjeannin, O., and Poulle, E., eds. (1996) *Autour de Gerbert d'Aurillac: le pape de l'an mil* (Paris).

Haase, W., ed. (1980) *Aufstieg und Niedergang der Römischen Welt* (Berlin).

Habiger-Tuczay, C. (1992) *Magie und Magier im Mittelalter* (Munich).

Hallberg, P. (1973) 'The concept of *gipta–gæfa–hamingja* in Old Norse literature', in *Proceedings of the First International Saga Conference* (London): 143–83.

— (1993) 'Eddic poetry', in Pulsiano (1993): 149–52.

Halpern, B. K., and Foley, J. M. (1978) 'Power of the word: healing charms as oral genre', *Journal of American Folklore*, 91: 903–24.

Halvorsen, E. F. (1981) 'Galder', in *KLNM*, V: 159–61.

— (1982a) 'Troll', in *KLNM*, XVIII: 655–7.

— (1982b) 'Trolldom', in *KLNM*, XVIII: 657–61.

Hampp, I. (1961) *Beschwörung, Segen, Gebet: Untersuchungen zum Zauberspruch aus dem Bereich der Volksheilkunde* (Stuttgart).

Hansen, J. (1900) *Zauberwahn, Inquisition und Hexenprozess im Mittelalter und die Entstehung der Grossen Hexenverfolgung* (Munich and Leipzig).

— (1901) *Quellen und Untersuchungen zur Geschichte des Hexenwahns und der grossen Hexenverfolgung im Mittelalter* (Bonn).

Hárbarðslióð: in the *Poetic Edda*.

Harmening, D. (1979) *Superstitio. Überlieferungs- und theoriegeschichtliche Untersuchungen zur kirchlich-theologischen Aberglaubensliteratur des Mittelalters* (Berlin).

— (1988) 'Hexenbilder des späten Mittelalters – Kombinatorische Topik und ethnographischer Befund', in Segl (1988): 177–94.

— (1989) 'Magiciennes et sorcières: la mutation du concept de magie à la fin du moyen âge', *Heresis*, 13–14: 421–45.

— (1990a) 'Spätmittelalterliche Aberglaubenskritik in Dekalog- und Beichtliteratur. Perspektiven ihrer Erforschung', in Dinzelbacher and Bauer (1990): 243–52.

— (1990b) 'Zauberinnen und Hexen. Vom Wandel des Zaubereibegriffs im späten Mittelalter', in Blauert (1990): 68–90.

Harris, J. (1985) 'Eddic poetry', in Clover and Lindow (1985): 68–156.

Harvey, M. (1973) 'Papal witchcraft: the charges against Benedict XIII', in Baker (1973): 109–16.

Hasquin, H., ed. (1984) *Magie, sorcellerie, parapsychologie* (Brussels).

Hastrup, K. (1981) 'Cosmology and society in medieval Iceland', *Ethnologia Scandinavica* (1981): 63–78.

— (1985) *Culture and History in Medieval Iceland* (Oxford).

— (1990a) *Iceland of Anthropology* (Odense).

— (1990b) *Nature and Policy in Iceland 1400–1800* (Oxford).

— (1992a) 'Uchronia and the two histories of Iceland', in *Other Histories*, ed. K. Hastrup (London): 102–20.

— (1992b) 'Den old nordiske verden', in *Den nordiske verden*, I, ed. K. Hastrup and O. Löfgren (Copenhagen): 21–37.

— and Löfgren, O. (1992) 'Lykkens økonomi', in *Den nordiske verden*, I, ed. K. Hastrup and O. Löfgren (Copenhagen): 240–57.

Haustein, J. (1990) *Martin Luthers Stellung zur Zauber- und Hexenwesen* (Stuttgart).

Haustein, J. (1995) 'Bibelauslegung und Bibelkritik. Ansätze zur Überwindung der Hexenverfolgung', in Lorenz and Bauer (1995): 249–67.

Hávamál: in the *Poetic Edda*.

Haver, J. van (1964) *Nederlandse incantatieliteratuur: een gecommentarieerd compendium van Nederlandse bezweringsformules* (Gent).

Head, T., and Noble, T. F. X., eds. (1995) *Soldiers of Christ: Saints and Saints' Lives from Late Antiquity and the Early Middle Ages* (University Park).

Heinrich, A. (1986) 'Annat er várt eðli: the type of the prepatriarchal women in Old Norse literature', in Lindow, Lönnrot and Weber (1986): 110–40.

Hen, Y. (1995) *Culture and Religion in Merovingian Gaul, A.D. 481–751* (Leiden and New York).

Herbert, C. (1991) *Culture and Anomie: Ethnographic Imagination in the Nineteenth Century* (Chicago).

Higley, S. (1995) 'Dirty magic: *seither*, science, and the parturating man in Old Norse and medieval Welsh literature', in *Figures of Speech: The Body in Medieval Art, History, and Literature* in *Essays in Medieval Studies*, 11: 137–47.

— (1997) 'The legend of the learned man's android' in *Retelling Tales: Essays in Honor of Russell Pick*, ed. T. Hahn and A. Lupack (Cambridge): 127–60.

Hildegard of Bingen, *Subtilitates Naturarum Creaturarum, De Lapidibus* in *Patrologia Latina*, ed. J. P. Migne, CXCVII: 1247 ff.

Hill, J., and Swan, M., eds. (1998) *The Community, the Family, and the Saint: Patterns of Power in Early Medieval Europe* (Turnhout).

Hill, T. D. (1978) 'The theme of the cosmological cross in two Old English cattle theft charms', *Notes & Queries*, n.s. 25: 488–90.

Hillgarth, J. N. (1980) 'Popular religion in Visigothic Spain', in James (1980): 3–60.

— (1986) *Christianity and Paganism, 350–750: The Conversion of Western Europe* (Philadelphia).

Historia Norvegiae (1880), ed. G. Storm, in *Monumenta Historica Norwegiae* (Oslo).

Hoak, D. (1985) 'Art, culture, and mentality in Renaissance society: the meaning of Hans Baldung Grien's *Bewitchced Groom* (1544)', *Renaissance Quarterly*, 38: 488–510.

Hollis, S. (1997) 'Old English 'Cattle theft charms': manuscript contexts and social uses', *Anglia*, 115: 139–64.

Holton, F. S. (1993) 'Literary tradition and the Old English bee charm', *Journal of Indo-European Studies*, 21: 37–53.

Holtsmark, A. (1980) 'Kjærlighetsmagi', in *KLNM*, VIII: 444–7.

Hrólfs saga kraka (1954), ed. Guðni Jónsson, Fornaldar sögur Norðurlanda, I (Reykjavík); *King Hrolf and His Champions*, in *Eirik the Red and Other Icelandic Sagas*, trans. G. Jones (Oxford, 1981).

Hsu, F. L. K. (1983) *Exorcising the Trouble Makers: Magic, Science and Culture* (Westport, CT).

Hugh of St Victor (1961) *The 'Didascalicon' of Hugh of St. Victor: A Medieval Guide to the Arts* trans. J. Taylor (New York).

Hunt, D. (1993) 'Christianising the Roman Empire: the Evidence of the Code', in *The Theodosian Code*, 143–58.

Hunt, L., ed. (1989) *The New Cultural History* (Berkeley).

Hunt, T. (1990) *Popular Medicine in Thirteenth-Century England: Introduction and Texts* (Cambridge).

Imbert, J. (1996) *Les temps carolingiens (741–891). L'Église: la vie des fidèles*, V, pt 2 of *Histoire du droit et des institutions de l'Église en Occident*, ed. G. le Bras and J. Gaudemet (Paris).

Isidore of Seville (1911), *Isidori Hispalensis Episcopi Etymologiarum sive Originvm Libri XX*, ed. W. M. Lindsay (Oxford).

Jackson, K. H., trans. (1971) *A Celtic Miscellany: Translations from the Celtic Literatures* (New York).

Jacobus de Voragine (1993) *The Golden Legend: Readings on the Saints*, 2 vols., trans. W. G. Ryan (Princeton).

Jacques-Chaquin, N., and Préaud, M., eds. (1993) *Le sabbat des sorciers en Europe (XVe–XVIIe siècles*, Colloque international E. N. S. Fontenay–Saint-Cloud (4–7 novembre, 1992) (Grenoble).

James, E., ed. (1980) *Visigothic Spain: New Approaches* (Oxford).

Jochens, J. (1993a) '*Hexerie eller blind allarm*: recent Scandinavian witchcraft studies', *Scandinavian Studies*, 65: 103–13.

— (1993b) 'Magie et réparation entre hommes et femmes dans les mythes et la société germanico-nordiques à travers les sagas et les lois scandinaves', *Cahiers de civilisation médiévale, Xe–XIIe siècles*, 36: 375–89.

— (1993c) 'Old Norse magic and gender', *Scandinavian Studies*, 63: 305–17.

— (1995) *Women in Old Norse Society* (Ithaca).

— (1996) *Old Norse Images of Women* (Philadelphia).

John of Salisbury (1938), *Frivolities of Courtiers and Footprints of Philosophers*, trans. J. B. Pike (London).

Jolly, K. L. (1992) 'Father God and Mother Earth: nature-mysticism in the Early Middle Ages', in *The Medieval World of Nature: A Book of Essays*, ed. J. E. Salisbury (Garland Press): 221–52.

— (1996) *Popular Religion in Late Saxon England: Elf Charms in Context* (Chapel Hill).

—, ed. (1997) *Tradition and Diversity: Christianity in a World Context to 1500* (Armonk, NY).

Jones , W. R. (1972) 'Political uses of sorcery in medieval Europe', *The Historian*, 34: 670–87.

Jonge, M. de (1985) *Outside the Old Testament* (Cambridge).

Jongeboer, H. (1984), 'Der Lorscher Bienensegen und der ags. Charm 'Wiþ ymbe'', *Amsterdamer Beiträge zur älteren Germanistik*, 21: 63–70.

Jordan, W. C. (1996) *The Great Famine: Northern Europe in the Early Fourteenth Century* (Princeton).

Karras, R. M. (1986), 'Pagan survivals and syncretism in the conversion of Saxony', *Catholic Historical Review*, 72: 553–72.

Kay, R. (1988) *The Broadview Book of Medieval Anecdotes* (Lewiston, NY).

Kee, H. C. (1983) *Miracle in the Early Christian World* (New Haven).

— (1986) *Medicine, Miracle and Magic in New Testament Times* (Cambridge).

Keefer, S. L. (1998) 'Ut in omnibus honorificetur Deus: the Corsnæd Ordeal in Anglo-Saxon England', in Hill and Swan (1998): 237–64.

Kelly, H. A. (1968, repr. 1974) *The Devil, Demonology, and Witchcraft* (New York).

— (1977) 'English kings and the fear of sorcery', *Medieval Studies*, 39: 206–38

— (1985) *The Devil at Baptism: Ritual, Theology, and Drama* (Ithaca and London).

Kieckhefer, R. (1976) *European Witch Trials: Their Foundations in Popular and Learned Culture* (London).

— (1987) 'Main Currents in Late Medieval Devotion', in Raitt (1987): 75–108.

— (1990) *Magic in the Middle Ages* (Cambridge).

— (1992) 'A Church reformed though not deformed?', *Journal of Religion*, 74: 240–9.

— (1994a) 'The holy and the unholy: sainthood, witchcraft, and magic in late medieval Europe', *Journal of Medieval and Renaissance Studies*, 24: 355–85.

— (1994b) 'The specific rationality of medieval magic', *American Historical Review*, 99: 813–36.

— (1994c) 'Magie et sorcellerie en Europe au moyen age', in Muchembled (1994): 17–44.

— (1997) *Forbidden Rites: A Necromancer's Manual of the Fifteenth Century* (Sutton Press, and University Park, PA).

King, P. D. (1972) *Law and Society in the Visigothic Kingdom* (Cambridge).

Kitson, P. (1989) 'From eastern learning to western folklore: the transmission of some medico-magical ideas', in Scragg (1989): 57–71.

Klaniczay, G. (1990) *The Uses of Supernatural Power: The Transformation of Popular Religion in Medieval and Early Modern Europe*, trans. S. Singerman, ed. K. Margolis (Princeton).

Klingshirn, W. E. (1992) *Caesarius of Arles: Life, Testament, Letters* (Liverpool and Philadelphia).

— (1994) *Caesarius of Arles: The Making of a Christian Community in Late Antique Gaul* (Cambridge).

KLNM (1981–88 2nd edn): *Kulturhistorisk leksikon för nordisk middelålder fra vikingetid til reformationstid* (Copenhagen and Malmö).

Köhler, R., ed. (1868) 'Segensprüche', *Germania*, 13: 178–88.

Kormáks saga (1938), ed. Einar Ól. Sveinsson, Íslenzk fornrit, 8 (Reykjavík); *Kormak's Saga*, trans. R. McTurk in *The Complete Sagas of the Icelanders*, I.

Kors, A. C. and Peters, E. (1972) *Witchcraft in Europe, 1100–1700: A Documentary History* (Philadelphia).

— (2001) *Witchcraft in Europe, 400–1700: A Documentary History*, rev. Edward Peters, (Philadelphia).

Krag, C. (1991) *Ynglingatal og Ynglinga saga* (Oslo).

Kramer, Heinrich (1991) *Malleus Maleficarum von Heinrich Institoris (alias Kramer) unter Mithilfe Jakob Sprengers. Aufgrund der dämonologischen Tradition zusammengestellt. Wiedergabe des Erstdrucks von 1487 (Hain 9238)*, ed. A. Schnyder (Göppingen).

— (1971) *The Malleus Maleficarum of Heinrich Kramer and James Sprenger*, trans. M. Summers (New York).

Kress, H. (1990) 'The apocalypse of a culture', in Pároli (1990): 279–302.

— (1993) *Máttugar meyjar:íslensk fornbókmenntasaga* (Reykjavík).

Kruger, S. F. (1992) *Dreaming in the Middle Ages* (Cambridge).

Kvideland, R., and Sehmsdorf, H. K. (1988) *Scandinavian Folk Belief and Legend* (Minneapolis).

Kyrkobalken: part of *Dalalagen* in *Corpus Iuris Sueo-Gotorum*.

La Roche, R. (1957) *La divination* (Washington, DC).

Lambert, M. (1992) *Medieval Heresy: Popular Movements from the Gregorian Reform to the Reformation* (Oxford and Cambridge, MA).

Larner, C. (1984) *Witchcraft and Religion: The Politics of Popular Belief* (Oxford and New York).

Larner, J. (1980) *Italy in the Age of Dante and Petrarch 1216–1380* (London and New York).

Larrington, C. (1992) "What does woman want?' *Mær* and *munr* in *Skírnismál*', *Alvíssmál*, 2: 3–16.

— (1993) *A Store of Common Sense* (Oxford).

Las siete partidas (1931), trans. and annotated by S. P. Scott (New York).

Laxdæla saga (1934), ed. ªl. Sveinsson, Íslenzk fornrit, 5 (Reykjavík); *The Saga of the People of Laxardal*, trans. K. Kunz in *The Complete Sagas of the Icelanders*, V.

Lea, H. C. (1955) *A History of the Inquisition of the Middle Ages*, III: 379–549 (New York).

— (1957) *Materials toward a History of Witchcraft*, I (New York).

Lear, F. S. (1965) *Treason in Roman and Germanic Law* (Austin).

Lecouteux, C. (1983) 'Hagazussa – Striga – Hexe. The Origins of these Terms and Concepts', *Études germaniques*, 38: 161–78.

— (1985) 'Hagazussa – Striga – Hexe', *Hessische Blätter für Volks- und Kulturforschung*, n.f. 18: 57–70.

Leites, E., ed. (1988) *Conscience and Casuistry in Early Modern Europe* (Cambridge and Paris).

Leofric Missal (1883), ed. F. E. Warren (Oxford).

Lerner, R. E. (1991) 'Werner di Friedberg intrappolato dalla lege', in Maire Vigueur (1991): 268–81.

Lesses, R. (1996) 'Speaking with angels: Jewish and Greco-Egyptian revelatory adjurations', *Harvard Theological Review*, 89: 41–60.

Levack, B. P. (1987) *The Witch-Hunt in Early Modern Europe* (London).

— ed. (1992) *Articles on Witchcraft, Magic and Demonology: A Twelve Volume Anthology of Scholarly Articles*, 12 vols. (New York and London).

Lincoln, B. (1994) *Authority, Construction and Corrosion* (Chicago).

Lindow, J. (1978) *Swedish Legends and Folktales* (Berkeley).

— (1985) 'Mythology and mythography', in Clover and Lindow (1985): 21–67.

— (1987) 'Fylgjur', in *Encyclopedia of Religion*, V: 460 (New York).

— (1993) 'Mythology', in Pulsiano (1993): 423–6.

—, Lönnrot, L., and Weber, G. W., eds. (1986) *Structure and Meaning in Old Norse Literature* (Odense).

Little, L. K. (1993) *Benedictine Maledictions: Liturgical Cursing in Romanesque France* (Ithaca and London).

Lokasenna: in the *Poetic Edda*.

Lönnroth, L. (1976) *Njáls Saga: A Critical Introduction* (Los Angeles).

Lorenz, S., ed. (1994a) *Hexen und Hexenverfolgung in deutschen Südwesten*, I: *Katalogband* (Karlsruhe).

— , ed. (1994b) *Hexen und Hexenverfolgung in deutschen Südwesten*, II, *Aufsatzband* (Karlsruhe).

— and Bauer, D. R., eds. (1995) *Das Ende der Hexenverfolgung* (Stuttgart).

Luck, G. (1985) *Arcana Mundi: Magic and the Occult in the Greek and Roman Worlds* (Baltimore).

MacKinney, L. C. (1943) 'An unpublished treatise on medicine and magic from the age of Charlemagne', *Speculum*, 18: 494–6.

MacMullen, R. (1966) *Enemies of the Roman Order: Treason, Unrest, and Alienation* (Cambridge, MA).

— (1997) *Christianity and Paganism in the Fourth to Eighth Centuries* (New Haven).

Maggioni, M. L. (1993) *Un manuale per confessori del quattrocento inglese (Ms. St. John's College, Cambridge S. 35)* (Milan).

Maguire, H., ed. (1995) *Byzantine Magic* (Cambridge, MA).

— (1997) 'Magic and money in the early Middle Ages', *Speculum*, 72: 1037–54.

Maier, A. (1952) 'Eine Verfügung Johanns XXII. über die Zuständigkeit der Inquisition für Zaubereiprozesse', *Archivum Fratrum Praedicatorum*, 22: 226–46; repr. in A. Maier, *Ausgehendes Mittelalter. Gesammelte Aufsätze zur Geistesgeschichte des 14. Jahrhunderts* (Rome, 1957): 59–80.

Maier, E. (1996) *Trente ans avec le diable: une nouvelle chasse aux sorciers sur la Riviera lémanique (1477–1484)* (Lausanne).

Maire Vigueur, J.-C., ed. (1991) *La parola all'accusato* (Palermo).

Malinowski, B. (1948), *Magic, Science and Other Essays* (Boston).

Malleus Maleficarum: see Kramer (1991), Schnyder (1993).

Malory, T. (1971) *Works*, ed. E. Vinaver, 2nd edn (Oxford).

Marcus, J. (1938) *The Jew in the Medieval World: A Sourcebook, 315–1791* (New York).

Markus, R. A. (1974) *Christianity in the Roman World* (London).

— (1990) *The End of Ancient Christianity* (Cambridge).

— (1992) 'From Caesarius to Boniface: Christianity and paganism in Gaul', in Fontaine and Hillgarth (1992): 154–72.

Markus, R. A. (1994) 'Augustine on magic: a neglected semiotic theory', *Revue des études augustiniennes*, 40: 375–88.

Mathiesen, R. (1995) 'Magic in Slavia Orthodoxa: the written tradition', in Maguire (1995): 155–77.

Matthews, J. (1989) *The Roman Empire of Ammianus Marcellinus* (London).

Max, F. (1993) 'Les premières controverses sur la réalité du sabbat dans l'Italie du XVIe siècle', in Jacques–Chaquin and Préaud (1993): 55–62.

McGinn, B. (1979) *Visions of the End: Apocalyptic Traditions in the Middle Ages* (New York).

McHugh, M. (1972) 'Satan in St. Ambrose', *Classical Folia*, 26: 94–103.

McKitterick, R. (1977) *The Frankish Church and the Carolingian Reforms, 789–895* (London).

—, ed. (1995) *The New Cambridge Medieval History*, II (Cambridge and New York).

McNamara, J. A. and Halborg, J. E., with E. G. Whatley, eds. and trans. (1992) *Sainted Women of the Dark Ages* (Durham and London).

McNeill, J. T. (1933) 'Folk-paganism in the penitentials', *The Journal of Religion*, 12: 450–66.

—, and Gamer, H. M. (1938, repr. 1965, 1990) *Medieval Handbooks of Penance* (New York).

Meaney, A. L. (1989) 'Women, witchcraft and magic in Anglo-Saxon England', in Scragg (1989): 9–40.

Meens, R. (1998) 'Magic and the early medieval world view', in Hill and Swan (1998): 285–95.

Medieval folklore: an encyclopedia of myths, legends, tales, beliefs, and customs (2000). Carl Lindahl, John McNamara and John Lindow (eds) (Santa Barbara).

Mélanges offerts à Edmond-René Labande: études de civilization médiévale (IXe–XIIe siècles) (1974) (Poitiers).

Menache, S. (1998) *Clement V* (Cambridge).

Merrifield, R. (1987) *The Archaeology of Ritual and Magic* (London).

Meulengracht Sørensen, P. (1983) *The Unmanly Man* (Odense).

— (1993) *Saga and Society: An Introduction to Old Norse Literature* (Odense).

Meyer, M., and Mirecki, P. (1995) *Ancient Magic and Ritual Powers* (New York).

— and Smith, R., eds. (1994) *Ancient Christian Magic: Coptic Texts of Ritual Power* (San Francisco).

Mierow, C. C., trans. (1915) *The Gothic History of Jordanes* (Princeton).

Milis, L., ed. (1998) *The Pagan Middle Ages* (Woodbridge).

Miller, W. I. (1986) 'Dreams, prophecy and sorcery: blaming the secret offender in medieval Iceland', *Scandinavian Studies*, 58: 101–23.

Mirecki, P. (1994) 'The Coptic wizard's hoard', *Harvard Theological Review*, 87: 435–60.

Mitchell, S. (1993) 'Óðinn', in Pulsiano (1993): 444–5.

— (1998) 'Anaphrodisiac charms in the Nordic Middle Ages: impotence, infertility and magic', *Norveg*, 41, 19–42.

Møller-Christensen, V. (1980) 'Impotens', in *KLNM*, VII: 368–9.

Momigliano, A. (1963) *The Conflict Between Paganism and Christianity in the Fourth Century* (Oxford).

Monter, W. (1983) *Ritual, Myth and Magic in Early Modern Europe* (Athens, OH).

Moore, R. I. (1985) *The Origins of European Dissent* (Oxford and New York).

— (1987) *The Formation of a Persecuting Society: Power and Deviance in Western Europe, 950–1250* (Oxford and New York).

Mordek, H., and Glatthaar, M. (1993) 'Vom Wahrsagerinnen und Zauberern. Ein Beitrag zur Religionspolitik Karls des Grossen', *Archiv für Kulturgeschichte*, 75: 33–64.

Mormando, F. (1998) *The Preacher's Demons: Bernardino of Siena and the Social Underworld of Early Renaissance Italy* (Chicago).

Morris, K. (1993) *Sorceress or Witch?* (Lanham).

Muchembled, R. (1987) *Sorcières: Justice et société aux 16e et 17e siècles* (Paris).

— (1993) *Le roy et la sorcière: L'Europe des bûchers (XVe–XVIIIe siècle)* (Paris).

—, ed. (1994) *Magie et sorcellerie en Europe du Moyen Age à nos jours* (Paris).

Mueller, M. M.: see under Caesarius of Arles.

Muir, E., and Ruggiero, G., eds. (1991) *Microhistory and the Lost Peoples of Europe*, trans. E. Branch (Baltimore).

Muldoon, J., ed. (1997) *Varieties of Religious Conversion in the Middle Ages* (Gainesville).

Müllenhoff, K., and Scherer, W. (1892) *Denkmäler deutscher Poesie und Prosa aus dem VIII. –XII. Jahrhundert*, 3rd edn (Berlin).

Mundal, E. (1974) *Fylgjemotiva i norrøn litteratur* (Oslo).

— (1993a) 'Women in sagas', in Pulsiano (1993): 723–5.

— (1993b) 'Supernatural beings: *fylgja*', in Pulsiano (1993): 624–5.

— and Steinsland, G. (1989) 'Kvinner og medisinsk magi', *Kvinnors rosengård*, ed. H. Gunneng *et al.* (Stockholm): 97–121.

Murdoch, B. (1989) 'Peri hieres nousou: an approach to the Old High German medical charms', in *Mit regulu bithungan*, ed. J. L. Flood and D. N. Yeandle (Göppingen): 142–60.

— (1991) "Drohtin, uuerthe so!': Funktionsweisen der altdeutschen Zaubersspruche', *Literaturwissenschaftliches Jahrbuch*, 42: 11–37.

Murphy, G. R. (1992) *The Heliand: The Saxon Gospel* (New York and Oxford).

Murray, A. (1978) *Reason and Society in the Middle Ages* (Oxford).

— (1992) 'Missionaries and magic in Dark-Age Europe', *Past and Present*, 136: 186–205.

Nässtrom, B.-M. (1995) *Freyja – the Great Goddess of the North* (Lund).

Naumann, H.-P. (1993) Supernatural beings: *dísir*', in Pulsiano (1993): 624.

Nelson, M. (1984) "Wordsige and worcsige': speech acts in three Old English charms', *Language and Style*, 17: 57–66.

Neusner, J., Frerichs, E. S., and Flesher, P., eds. (1989) *Religion, Science, and Magic: In Concert and in Conflict* (Oxford and New York).

Nie, G. de (1995) 'Caesarius of Arles and Gregory of Tours: two sixth-century bishops and 'Christian magic'', in Edel (1995): 170–96.

Nirenberg, D. (1996) *Communities of Violence: Persecution of Minorities in the Middle Ages* (Princeton).

Njáls saga: Brennu-Njáls saga (1954), ed. ªl. Sveinsson, Íslenzk fornrit, 12 (Reykjavík); *Njal's Saga*, trans. R. Cook in *The Complete Sagas of the Icelanders*, III.

Nock, A. D. (1972a) 'Paul and the Magus', in Nock (1972b), II: 308–30.

— (1972b) *Essays on Religion and Magic in the Ancient World*, 2 vols. (Cambridge, MA).

Norges gamle love indtil 1387 (1846–1985), ed. R. Keyser and P. A. Munch, 5 vols. (Christiania).

Norna-Gests þáttr (1954), ed. Guðni Jónsson, Fornaldar sögur Norðurlanda, I (Reykjavík); *Stories and ballads of the far past*, trans. N. Kershaw (Cambridge, 1921).

Nöth, W. (1977), 'Semiotics of the Old English charm', *Semiotica*, 19: 59–83.

Ohrt, F. (1921) *Danmarks trylleformler* (Copenhagen).

Oldoni, M. (1987) *Fantasmi e fantasia nel Medioevo. Gerberto e il suo doppio* (Naples).

Qrvar Odds saga (1954), ed. Guðni Jónsson, Fornaldar sögur Norðurlanda, II (Reykjavík); *Arrow Odd* in *Seven Viking Romances*, trans. Hermann Pálsson and P. Edwards (Harmondsworth, 1985).

Ostorero, M. (1995) *'Folâtrer avec les démons': sabbat et chasse aux sorciers à Vevey, 1448* (Lausanne).

—, Paravicini Bagliani, A., and Utz Tremp, K., eds. (1999) *L'imaginaire du sabbat: édition critique des textes les plus anciens (1430c. – 1440c.)*, Cahiers lausannois d'histoire medievale (Lausanne).

Owst, G. R. (1957) '*Sortilegium* in English homiletic literature of the fourteenth century', in Davies (1957): 272–303.

Pack, R. A. (1976), 'A treatise on prognostications by Venancius of Moerbeke', *Archives d'histoire doctrinale et littéraire du Moyen Age*, 43: 311–22.

Page, R. I. (1963) 'Lapland sorcerers', *Saga Book*, 16: 215–32.

— (1964) 'Anglo-Saxon runes and magic', *Journal of the Archaeological Association*, 27: 14–31.

— (1995) *Chronicles of the Vikings: Records, Memorials and Myths* (London).

Pagels, E. (1995) *The Origin of Satan* (New York).

Pálsson, Gísli (1991) 'The name of the witch', in *Social Approaches to Viking Studies*, ed. R. Samson (Glasgow): 157–68.

Pálsson, Herman (1990) *Heimur Hávamála* (Reykjavík).

Paravy, P. (1979) 'À propos de la genèse médiévale des chasses aux sorcières: le traité de Claude Tholosan, juge Dauphinois (vers 1436)', in *Mélanges de l'École française de Rome. Moyen Age–Temps Modernes* 91: 373–9; German trans. in Blauert (1990): 118–59.

— (1981) 'Faire croire. Quelques hypothèses de recherche basées sur l'étude des procès de sorcellerie du Dauphiné au XVe siècle', *Faire Croire*, 119–30.

— (1993) *De la chrétienté romaine à la Réforme en Dauphiné: evêques, fidèles et déviants (vers 1340–vers 1530)*, 2 vols., Collection de l'Ecole Française de Rome, 183 (Rome).

Parnell, S. S., and Olsan, L. T. (1991) 'The index of charms: purpose, design, and implementation', *Literary and Linguistic Computing*, 6: 59–63.

Pároli, T., ed. (1990) *Poetry in the Scandinavian Middle Ages* (Spoleto).

Parsons, J. C., ed. (1993) *Medieval Queenship* (New York).

Partner, P. (1982) *The Murdered Magicians: The Templars and Their Myth* (Oxford).

Paton, B. (1991) "To the fire, to the fire! Let us burn a little incense to God': Bernardino, preaching friars, and *maleficio* in late medieval Siena', in Zika (1991): 9–14.

— (1992) *Preaching Friars and the Civic Ethos: Siena, 1380–1480* (London).

Pennington, K. (1993) *The Prince and the Law 1200–1600: Sovereignty and Rights in the Western Legal Tradition* (Berkeley and Los Angeles).

Peters, E. (1972): see Kors and Peters (2001).

— (1978) *The Magician, the Witch, and the Law* (Philadelphia).

— (1980) *Heresy and Authority in Medieval Europe* (Philadelphia).

— (1996a) *Torture*, expanded edn (Philadelphia).

— (1996b) '*Rex curiosus*: a preface to Prospero', *Majestas* 4: 61–84.

Pharr, C. (1932) 'The interdiction of magic in Roman law', *Transactions of the American Philological Association*, 63: 269–95.

— (1952): see under *The Theodosian Code*.

Pinto, L. B. (1973) 'Medical science and superstition: a report on a unique medical scroll of the eleventh-twelfth century', *Manuscripta*, 17: 12–21.

Platt, C. (1996) *King Death: The Black Death and Its Aftermath in Late-Medieval England* (Toronto).

Poetic Edda: *Edda: die Lieder des Codex regius* (1985), ed. G. Neckel and H. Kuhn, 5th edn; *The Poetic Edda*, trans. C. Larrington (Oxford, 1996).

Polo, Marco (1958) *The Travels of Marco Polo*, trans. R. Latham (New York).

Poole, R. (1993) '*Darraðarljóð*', in Pulsiano (1993): 121.

Poulin, J.-C. (1979) 'Entre magie et religion. Recherches sur les utilisations marginales de l'écrit dans la culture populaire du haut moyen âge', in Boglioni (1979): 121–43.

Pratt, M. L. (1992) *Imperial Eyes* (London).

Pulsiano, P., ed. (1993) *Medieval Scandinavia* (New York).

Purkiss, D. (1996) *The Witch in History: Early Modern and Twentieth-Century Representations* (London and New York).

The Quest of the Holy Grail (1969) trans. P. M. Matarasso (New York).

Raitt, J., ed. (1987) *Christian Spirituality: High Middle Ages and Reformation* (New York).

Rather (1991) *The Complete Works of Rather of Verona*, ed. and trans. P. L. D. Reid (Binghamton).

Raudvere, C. (1993) *Föreställningar om maran i nordisk folktro* (Lund).

— (1995) 'Analogy narratives and fictive rituals', *Arv: Nordic Yearbook of Folklore*, 51: 41–62.

— (1998) 'Sigdrivas råd: erövring av kunskap i den norröna diktningen', *Svensk religionshistorisk årsskrift*, 128–46.

Rausing, G. (1993) '*Ynglinga saga*', in Pulsiano (1993): 739–40 (New York).

Remly, L. L. (1979) 'Magic, myth, and medicine: the veterinary art in the Middle Ages (9th–15th centuries)', *Fifteenth Century Studies*, 2: 203–9.

Reynolds, R. E. (1986) 'Law, canon: to Gratian', in *Dictionary of the Middle Ages*, VI: 395–413.

Riché, P. (1973) 'La magie a l'époque carolingienne', *Comptes rendus des séances de l'Académie des Inscriptions et Belles-lettres*, 1: 127–38.

— (1978a) *Education and Culture in the Barbarian West from the Sixth through the Eighth Century*, trans. J. Contreni (Columbia, SC).

— (1978b) *Daily Life in the World of Charlemagne*, trans. J. A. McNamara (Philadelphia).

— (1987) *Gerbert d'Aurillac, le pape de l'an mil* (Paris).

Ridder-Symoens, H. de (1987) 'The intellectual and political backgrounds of the witch-craze in Europe', in Dupont-Bouchat (1987): 37–64.

Rigault, A. (1896) *Le procès de Guichard, Evêque de Troyes (1308–1313)* (Paris).

Rivers, T. J. 1977) *The Laws of the Alemans and Bavarians* (Philadelphia).

Robert of Jumièges (1896, repr. 1994) *Missal*, ed. H. A. Wilson (London).

Roberts, G. (1996) 'The descendants of Circe: witches and Renaissance fictions', in Barry, Hester and Roberts (1996): 183–206.

Rousseau, P. (1979) 'The death of Boethius: the charge of *Maleficium*', *Studi Medievali*, ser. III, 20: 871–89.

Rubin, M. (1991) *Corpus Christi: The Eucharist in Late Medieval Culture* (Cambridge).

Rubin, S. (1974) *Medieval English Medicine* (New York).

— (1989) 'The Anglo-Saxon physician', in *Medicine in Early Medieval England*, ed. M. Deegan and D. G. Scragg (Manchester): 7–15.

Russell, J. C. (1994) *The Germanization of Early Medieval Christianity: A Sociohistorical Approach to Religious Transformation* (Oxford).

Russell, J. B. (1972) *Witchcraft in the Middle Ages* (Ithaca, NY).

— (1977) *The Devil: Perceptions of Evil from Antiquity to Primitive Christianity* (Ithaca and London).

— (1980) *A History of Witchcraft, Sorcerers, Heretics and Pagans* (London).

— (1981) *Satan: The Early Christian Tradition* (Ithaca and London).

— (1984) *Lucifer: The Devil in the Middle Ages* (Ithaca and London).

— (1987) 'History and truth', *The Historian: A Journal of History*, 50: 3–13.

Salzman, M. R. (1987) '*Superstitio* in the Codex Theodosianus and the persecution of pagans', *Vigiliae Christianae*, 41: 172–88.

Sands, D. B., ed. (1966) *Middle English Verse Romances* (New York).

Sandvik, G. (1993) 'Þing', in Pulsiano (1993): 663–4.

Sas, N. C. F. van, and Witte, E., eds. (1992) *Historical Research in the Low Countries* (The Hague).

Saxo Grammaticus (1931) *Gesta Danorum*, 2 vols., ed. J. Olrik and H. Ræder (Copenhagen); *The History of the Danes*, 2 vols., trans. P. Fisher, ed. H. Ellis Davidson (Cambridge, 1979–80).

Sayers, W. (1992) 'Sexual identity, cultural integrity, verbal and other magic in episodes from *Laxdœla saga* and *Kormáks saga*', *Arkiv för nordisk filologi*, 107: 131–55.

Schäfer, P. (1990) 'Jewish magic literature in late Antiquity and early Middle Ages', *Journal of Jewish Studies*, 41: 75–91.

Schjødt, J. P. (1990) 'Horizontale und vertikale Achsen in der vorchristlichen skandinavischen Kosmologie', in *Old Norse and Finnish Religious and Cultic Place-Names*, ed. T. Ahlbäck (Åbo): 35–57.

— (1993) 'The relation between the two phenomenological categories initiation and sacrifice as exemplified by the Norse myth of Óðinn on the tree', in *The Problem of Ritual*, ed. T. Ahlbäck (Åbo): 261–73.

Schmidt, T. (1989) *Der Bonifaz-Prozess: Verfahrender Papstanklage in der Zeit Bonifaz' VIII und Clemens' V* (Cologne and Vienna).

Schmitt, J.-C. (1983) *The Holy Greyhound: Guinefort, Healer of Children since the Thirteenth Century* (Cambridge and Paris).

Schnyder, A. (1991): see under Kramer.

— (1993) *Malleus Maleficarum. Kommentar zur Wiedergabe des Erstdrucks von 1487(Hain 9238)* (Göppingen).

Schönbach, A. (1883) 'Segen', *Zeitschrift für deutsches Altertum*, n.f. 15: 308.

Schüssler-Fiorenza, E., ed. (1976) *Aspects of Religious Propaganda in Judaism and Early Christianity* (Notre Dame).

Scott, J. (1992) 'Women's history', in Burke (1992b): 42–66.

Scragg , D. G., ed. (1989) *Superstition and Popular Medicine in Anglo-Saxon England* (Manchester).

Segl, P., ed. (1988) *Der Hexenhammer. Entstehung und Umfeld des Malleus Maleficarum von 1487* (Cologne and Vienna).

— (1990) 'Spätmittelalterliche Volksfrömmigkeit im Spiegel von Antiketzertraktaten und Inquisitionsakten des 13. und 14. Jahrhunderts', in Dinzelbacher and Bauer (1990): 163–76.

— (1993) 'Der Hexenhammer – eine Quelle der Altags– und Mentalitätsgeschichte', in Tanz (1993): 127–54.

Selmer, C. (1952) 'An unpublished Old High German blood charm', *Journal of English and Germanic Philology*, 51: 345–54.

Sharpe, J. (1992) 'History from below', in Burke (1992b): 24–41.

— (1997) *Instruments of Darkness: Witchcraft in Early Modern England* (Philadelphia).

Sheingorn, P., trans. (1995) *The Book of Sainte Foy* (Philadelphia).

Shinners, J. (1997) *Medieval Popular Religion, 1000–1500: A Reader* (Peterborough, Ontario).

Sigrdrífumál: in the *Poetic Edda*.

Siller, M. (1982) 'Zauberspruch und Hexenprozess: Die Rolle des Sauberspurchs in den Zauber- und Hexenprozessen Tirols', in W. M. Bauer *et al.*, eds., *Tradition und Entwicklung: Festschrift Eugen Thurnher* (Innsbruck): 127–54.

Simek, R. (1993) *Dictionary of Northern Mythology* (Cambridge).

Simpson, J. (1988) *Scandinavian Folktales* (London).

Siraisi, N. (1990) *Medieval and Early Renaissance Medicine* (Chicago).

Smallwood, T. M. (1989) "God was born in Bethlehem … ': the tradition of a Middle English charm', *Medium Ævum*, 58: 206–23.

Smart, N. (1983) *Worldviews: Crosscultural Explorations of Human Beliefs* (New York).

Smelik, K. A. D. (1977) 'The witch of Endor: 1 Samuel 28 in Rabbinic and Christian exegesis till 800 A.D.', *Vigiliae Christianae*, 33: 160–79.

Smith, J. M. H. (1992) 'Review article: early medieval hagiography in the late twentieth century', *Early Medieval Europe*, 1: 69–76.

Snorri Sturluson, *Edda*, ed. A. Faulkes. 1: *Prologue and Gylfaginning* (Oxford, 1982); 2: *Skáldskaparmál*, 2 vols. (London, 1998); 3: *Háttatal* (Oxford, 1991); *Edda*, trans. A. Faulkes (London, 1987); *The Prose Edda of Snorri Sturluson: Tales from Norse Mythology,* trans. J. Young (Berkeley, 1954).

Snorri Sturluson (1941) *Heimskringla,* I, ed. Bjarni Aðalbjarnarson, Íslenzk fornrit, 26 (Reykjavík); *Heimskringla II: Sagas of the Norse Kings*, trans. S. Laing, rev. P. Foote (London, 1961).

Spamer, A., and Nickel, J. (1958) *Romanusbüchlein: Historisch-philologischer Kommentar zu einem deutschen Zauberbuch* (Berlin).

Spargo, J. W. (1934) *Virgil the Necromancer: Studies in Virgilian Legends* (Cambridge, MA).

Speyer, W. (1992) 'Das Buch als magisch-religiöser Kraftträger im griechischen und römischen Altertum', in Ganz (1992): 59–86.

Staat, Kirche, Wissenschaft in einer pluralistischen Gesellschaft. Festschrift zum 65. Geburtstag von Paul Mikat (1989) (Berlin).

Stafford, P. (1993) 'The portrayal of royal women in England, mid-tenth to mid-twelfth centuries', in Parsons (1993): 143–67.

Stancliffe, C. (1992) *Saint Martin and His Hagiographer: History and Miracle in Sulpicius Severus,* (Oxford).

Stanley, E. G. (1975) *The Search for Anglo-Saxon Paganism* (Cambridge).

Stannard, J. (1977) 'Magiferous plants and magic in medieval medical botany', *Maryland Historian*, 8, no. 2: 33–46.

Steinmeyer, E. (1916) *Die kleineren althochdeutschen Sprachdenkmäler* (Berlin).

Steinsland, G., and Vogt, K. (1981) 'Aukinn ertu Uolse ok vpp vm tekinn: en religionshistorisk analyse av *Vǫlsaþáttr* i *Flateyjarbók*', *Arkiv för nordisk filologi*, 96: 87–106.

Sticca, S. (1996) *Saints: Studies in Hagiography* (Binghamton).

Storms, G., ed. and trans. (1948, repr. 1975) *Anglo-Saxon Magic* (Halle; Folcroft, PA).

Strayer, J. R. (1980) *Philip the Fair* (Princeton).

Strobino, S. (1996) *Françoise sauvée des flammes? Une Valaisienne accusée de sorcellerie au XV siècle* (Lausanne).

Strömbäck, D. (1935) *Sejd* (Uppsala).

Stuart, H. (1977) 'Spider in Old English', *Parergon*, 18: 37–42.

— (1985) 'Utterance instructions in the Anglo-Saxon charms', *Parergon*, 3: 31–7.

Sturluson: see under Snorri Sturluson.

Suger (1992) *The Deeds of Louis the Fat*, trans. R. Cusimano and J. Moorhead (Washington, DC).

Sullivan, D. (1974) 'Nicholas of Cusa as a reformer: the papal legation to the Germanies, 1451–1452', *Medieval Studies*, 36: 382–428.

Summers, M. (1971): see under Kramer.

Swanson, R. N. (1995) *Religion and Devotion in Europe c. 1215 – c. 1515* (Cambridge).

Tacitus, Cornelius, works in 5 vols., Loeb Classical Library (Cambridge, MA, London); *Germania* in vol. I (1970); *Historiae* in vol. II (1925).

Tambiah, S. J. (1990) *Magic, Science, Religion, and the Scope of Rationality* (Cambridge).

Tanz, S., ed. (1993) *Mentalität und Gesellschaft im Mittelalter. Gedenkschrift für Ernst Werner*, (Frankfurt, Berlin and New York).

Tavenner, E. (1916, repr. 1966) *Studies in Magic from Latin Literature* (New York).

Thee, F. C. R. (1984) *Julius Africanus and the Early Christian View of Magic* (Tübingen).

The Theodosian Code (1993) ed. J. Harries and I. Wood (Ithaca, NY).

— (1952), ed. and trans. C. Pharr (Princeton).

Thomas, K. (1971) *Religion and the Decline of Magic* (New York).

Thompson, S. (1955–8), *Motif-Index of Folk-Literature: A Classification of Narrative Elements in Folktales, Ballads, Myths, Fables, Mediaeval Romances, Exempla, Fabliaux, Jest-Books, and Local Legends*, 6 vols. (Bloomington).

Thorndike, L. (1905) *The Place of Magic in the Intellectual History of Europe* (New York).

— (1923–58, repr. 1964) *A History of Magic and Experimental Science*, 8 vols. (New York and London).

— (1944, repr. 1975) *University Records and Life in the Middle Ages* (New York).

— (1965) *Michael Scot* (London).

Tolan, J. (1998) 'Peter the Venerable on the 'Diabolical Heresy of the Saracens'', in Ferreiro (1998): 345–67.

Townsend, D. (1996): see under Walter of Châtillon.

Trachtenberg, J. (1939, repr. 1970) *Jewish Magic and Superstition* (New York).

— (1943) *The Devil and the Jew* (New Haven).

Translations and Reprints from the Original Sources of European History (1897–1907) (Philadelphia); see also *The Internet Medieval Sourcebook* at http://www.fordham.edu/halsall/sbook.html

Trusen, W. (1989) 'Vom Inquisitionsverfahren zum Ketzer- und Hexenprozess. Fragen der Abgrenzung und Beeinflussung', in *Staat, Kirche, Wissenschaft*, 435–50.

Turner, V. (1971) 'An anthropolocial approach to the Icelandic saga', *The Translation of Culture*, ed. T. O. Beidelman (London): 349–74.

Tylor, E. B. (1889) *Primitive Culture: Researches into the Development of Mythology, Philosophy, Religions, Language, Art, and Custom* (New York).

Van Dam, R. (1993) *Saints and Their Miracles in Late Antique Gaul* (Princeton).

Van Engen, J. (1986) 'The Christian Middle Ages as an historiographical problem', *American Historical Review*, 91: 519–52.

—— (1994) 'The Church in the fifteenth century', in Brady, Oberman and Tracy (1994): 305–30.

Vatnsdœla saga (1939), ed. Einar Ól. Sveinsson, Íslenzk fornrit, 8 (Reykjavík); *The Saga of the People of Vatnsdal*, trans. A. Wawn in *The Complete Sagas of the Icelanders*, IV.

Vauchez, A. (1997), *Sainthood in the Later Middle Ages*, trans. J. Birrell (Cambridge).

Vaughan, R. (1979) *John the Fearless* (London and New York).

Veenstra, J. R. (1998) *Magic and Divination at the Courts of Burgundy and France: Text and Context of Laurens Pignon's 'Contre les devineurs' (1411)* (Leiden, New York, Cologne).

Vickers, B., ed. (1984) *Occult and Scientific Mentalities in the Renaissance* (Cambridge and New York).

Víga-Glúms saga (1956), ed. Jónas Kristjánsson, Íslenzk fornrit, 9 (Reykjavík); *Killer-Glum's Saga*, trans. J. McKinnell in *The Complete Sagas of the Icelanders*, II.

Vogel, C. (1994) *En rémission des péchés: recherches sur les systèmes pénitentiels dans l'Église latine* (Aldershot and Brookfield).

Vǫluspá: in the *Poetic Edda*.

Vriend, H. J. de (1984), *The Old English Herbarium and Medicina de Quadrupedibus*, Early English Text Society, 286 (Oxford).

Wagner, R.-L. (1939) *'Sorcier' et 'Magicien'* (Paris).

Wahlgren, E. (1993) '*Vinland saga*', in Pulsiano (1993): 704–5.

Wakefield, W. L. and Evans, A. P., trans. and eds. (1969, rev. 1991) *Heresies of the High Middle Ages: Selected Sources Translated and Annotated* (New York).

Wallace-Hadrill, J. M. (1983) *The Frankish Church* (Oxford).

Walter of Châtillon (1978) *Alexandreis: Galteri de Castellione Alexandreis*, ed. M. Colker (Padua); *The Alexandreis of Walter of Châtillon: A Twelfth-Century Epic*, trans. D. Townsend (Philadelphia, 1996).

Ward, B. (1982) *Miracles and the Medieval Mind: Theory, Record and Event 1000–1215* (Philadelphia).

Ward, E. (1990) 'Caesar's wife: the career of the Empress Judith, 819–829', in Godman and Collins (1990): 205–27.

Ward, J. O. (1980) 'Witchcraft and sorcery in the later Roman Empire and the early Middle Ages: an anthropological comment, *Prudentia*, 12: 93–108.

—— (1993): see Davidson (1993).

Weston, L. M. C. (1995) 'Women's medicine, women's magic: the Old English metrical childbirth charms', *Modern Philology*, 92: 279–93.

Whitelock, D. (1955) *English Historical Documents c. 500–1042* (New York).

Wickham-Crowley, K. (1996) 'Tangled webs: weaving and the supernatural', paper delivered at the Thirty-First International Congress on Medieval Studies, the Medieval Institute, Western Michigan University, May 1996.

Williams, G. S. (1995) *Defining Dominion: The Discourses of Magic and Witchcraft in Early Modern France and Germany* (Ann Arbor).

Wipf, K. A. (1975) Die Zaubersprüche im Althochdeutschen', *Numen*, 22: 42–69.

Wolff, L. (1963) 'Die Merseburger Zaubersprüche', in *Die Wissenschaft von deutscher Sprache und Dichtung*, ed. S. Gutenbrunner *et al.* (Stuttgart): 305–19.

Wolfram, H. (1988) *History of the Goths*, trans. T. J. Dunlap (Berkeley, Los Angeles and London).

Yarnall, J. (1994) *The Transformations of Circe* (Urbana).

Ynglingatal (1925), ed. A. Noreen (Stockholm).

Zenkovsky, S. A., ed. and trans. (1974) *Medieval Russia's Epics, Chronicles, and Tales* (New York).

Ziegler, P. (1969) *The Black Death* (New York).

Zier, M. (1992) 'The healing power of the Hebrew tongue: an example from late thirteenth-century England', in Campbell, Hall and Klausner (1992): 103–18.

Zika, C., ed. (1991) *No Gods Except Me: Orthodoxy and Religious Practice in Europe, 1200–1600* (Melbourne).

— (1998) 'Dürer's witch, riding women, and moral order', in Eichberger and Zika (1998): 118–40.

Þáttr Þiðranda (1860), in *Flateyjarbók,* I, ed. Guðbrandr Vigfússon and C. R. Unger (Christiania); *Thidrandi Whom the Goddesses Slew*, in *Eirik the Red and Other Icelandic Sagas*, trans. G. Jones (Oxford, 1981).

Index

Burgundy, 236
Burning, 244
Byzantium, 51

Caesarius of Arles, 184, 197
Caesarius of Heisterbach, 50, 56, 61-6
Calendar, 55
Cannibalism, 86, 211
Ceremony, 110-11, 120, 122, 124-29,
    131-3, 139-42, 145, 150
Charlemagne, 36, 45, 176, 190, 193-4,
    197-200
Charles the Bald, 201
Charles V of France, 221
Charm, 29, 36, 39-42, 48-9, 52, 59,
    89-90, 117, 123, 134, 144-6, 150,
    182, 189-90, 229
China, 70
Chiromancy, 56
Christianization, 109
Circe, 175, 185
Claude Tholosan, 234, 236
Clement V, 220
Clergy, 31, 36
Clovis, 15
Cnut of England, 202
Cologne, 239, 242
Confession, 209-10, 212, 225
Conflict, 133, 136, 141-2, 146, 151-3,
    155-7, 210
Conjuration, 59, 213, 229
Constantine, 15, 45, 179
Corpse, 51
Corsica, 39
Cosmology, 35, 208
Council, 176, 181-2, 184, 194-5,
    197-99, 218; Basel, 226-8, 233,
    235-6; Constance, 226-7; Lateran,
    212; Nicaea, 194; Pavia-Siena, 227
Court, 176, 200, 211, 214, 218-9, 225
Crime, 152, 155, 210, 212, 232, 234,
    243-4
Criminal, 211
Cross, 38, 43-5, 47
Crucifixion, 180
Crusades, 21
Cú Chulainn, 68

Cult, 101, 129, 131-2
Curse, 30, 35, 42, 60, 92, 96, 104-05,
    120, 126, 134, 136-7, 148, 157-9,
    230
Cyprian, 61, 216-7

Dante, 217
Dauphiné, 232
Decretum, 205
Defamation, 154, 161
Demon, 30-1, 46, 49-50, 57-9, 62-3,
    65-6, 68, 81-88, 131, 134-5, 140,
    144, 147, 162, 178, 182-5, 188,
    195, 200, 202-4, 208-9, 211-6, 220,
    223, 228-31, 234
Demonology, 182, 184, 215, 232,
    236-8, 243
Demon-worshipper, 211
Denmark, 76, 152
Desecration, 211
Destiny, 137
Devil worship, 220
Devil, 18, 24, 26, 35, 43, 49-50, 52,
    59-60, 62-3, 77, 88, 102, 131, 137,
    140, 162, 183-5, 198-200, 202, 204-5,
    207-8, 223, 230-1, 234, 236, 240, 243
Devil's mark, 240
Devil's pact, 62, 208, 231, 242
Diana, 18, 189, 203-4
Dionysius Exiguus, 181
Dioscorides, 33-4
Directorium Inquisitorum, 215
Discipline, 210
Disease, 142
Divination, 17, 29-30, 53-6, 58, 84-7,
    106, 110-11, 113-14, 116, 119-20,
    122, 126-7, 133, 136, 148, 152, 178,
    185, 188-92, 195-6, 198-9, 201, 203,
    213-5, 217, 231
Diviner, 7, 22, 99, 126, 129, 179-80,
    195-6, 203, 209-10, 213, 217
Dragon, 45, 54
Dream, 137
Druid, 61

Eagle, 98
Edda, 58, 78-9, 92, 115, 117, 143, 146,
    150